H. Rider Haggard

H. Rider Haggard on the Imperial Frontier:
The Political and Literary Contexts of His African Romances

GERALD MONSMAN

ELT Press
UNIVERSITY OF NORTH CAROLINA AT GREENSBORO

ELT Press English Department PO Box 26170
University of North Carolina Greensboro, NC 27402–6170
e–mail: langenfeld@uncg.edu

NUMBER TWENTY–ONE : 1880–1920 BRITISH AUTHORS SERIES

ELT Press © 2006
All Rights Reserved
Acid–Free Paper ∞

ISBN 0–944318–21–5
Library of Congress Control Number: 2005938753

Front Cover   *Map Of Africa, Showing Its Most Recent Discoveries* (1867)
Constructed & Engraved by W. Williams, Philadelphia

Back Cover   *H. Rider Haggard* (c. 1890)
The Norfolk Record Office

TYPOGRAPHY & DESIGN

Display Type: Galliard
Text Type: New Century Schoolbook

TEXT
Designed by Robert Langenfeld
COVER
Designed by Michelle Coppedge

Printer : Thomson–Shore, Inc. Dexter, Michigan

In Memoriam

Diana DeKryger-Monsman

❧ CONTENTS

        Acknowledgments viii–ix
        Introduction 1–12

ONE
Empire and Colony   13–40

TWO
Heretic in Disguise   41–71

THREE
Diamonds and Deities: The Spoils of Imperialism   72–101

FOUR
Zululand: Native Auto/Biography   102–130

FIVE
From the Cape to the Zambezi: Boer and British   131–162

SIX
From Zululand to the Far Interior: Natives and Missionaries   163–190

SEVEN
Romances of the Lakes Region: Tales of Terror and the Occult   191–224

EIGHT
In Concluding: "'I Have Spoken,' as the Zulus Say"   225–236

        Notes   237–267
        Appendix: Bertram Mitford: Profile of a Contrarian   268–288
        Index   289–294

ACKNOWLEDGMENTS

For his unstinting advice and support, grateful acknowledgment is made to Dr. Robert Langenfeld, my ELT Press editor at the University of North Carolina, Greensboro, and to his hawk-eyed proofreader, designer, and editorial assistant, Michelle Coppedge. Two of my essays in *English Literature in Transition* are here particularly integral to chapters three and four: "Of Diamonds and Deities: Social Anthropology in H. Rider Haggard's *King Solomon's Mines*," 43.3 (2000), 280–97, and "H. Rider Haggard's *Nada the Lily*: A Triumph of Translation," 47.4 (2004), 371–97. Pertaining to the appendix on Bertram Mitford, I wish to thank the Manuscripts Department, Wilson Library, the University of North Carolina-Chapel Hill, for permission to publish from the A. P. Watt and Company Records #11036, General Manuscripts.

Individuals who have helped me along on this intellectual exploration are many. In the United States, I thank Frieda Rosenberg, Head of Serials Cataloging, University of North Carolina-Chapel Hill; and Rives Nicholson in the School of Information and Library Science, University of North Carolina-Chapel Hill.

In England, I thank Brian Stringer; Fiona Mitford; Dennis Savage, to whom I apologize for not showing up because I underestimated the slowness of the Tube; Wendy Sterry, Archive Specialist, Norfolk Heritage Centre; Liz Evans; Father David Goddard; and Madeleine Beard.

In Africa, I thank Dennis Pretorius; Dr. Keith Tankard; Sharon Warr, who substantiated for me the impenetrability of the Colonial Office files; and several cherished academic friends from KwaZulu-Natal, who though wishing to remain unnamed nevertheless are the enliveners of my convictions and comprehension.

Finally, and more particularly, I am pleased to thank my colleague at the University of Arizona, Roger Bowen, who formally endorsed this sabbatical enterprise to the Powers in high places.

The ideas here advanced arise from an ongoing investigation into the narrative patterns of the nineteenth century's struggle to interpret the good and decipher the diabolic in human affairs. Recontextualized in this current analysis by new arguments and their surrounding applications, diverse elements hark back to widely assorted drafts maturing among my papers, as well as to my study of colonial allegory in the *Victorian Review*, 18:2 (1992), 49–62. For permission to draw upon those last-named insights, I thank the Victorian Studies Association of Western Canada.

During this career-long undertaking, I have been supported in one project or another by the American Council of Learned Societies, the John Simon Guggenheim Foundation, and the American Philosophical Society.

However, I dedicate this capstone study to my first guide and abecedary, Diana DeKryger-Monsman, who through songs when I was a child taught me enough Dutch so that fortuitously I could muddle through Afrikaans in later years. "Dena" was taken out of school after the eighth grade to work in the "pickle fields" (i.e., cucumbers) and at Gerber's canning factory. She escaped field and factory, compressed high school into a year and a half, married happily, and took her Bachelor of Science degree at Johns Hopkins. When that ancient queen of all the sciences, "divine philosophy," beckoned, she took a Ph.D. with Arthur Lovejoy as supervisor. She then returned to The Hopkins to take an M.A. in yet another department, which led to her writing and producing, in the early days of television, live plays for WBAL. If the birth of her only child did not quite derail her career, said son has it on good authority that for her the event eclipsed the simultaneous appearance in the *Philosophical Review*, 49 (1940), 324–45, of her first essay on Josiah Royce's conception of the self. Well into her 80s she still gravitated toward any nearby university like iron to a magnet. And from the first she never doubted I would publish—and always took it for granted that I would publish boldly.

Gerald Monsman
Sierra de Santa Catarina
3 March 2006

❧ Introduction

This is the first book-length study of the African fiction of H. Rider Haggard (1856–1925) from the perspective of literary criticism, encompassing both his biography and the ideologies of the nineteenth century. In it, I hope to revise the image of Haggard as a mere writer of adventure stories or as an unreconstructed British imperialist. His other fiction (with Scandinavian, Egyptian, or European settings) does not lack narrative panache; rather, the African tales in particular have an unsettling relevance both to the politics and to the associated history of ideas of the nineteenth-century metropolitan centers of empire—and, even, to contemporary issues. The context for Haggard's African tales was a triad of extraordinary nineteenth-century cultures in conflict—British, Boer, Zulu—and this study will attempt to place his imaginative works in that context of colonial fiction writing and subsequent postcolonial debates about history and its representation. I will show how his fiction reflects an agenda of imperial dissent, suggests an idealistic belief in the value of Anglo-African cultural rapport, and anticipates innovative anthropological and cultural principles. Many of Haggard's novels and romances are complex works that open themselves to multiple levels of interpretation: historical, mythic, gender, political, and religious. My focus, then, will be on the narrative patterns of these romances in the widest sense of Aristotle's *mythos*: the physical actions and the underlying attitudes of the characters *in relation* both to the author's intentions and to the cultural issues surrounding his stories and their reception.

Colonial African literature written during Haggard's period, from the late nineteenth and well into the early twentieth century, including such empire writers as Rudyard Kipling, Bertram Mitford, and Olive Schreiner, tends to represent the indigenous populations in paradigms that derive initially from the metropolitan centers. Certainly the bowdlerized and transmuted cinematic versions of *King Solomon's Mines* (1885) and *She* (1887) may well be so described. All such works have been characterized by a twenty-first-century South African scholar, Sola Adeyemi, as "frequently inaccurate, ambiguous, amusing or downright malicious." Adeyemi further introduces the term "post-scription" (as in postscript) to describe, in connection with Haggard's recently published *Diary of an African Journey* (2000), later exculpatory critiques "whose aim is to explain or re-present colonial narratives in a more acceptable manner, acceptable in the sense of erasing original prejudices expressed by the original narratives, a kind of rationalisation after the fact." Haggard's diary of his visit to South Africa in 1914 is unexpectedly, says Adeyemi—given the politics of his earlier novels—*not* one of these "exercises in colonial apologia, so current nowadays." Haggard there both wrote objectively and departed Africa "with a deep disenchantment about the future of the empire."[1] Yet when Adeyemi implies that Haggard's early 1880s and 1890s characters, such as Gagool and Umslopogaas, were "suffused" with imperial ideology and that only his later imaginative progeny from the 1910s and 1920s, such as Mameena and Zikali, are pro-native or "counter-narrative" portrayals, one must object on the grounds of oversimplification.

Even Haggard's early fiction consistently transcended the dominant imperial mindset of newspapers, schools, and missions, in part because for him, as for Richard Burton, a knowledge of history and ethnography enriched his perspective. And Haggard's presentation of the common man's racism, as in *Queen Sheba's Ring* (1910), can be trenchantly satiric: for Sergeant Quick, "all African natives north of the Equator were Arabians, and all south of it, niggers."[2] To be scrupulous here, Haggard's readers are expected to admire the loyal and practical, if unreflective, Quick, whose parsing of African humanity is more a comic educational limitation than a tragic moral shortsightedness. Yet in such satiric thrusts, Haggard anticipates later irreverent lampoons such as those, say, in Evelyn Waugh's *Scoop* (1938), in which Fleet Street's frenzied race for the news of an ostensible war "in the North-Easterly quarter of Africa"[3] has Lord Copper explaining the imperial policy of his paper to novice reporter William Boot: "'the Patriots are in the right and are going to win'"; and Boot is told to file a story on "'the first victory about the middle of July.'" Lord Copper's assistant clarifies: "'Lord Copper only wants Patriot victories and both sides call themselves patriots and of course both sides will claim all the victories. But of course it's really a war between Russia and Germany and Italy and Japan who are all against one another on the patriotic side. I hope I make myself plain?'"[4] On occasion Haggard's more "realistic" fiction (a realism within fantasy, like the dragon "sniffing along the stones" in *Beowulf*) also can rise to such irreverent satire of the empire's insensitivity and mercenary hypocrisy.

Haggard transposed into his adventure tales not only his personal experiences with African colonial politics and those contemporary issues such as diamonds, gold and ivory, but also *in transitu* contributed, in his tales of magic and religion among strange deities, to an emerging aesthetic indebted intellectually, thematically and formally to "the primitive." He reflected something of Roger Fry's response in "Art of the Bushman" (1910) and "Negro Sculpture" (1920) to African aesthetic and spiritual capacities. Far from gloating that African behavior and ritual epitomized an earlier, primitive stage of European cultural development, Haggard extolled the natives as closer to humanity's primal springs of being. The expansion of exploration, trade, and colonial settlement in the late nineteenth century had stimulated a curiosity about primitive peoples, an interest first provoked by colonial contacts going back to the Spanish conquest of the Americas and by the writings of Hobbes, Rousseau, and Montaigne (on cannibals). Thus after imperial rule had opened primitive societies to investigations of cultural history, an adventure such as *King Solomon's Mines,* although in an alien land where the marvelous abounds, is potentially also implicated in Victorian politics and anthropological theories. The *Popular Magazine of Anthropology* (inaugurated 1866) and the public meetings of the Ethnological Society (founded 1843)—from which sprang the Anthropological Society of London (1863)—signaled a Victorian surge of interest. In those lectures and in ethnographically oriented fiction such as that of G. A. Henty on Ashanti warfare, a fascination with primitive man grew into, ultimately by the century's end, what Andrew Lang had declared a new "exotic" literature, "whose writers have at least seen new worlds for themselves; have gone out of the streets of the overpopulated lands into the open air; have sailed and ridden, walked and hunted; have escaped from the smoke and fog of town. New strength has come from fresher air into their brains and blood."[5] Haggard quickly discovered that the exoticism of his new ethnographic fiction could successfully challenge the popularity of both the domestic novel and the scandalous naturalism of Zola.

Like Bertram Mitford or his admired contemporary Olive Schreiner, Haggard was an Anglo-African writer straddling the moral divide of mixed allegiances, with one foot in Africa and the other in England. In fantasy, Haggard gave expression to feelings of cultural conflict, probing and subverting the dominant economic and social forces of imperialism. His narratives covertly support racial mixing in their love plots; they endorse native religious powers as superior to the European empirical paradigm; and they celebrate autonomous female figures who defy patriarchal control. Like a Renaissance play, Haggard's fiction appealed—even as England's grip on empire gradually slipped in the decades of post-Victorian disillusionment—to both the gentry in the seats and the commonality in the pit. Perhaps this was because Haggard not only mined his characters from the ore of real-life Africa but also from the depths of his subconscious, turning mundane reality into thrilling storylines by infusing the social and quotidian with the exoticism of lived nightmares and extraordinary ordeals.

⚜ ⚜

Among contemporary South Africa's confused mosaic of differing identities, historically that of the Zulus has been most conflicted, portrayed as blood-crazed savages (by the British officials of the Zulu War), as noble romanticized warriors (in Haggard's novels), or as a once-great culture founded by a nationalist Zulu hero (by contemporary Inkatha apologists). Although this analysis embraces all Haggard's sub-Saharan fiction, some fourteen or fifteen of his novels are set more particularly either before, during, or after the Zulu War and deal with the adventures of Allan Quatermain, Haggard's Anglo-African alter ego, hunter and trader.[6] Quatermain's life, the implicit fictional dates of which are circa 1817–1887,[7] spans the decades from the emergence of Shaka to the Berlin Conference; that is, from the rise of the Zulu nation through the rapid European penetration of the interior of Africa—the so-called "scramble for Africa"—to just after 1885, the fateful year of Africa's partitioning in Berlin by the colonial powers. Allan Quatermain is thus an emblem of the European in darkest Africa. Haggard's hero was the son of an idealistic missionary: "one of the gentlest and most refined men that I ever met; even the most savage Kaffir loved him, and his influence was a very good one for me. He used to call himself one of the world's failures. Would that there were more such failures."[8] Quatermain is certainly aware of those colonial administrators and Boers who as exploitative imperialists detested the pro-native "meddling missionaries."[9] Yet at the same time, Haggard's own distrust of zealous missionaries who condemned colonial abuses of the natives reflected an awareness of the pervasive mentality of imperialism even at the heart of religious charity. Thus in *King Solomon's Mines* even Ignosi lumps "praying-men" in with all those "traders with their guns and rum" as foes to a Zulu utopia.[10]

| Introduction |

Although the overly fastidious moral sensibility of Quatermain disapproves of Good's affair with Foulata, which colonials referred to as "going native," surely Haggard's readers (and even more so, contemporary ones) sympathized with her vision of a future apotheosis among the stars. Good's sin as implied by Haggard is nothing less than his failure to go native; and his punishment of permanent bereavement is for leaving his consort in order to pursue treasure. This interpretation contradicts Wendy Katz, who finds that Haggard is "unaware of the depths of his racial antagonism" and that his culturally broad-minded comments carry only "an aura of liberal tolerance."[11] Of course, Haggard could not have gotten away with explicitly condoning miscegenation in print, a variant of what in his private correspondence he called biting the "red apple"; Captain Robertson in *She and Allan*[12] is Haggard's most unreserved and sympathetic public presentation of racial mixing. After Darwin's *Origin of Species* (1859) and *Descent of Man* (1871), widely accepted but by no means empirically grounded anthropological theories maintained that primitive peoples were evolutionarily arrested and that such inferior races should not intermarry with Europeans. In the popular literature of imperialism such ideas often combined with the belief that the annihilation of aboriginals was justified by natural selection and the survival of the fittest. With their sense of racial superiority, the British applied Hobbes's phrase to describe the natives' lives as "nasty, brutish, and short"—though one postcolonial wit remarked that native life in pre-independence times was, more accurately, "nasty, *British*, and short."

Certainly popular nineteenth-century writers other than Haggard also condemned racist views. In the opening pages of H. G. Wells's *The War of the Worlds* (1898), the Martian observers of mankind are malevolent spies; but man, the arrogant observer of the protozoans (ironically, his ultimate savior), is the noble scientist. For Wells, privileging the terrestrial perspective resembles an ethnocentric British imperialism, implying that the Martians, the technologically superior invaders, are only the British themselves in another guise:

> And before we judge of them too harshly we must remember what ruthless and utter destruction our own species has wrought, not only upon animals, such as the vanished bison and the dodo, but upon its own inferior races. The Tasmanians, in spite of their human likeness, were entirely swept out of existence in a war of extermination waged by European immigrants, in the space of fifty years. Are we such apostles of mercy as to complain if the Martians warred in the same spirit?[13]

And despite Chinua Achebe's indictment of Joseph Conrad as a "bloody racist" (because he ignored native history and culture and used all of Africa merely as a backdrop for the breakup of a single European mind), Conrad's *Heart of Darkness* (1899) did pose the difficult moral issue of the legitimacy of *any* colonial intrusion—even a well-intentioned enhancement of "waste spaces" as ostensibly benign as that envisioned by Ruskin[14]—inasmuch as the noble-sounding justifications of the imperial agenda swiftly became mere rationalizations for greed.

As with other nineteenth-century liberals, Haggard lacks our contemporary awarenesses, but substantive allowances must be made for his geographical-historical "context." From Olive Schreiner to Isak Dinesen, the language of liberal colonialism (if that is not an oxymoron) simply did not require the scrupulous tolerance we came to expect in the last half of the twentieth century. Although Haggard's Quatermain cancels the word "nigger" because "I don't like it,"[15] yet the liberal Schreiner did use it in her narrative "Diamond Fields," though not with racist intent according to Richard Rive: "The word *nigger* as used by Olive Schreiner and other white, liberal South African writers and thinkers in the late 19th century was more paternalistic and condescending than overtly derogatory, and should be read in such a context."[16] Rive's is a harsh enough accusation; but if I understand him, such an epithet was not a racial slur but an economic-class designation—though to us it is obvious that such class status in the colonies probably was not unrelated to *somebody's* belief that human traits and capacities are determined by racial differences. And consonant with imperialism's nationalistic rationale, Haggard's primary reason for being in Africa was colonial administration and capitalistic enterprise, not the celebration of African nature—or love. He went back to England to find his wife. But to judge past actions by contemporary guidelines both is and is not acceptable. If that judgment condemns others because it privileges one's own subjective morality within the sharp apex of the present moment, then the result is self-righteous and fraudulent; but if it acknowledges that the composite experience of earlier generations constructively contributed to our present-day moral ethos, then historical sensitivity has replaced arrogance. Haggard is better than an unconscious racist with a mere "aura of liberal tolerance." T. S. Eliot's riposte on the sense of distance between our "now" and lives in the past seems especially applicable both to Haggard and to the more enlightened of his contemporaries: "Some one said: 'The dead writers are remote from us because we *know* so much more than they did.' Precisely, and they are that which we know."17

※ ※

In his short stories or longer romances, Haggard excels as a storyteller. Several of the Quatermain subseries—*Allan and the Holy Flower* (1915) and its sequel *The Ivory Child* (1916)—rate as among the best-ever mystery romances, though among this writer's favorites, after *King Solomon's Mines* and *She*, are two of the Zulu historical novels, *Nada the Lily* (1892) and *Child of Storm* (1913), as well as the neglected adventure romance, *The Yellow God* (1908). Haggard is not often recognized as a master of the short romance. But one of his "romancettes" or "romancellas" (the "romance" form of a novelette or novella), *Maiwa's Revenge* (published 1888; set 1859), undoubtedly had a major impact on Ernest Hemingway's safari stories and narrative style; another, *The Wizard* (1896), probably had a profound thematic and imagistic impact on Olive Schreiner's famously polemical allegory, *Trooper Peter Halket* (1897). Every tale offers fighting, revenge, mystery and monsters, chases and escapes, true love and occult phenomena—together with a few pauses to catch one's breath. Haggard's actual life in Africa never maintained such dramatic intensity; but unlike those who merely undergo exploits without internalizing them, Haggard, back in England and leading a very practical, sedate life, imagined these events with an intensity that became a living reality—the reality of vision being always a deeper way of experiencing, for both author and reader. If, in the unreflective imperialism of the "penny-dreadfuls," the noble savage is displaced and outstripped by the virtuous white hero, in *King Solomon's Mines* Haggard offers a better imaginative experience. Umbopa tellingly remarks to Quatermain's companion, Sir Henry, "We are men, you and I";18 and throughout this narrative a Berserker/Zulu knighthood, epitomized by mail shirts and oxtails, imbues both European and African. Andrew Lang in "The Sagas" had called the Zulus because of their warlike ways "a kind of black Vikings of Africa."19 And in much this same spirit of assimilation, Sir Henry, a sort of Nordic epitome of military masculinity like Charles Kingsley's Hereward the Wake, becomes in Haggard a white Zulu. In connection with the rejuvenation of British masculinity, Wendy Katz quotes from *Allan Quatermain* the eponymous hero's disgust with the primness of British life vis-à-vis the ethos of the Zulu warrior;20 and Patrick Brantlinger notes Haggard's preoccupation with "the diminution of opportunities for adventure and heroism in the modern world."21 In Haggard's fiction the reader becomes, with breath-taking virtuality, one of the warriors among the African mountains and veldts.

Samuel Taylor Coleridge coined the famous phrase "willing suspension of disbelief"; and when applied to realistic fiction, one could say that the reader need practice only a little suspension. But fantasy often demands more. Historical and fictional events are real or could be real; fantasy is unreal, could never happen. Before the advent of special effects in film and virtual reality, one often heard from bottom-line, nuts-and-bolts folk some variation of "Why bother with the unreal, that which can never happen, when we live in reality?" The answer is simply that we need to be jogged out of our "reality ruts," the windows of our psyches need to be opened to unsuspected possibilities—not the possibility that the fantastic may be *literally* true, but the possibility that things as we assume them to be (and of which we often despair) somehow might be otherwise. Haggard's was, after all, an age of arrogant "scientific" confidence in which Lord Kelvin was quoted as saying that "the grand underlying principles" of physical reality "have been firmly established" and all that remained was "determining values to a greater number of decimal places."[22] Despite Haggard's pride in the factual justifications and predictive power of his fantasies, as alluded to in several of his introductions—*Heu-Heu* (1924) or *People of the Mist* (1894), for example—his prescience is merely an incentive to our "willing suspension of disbelief." What his fantasies preeminently do is deliver possibilities for triumph in the moment of loss, for joy and love, for dying the right sort of death, and even, as T. S. Eliot observed of Baudelaire, for damnation instead of mere boredom. Haggard's appeal to readers lies in his capacity for liberating them from the routines and expectations of daily life. He brings them for a time into fruitful contact with emotion, imagination, and "the unknown" so that when they return to their trades and professions, they have a richer context for their lives' possibilities.

After the initial two chapters that present the context for both Haggard's colonial Natal years and his fictional reputation, the following chapters will focus on those works of Haggard that best weather a modern reading. With few exceptions, these are his African novels and the romances that feature his alter ego, Allan Quatermain. The *Cleveland Plain Dealer*, reviewing *Allan and the Holy Flower* in a long-forgotten, inconsequential notice, wrote: "The series of romances about Allan Quatermain . . . will some day be read even as the great series by Dumas is read."[23] Alexandre Dumas's series of romantic novels then and even now enjoys a highbrow reputation that Haggard's popular fiction has not as yet attained. This study aims to make that "some day" "now" and to bring Haggard's African romances into the circle of serious literature. The fiction discussed is grouped geographically, inasmuch as each region has its unique historical, socio-cultural, and/or spiritual traditions. As for Haggard's original readers, *King Solomon's Mines* (published 1885 and set in 1880–1881) supplies background and context not only for his Allan Quatermain sequels but for all his African romances. This novel is thus foregrounded here as the first to be discussed. Most of Haggard's successive works are, from the perspective of their historical settings, actually prequels. All later Quatermain tales also have a secondary location in the sense that although their primary events occurred in Africa in previous decades, they are envisioned as narrated to Haggard-the-editor by Allan on his Yorkshire estate after his return from the mines of King Solomon and before he once again sets out for Africa and his death, as described in *Allan Quatermain* (1887). A sort of "recollection in tranquillity" operates here to frame these narratives with a powerful *Ubi sunt* resonance, an elegiac lament for a past irretrievably lost but for the telling of it. Now, a century past the midpoint of Haggard's literary career, his novels—as well as those of Bertram Mitford and others—have become fascinatingly problematic in hindsight. When Haggard revisited Africa in 1914 things already had gone clearly wrong. Today the Africa that Haggard, Mitford, or Schreiner had envisioned, a fully Europeanized one with whites and blacks in harmonious accord, has been replaced by a reality of rancorous racial tensions. Was it a failure of the earlier participants to recognize differences or distinctions between peoples or cultures? And was it their ingenuous utopianism that produced its opposite, strife? Or was it the failure of a "good" imperialism in the face of economic greed? *Is* there such a thing as a "good" imperialist; and, if so, do destructive moral ambiguities still exist? Definitive answers are inaccessible; yet an examination of Haggard's rich output may put us on the track to asking better questions in discerning what the inevitable decolonizing of the land and its history implies for the colonizer and the colonized.

I am perfectly aware of the subtlety of colonial self-deception and may be vulnerable to a *tu quoque* in my own readings of his novels, but recent critics propose (too often in dismal, turgid prose) not only divergent but sometimes self-contradictory estimates of Haggard's colonial politics. The critics' sentimental fantasies of Haggard's misconstruction of native "otherness" and the invariable evils of his imperial models seem almost shadow plays for unspoken discussions of our own cultural shifts and disputes. For example, Anne McClintock notes that "missionaries and colonists voiced their repugnance for polygyny" and includes Haggard in this;[24] however, she ignores Haggard's two-page endorsement in *Days of My Life: An Autobiography*[25] of Bishop Colenso's support for polygamy. Again, Carolyn Hamilton claims Haggard endorses and portrays Shepstone's politics, including indirect colonial rule by a strong central authority expressed through the tribal system of autocratic Zulu kingship;[26] but if we assume that the stabilized government of Kukuanaland in *King Solomon's Mines* reflects Haggard's ideal, then Ignosi's prohibition of missionaries and traders directly contravenes one of Shepstone's main principles of colonial administration. One critic even asserts that Haggard did not know Zulu![27]—this in the face of historical evidence that Haggard and his campfire buddy Fred Fynney were diplomatic interpreters on several Zulu missions. I also suspect a holistic political interpretation may encourage atomistic misreadings: Hamilton claims that "the telling of the story that Haggard records in *Nada the Lily* takes place on the grave of Shaka, where the elderly Mopo has retired."[28] But Fynney makes it clear this grave is "guarded by the spirits of the Zulu nation, and no native will venture near."[29] Though Shaka's grave clearly lies at the lower end of "the great plains rising by steps,"[30] Hamilton applies the word "beneath" with simple literalism. In a similar vein, Laura Chrisman asserts that "Haggard omits allusions to Shaka's technical military innovations" in *Nada* and "reduces any reference to the actual battles and conquests to an occasional throwaway remark or casual description."[31] Although a novel cannot be a historical treatise, much of the first paragraph of the preface is devoted to Shaka's "Zulu military organisation";[32] and describing the historical battle with Zwide, Haggard begins a *four-page description* of Shakan tactics with: "Chaka moved out to meet him with ten full regiments, now for the first time armed with the short stabbing-spear...."[33]

Haggard's speed of composition—he avowed he wrote *She: A History of Adventure* (1887) in only six weeks[34]—was a proficiency he shared with Bertram Mitford, G. A. Henty and many other fashionable adventure writers. Such a boast or admission might suggest the negligible literary value of popular late-nineteenth-century fiction, trivial adventures—and here the indictment grows even worse—pandering to adolescent longings. Quatermain's assertion in *King Solomon's*

Mines that there is "no petticoat"³⁵ in his tale is the key signature of nineteenth-century boys' adventures; indeed, Haggard even dedicated this novel to "big and little boys." Boys and petticoats being inimical in the repressive mind of the period, a publisher's ad for Mitford's *Gerard Ridgeley* (1894) describes that novel also as for "boys"; thus its romance is "subordinate."³⁶ The onus of a debased, artless genre, deeply mired in adolescent culture, has the added burden—and now the presentment becomes damning—of its "Victorian flaws" of narration: the stilted eroticism (the sexuality of native girls is broached only to be tabooed, blatantly so in Mitford's *Seaford's Snake*³⁷); the long descriptive passages of scene and character painting; the tendency to contrast simplistically innocence and guilt; hairbreadth escapes; and unbelievable plot coincidences. But as with all literary conventions and codes, one must consider the intended effect of these ostensible flaws on the urbanized reader. Such cosmopolites interpret or naturalize these allegedly flawed artifices in accord with a way of seeing specific to their historical moment; indeed, they construed the ethos (if not the fantasy) of these texts as an accurate reflection of race, class, gender, and morality in the colonies. What to us may seem risible in these narratives—e.g., the bizarre significance placed on a young man's sudden use of a young lady's Christian name, as in Mitford—truly reflected colonial social practice. Or consider the more complex issue of coincidence used as a mere plot device to forward the narrative (here even the celebrated Dickens allowed himself wide latitude): is there not a psychological truth in coincidence that overrides realism, providing a non-objective or intrinsic representation more psychological than logical? This wrenching of the empirical satisfied profoundly felt needs seldom met fully in life as Haggard's readers knew it, tapping a poetic truth that lies below the surface of external events to supply emotional closure.

In *The Seven Types of Adventure Tale* (1991), Martin Green included works like those of Haggard and Mitford in the etiology of this genre. But such differentiation and classification of central characters by type—thus legitimating adventure fiction as archetypal—might be extended to new categories, elements, or patterns indefinitely. More pertinently, one might begin with the word "adventure" itself: *ad* (toward) + *venire* (to come), from *bainein* (to walk). What is it one walks or treks toward? Here Joseph Campbell's *Hero with a Thousand Faces* (1949) suggests a journey-ordeal that produces a newly empowered identity for the reader of Haggard's work, a reborn sense of self in which the rigors of colonial life, as earlier noted, are presented as an antidote to

England's increasing softness. Such narratives, moreover, have distinguished antecedents in tales of human conflict outside the adventure genre; they are often constructed around patterns of opposition that progress to the resolution of conflict; and they are informative about the peculiarities of their regions—the inhabitants, customs, and topography. In mere formula-driven adventures the "flaws"—externalities of action and scene described without imagination, not to mention the stilted, cliché-ridden dialogue—really *are* flaws. Reading such tales is sort of like eating the menu, not the meal. I hesitate to cite Captain F. S. Brereton's excellently titled *With Shield and Assegai* (1900), but unquestionably it's a better menu than meal. Whereas literary theorists, perhaps, may nominate masterpieces, they never ratify them. Although largely neglected by theorists, the reputation of a novel such as *King Solomon's Mines* nonetheless has grown over the years to the status of a masterpiece. As much as Haggard's adventures seem to rely on a mix of sensationalism and low-mimetic formal realism, they *do* in fact push toward literature's extended levels of meaning and epiphany. British against Boers; Africans against both British and Boers; Africans also against themselves, tribe by tribe; and *all* against the wilderness of land and beast—this struggle for survival in a post-Darwinian universe red in tooth and claw of course *changes* the fictional Haggard protagonist—but also, sometimes as profoundly, Haggard's readers. What more does good literature need to do?

ONE

Empire and Colony

Two definitions open the door to an interpretive reading of H. Rider Haggard's African fiction: first, "imperialism" which derives from the Latin *imperium* (i.e., command, empire), and applies to the extension of any nation's supremacy over a foreign area, either by direct territorial appropriation or by indirect control over its political, economic, or cultural life. And second, the traditional manner of this territorial appropriation: "colony" which comes from *colonia* (farm), the cultivation or development by settlers of this annexed land for its agricultural or (increasingly in nineteenth-century Africa) mineral products.

In ancient times Phoenicians, Romans, and Arabs settled the Mediterranean coast of North Africa, trading gold and salt across the Sahara. But Africa remained beyond European contact until the Renaissance when in 1471 the Portuguese established a coastal trade in gold, spices, and slaves. Then in 1652 the Dutch colonized the Cape of Good Hope as a resupply station, and sailors-turned-farmers were provided with Dutch servant girls shipped out from Amsterdam to fulfill the injunction of Genesis to be fruitful and multiply. Not long after, in the wake of the Religious Wars in France, Protestant Huguenots immigrated to South Africa where they intermarried with the Dutch. These Dutch-French settlers became the South African Boers (the Dutch word for "farmers"), and their spoken "Nederlands," adulterated with the native French of the Huguenots, became "Afrikaans" or "the Taal." After the Napoleonic wars and with a need for raw materials to feed its industries, Britain invaded the Cape; and by the second half of the nineteenth century, English superseded Afrikaans as the dominant colonial language. In response to British empire-building and in search of cultural and religious freedom (and, to tell the crude truth, native slave labor), the Boers then pushed north to settle the South African interior.

But attracted by the discovery of diamonds and gold, the British then invaded the interior also.

The industrial revolution had set off a European scramble for land that culminated in The General Act of the Berlin Conference (26 February 1885) to regulate the partition of Africa, not into autonomous indigenous ethic kingdoms but into Anglophone, Francophone, Lusophone, and Germanophone colonies under European control. There are three kinds of "African" writers of English whose viewpoints trisect colonial/postcolonial events. First, those tribally native authors, largely of the twentieth century, both born in and culturally indigenous to Africa, whether permanently domiciled there or not: Sol Plaatje, Ngugi wa Thiong'o, Chinua Achebe, and others. Next are those authors who have written of Africa but have not settled there: Joseph Conrad, V. S. Naipaul, G. A. Henty. And finally, those Euro-centered authors who were born or had settled for a period in Africa: in the last century Isak Dinesen or Nadine Gordimer, and in the nineteenth century Olive Schreiner, Bertram Mitford, and H. Rider Haggard. Among such Euro-centered authors as Haggard, the propagandization and contestation of the ideology of empire is complicated by autobiographical involvement.

Did the experience of being an Anglo-African frame the attitudes of these writers toward themselves in such a way that their European status complicated the evaluation of their private thoughts and acts? Nadine Gordimer speculates, for example, that Schreiner, anticipating the careers of so many South African writers up until about the 1970s, sailed to England to seek a culture: "They went because the culture in which their writings could take root was not being created: one in which the base would be the indigenous black cultures of the country, acting in interpenetration with imported European cultural forms, of which literature was one."[1] One recalls Schreiner's account of how Willie Bertram's gift of Herbert Spencer's *First Principles* opened new vistas for her[2]—an episode transposed into her fictional scene in *The Story of an African Farm* (1883) of the Stranger giving a book to Waldo.[3] This book and that box of books locked away in the loft for which Waldo is punished, like some errant Adam eating the forbidden fruit, are really the beckoning cultural heritage that will allow the artist to find his or her voice. But that culture remains largely European: "The solitary white child, who grows up in the mission house ... may discover ... that from the old book-shelf with its score of volumes read and reread and long pored over, and from the mail-bag arriving once a month,... it had learnt most of what London and Paris had to teach it."[4] Although Sch-

| ONE: Empire & Colony |

reiner discovered a bigger shelf of books in Europe, it wasn't a South African shelf. Even the books from Durban and Cape Town, the metropolitan British centers *in* colonial Africa, were not *of* Africa. Thus when Haggard notes in *Jess* that even in the Transvaal John was "not greatly troubled by the lack of civilized society, for he was a man who read a great deal, and books could be ordered from Durban and Cape Town, while the weekly mail brought up an ample supply of papers";[5] these books were British—but note that in a short generation, from the later 1860s to the early 1880s, the monthly mail-bag to the outback had become weekly.

According to the timeless imperial agenda first scripted by Homer's Ulysses, among the first of Western imperialists, the stock and fertile land belonging to the sparsely settled Cyclopes are there for the technologically superior adventurer to take:

> Wild goats in hundreds breed there; and no human being comes upon the isle to startle them—no hunter of all who ever trekked with hounds through forest or had rough going over mountain trails. The isle, unplanted and untilled, a wilderness, pastures goats alone. And this is why: good ships like ours with cheekpaint at the bows are far beyond the Cyclopes. No shipwright toils among them, shaping and building up symmetrical trim hulls to cross the sea and visit all the seaboard towns, as men do who go and come in commerce over water. This isle—seagoing folk would have annexed it and built their homesteads on it: all good land, fertile for every crop in season: lush well-watered meads along the shore, vines in profusion, prairie, clear for the plow, where grain would grow chin high by harvest time, and rich sub-soil.[6]

In the absence of "shipwrights," owing to their technological backwardness, and because of their isolation in the surrounding ocean, they are an undiscovered prize ripe for plunder. A few lines later Ulysses notes that when they unexpectedly made landfall, "some god guided us that night." Ulysses thus invokes divine guidance as a justification for the incursion of his mariners. Admittedly Polyphemus's cannibalistic predilections are unattractive, but Ulysses's characterization of him as "all outward power, a savage, ignorant of civility" and as "raging mad"[7] overlooks the provocation of the Greeks' invasion of his cave and attempt to intimidate him with bluster about the sack of Troy and the avenging power of Zeus. The future role of colonial technology is imagisticly implicit in the olive beam that blinds him: resembling the ship's mast, its stab is like the shipwright's drill in timber and its hot crackling in Polyphemus's blood is like the "scream" of a hissing ax blade tempered in cold water.[8] Polyphemus's subjection and pain are thus figured by Homer in terms of the superior power and accomplishments of technology.

Isak Dinesen in her autobiographical recreation of a coffee plantation, her *colonia* in Kenya, discusses with her houseboy Kamante the writing of *Out of Africa* (1936). Entering in a breeze, Kamante has scattered Dinesen's typescript on the floor; he then lays a copy of the *Odyssey* on her writing table, pointing to the evident superiority of Homer's narrative, inasmuch as it is heavier and harder as well as more tightly bound than her loose pages:

> He ... then asked me gravely: "Msabu, what is there in books?" As an illustration, I told him the story from the Odyssey of the hero and Polyphemus, and of how Odysseus had called himself Noman, had put out Polyphemus' eye, and had escaped tied up under the belly of a ram. Kamante listened ... and asked me if [Polyphemus] had been black, like the Kikuyu. When I said no, he wanted to know if Odysseus had been of my own tribe or family. "How did he," he asked, "say the word *Noman*, in his own language? Say it." "He said *Outis*," I told him.... "Must you write about the same thing?" he asked me. "No," I said, "people can write of anything they like. I might write of you." Kamante who had opened up in the course of the talk, here suddenly closed again.... After a pause ... he said firmly, "all the boys on the plain are afraid sometimes." "Of what were you afraid?" I said...."Of Outis," he said. "The boys on the plain are afraid of Outis."9

The charm of this passage is that initially Kamante naively misreads a book's physical accidentals as its essential character, although his suspicion of another possible level of significance in the pages Dinesen writes prompts him to seek her help in demystifying their meanings.

Likewise, Dinesen's allusion to Homer itself invites a demystifying by her readers. Dinesen's memoir both describes its own process of composition and simultaneously offers the story of Ulysses's invasion of Polyphemus's home and homeland as an illustration of what such a book might contain. The story of the wily Ulysses tricking the savage Polyphemus may at first glance seem only arbitrarily connected to the framing account of the autobiography's composition and to its description of a Kenyan coffee plantation overseen by a paternalistic Karen Blixen ("Dinesen" is her authorial "Outis"), but this juxtaposition actually reveals a deep-seated continuity between Dinesen and Ulysses. The story's disguised and ominous undertones disclose not an innocently romantic Africa in which Dinesen unproblematically enjoys all her roles of power—benevolent aristocrat, landowner, hunter, doctor and teacher to the natives, author—but a morally ambiguous colonialism of which she is a part. A woman, and so literally "no man," Dinesen prefers her status in Africa to the European woman's subservience and, her anti-imperial and pro-native sentiments notwithstanding, her story reveals her participation in the racial hierarchy of colonialism. This imperial paradigm as it unfolded in British history was a familiar story that used paternalistic rhetoric to justify racial domination and to disguise greed and the technological destruction of the land and its people. Often ethnocentric, materialistic, and indifferent to the world of nature, colonial society at times was able to turn even the noblest of missionary ideals into mere ancillary camouflage for its greedy exploitation of the territory and its natives. In much the same fashion that Ulysses disguised his invasion by appeals to the power and will of Zeus, so the imperial agenda can be said to have concealed its coercive face behind a moral façade, hiding the aggression of Ulysses within the figure of a humane and decent Blixen. This subliminal cunning of the European autobiography on the imperial frontier would have been as startling an insight for Dinesen's intended readers as the discovery of her book's deeper and more personally applicable levels of meaning was to Kamante.

Turning to England's older colony in South Africa and to Dinesen's colonial predecessor, Haggard (and, not surprisingly, before he left Africa Haggard also presided over a *colonia* with ostriches), one may ask how aware he also might have been about the problematics of even the best-intentioned actions on the colonial frontier and what this might imply when he assessed his own character, conduct, and motives. Ulysses's ruminations describing the potential productivity of the land of the savage cannibal Polyphemus are repeated in spirit by a host of subsequent commentators, not least of whom are Haggard's trio of adventurers in *King Solomon's Mines* when they espy the land of the Kukuanas:

> Behind and over us towered Sheba's snowy breasts, and below, some five thousand feet beneath where we stood, lay league on league of the most lovely champaign country. Here were dense patches of lofty forest, there a great river wound its silvery way. To the left stretched a vast expanse of rich undulating veldt or grass land, on which we could just make out countless herds of game or cattle, at that distance we could not tell which. This expanse appeared to be ringed in by a wall of distant mountains. To the right the country was more or less mountainous, that is, solitary hills stood up from its level, with stretches of cultivated lands between, amongst which we could distinctly see groups of dome-shaped huts. The landscape lay before us like a map, in which rivers flashed like silver snakes, and Alp-like peaks crowned with wildly twisted snow wreaths

rose in solemn grandeur, whilst over all was the glad sunlight and the wide breath of Nature's happy life.[10]

Whereas Haggard's passage has an iconic Edenic quality, this map-cum-snake imagery reappears at the opening of Conrad's *Heart of Darkness* with a markedly more sinister coloration, Conrad intending to present "the criminality of inefficiency and pure selfishness when tackling the civilizing work in Africa."[11]

Such a glorious panorama occurs not just in *King Solomon's Mines* but as early as Haggard's first published work, "A Zulu War-Dance," in the *Gentleman's Magazine* (1877):

> Before we dismounted we rode to the extreme western edge of the plateau, to look at one of the most perfectly lovely views it is possible to imagine. It was like coming face to face with great primeval Nature, not Nature as we civilised people know her, smiling in corn-fields, waving in well-ordered woods, but Nature as she was on the morrow of the Creation. There, to our left, cold and grey and grand, rose the great peak, flinging its dark shadow far beyond its base. Two thousand feet and more beneath us lay the valley of the Mooi river, with the broad tranquil stream flashing silver through its midst. Over against us rose another range of towering hills, with sudden openings in their blue depths through which could be seen the splendid distances of a champaign country.[12]

In the scene-painting of African travel literature, a sense of the land as a potential colony, its fertility, had been a commonplace. M. L. Pratt in *Imperial Eyes* labeled this the panoramic moment of the imperial gaze, her title punning on the subjective "I"s of the viewers' motives. As late as Bertram Mitford's *A Veldt Vendetta* (1903), when conflict between natives and settlers was overt, the rhetoric of an exotic prelapsarian beauty persisted:

> What is there about that marvellous African sunset glow?... It was as a scene cut out of Eden, that wondrous changing glow which rested upon the whole valley, playing upon the rolling sea of foliage like the sweep of golden waves, striking the iron face of a noble cliff with a glint of bronze, then dying, to leave a pearly atmosphere redolent of distilling aromatic herbs, tuneful with the cooing of myriad doves and the whistle of plover and the hum of strange winged insects coming forth on their nightly quests.[13]

Curiously, colonial accounts more often than not reveal a subconscious awareness of the paradox at the core of an imperialism that combines military and economic domination with benevolent aspirations for the Africans. Numerous clues suggest how easily commercial expansionism and religious paternalism coalesced. If, on the one hand, Mungo Park can unabashedly describe his travels as of value "in rendering the geography of Africa more familiar to my countrymen, and in opening to their ambition and industry new sources of wealth, and new channels of commerce,"[14] this secular expansionism combined, on the other hand, with the latent paternalism of the missionary, as Livingstone's *Missionary Travels* (1858) evinces. Livingstone's first expedition had begun with five hundred New Testaments in a native language, but its outcome produced a testament of another sort—the explicit endorsement of African commerce: "The prospects there disclosed are fairer than I anticipated, and the capabilities of the new region lead me to hope that by the production of the raw materials of our manufactures, African and English interests will become more closely linked."[15] But Livingstone betrays, in part by his disavowals, an apprehension that the symbiosis of missionary and trader may disguise divergent aspirations and results:

> Wherever a missionary lives, traders are sure to come; they are mutually dependent, and each aids in the work of the other; but experience shows that the two employments can not very well be combined in the same person. Such a combination would not be morally wrong, for nothing would be more fair, and apostolical too, than that the man who devotes his time to the spiritual welfare of a people should derive temporal advantage from upright commerce, which traders, who aim exclusively at their own enrichment, modestly imagine ought to be left to them. But, though it is right for missionaries to trade, the present system of missions renders it inexpedient to spend time in so doing. No missionary with whom I ever came in contact, traded; and while the traders, whom we introduced and rendered secure in the country, waxed rich, the missionaries have invariably remained poor, and have died so.[16]

Later in his introduction to *Narrative of an Expedition to the Zambesi* (1866), Livingstone once again acknowledges that his account "is written in the earnest hope that it may contribute to that information which will yet cause the great and fertile continent of Africa to be no longer kept wantonly sealed, but made available as the scene of European enterprise."[17] In fairness, one must note that the commercial apologias for both of Livingstone's books concluded with the hope that "happiness," "prosperity," "freedom," and "the blessings of the Gospel" will result for the native tribes also. It may be that the Wesleyan Mission Society that sponsored Olive Schreiner's father, Gottlob, had a keener sense of the practical moral defects of trading than did Livingstone; Gottlob lost his missionary post in 1865 precisely because he attempted to supplement his meager stipend with Livingstone's "upright commerce." Interestingly, Gottlob originally had gone to Africa in 1838 under the auspices of the London Missionary Society that in 1840 had sent Livingstone to the same South African field; the London Missionary Society in 1842 likewise had made inquiries into Gottlob's unauthorized trading activities.

Although Haggard's novella or "romancella," *The Wizard* (1896), presents a heroic missionary-martyr, Haggard elsewhere is fully aware of the downside of missionary teaching. Perhaps in *Allan and The Holy Flower* and *The Ivory Child* we are most acutely made aware of Allan's sainted father, "the Predikant" (Afrikaans for preacher), and of his unavailing efforts to inculcate doctrine in Hans the Hottentot (nowadays the Khoi-Khoi). Hans's amusing sense of the Christian afterlife is mainly of hell fire for everyone, missionaries included; and, indeed, the early missionaries did stress damnation and hell to the disregard of love and salvation. Olive Schreiner, daughter of a missionary, shows the boy Waldo at the opening of her *Story of an African Farm* psychologically traumatized by the thought of a soul damned at every tick of the watch: "'Dying, dying, dying!' said the watch; 'dying, dying, dying!' He thought of the words his father had read that evening—*'For wide is the gate, and broad is the way, that leadeth to destruction, and many there be which go in thereat.'"*[18] Schreiner contrasts these socially constructed values of patriarchal religion, embodied in the harshly mechanical watch, to the beauty and love in nature, reflected in the moon and its fluid rhythms. Watch and moon are both silver and round; but the former is artificial, whereas the latter divine. Elsewhere Bertram Mitford in *The Induna's Wife* (1898) depicts Dingaan insisting that he is more merciful than God because although Zulus torture guilty men to death on stakes, God condemns evil-doers to much longer torment after death. Amusingly, the spluttering Francis Owen helps Dingaan prove his point:

> "Who art thou, thou man of blood, to wreck and mangle God's Image thus?" pointing to those upon the stakes. "Tremble and know that a judgment awaits thee—yea, a burning fiery looking-for of judgment to come. Then the torment that these undergo now shall be a bed of flowers beside such as thine, for thy part shall be in the lake that burneth with fire for ever and ever and ever."[19]

The king only laughs and dismisses the missionary as "mad." In the light of Haggard's running joke on Hans's unorthodox Christianity, one suspects that in *The Holy Flower* the feigned lunacy that protects the American missionary with a butterfly net, "Brother John," from native attack may imply that from a tribal point of view such missionary preachments as those on the afterlife, the Trinity, the Resurrection, and monogamy were as mad as chasing butterflies among the lions. The hymns of the missionaries, of course, were perennially a hit.

But potentially the scripts of the benevolent missionary, of Predikant Quatermain, or of a David Livingstone or a Gottlob Schreiner, may reflect less the gospel of equality than the cultural hegemony or master plot of the dominant culture. To bestow a spiritual power upon those who have no prospects of social or economic power—natives, women and children—may be another more subtle form of cultural domination. Thus when the Reverend George Browne's *History of the British and Foreign Bible Society* (1859) recounts a missionary's anecdote of how two little native girls from the mission station (female, native, and children—a cliché in these accounts for pure innocence) converted members of the Bushmen tribe by reading from their Testaments, the issue arises whether theirs was the divine Word, the unmediated voice of God, or whether the self-effacing missionary may not somehow be concealing in the innocent mouths of "babes and sucklings" (Browne's phrase, from Psalm 8) the patriarchal script of England's cultural dominance of her colonies and its peoples.[20] May not the worldly powerlessness itself of the missionary's surrogates be the message, inasmuch as the natives are frequently represented as children who are never intended to grow up and challenge colonial authority? Africa ideally was a world in which, according to Dinesen, "the white pioneers lived in guileless harmony with the children of the land" and in which, according to J. W. Colenso, Bishop of Natal, "the name for Deity among Zulus ... is derived [from] the word *umlunga*, commonly used in this colony for 'white-man.'"[21]

The frequent comparison also of natives to animals in nineteenth-century accounts is not simply an inconsequential rhetorical formula, but an indication of an ingrained way of looking at them, of a reading and a writing resistant to more tolerant formulations, of the script of their subjugation. Thus Dinesen's natives resemble bats, hyenas, dogs, ticks on a sheep, or elephants: "The old dark clear-eyed Native of Africa, and the old dark clear-eyed Elephant,—they are alike; you see them standing on the ground, weighty with such impressions of the world around them as have been slowly gathered and heaped up in their dim minds";[22] and the Bushman is described by Schreiner, late in her career, as having an "ape-like body" and a "simple" mind unable to perform the "mental operations necessary for the maintenance of life under civilized conditions."[23] Early settlers, she notes, supposed the Bushmen "absolutely incapable of feeling, and the Boers, and even the Kaffirs, still regard them as only half-human, and probably descended from baboons. They will bear resentment for long years with the persistency of many wild animals, but have also a curiously strong sense of gratitude, and are not incapable of powerful affection of a dog-like kind."[24] As her language reveals, Schreiner is not very far from the rhetoric of the early settlers. However, the Bushmen also "possess a curious imitative skill, and under shelving rocks and in caves all over South Africa their rude etchings and paintings of men and animals are found, animated by a crude life and vigour."[25]

And even when the natives do have civil power, successful proselytizing undermines it. One may cite Livingstone's inadvertently droll description of the tribal chief Sechele's conversion, the occasion of whose baptism Livingstone himself unintentionally suggests is political "suicide":

> He felt the difficulties of his situation long before I did, and often said, "Oh, I wish you had come into this country before I became entangled in the meshes of our customs!" ...He went home, gave each of his superfluous wives new clothing, and all his own goods, which they had been accustomed to keep in their huts for him, and sent them to their parents with an intimation that he had no fault to find with them, but that in parting with them he wished to follow the will of God.... Seeing several of the old men actually in tears during the service, I asked them afterward the cause of their weeping; they were crying to see their father, as the Scotch remark over a case of suicide, "*so far left to himself.*" ...All the friends of the divorced wives became the opponents of our religion. The attendance at school and church diminished to very few besides the chief's own family. They all treated us still with respectful kindness, but to Sechele himself they said things which, as he often remarked, had they ventured on in former times, would have cost them their lives.[26]

Livingstone does not quite singlehandedly overthrow a native governmental system nor is he solely guilty of initiating the detribalization of South African blacks. But what he has done is to precipitate the breakdown of an indigenous system without generating any noticeable social improvement; instead, into this erosion of power come the European cattle herders, the prospectors, the traders and speculators—in short, all the folk of imperial rule:

> Speculator and Capitalist ... have [contrived] ... that, by the passing of laws dispossessing the native by indirect means of his hold on the land, and breaking up his tribal tenure, and by the making of direct wars upon him, the native, at last being absolutely landless, may be unable to resist any attempt to lower wages, and may then sink into the purely proletariat condition ... on the border of starvation.27

If the meek can only inherit the earth by starvation and death, then theirs is a sentimental and ironic inheritance at best, a most ambiguous sort of power. Yet admiration of Livingstone was so intense that one suspects his readers would not have found his final comment on the Christianizing of Sechele politically ironic: "It was trying, after all we had done, to see our labors so little appreciated; but we had sown the good seed, and have no doubt but it will yet spring up, though we may not live to see the fruits."28

§§ §§

The invaders disguise or misrepresent their predatory expansion by denying that they are destroying anything of value, defining the natives' oral traditions and their land as an emptiness waiting to be filled, either with a European spiritual message as in the Bible Society's innumerable translations or with gold and diamond mining, not to mention Mistah Kurtz's dark-hearted ivory trading. John Ruskin, one of the most influential professors at Oxford, in his 1870 Oxford Inaugural Lecture had exhorted the "youths of England" to assist their motherland. Ruskin "describes the present passage as 'the most pregnant and essential' of all his teaching."29 It is a quintessential statement of British imperialism, ripe with sinister idealism. Cecil Rhodes may have heard this lecture:

> There is a destiny now possible to us—the highest ever set before a nation to be accepted or refused. We are still undegenerate in race; a race mingled of the best northern blood. We are not yet dissolute in temper, but still have the firmness to govern, and the grace to obey. We have been taught a religion of pure mercy, which we must either now betray, or learn to defend by fulfilling. And we are rich in an inheritance of honour, bequeathed to us through a thousand years of noble history, which it should be our daily thirst to increase with splendid avarice, so that Englishmen, if it be a sin to covet honour, should be the most offending souls alive. Within the last few years we have had the laws of natural science opened to us with a rapidity which has been blinding by its brightness; and means of transit and communication given to us, which have made but one kingdom of the habitable globe. One kingdom;—but who is to be its king? Is there to be no king in it, think you, and every man to do that

which is right in his own eyes? Or only kings of terror, and the obscene empires of Mammon and Belial? Or will you, youths of England, make your country again a royal throne of kings; a sceptred isle, for all the world a source of light, a centre of peace; mistress of Learning and of the Arts;—faithful guardian of great memories in the midst of irreverent and ephemeral visions;—faithful servant of time-tried principles, under temptation from fond experiments and licentious desires; and amidst the cruel and clamorous jealousies of the nations, worshipped in her strange valour of goodwill towards men?30

Ruskin's vision of a utopian global unity is challenged by Mammon and Belial, devils in the pandemonium of Milton's *Paradise Lost*, distinguished princes of darkness.

Ruskin's young men were to go forth like soldiers, as the first line of the hymn of Bishop Venantius Fortunatus (530–609 AD) announces: "The royal banners forward go." But those "oriflammes" that were the ancient banners of the French kings, will they be the "flames of gold" of the princes of light or of darkness?

"*Vexilla regis prodeunt.*" Yes, but of which king? There are the two oriflammes; which shall we plant on the farthest islands,—the one that floats in heavenly fire, or that hangs heavy with foul tissue of terrestrial gold? There is indeed a course of beneficent glory open to us, such as never was yet offered to any poor group of mortal souls. But it must be—it *is* with us, now, "Reign or Die." And if it shall be said of this country, "*Fece per viltate, il gran rifiuto,*" that refusal of the crown will be, of all yet recorded in history, the shamefullest and most untimely.31

Ruskin here is quoting Dante's *Inferno*: "I saw and recognized the shade of him / Who made, through cowardice, the great refusal."32 But though Ruskin's emissaries of England were not cowards, in history's clarifying hindsight they might be villains. The dark side of Ruskin's idealism weighs heavy in our century:

And this is what she must either do, or perish: she must found colonies as fast and as far as she is able, formed of her most energetic and worthiest men;—seizing every piece of fruitful waste ground she can set her foot on, and there teaching these her colonists that their chief virtue is to be fidelity to their country, and that their first aim is to be to advance the power of England by land and sea: and that, though they live on a distant plot of ground, they are no more to consider themselves therefore disfranchised from their native land, than the sailors of her fleets do, because they float on distant waves. So that literally, these colonies must be fastened fleets; and every man of them must be under authority of captains and officers, whose better command is to be over fields and streets instead of ships of the line; and England, in these her motionless navies (or, in the true and

> mightiest sense, motionless *churches*, ruled by pilots on the Galilean lake of all the world), is to "expect every man to do his duty"; recognizing that duty is indeed possible no less in peace than war; and that if we can get men, for little pay, to cast themselves against cannon-mouths for love of England, we may find men also who will plough and sow for her, who will behave kindly and righteously for her, who will bring up their children to love her, and who will gladden themselves in the brightness of her glory, more than in all the light of tropic skies.33

The Christianizing of the pagan lands goes hand in hand with its political pacification. Ruskin's Sea of Galilee, frequented by Christ and his disciples, is the Christian world; this he combines with Nelson's challenge at the Battle of Trafalgar—and the collapse of Napoleon's imperial plans to invade England. Ruskin's other image of "cannon-mouths" echoes Tennyson's "Charge of the Light Brigade" in the Crimean War.

If the unholy polluting clouds are the future industrial smudge-pots of the midlands, then apparently Ruskin would have the unsightly effects of manufacturing banished to the colonies as well. But for England to enable her men to do their imperial duty, England

> must make her own majesty stainless; she must give them thoughts of their home of which they can be proud. The England who is to be mistress of half the earth, cannot remain herself a heap of cinders, trampled by contending and miserable crowds; she must yet again become the England she was once, and in all beautiful ways,—more: so happy, so secluded, and so pure, that in her sky—polluted by no unholy clouds—she may be able to spell rightly of every star that heaven doth show; and in her fields, ordered and wide and fair, of every herb that sips the dew; and under the green avenues of her enchanted garden, a sacred Circe, true Daughter of the Sun, she must guide the human arts, and gather the divine knowledge, of distant nations, transformed from savageness to manhood, and redeemed from despairing into peace.34

His English Circe is not the malign enchantress (*cf.* Milton, *Comus*, 50–53) but goddess of enlightenment. Circe's enchantment entails not only the voluptuousness that enslaves the soul but also the soul's quest for the divine light of reason, as Giordano Bruno epitomized her in Diana, the virgin English queen, Elizabeth I (see discussion of Haggard's Circe, Ayesha, in chapter seven). Does the beauty-evil duality of Homer's goddess allegorize Ruskin's alternatives of altruistic idealism and selfish materiality?

Afterwards, Ruskin's admirer, Cecil Rhodes, had few moral qualms about seizing Mashonaland, which till then apparently had neither "human arts," nor "divine knowledge," nor redemptive "peace." In postcolonial times, the Nigerian writer, Chinua Achebe, addressed this cultural-wasteland/emotional-void premise of the colonial script: it must be recognized, he says, "that African people did not hear of culture for the first time from Europeans; that their societies were not mindless but frequently had a philosophy of great depth and value and beauty, that they had poetry and, above all, they had dignity. It is this dignity that African people all but lost during the colonial period, and it is this that they must now regain."[35] Like Homer's archetypal narrative of imperial aggression, any European's account of life on the imperial frontier is seemingly implicated in the doubleness of this canonical story of Africa, in the colonial paradigm that plays out the confrontation between "god-fearing" Europeans and "wild savages"[36]—a confrontation that proclaims a moral mandate but wounds Cyclopes, frightens the Kikuyu on the plain, and eliminates the African. Schreiner's fictional character, Trooper Peter Halket, recollects the following from Rhodes's campaign of conquest:

> Then—he saw the skull of an old Mashona blown off at the top, the hands still moving. He heard the loud cry of the native women and children as they turned the maxims on to the kraal; and then he heard the dynamite explode that blew up a cave. Then again he was working a maxim gun, but it seemed to him it was more like the reaping machine he used to work in England, and that what was going down before it was not yellow corn, but black men's heads; and he thought when he looked back they lay behind him in rows, like the corn in sheaves.[37]

In point of fact, Rhodes is said to have demonstrated on several occasions the lethality of the Maxim by mowing down fields of corn before the chiefs of several kraals, thereby effortlessly securing the land without a fight. (And this, in turn, is not without relevance to Quatermain's demonstration of the superiority of his armaments by shooting an assegai to fragments in *King Solomon's Mines*.[38]) Trooper Peter sees the annihilation of the blacks as nature's bountiful harvest—the grim reaper is imaged as a husbandman and the dead natives are presented as the land's crop.

The alternative to slaughter is enslavement, also masquerading in the colonial script as its opposite. According to Peter's story of his "nigger girls,"[39] their sexual subjugation is supported by an economic exploitation under the pretense that the native women are somehow benefitted or at least should not be ungrateful:

> "They've got the damned impertinence to say, that the Matabele oppressed them sometimes, but the white man oppresses them all the time!

"Well, I left those women there," said Peter.... "Mind you I'd treated those women really well. I'd never given either of them one touch all the time. I was the talk of all the fellows round, the way I treated them.... Why, I hadn't been gone six hours when those two women skooted!"40

Peter's "never . . . one touch" simply means he didn't hit them; he was sexually violating them all the while, of course. Blindness to preexisting native marriage ties or any native values was disguised by Peter's premise that natives do not have feelings.41

Two factually true incidents, one from the first phase and one from the later period of British colonial administration in Africa, illustrate this scripting of the natives as their own victims. John Barrow, the official representative of the English governor, describes in his *Account of Travels into the Interior of Southern Africa* (1801) the massacre of a sleeping Bushman village by his Boer guides, who claimed to be responding to a shower of Bushmen arrows. "I . . . had heard enough to pierce the hardest heart,"42 remarks the somewhat shaken Barrow of the shrieking and cries. He then proceeds to distribute tobacco to the survivors to mitigate the effects of the attack:

> The manner indeed in which their village was attacked was certainly not calculated to inspire them with much confidence. On the contrary, it was so directly hostile as perfectly to justify their shooting a volley of arrows among us.... The conclusion of the business, however, must have appeared to them very different from what, on former occasions, they had always experienced, when those who escaped from immediate death were incessantly pursued and fired upon, and their wives and children seized and carried away into slavery.43

Not only does Barrow here assume that the natives have cause to be thankful for not being wholly slaughtered or enslaved, but he exonerates the Boers, albeit reluctantly; and with all "appearances" pointing to this tribe's never having "committed depredations on the colonists," he programmatically places the onus on the natives: if the Bushmen when starving beg for Dutch cattle rather than stealing these cows, they won't be massacred: "our present journey into their country was for no other intention than to give them an opportunity of putting a final stop to all expeditions against them, if, by a change of conduct, they were inclined to avail themselves of it; and they were assured that not a single shot would have been fired upon their horde had they not first discharged their arrows upon the farmers."44

Didn't Polyphemus deserve the stick in the eye for eating Odysseus's sailors? Never mind the fact that the Greeks had invaded his cave, attempted to intimidate him with their boasts of the sack of Troy, and threatened him with the wrath of Zeus. Polyphemus is not given much of a choice: either beggared by the sailors or declared their enemy. The same goes for these Bushmen. They won't be massacred if they renounce their hunting-gathering life to beg or starve when hungry, and Barrow's distribution of tobacco symbolically links their future access to provisions with submission to imperial rule. The English might appear anxious to curb the Boer's slaughter or enslavement of the natives, but by continuing to define the natives as predators and by limiting their right to live off their land, the British distort the Boers' direct contestation over resources into a far more devious script.

More than a century later, Dinesen retells "Kitosch's Story" from the ironic perspective of a colonial jury that faults the native himself for the consequences of an assault, the colonist once again being largely "innocent" of his actions. A white settler had a young native sadistically flogged and bound for an offense so trivial as to make the punishment a purely symbolic assertion of power:

> The boy, beaten to the point of deafness, tied and retied tighter, moaned all night and said that he wanted to die. At four ... he again said that he wanted to die. A little while after, he rocked himself from side to side, cried: "I am dead!" and died. Three doctors gave evidence in the case. The District Surgeon ... pronounced death due to the injuries and wounds that he had found on the body.... The two doctors from Nairobi, called in for the defence, were, however, of a different mind: ... the wish to die, in a Native, had actually caused death. In the present case the matter was particularly clear, for Kitosch had himself said that he wanted to die. The second doctor bore him up in this point of view. It was very likely, the doctor now went on, that if Kitosch had not taken this attitude, he would not have died.... He added that the wound on the lip might not be due to a kick, but might be just a bite by the boy himself, in severe pain.[45]

Somewhere in the auxiliaries of that last sentence the settler becomes as invisible as Odysseus to the blinded cyclops. The boy "might" just have bit himself because he "might not" necessarily have been kicked on the lip. Dinesen's English publishers, sensitive to the British image in Kenya, wanted to delete this too trenchant incident from their edition. But the greatest irony may be that when commenting *in propria persona* on the meaning of the boy's death for her, Dinesen is co-opted by the identical imperial script that she had found so grotesquely obtuse. Though the settler was absolved of murder, guilty only of "grievous hurt," Dinesen leaves her readers to conclude that blame for the death was inappropriately displaced onto the native child himself;

yet for her, Kitosch's story really illustrated "a strange, a humiliating fact that the Europeans should not, in Africa, have power to throw the African out of existence. The country is his Native land, and whatever you do to him, when he goes he goes by his own free will, and because he does not want to stay."[46] According to Dinesen's sentimental myth-making, when the colonist murders the native, it is the native who is humiliating the imperialist by his freedom, nobly displaying his unwillingness to live!

Such narratives reinforce hegemonic interpretations of the colonized. One might compare Jomo Kenyatta's satiric Gikuyu parable in *Facing Mount Kenya: The Tribal Life of the Gikuyu* (1938)[47] to Ruskin's advice about "seizing every piece of fruitful waste ground." Kenyatta, Kenya's Prime Minister and first President after the country's independence in 1963, illustrates the land relations between the indigenous Gikuyu and the Europeans by recounting one of the oral tales of his people, a brief beast fable later retitled by Achebe "The Gentlemen of the Jungle." In it, the native is the "man"; the Europeans are, in an amusing narrative reversal, the jungle animals. The elephant, with the complicity of other beasts with claws and teeth, pushes the man from his house. The ensuing government panel of inquiry is loaded with jungle lords more "educated" than the man, self-avowedly honorable and divinely chosen—how can "the man" complain if the "unoccupied space" in his hut is awarded to the elephant? The tale ends with the annihilation of the imperialist: "'Ng'enda thi ndagaga motegi,' which literally means 'there is nothing that treads on the earth that cannot be trapped,' or in other words, you can fool people for a time, but not for ever."[48] Kenyatta's use of a proverb in the Gikuyu tongue is a display of an aroused native empowerment.

The trap is sprung when the dispute between the imperialist and native ripens into imperialists greedily fighting among themselves for the spoils: "Presently they all began disputing about their rights of penetration, and from disputing they came to fighting, and while they were all embroiled together the man set the hut on fire and burnt it to the ground, jungle lords and all. Then he went home, saying: 'Peace is costly, but it's worth the expense,' and lived happily ever after."[49] The legalistic phrase "rights of penetration" (Kenyatta presumably supplies this equivalent for whatever the Gikuyu locution) crystallizes the allegorical significance of the ending. When the natives cease to cooperate and the imperialists kindle internecine squabbles (perhaps an echo of World War I belligerence among the colonies) the solution of the "man" is to burn out the jungle lords, throwing their imperial rhetoric of "peace and tranquility" back at them. Homer's tale of Polyphemus had ended nearly similarly, with a narrow escape and a lasting curse for Odysseus. The frontispiece of Kenyatta's volume, heavy with symbolism, shows the highly educated author in native dress, assegai in hand, almost as if the Mau-Mau insurrection and the massacre at Lari in 1953 were foreseen.

Not surprisingly the modern African writer rejects the imperialist's "story" of peace and knowledge, the sort of incursion that Mungo Park unabashedly described as opening "new sources of wealth," but also the missionary's "story" as he encountered it in his mission school—the former because it was exploitative, the latter because it was paternalistic. The boys on the plain are afraid of the Boogie with no name; indeed, to cry out against him, like Polyphemus among his fellow cave dwellers, is merely to have been tricked into disavowing "no man's" instrumentality in their anguish: "I was filled with laughter to see how like a charm the name deceived them."[50] The contemporary African writer must cry out against Noman, not in the preordained, self-serving rhetoric of the imperialist but in a new voice. If Noman has coopted written language to his purposes, a writer such as Kenyatta must throw back at him in the native tongue the arrogant words of the Lion, who, with no mention of justice, only wanted "'peace and tranquillity' in his kingdom."

Kenyatta's parable appeared only two years after Isak Dinesen in *Out of Africa* had described autobiographically her experiences among the Kikuyu (same tribe, alternate spelling) on her plantation outside of Nairobi. For Dinesen, the Kikuyu squatters on her farm were, as we have noted previously, "the children of the land" with whom, ideally, "the white pioneers lived in guileless harmony."[51] Much more ironically she had observed in *Out of Africa*:

> The squatters are Natives, who with their families hold a few acres on a white man's farm, and in return have to work for him a certain number of days in the year. My squatters, I think, saw the relationship in a different light, for many of them were born on the farm, and their fathers before them, and they very likely regarded me as a sort of superior squatter on their estates.[52]

Her readers certainly saw this as a joke on the native's failure to fathom the legalities of modern ownership; but there is no clue that Dinesen saw it any differently—though in that case its irony is devastatingly turned back upon her!

| ONE: Empire & Colony |

Certainly in 1877, not long after Haggard arrived in Natal, the level of his political self-awareness did not seem high, inasmuch as he complacently describes the Boers' *modus operandi* for stealing the native's land in the Transvaal in precisely the same way the Gikuyu to the north described the British grasping the natives' homesteads: hospitable Africans and polite Europeans; then trickery, lies, and intimidation fobbed off as justice and divine authority.[53] Haggard's "Zulu War-Dance" begins with a discussion of what he and his contemporaries called "the Native Question," how to manage the competing claims of Europeans and Africans to Natal, the growing *colonia:*

> In all that world-wide empire which the spirit of English colonisation has conquered from out of the realms of the distant and unknown, and added year by year to the English dominions, it is doubtful whether there be any one spot of corresponding area, presenting so many large questions— social and political—as the colony of Natal. Wrested some thirty years ago from the patriarchal Boers, and peopled by a few scattered scores of adventurous emigrants ... the seeds of great political trouble were planted in the young colony, seeds whose fruit is fast ripening before our eyes. When the strong aggressive hand of England has grasped some fresh portion of the earth's surface, there is yet a spirit of justice in her heart and head which prompts the question, among the first of such demands, as to how best and most fairly to deal by the natives of the newly-acquired land.[54]

The paradoxical quality of this last sentence can hardly be more ironic: Haggard's ideal is of a virtuous liberal imperialism that will treat the natives with justice and fairness, yet the government already "has grasped" with "strong aggressive hand" the land that the natives, formerly under their indigenous rulers, had cultivated or upon which they had hunted.

Of course, Haggard's argument would be that the Boers, the first Dutch-Huguenot settlers, originally conquered Natal and that the British merely annexed the territory from them, inheriting the Native Question. But the natives put the issue more simply: "When the missionaries came to Africa they had the Bible and we had the land. They said 'Let us pray.' We closed our eyes. When we opened them we had the Bible and they had the land."[55] Haggard as early as 1877 was not unaware of this contradiction at the heart of the British colonizing effort—but he hoped the "heart and head" of a virtuous liberal imperialism could somehow dissolve the simmering contradictions before they exploded in violence:

There is now at work among the Kafir population the same motive power which has raised in turn all white nations, and, having built them up to a certain height has then set to work to sap them until they have fallen—the power of civilisation. Hand in hand the missionary and the trader have penetrated the locations. The efforts of the teacher have met with but a partial success. "A Christian may be a good man in his way, but he is a Zulu spoiled," said Cetywayo, King of the Zulus, when arguing the question of Christianity with the Secretary for Native Affairs [Theophilus Shepstone]; and such is, not altogether wrongly, the general feelings of the natives. With the traders it has been different. Some have dealt honestly—and more, it is to be feared, dishonestly—not only with those with whom they have had dealings, but with their fellow-subjects and their Government. It is these men chiefly who have, in defiance of the law, supplied the natives with those two great modern elements of danger and destruction, the gin-bottle and the rifle. The first is as yet injurious only to the recipients, but it will surely re-act on those who have taught them its use; the danger of possessing the rifle may come home to us any day and at any moment.[56]

The Zulu War was less than two years away.

As with Schreiner's *Thoughts on South Africa*[57] and Livingstone's *Missionary Travels*,[58] so Haggard in "The Transvaal" applied imagery from the biblical accounts of the Israelites' conquest of the Promised Land to describe the subjugation of Africa by the Boers, showing how the Victorians supplemented the ancient Homeric imperial paradigm with a religious precedent of equal cultural influence: "For many years they had, like the children of Israel, to contend with fierce tribes who gave and took no mercy; for many years their hand was to be against every man's and every man's hand against them."[59] But submerged in the imagery of that "hand against" is the further biblical analogue of Hagar's child, "a wild ass of a man,"[60] making the natives and Boers children of the flesh, endowing the British as the heirs of promise. Bertram Mitford in *The Induna's Wife* (1898) makes dramatic use of this paradigm, when just before the famous historical massacre by the Zulus of Piet Retief's delegation, the Boers proclaim: "We crossed the mountains in obedience to the will of God. It was His will that we should seek out a new land for our wives and our children, and His finger it was that guided us hither. We are even as the People of God in old times, who went to dwell in the land which He had promised them; and, even as they, we are ruled and led by the Great Book."[61]

Although even a broad-minded liberal like Schreiner never attempted to integrate native culture explicitly into her colonial identity, she begins her autobiographical novel with a symbolic and inescapable relationship to the "savage." As Schreiner's autobiographical stand-in, the boy Waldo in *The Story of an African Farm* discovers in the aboriginal artist a "writing of the self," the Bushman's petroglyphs comprising an intuitive native autobiography that brings the hidden self to light. This passage on the primitive artist is very likely a fictionalized adaptation of Barrow's passage on an aboriginal drawing of a unicorn in *Travels*:[62]

> They sat under a shelving rock, on the surface of which were still visible some old Bushman-paintings, their red and black pigments having been preserved through long years from wind and rain by the overhanging ledge; grotesque oxen, elephants, rhinoceroses, and a one-horned beast, such as no man ever has seen or ever shall....
>
> "Sometimes ... it seems the stones are really speaking—speaking of . . . the time when the little Bushmen lived here, so small and so ugly, and used to sleep in the wild dog holes, and in the 'sloots,' and eat snakes, and shot the bucks with their poisoned arrows. It was one of them, one of those old wild Bushmen, that painted those," said the boy, nodding towards the pictures—"one who was different from the rest. He did not know why, but he wanted to make something beautiful—he wanted to make something, so he made these. He worked hard, very hard, to find the juice to make the paint; and then he found this place where the rocks hang over, and he painted them. To us they are only strange things, that make us laugh; but to him they were very beautiful."
>
> The children had turned round and looked at the pictures.
>
> "He used to kneel here naked, painting, painting, painting; and he wondered at the things he made himself," said the boy, rising and moving his hand in deep excitement. "Now the Boers have shot them all, so that we never see a yellow face peeping out among the stones."[63]

In her novel's preface, Schreiner, in summing up her craft, had applied to herself as author this same activity of "painting": the novelist, she says, "must paint what lies before him,"[64] whether that be a truthful inward reality or a scientifically accurate external world. If Waldo Farber's patronym (*farber* as a colorist) paints him as a double of his admired Bushman, both Waldo and the Bushman are again doubled in Schreiner the autobiographical novelist who "paints." Could Schreiner's analogues be sensitive to differently constructed cultures, providing an image for the novelist that mitigates the oppression of oral cultures that Claude Lévi-Strauss finds inherent in writing, implicit perhaps even in the missionaries' dispersion of biblical translations? Waldo's eerie observation on the fate of the Bushmen—the boys on the plain, as it were—is perhaps so laconic not only because it reflects a genocide that was an all-too-familiar and irremediable fact by the year 1862 (the time-setting of her novel) but also because he is echoing Schreiner's resignation at colonial society's hostility to the artist's visionary quest. Schreiner knew that the scripts colonial Victorianism furnished were not those she wished for her fiction or her life—tales of racial loyalty well rewarded, of marriage for wealth and position, of the fallen woman as pariah, of "hair-breadth escapes"[65] by great white hunters, or of the South African plains and its frightened boys as the fitting scene of commercial enterprise.

Indeed, Homer's imperialist Ulysses constantly recurs as a prototype for colonial awarenesses and attitudes. For example, Dinesen's pen-portrait of old Knudsen presents an ironic imperialist—a seafarer, and thus like Tennyson's intrepid Ulysses, he is marooned by age on land: "He had experienced many things: shipwrecks, plague, fishes of unknown colouring, drinking-spouts, water-spouts, three contemporaneous suns in the sky, false friends, black villainy, short successes, and showers of gold that instantly dried up again. One strong feeling ran through his Odyssey: the abomination of the law, and all its works, and all its doings."[66] Small, weak, he had "the soul of a Berserk."[67] And like Tennyson's restless king, his ambition in the face of his mortality knew no bounds: "A short time before he died he confided to me, under the promise of secrecy, a tremendous plan.... He was, he told me, going to lift, from the bottom of Lake Naivasha, the hundred thousand tons of guano dropped there, from the time of the creation of the world, by the swimming-birds."[68] Dinesen's epic, mythologizing diction ironizes his quest for wealth. Knudsen's is the imperial dream gone haywire. Here Knudsen pursues neither the diamonds of Haggard's adventurers nor, even, the ivory of Conrad's insane Kurtz, but birdshit—presumably for fertilizer, although it also was and still is an ingredient in some expensive feminine cosmetics. The question his figure poses is this: might Dinesen have surmised that on some level her mock-epic pen-portrait could very well apply to her, as much as to her fellow Dane Knudsen? Might she not be naively misreading Knudsen's physical accidentals of person (akin to a book's hardness and color) as his essential significance living there on her farm in Africa? This is also the interpretive problem that we encounter in Haggard: not what he says—or says he says—but what he means. In this one must separate the sentimental fantasies of current political agendas from the unvarnished realities of what can be known or inferred about Haggard's own limitations and accomplishments.

| ONE: Empire & Colony |

಼಻ ಼಻

Haggard's early manhood was the stuff of fiction—quite literally. Whatever praise or blame his many novels may deserve, one fact is indisputable: when he wrote of Africa, he wrote of what he had seen, done, or heard from eyewitnesses, although he also deliberately intermixed with his facts elements of the fantastic, of the supernatural and of fictional history to give his tales an aura of exoticism. Certainly no one would have predicted literary fame for young Haggard. He was born in 1856 in Norfolk, England, sixth son (eighth of ten children) of William and Ella Haggard. Haggard's mother, who spent her early years in colonial Bombay, imparted to him something of that British construction of the mystical and erotic East—Hindu beliefs in reincarnation and, as later described by E. M. Forster in *A Passage to India* (1924), the mystery or muddle of "God si Love" and those equivocal echoes in the Malabar Caves. Ella Haggard was also a poet, and lines from her "Life and Its Author" might have engraved themselves deeply on her son's imagination: "Life infinite, diverse, pervading all..../ Dark web involved! Oh mystery profound!"[69]

Haggard's father was a barrister and country squire who seems either not to have recognized his son's abilities or to have tired of paying for Rider's older brothers at the university. At any rate, after Ipswich Grammar School, Haggard did not prepare to enter the university. Instead, he failed an army entrance examination, studied for the Foreign Office examinations, experimented with spiritualism, and fell in love with Lilly ("Lilith") Jackson. He seems to have been that typical Victorian younger son of the gentry—dreamy, melancholy, and professionally unfocused, lying about on the hearth rug waiting for the light to dawn on his life.

But when Sir Henry Bulwer, Squire Haggard's friend, was newly named Lieutenant-Governor of Natal Colony, Haggard's father wrote to inquire if Bulwer could somehow make use of Rider in Africa. Possibly the squire pressured his son into the job to put some distance between Rider and the girl he wanted to marry. Bulwer's answer was positive; and Haggard, duties undefined, embarked for South Africa with Sir Henry in 1875 for what became the defining half-dozen years of his life. At that time, present-day South Africa consisted of independent territories, among them the Cape Colony and Natal (chiefly British), the Orange Free State and the Transvaal (Boer, i.e., Dutch), Zululand and Basutoland (tribal). Africa galvanized him, awakened his latent abilities. He became the governor's trusted aide, hobnobbed with the imperial elite, learned to speak Zulu (probably the autodidact's way: "learn a little, use it a lot"), negotiated with African chieftains, hunted from galloping horses, and, as he later told his brother, found the world a very red apple—observing that even if women sometimes have rotten hearts, the outside of the apple is no less red and women are not less beautiful because they are false! Although he determined not to bite that red apple of love too deeply, Haggard undoubtedly enjoyed its casual flavors in Africa.

Haggard-the-attaché becoming Haggard-the-romance-writer can be traced in his early descriptive and polemical prose written during his time in Africa: "A Zulu War-Dance" (1877), "The Transvaal" (1877), and "A Visit to the Chief Secocoeni" (1877). In particular, the relation between the Zulu warriors and the British as presented in these essays became the political and imaginative context for Haggard's work. In Haggard's description of his first diplomatic excursion into a Natal-protected tribal area, where he observes that "when the strong aggressive hand of England has grasped some fresh portion of the earth's surface," despite "a spirit of justice in her heart and head"—all the game gets shot: "All around rose the great bush-clad hills, so green, so bright in the glorious streaming sunlight, and yet so awfully devoid of life, so solemnly silent. It was indeed a sight never to be forgotten, this wide panoramic out-look, with its towering hills, its smiling valleys, its flashing streams, its all-pervading sunlight, and its deep sad silence...."[70]

He draws an implicit analogy here between the game and the natives—the imperialist annihilates the former and emasculates the latter. In a passage that later in his romance served to model Sir Henry Curtis, who went native before the climactic battle, Haggard paints the once-heroic Zulu warrior

> arrayed in the full panoply of savage war. With his right hand he grasped his spears, and on his left hung his large black ox-hide shield, lined on its inner side with spare assegais. From the "man's" ring round his head arose a single tall grey plume, robbed from the Kafir crane. His broad shoulders were bare, and beneath the arm-pits was fastened a short garment of strips of skin, intermixed with ox-tails of different colours. From his waist hung a rude kilt made chiefly of goat's hair, whilst round the calf of the right leg was fixed a short fringe of black ox-tails. As he stood before us with lifted weapon and outstretched shield, his plume bending to the breeze, and his savage aspect made more savage still by the graceful, statuesque pose, the dilated eye and warlike mould of the set features, as he stood there, an emblem and a type of the times and the things which

are passing away, his feet resting on ground which he held on sufferance, and his hands grasping weapons impotent as a child's toy against those of the white man,—he who was the rightful lord of all,—what reflections did he not induce, what a moral did he not teach![71]

Because Haggard's "reflections" and moralizing are interrupted by the appearance of the native chief and the staging for entertainment of the war-dance, his readers are left to draw their own conclusions about the relation between weaponry and territorial control.

Already in 1877 when Haggard was writing his first essays, tens of thousands of Zulus had begun massing on the boarders of the Boer Republic of the Transvaal to attack five thousand armed Dutch, men and boys. Spear against rifle, it would have been a bloodbath destabilizing native-imperial relations in the surrounding territories, including Natal. Since at that moment the Zulus respected the British, if the Transvaal became a British crown colony the catastrophe could be averted. Gold and diamonds in the Transvaal provided the final incentive for British intervention. Haggard was recruited by the charismatic chief of native affairs, Sir Theophilus Shepstone, for this diplomatic mission; and their small group trekked to Pretoria, the capital, to inform the Dutch that the British were taking over their republic. Haggard's autobiography crystallizes this personal-national rite of passage with a strikingly posed photograph of the Commission to the Transvaal in front of their military-style tent, with the banner soon to be unfurled over Pretoria draped on a guy line and with the youthful but manly Haggard, his eyes boring straight into the camera, seated at the feet of his newfound spiritual father, Sir Theophilus Shepstone, the "white chief" (politically and unironically) of the Zulu nation. Standing in front of an armed, ominously silent crowd of Dutchmen, Haggard personally hoisted the Union Jack over Pretoria and, he recalled, "when the late Sir Melmoth Osborn grew nervous in reading the proclamation, I took it from his hand and finished the business," thereby claiming for his Queen (on her birthday) a territory as big as Great Britain itself.[72] For a young man, all but a boy, that certainly compensated for bypassing *Literae Humaniores* at Oxford! Years later, Haggard's romance *Finished* (1917) dramatized this moment of glory in full.[73] One suspects a *quid pro quo* between Haggard's ceremonial flag-raising and his early essay on the looming Transvaal crisis in *Macmillan's Magazine* the same month, inasmuch as the essay's rhetoric had culminated with a vision of the British flag about to be unfurled over the Dutch Republic. On the way back to Natal the small group escaped a fatal night ambush by the Boers only because Haggard had convinced his companions to take the scenic moonlit route.

Afterwards, Haggard served as assistant to the Transvaal colonial secretary and was appointed as Registrar and Master of the Transvaal High Court. But news of Lilly Jackson's marriage back in England devastated him. On a trip back to England, Haggard met and married a Norfolk heiress with whom he returned to Africa to take up ostrich farming on the border of Natal and the Transvaal. But beyond any doubt, the Zulu War (1879) was the global event of Haggard's 1875–1881 African years. Describing the battleground at the outbreak of the Anglo-Zulu War in *Finished*, Haggard has Allan Quatermain report: "To the right of us was a stony eminence and to our left, its sheer brown cliffs of rock rising like the walls of some cyclopean fortress, the strange, abrupt mount of Islandhlwana."[74] Either words have a mysterious life of their own or, more likely, Haggard's subconscious opened itself to the romantic influence of classical allusion. Or was Haggard here fully cognizant and Quatermain merely subliminally aware? At any rate, "cyclopean" designates not only large, irregular blocks but also connotes both the Cyclopes as a class of early builders—mythical artists—and the rocks Polyphemus hurled at the ship of the boasting Ulysses. As Ulysses's imperial violation and pride was punished by the gods, so, on this day of the new moon, the overly confident British at Islandhlwana are about to be overwhelmed by the Zulu army.

After the British debacle at Islandhlwana, Haggard served briefly in 1879 in the Pretoria Horse:

> In those pre-cable times it must take a long while before reinforcements could arrive from England, and as the situation in Zululand was very urgent after this disaster, there was a great demand for volunteers, and especially for volunteers who could ride, shoot, and knew the country and the natives. Under these circumstances the authorities allowed a mounted corps of Englishmen to be raised at Pretoria, of which corps I was elected adjutant and lieutenant.... This corps, which was named the Pretoria Horse, was about sixty strong, and for the most part composed of Colonial-born men of more or less gentle birth. A smarter body of irregular cavalry than it became after a month or so of steady drill, it would, I think, have been difficult to find, as every trooper in it could ride well, while many were fine rifle shots, and almost all of them were thoroughly acquainted with the country and the natives whom they were to fight.[75]

But whereas Haggard knew Natal and the Transvaal intimately, his autobiography, *Days of My Life* (1926), shows he never travelled into Zululand as a young man. Although he wrote an account of Islandhlwana and Rorke's Drift for Andrew Lang's *The True Story Book* (1900) and fictionally described the bloodshed of Islandhlwana in three works, *The Witch's Head* (1884), *Black Heart and White Heart* (1896) and *Finished* (1917), he did not visit the Anglo-Zulu battlegrounds until he returned to Africa as a government commissioner in 1914, as described in his *Diary of an African Journey* (2000).

More political trouble loomed in 1881. The Boers wanted their country back, and a commando of old men and boys slaughtered the *rooibaatjes* at Majuba Hill (properly Amajuba, Zulu for "the hill of doves"). Strangely, because Haggard's farm was on the border, his kitchen was used to negotiate the treaty reestablishing Dutch independence. Haggard felt the retrocession of the Transvaal to the Boers to be a "great betrayal" of settlers and natives alike by the Gladstone government. Recalling that moment years later in a 1905 speech in Canada in the wake of the Boer War, he declared with sonorous Edwardian pomposity:

> I was with Sir Theophilus Shepstone when we annexed the Transvaal; ... I had the honour of hoisting the flag of England over it. Gentlemen, I lived, too, to see the flag pulled down and buried. And I tell you this— ... it was the bitterest hour of my life; ... my old chief, Sir Theophilus Shepstone, was right, and they disgraced him; and even I, humble as I was, was right, and they mocked at me. We know the end. Thus my residential and official connection with South Africa came to an end—I would not stop there any longer.[76]

Haggard believed England paid for its expedient capitulation in 1881 when later in the Anglo-Boer War it attempted to regain the control it had relinquished.

Having escaped one ambush in 1877, Haggard thought it safest to return to England with his wife and child to study law—and write, at first with only modest success. Upon his return from Africa Haggard had found England by comparison a spiritually barren society spawning a crude mass of worthless fiction. Haggard's first book was not fiction, however, but came in the wake of the Zulu War: *Cetywayo and His White Neighbours* (1882), a study of British relations with the Zulus and Boers before 1879. It appeared shortly after he returned to England and was essentially a greatly expanded version of his 1877 essays on the political and social system of the Zulus, particularly that on the Transvaal, with his other two essays reprinted as appendices. In the broadest sense, this polemical analysis was designed to defend Shepstone as the guardian of peace, happiness, and prosperity for Zulus,

Boers, and British alike and to attack critics for scapegoating Shepstone when political events went wrong. Haggard maintained that Shepstone did not incite the Zulus to threaten invasion of the Transvaal so that the Boers would accept British protection; nor was Shepstone cynical enough to allow the Zulus and Boers to go to war so that the British could mop up afterwards; rather, from the highest principles of humanitarianism (so Haggard believed), Shepstone quickly annexed the region to prevent a Zulu invasion and avoid a slaughter that might well have spilled over into the rest of southern Africa—specifically, Natal and the Cape. Haggard knew his "spiritual father" well and told the truth as he understood it. Haggard's truth, however, did postulate the right of the Boers and British to settle Africa. Certainly territorial encroachment and bloody internecine warfare were part of Africa long before the Europeans arrived, *à la* Sol Plaatje's descriptions in *Mhudi* (1930), but the British and Boers brought new weapons and vastly different cultural practices—minorities with overwhelming technology. On this political asymmetry Haggard's fiction was about to be built.

❧ TWO

Heretic in Disguise

The injury to Haggard's reputation occurred early in his career when he ripped into the dominant fictional practices of realism and naturalism. His manifesto, "About Fiction" (1887), earned him the sort of vituperation that better known pronouncements—such as the Preface to the second edition of *Lyrical Ballads* (1800) or Virginia Woolf's "Modern Fiction" (1925)—largely escaped. Between a bowdlerized realism and a harsh naturalism at the end of the century lay Haggard's romances. Haggard knew that realism ought to recognize the failure of mimesis and to question how objective reality could be represented. But his solution was not to strip back the polite surfaces of an earlier infatuation with simple appearances to expose the harsh realities of naturalism; nor was it to disavow action in favor of attitudes, those finely discriminated sensations and ideas of the psychological novel epitomized by Woolf's absorption in the "moment of being." For Haggard the Aristotelian *mythos* is constituted as much by dramatic physical action as by inner states of being. In a sense, however, what Woolf describes in "The Moment: Summer Night"[1] as "the terror, the exultation" as the walls of the moment open and the self is freed reappears in Haggard as a romantic interest in the exotic and mysterious, the depths of the occult imagination.

In his day Haggard was dismissed by the literary inner circle as the beneficiary of a mere momentary commercial popularity, a repudiation doubtless attributable to his explicitly voiced patriotism and piety; also, perhaps as Andrew Lang suggested, even those accusations of plagiarism against *King Solomon's Mines* and *Jess* were triggered by envy at Haggard's astonishing success.[2] Obviously similarities among passages, in and by themselves, are not necessarily evidence of derivation; but more to the point, a *transformative* use of preexisting historical material for an altogether new creation is the *essence* of originality.

One may also note that Haggard reinvents the stock characters and plot devices employed in mass-market boy's adventure stories so that mature readers, ordinary and discriminating alike, find his plots fresh and exciting. Afterwards in the twentieth century, Haggard was additionally censured as an exponent of colonial racism; but even in that shifting climate of opinion his popularity was not effaced. As C. S. Lewis observed: "The promised time 'when the Rudyards cease from kipling and the Haggards ride no more' has failed to arrive. Obstinately, scandalously, Haggard continues to be read and re-read. Why?"[3] Of course, Lewis wrote that well-nigh a half century ago. But it is still true. So, again, why? Because Haggard can tell a story, a story that outwardly may conform to Victorian-Edwardian standards but that also fosters a progressive and perspicacious cultural vision. These African romances have a disturbing relevance not merely to the British Empire and its past cultural ideals but equally to events and anxieties in the twenty-first century.

In his life, beliefs, and fiction Haggard thoroughly assimilated the mythologies and social codes of his time and took their measure. Yet he was an authentic heretic in the root sense of that word: *hairetiós, haireîsthai*, one who chooses; that is, one who makes choices contrary to the socially constructed, regnant ideals and practices of his culture. In biographical accounts, Haggard is now widely acknowledged to have violated the taboo of miscegenation by taking a native mistress; in his cultural observations he seconded the subversive endorsement by Bishop J. W. Colenso of polygamy among native converts; and in his fiction he rejected the dominant mode of realism in favor of romance and its intimations of darkly disturbing cultural practices and occult experiences. Incidentally, with respect to Haggard's native mistress, even the saintly David Livingstone did not quite escape suspicion, at least if Frank Harris is taken at face value. Alluding to the numerous natives of mixed ancestry he met while taking the route of Livingstone, Harris commented that "It grew to be a joke with us that we were following in the missionary's footsteps."[4] Whatever Livingstone's venal transgressions, his deeply held Scottish Presbyterianism is not in doubt; even that great father of the church, Augustine, sowed his oats in Carthage, albeit in his early years. But with Victorian respectability attaining epidemic proportions, a disconnect between Haggard's overt stance and covert feelings must have become an inevitability. He remains a member of the English gentry, but one whose vision has been camouflaged, not obliterated, by the conventions of his social role as "gentleman," the highest accolade he can envision.[5] That Haggard in numerous ways was in advance of popular opinion will be shown herein; but that he exceeded the liberalism of Bishop Colenso's social preachments would be, of course, a preposterous anachronism. Yet he is able to set aside his own caste convictions when analyzing the agricultural issues of England; at other moments, his cultural relativism and religious skepticism led him to create personae who promulgate for him his progressive or subversive views: his liberal views on native polygamy and his skepticism in weighing the tenet of eternal punishment (Colenso, again), his support for the natives against Boer oppression and governmental disenfranchisement—in these and many other areas he was an empirical and probing, even at times crusading, novelist.

Haggard's fiction is ideally suited to a freely applied New Historicist interpretation of the interconnections among his textual personae, his own personal life and behavior, and the cultural belief systems that both bind him and are subverted by him. Like Joseph Conrad and Rudyard Kipling, Haggard was intrigued by cultural differences. Ian Fletcher's judgment on Haggard's "interest in the relativity of cultures," however, is dismissive: "He is a much more naive writer, of course, than either, but he worries over the same questions as the more profound writers of his time. The novels and romances reflect his wavering moods. Sometimes he is sceptical about the European virtues and highly pessimistic about progress, enlightenment and civilisation. At others, he exalts the white man, and particularly the English gentleman."[6] Certainly Haggard's novels did not propagate the popular ideology of "the white man's burden"; rather, he incisively and (*contra* Fletcher) astutely criticized the racism, commercial greed, and moral narrowness of the imperial enterprise. Further, Haggard promoted an ideal of Zulu national consciousness; supported the political, economic, and social equality of the sexes; and expounded groundbreaking theories of anthropology and psychology.

Progressively and proactively, he introduced in his fiction contesting representations, celebrating traditional Zulu values that had been destroyed, thus humanizing the Zulus and their history for the British public in the wake of the Zulu War. In his dedication of *Child of Storm* (1913), Haggard included a paragraph on their loss of past glory and present demoralization:

> Now everything is changed, or so I hear, and doubtless in the balance this is best. Still we may wonder what are the thoughts that pass through the mind of some ancient warrior of Chaka's or Dingaan's time, as he suns

himself crouched on the ground, for example, where once stood the royal kraal, Duguza, and watches men and women of the Zulu blood passing homeward from the cities or the mines, bemused, some of them, with the white man's smuggled liquor, grotesque with the white man's cast-off garments, hiding, perhaps, in their blankets examples of the white man's doubtful photographs—and then shuts his sunken eyes and remembers the plumed and kilted regiments making that same ground shake as, with a thunder of salute, line upon line, company upon company, they rushed out to battle.[7]

Picturing this tarnished old Africa in the opening decades of the new twentieth century, Haggard betrays an immense disillusionment; indeed, because the old Africa already had been disappearing gradually long before the end of the nineteenth century, Haggard perceived not only that it had faded but that it soon would be forgotten. He could not let that happen.

In recent years, countering the natives' demoralization has become a task that Chief Gatsha Buthelezi—the Chief Executive Officer of the KwaZulu Government and great-grandson of Mnyamana, Cetshwayo's Prime Minister and army commander at the battles of Isandhlwana and Khambula—undoubtedly would consider fundamental to reestablishing "the Zulu national consciousness." A recent South African press release quotes Chief Buthelezi:

> another of my hopes for my people is the return of Zulu pride—pride in what they were, are and can be. Somehow, without the intention to do so, a feeling has been inculcated that we should be ashamed of everything that constitutes our past. To many people the old Zulu kingdom means just bloodshed, but it had other positive aspects in the sense that our political and social system was based on it. With the overthrow of the Zulu kingdom came the shattering of much of the Zulu national consciousness. We can get back this national consciousness, step by step, in the best possible way, if our people have the right once more to make decisions about their own future.[8]

Haggard was supportive of "the Zulu national consciousness" but aware of its moral ambiguities—as Buthelezi's use of the adverb, not adjective, in the phrase "just bloodshed" evidently implies.

Also among Haggard's progressive and proactive concerns is the presentation of woman's lives, both native and European, within a patriarchal colonialism. If such powerfully aggressive females as Ayesha and Mameena threaten familial and political stability, nonetheless other figures such as Allan's wives and heroines such as those in *Maiwa, Ghost Kings, Benita, Treasure of the Lake, Yellow God* and numerous other novels are strong, passionate, and principled women. One can certainly see in Haggard's fiction feminist resemblances to the radical opinions of his co-colonist, Olive Schreiner. After the success of *She*, Haggard observed in "About Fiction" (1887) that contemporary Anglo-American writing was either dreary and insipid or decadently naturalistic. Haggard invited his reader to "consult his own mind, and see how many novels proper among the hundreds that have been published within the last five years, and which deal in any way with every day contemporary life, have excited his profound interest. The present writer can at the moment recall but two—one was called 'My Trivial Life and Misfortunes,' by an unknown author, and the other, 'The Story of a South African Farm,' by Ralph Iron."9 According to Haggard, who cited Olive Schreiner's male pseudonym and somewhat inattentively annexed "South" to the title of this most famous novel of a *"colonia"* written in that century, *The Story of an African Farm* (1883) is a notable contemporary narrative of "spiritual intensity." Among all empire writers, Schreiner comes closest in her pro-native politics, her African animistic beliefs, her mythic-allegorical allusiveness, and in her vision of the political, economic, and social equality of the sexes. In Schreiner's thought and career one can catch the iconoclastic voice of Haggard's own colonial resistance, although neither Haggard nor Schreiner questioned the morality of colonization per se since they both believed in the possibility of a nonexploitative, Anglo-African settlement.

Like Haggard, Schreiner stood to benefit from the political and economic structures of imperialism, though as a daughter in the patriarchal household she would have gained less than her brothers. And precisely because of this marginalization, she ultimately may have floundered in her role as a colonial wife and mother, impatient with her traditional options yet also, as author, in need of a social script that would allow her to define what was distinctively African in herself or to connect with the indigenous populations either in their subjugation or in their latent power. Like her young heroines, Schreiner inhabited an almost wholly insular European cultural domain from which she gradually had to surmount the racial impediments of the colonial venture and reach toward other peoples:

> One of my earliest memories is of walking up and down on the rocks behind the little Mission House in which I was born and making believe that I was Queen Victoria and that all the world belonged to me. That being the case, I ordered all the black people in South Africa to be collected and put into the desert of Sahara, and a wall built across Africa shutting it off; I then ordained that any black person returning south of that line should

have his head cut off. I did not wish to make slaves of them, but I wished to put them where I need never see them, because I considered them ugly. I do not remember planning that Dutch South Africans should be put across the wall, but my objection to them was only a little less.10

This confession appears almost identically again in her last major fictional effort, the unfinished novel *From Man to Man,* as part of little Rebekah's vision of the colonial world.11 The young Olive, like the fictional Rebekah, observes the varied and numerous indigenous populations of her land but fails to appreciate them as people like herself who, together with her family, should be the real determinants of her life and of the land in which she will live.

Ironically, this racist wall of apartheid that the real and fictional girls erect in fantasy is the same gendered wall that a colonial patriarchy begins to construct around them in *reality* as they grow older. As Schreiner's heroine Lyndall remarks in *The Story of an African Farm*:

> "They [parents] begin to shape us to our cursed end ... when we are tiny things in shoes and socks. We sit with our little feet drawn up under us in the window, and look out at the boys in their happy play. We want to go. Then a loving hand is laid on us: 'Little one, you cannot go,' they say, 'your little face will burn, and your nice white dress be spoiled.' We feel it must be for our good, it is so lovingly said; but we cannot understand; and we kneel still with one little cheek wistfully pressed against the pane. Afterward we go and thread blue beads, and make a string for our neck; and we go and stand before the glass. We see the complexion we were not to spoil, and the white frock, and we look into our own great eyes. Then the curse begins to act on us. It finishes its work when we are grown women, who no more look out wistfully at a more healthy life; we are contented. We fit our sphere as a Chinese woman's foot fits her shoe, exactly, as though God had made both—and yet he knows nothing of either."12

Gender stereotyping begins in earliest childhood, differentiating the robust outdoor play of the boys from the girls whose face and dress are to be their passports to successful marriage—white skin and white dress, the sheltered gentry's symbols of race and class. In Haggard and Schreiner's Africa, the female's choice was between marriage with motherhood and very little else—spinsterhood or prostitution. As a young adult, Lyndall decries the construction of this entrapping system of values. In the place of athletic activity is adorning the self with "blue beads" (precisely what Haggard's native Mameena wore also) and a narcissistic contemplation of oneself in the pool of the looking-glass. The restriction laid upon the child is "lovingly said," engendering a far stronger hold than fear and cruelly meant prohibitions. The child here is as unaware of the hidden coercion in the parent's "loving hand" as the native is of the cultural control implicit in the missionaries' proselytizings. This passage may well remind the reader of Haggard's paradoxical description in his first published work of the "strong aggressive hand of England" that "has grasped some fresh portion of the earth's surface" which nevertheless it purportedly does with "a spirit of justice in her heart and head," prompting the imperial question of "how best and most fairly to deal by the natives of the newly-acquired land."[13]

Schreiner's passage ends with a brilliant analogy to Chinese foot-binding. Like Quatermain's ordained Church of England father, Schreiner's father also had been a missionary. And in the missionary literature to which the young Schreiner would have been exposed, Christians protested this deforming practice. But the girl-child's "cursed end" is to be bound, no less than the foot of the Chinese woman, by a socially encouraged narcissism advertising her as a commodity. She is also encumbered, in the vernacular sense of the menstrual "curse," with the biological burden of being a woman destined for a narrow reproductive role in a male world. That this "curse" of menstruation should condemn the girl to a life of childbearing is no more seen as a distortion of nature in British and colonial culture than that the woman's foot should be crushed to fit her shoe is seen as inhuman by the Chinese. Thus socially constructed gender roles are understood by the grown woman to be natural and inevitable. Looking into the mirror the child and woman sees herself exactly as society wants her to see herself, as unconstrained, invisibly distorted according to a social plan. That Haggard sympathized with the plight of a woman such as Schreiner's Lyndall is evident from these remarks:

> Whatever her nature may be, however deep are her maternal and affectionate instincts, without sin and sorrow she may not gratify them except first she pass the lawful gate of holy matrimony.... Nature, in her simplicity, made certain arrangements to meet these difficulties; civilization in its wisdom has altered those arrangements,... has laid down new and stricter rules for the game, and, in consequence, too often the individual player must suffer and smile.... How long will the dam of custom and training resist these pent-up waters of disappointment and empty loss? And when Nature at last reasserts her sway (if she ever does) what will happen?... Which will win in the end, primary human impulse or inherited custom and tradition? That is one of the many problems of the unborn twentieth century. Or will the question settle itself in some fashion at present quite unforseen?[14]

In *Child of Storm* Haggard creates one of his greatest characters, a rebellious and deadly native beauty, Mameena, a "Zulu Helen" who rose from obscurity to seduce, to betray, to murder a Zulu prince, to cripple fatally a dynastic house, and to take poison on her lips with greater nobility than Cleopatra holding the asp to her bosom. She displays sexual resistance towards her unsuitable lovers, yet offers her coveted body to the champion of her own choosing. Schreiner's Lyndall might have spoken for Mameena, had Mameena been a white colonial South African. Mameena is perfectly aware of her gender restraints and stereotypes. When she proposes to Allan that he could become a white Zulu chief, he gasps "'You are mad! How would you do all these things?'" Her reply: "'I am not mad.... I am only what is called great, and you know well enough that I can do them, not by myself, who am but a woman and tied with the ropes that bind women, but with you to cut those ropes and help me.'"15 This is the classic feminist strategy of an indirect exercise of power brazenly exposed. There is also here a candid recognition of the political utility or, even, commercialization of desire, not its idealism: "'Every man wants power.... There is wealth in the land.... If you wished it even you could sweep out Natal and make the whites there your subjects, too.'"16 Since that first gloriously ironic opening sentence of *Pride and Prejudice* (1813)—"It is a truth universally acknowledged, that a single man in possession of a good fortune, must be in want of a wife"—marriage has been seen to hold an economic ingredient. Mameena tells the impatient Saduko: "As for the waiting, you must ask my father of that. Am I not his heifer, to be sold, and can I disobey my father?'"17 Perhaps her most revealing moment is when she says to Quatermain: "'I love you, Macumazahn, as you will never be loved till you die, and I shall never love any other man, however many I may marry.'"18 Oscar Wilde in *The Importance of Being Earnest* (1895) gives nearly the same line to Gwendolen saying farewell to Jack toward the end of Act I. But what could be farce in London was still brutal reality in Zululand.

When one recalls Dickens's near-caricature of Dora Copperfield, the child-wife of David, and then compares with that Haggard's depiction of Mameena, the difference is diametric. Of course, Mameena's love is destructive; but she is balanced with the constructive love of so many other Haggard heroines, such as Nada in *Nada the Lily* (1892) or Rachel in *Ghost Kings* (1908). What empowers these normative folk-pastoral heroines as they venture beyond Africa's imperial frontiers is the replacement of a Victorian image of correct, submissive womanhood with a combative, high-spirited feminist appropriation of virile and primitive energy. The sheltered, dependent middle-class woman whose wifely duty was to her husband alone may have been challenged by Alfred Tennyson's Lilias in *The Princess* (1847–1853), but only perhaps because the rights of women were displaced into a distant medieval setting. As late as John Ruskin's *Sesame and Lilies* (1865) in "Lilies: Of Queens' Gardens" the purity of the lily represented for women a life sheltered from all realities save those of birth and death. But on the African frontier one has only to recall Isak Dinesen's multiple "roles" on the coffee plantation to realize that the difficulties and perils shared by the sexes in Haggard's romances offer greater opportunities for equal partnership. Tennyson's neo-medieval fantasy became in Africa a real possibility. Thus in Haggard's *Nada the Lily*, the beautiful Zulu "lily" finally breaks the patriarchal mold by choosing for herself. Similarly, only by entirely dissolving his gender role does Schreiner's womanly Gregory Rose, crossdressed in woman's clothes, find an authentic identity by nursing Lyndall. Schreiner's novel had indicted traditional gender roles for deceit, cynicism and violence within and between the sexes. Gregory's escape from his biological identity was a direct result of his social autonomy on the Transvaal frontier.

Finally, Haggard's romances also reflect a progressive and active approach to anthropological and psychological investigations, dramatizing the problematics of using empirical methods to arrive at theoretical understandings. No explanation of reality can have meaning for Haggard unless it arises from the temporal and historical structure of human life. In much the same fashion as his contemporary, the German phenomenological historian Wilhelm Dilthey, Haggard begins fiction writing with the radical empiricism of psychological introspection, that is, with lived experience and its memories. Then, by virtue of the self's direct apprehension of relations and connections, he passes from autobiography to biography, to cultural history and, finally, to a near-mystic interpretation of fact. As Dilthey observed: "The power and breadth of our own lives and the energy with which we reflect on them are the foundation of historical vision. It alone enables us to give life back to the bloodless shadows of the past. Combined with an infinite desire to surrender to and lose one's self in the existence of others, it makes the great historian."[19] These stages in the historical method, as Dilthey discovers, are made possible by a "whole web of connections which stretches from individuals concerned with their own existence to cultural systems and communities and, finally, to the whole of mankind, which makes up the character of society and history."20 When in *She* the native guide inquires of Holly—"'Are there none in your land who can see without eyes and hear without ears?'"21—Billali is here presenting the ethnographer's and historian's challenge to hold to scientific principles and yet to transcend pragmatic observational limitations. Thus too Ayesha denies that the images in her incantation bowl are merely magical illusion: "'it is no magic; that is a fiction of ignorance. There is no such thing as magic, though there is such a thing as a knowledge of the secrets of Nature.'"22

For Haggard the body is surrounded by a phenomenal soul,23 much as Woolf's "nimbus" of consciousness surrounds the body. In *Benita* Haggard identifies Hegel as the exponent of the idea that visionaries with strangely sharp percipient powers tap into latent reflections and historic memories by merging the lesser private self into the wider or greater "sub-conscious self" which is the spirit of the universe.24 Such occurrences of "animal magnetism" or hypnotism were presented by Hegel as defying mere empirical concepts. Lecturing on "Mysticism," William James, in a footnote to *Varieties of Religious Experience* (1903), asks: "What reader of Hegel can doubt that the sense of a perfected Being with all its otherness soaked up into itself, which dominates his whole philosophy, must have come from the prominence in his consciousness of mystical moods like this [i.e., J. A. Symonds's "mystic state of mind"], in most persons kept subliminal? The notion is thoroughly characteristic of the mystical level, and the Aufgabe [duty] of making it articulate was surely set to Hegel's intellect by mystical feeling."25

Haggard did not benefit directly from Freud's "scientific" writing on dream interpretation; but he clearly assimilated classical, biblical, and contemporary spiritualist doctrines, as well as such theories as those of J. A. Symonds, M.D. (father of the well-known poet) in *In Sleep and Dreams* (1851). Symonds describes how an irrational dream-world may be superimposed upon the reality to which the dreamer awakes, the surreal and real thus experienced simultaneously. Perhaps Haggard also may be understood as a dissenting precursor to Sigmund Freud's essay "The Uncanny" (1919) on the perception of that which is "beyond" or "daemonic." The experience of Freud's *unheimlich* derives solely from the atavistic power of the mind over material reality and is implicit in animistic conceptions of the natural world. Although in *The Interpretation of Dreams* (third edition, 1911) Freud found Haggard's "fantastic" romance *She* (1887) to be "a *strange* book, but full of hidden meaning" about "the eternal feminine, the immortality of our emotions" (Chap. 6, "The Dream-Work"),26 he nonetheless considered the uncanny a mere psychic defense, not unlike Allan Quatermain's persistently explaining away such events in terms of "a natural interpretation."27 But for Haggard, the uncanny affirmed transcendence; almost like Tertullian's *credo quia absurdum*, Haggard kept faith even in the face of logical explanations—whether of Quatermain's sort or of Freud's.

Psychic investigators among the Victorians differed as to whether evolution implied that humans were gaining or losing psychic aptitudes. For such figures as Frederick Myers and J. Milne Bramwell, so Frank Podmore has argued, the evolutionary process impoverished modern individuals by eliminating or diminishing their occult gifts—precognition, prestidigitation, clairvoyance, extrasensory perception, telepathy, divination, materializations, and (for Haggard) shape-shifting.28 Is the Victorian afraid that the savage may destroy the civilized self? Does the bestial simian Mr. Hyde of Stevenson's allegory cause every educated Dr. Jekyll to repress and vanquish his primitive side? Or does the white man need the assistance of primitive strength and virility to reanimate? If so, is "the primitive" Africa's darkness or Africa's enlightenment? Thus Haggard maps and champions the important area of African spirituality, including a nobility of vision that even, as for W. B. Yeats, included good manners. If Haggard believed along with other colonists that the natives were less evolved, their supernatural skills lost by ostensibly more-advanced civilizations gave them genuine superiority: Quatermain says at one point that Umslopogaas understood "'perchance because such primitive natures are in closer touch with high and secret things than we imagine, perchance for other reasons.'"29 This is given splendid expression in *Allan and the Holy Flower* (1915) when a prophetic Zulu witch-doctor tells Quatermain: "'Ah,' said Mavovo, 'you white men are very clever, and think that you know everything. But it is not so, for in learning so much that is new, you have forgotten more that is old. When the Snake [spirit] that is in you, Macumazahn, dwelt in a black savage like me a thousand thousand years ago, you could have done and did what I do.'"30 Later the novel's "wandering Jew" figure—actually an American Episcopal missionary—observes that there is no explanation for "'native vision ... except the old one that there are more things in heaven and earth, etc., and that God gives different gifts to different men.'"31

In "Lost on the Veld" Haggard attributes to the natives a superior, atavistic sense of direction: "Natives are, of course, much less likely to be lost than white men, since, even in stretches of country which they do not know, the instinct of locality and direction is far stronger in them than in us, out of whom, in many instances, it has been bred in the course of generations."32 Some traces of psychic powers still remain in gifted Anglos, though perhaps like Lady Ragnall in *The Ivory Child* these often are prompted by means of the "Taduki" drug. But certainly in *The Wizard*, one of Haggard's finest novels, the power of the uncanny derives from a spiritual disrobing of Western materialism. Not only did Haggard describe in his autobiography such instances as a native woman who gave news of the battle at Roark's Drift before it could have been known, but he noted a personal instance of psychic affinity between himself and the family's black retriever in which he sensed the animal's dying distress.33 And when in *The Ivory Child* Haggard compared Hans's loyalty to the love of a dog—indeed allowed Mameena to disparage him as a "little Yellow Dog"34—his apparent lapse of taste in combining animal and human qualities may actually be a Wordsworthian maneuver that sees all the rich thicket of phenomenal reality as instinct and inspired with divine spirit. Wordsworth often spoke as though he didn't know the difference between rocks, daffodils, fallen women, and Very Right Reverends in the Church of England. And when the critic Ivor Winters once sputtered that G. M. Hopkins's use of a small kestrel hawk, a windhover, to symbolize Christ was as irreverent as if he, Winters, were to use his pet Airedale for that purpose, Winters apparently overlooked the fact that Francis Thompson in "The Hound of Heaven" had done just that. Should Haggard be far behind? If many of the British and most of the Boers took the natives' land and enslaved them, Haggard more sympathetically appropriated or assimilated their rituals and spirituality into his notions of the occult. By this acculturative gesture, Haggard subverts the familiar colonial ethos of native victimization and locates Zulu power not in failed military campaigns but in their greater spirituality. As a matter of fact, when Haggard highlights the Zulu's imperial tendencies in *Nada the Lily* and elsewhere, he is perhaps comparing Lord Chelmsford to Shaka, suggesting that armed force cannot bring peace—an example of countercolonial narrative resistance by analogy to the colonized.

🙰 🙰

But Haggard was not a twenty-first century theorist, as his 1877 essays make eminently clear, although his later fictional presentations of the values and aspirations of jingoistic imperialism are skillfully deflected by his alter ego, Allan Quatermain. Quatermain in one sense is the generic imperial adventurer; indeed, he is the Tennysonian Ulysses. And here I am thinking not only of Tennyson's magnificent dramatic monologue "Ulysses," but of the much paler "To Ulysses" in which the poet, like Haggard's British readers "soaking here in winter wet," gives thanks for stories to the adventurer he once wished to be:

> I, once half-crazed for larger light
> On broader zones beyond the foam,
> But chaining fancy now at home
> Among the quarried down of Wight,
> Not less would yield full thanks to you
> For your rich gift, your tale of lands
> I know not.35

But though Haggard employed Quatermain as his second self to undercut the imperialistic agenda of foreign rule and native dispossession, his character is also what may be called, in technical discussions of narrative point of view, the "innocent eye" or, more darkly, an "obtuse narrator." Quatermain is an unpolished trader and ivory hunter, though born the son of a parson, hence he considers himself a gentleman; and Haggard repeatedly jokes about Quatermain's limited bookish exposure to only the *Ingoldsby Legends* and the Bible. But his raw intelligence and intuition, like that of Ulysses, is exceptional. This allows Haggard to subject British assumptions, practices, and jingoistic persiflage to the sound common sense of Quatermain's practical experience—not unlike Huck Finn's candid appraisal of the Grangerfords' feuding or Jim's perplexed pondering on the ways of royalty in Mark Twain's novel of the same year as *King Solomon's Mines*. Huck and Jim skewer with innocent but deadly literalism the excesses of a decayed romanticism. Twain's innocents also become mouthpieces for socially constructed contemporary evils, as when Aunt Sally asks if anyone was injured in a boiler explosion on a steamboat, Huck, as a boy bred in a slaveholding community, replies: "No'm. Killed a nigger."36

Twain's clearly ironic manipulation of Huck allows us to separate the author's social values from those of his boyish stalking horse; but Haggard is more subtly entwined with Quatermain, and the problem arises how to separate Allan's plainness, his pragmatic responses to situational urgencies, and his social background from Haggard's own perceptions and political values. In Haggard's second essay, "The Transvaal," printed in the influential *Macmillan's Magazine*, the young author unconsciously disguises British intervention with a rhetoric of protection, productivity, and enlightenment: the Boers are about to be exterminated by the Zulus, whereas the Basutos need protection from the Boers; both Boers and Basutos need British "law, justice and order"; and under British control the Transvaal will "repay the enterprise of thousands." Haggard even justified the annexation of the Transvaal as a specific rescue mission, not unlike the expeditionary foray for the lost brother in *King Solomon's Mines*: four hundred British "souls" have found themselves caught in the hostilities between Boers and natives and "have transmitted numerous and piteous applications for protection to the governments of the Cape and Natal."[37] The welter of motivations here suggests an overly idealistic vision of peace, order, and coexistence, though the rhetoric of intervention for humanitarian reasons has never had a better formulation: "The only thing that can excuse the annexation of lands, belonging by nature and by right to savage races, is the introduction of a just and merciful policy towards the original owners, the prevention of unnecessary bloodshed, and the assurance, in return for their birthright, of safety from foreign aggression, and of peace and security at home."[38] Another even stronger statement of native rights within imperialism is given in *Cetywayo*.[39] Haggard's imperial humanitarianism, however, always predicates the right of the Boers and British to settle Africa.

In *Allan Quatermain*, Haggard allows his hero to introduce his tale with an essay on human "kinship":

> I say that as the savage is, so is the white man, only the latter is more inventive, and possesses a faculty of combination; save and except also that the savage, as I have known him, is to a large extent free from the greed of money, which eats like a cancer into the heart of the white man. It is a depressing conclusion, but in all essentials the savage and the child of civilisation are identical. I dare to say that the highly civilised lady reading this will smile at an old fool of a hunter's simplicity when she thinks of her black bead-bedecked sister; and so will the superfine cultured idler scientifically eating a dinner at his club, the cost of which would keep a starving family for a week. And yet, my dear young lady, what are those pretty things round your own neck?—they have a strong family resemblance, especially when you wear that *very* low dress, to the savage woman's beads. Your habit of turning round and round to the sound of horns and tom-toms, your fondness for pigments and powders, the way in which you love to subjugate yourself to the rich warrior who has captured you in marriage, and the quickness with which your taste in feathered headdresses varies,—all these things suggest touches of kinship; and remember that in the fundamental principles of your nature you are quite identical. As for you, sir, who also laugh, let some man come and strike you

in the face whilst you are enjoying that marvellous-looking dish, and we shall soon see how much of the savage there is in *you*.40

Today, of course, the word "savage" sounds oddly pejorative, though for Haggard the word may be more positive than "native" because of its overtones of occult power; and *we* would avoid all tendency to stereotype racially, though European inventiveness fares poorly in contrast to African freedom from greed. And, of course, why is it a "depressing" conclusion that society at the metropolitan center of empire is little different from life in an African kraal? Perhaps because technology has done so little for the spirit. No matter what, Haggard's basic respect for the "savage" Zulu is evident in *The Days of My Life* also:

> True gentility, as I have seen again and again, is not the prerogative of a class but a gift innate in certain members of all classes, and by no means a common gift. With it rank, station, wealth have nothing to do; it either is or is not born in a man, and still more so in a woman.... Like others, savages have their gentlefolk and their common people, but with all their faults even those common people are not vulgar in our sense of the word. In essential matters they still preserve a certain dignity.41

Making due allowances, are not the above passages calculated manifestos, radical and didactic, supportive of essential human identity and affiliated rights?

Or might Haggard's words disguise a conflict? What Haggard preaches and what he reveals in his novels may diverge. At times animals fill the role pattern of belligerent natives, as when in *Allan's Wife* a deranged white woman leads hostile baboons and when in *Heu-Heu* the subhuman "Hairy Folk" attack the reader's fellow humans. If Haggard believes that a developing liberal democracy is attainable by Africans, why in so many of his novels does he write about a secret civilized white race in the heart of Africa when, given the preachments in *Allan Quatermain*, it would have been both more broad-minded and fictionally more plausible for such a civilized race to be black? Perhaps these secret white civilizations are Haggard's ideal of an Anglo-African coexistence, though they are racial enclaves, not integrated social communities. Quatermain's recurrent assumption, as in *King Solomon's Mines* or *Allan Quatermain*, that intricate structures must have been built by whites certainly was consistent with prevalent assumptions and must have been endorsed by Haggard himself. But, of course, central Africa had been so recently an "unexplored" and "unknown" territory (words found on many a nineteenth-century map) that readers almost believed anything might be possible. Nevertheless, where are the civilized black Africans?

Perhaps Haggard's answer is, in Africa: "What is a gentleman? I don't quite know, and yet I have had to do with niggers—no, I'll scratch that word 'niggers' out, for I don't like it. I've known natives who *are* ... and I have known mean whites with lots of money and fresh out from home, too, who *ain't*."[42] In *King Solomon's Mines* Quatermain explicitly rejects the epithet, as does Haggard's altar ego Ernest in *The Witch's Head*: "he objected to the word 'nigger' as applied to a people who, whatever their faults may be, are, as a rule, gentlemen in the truest sense of the word."[43] And in the dedication to *Child of Storm* Haggard warily admires the Zulu's "superstitious madness and bloodstained grandeur" and then observes that "at least they were not mean or vulgar. From those who continually must face the last great issues of life or death meanness and vulgarity are far removed."[44] Certainly territorial encroachments and bloody internecine warfare were part of Africa long before the Europeans arrived; but the British and Boers brought new weapons, vastly different cultural practices, and for many a pragmatic disregard for the native ways of life: "savage customs." However, Haggard's natives are presented as they were or at least as he saw them—nobler, braver and often better mannered than Europeans:

> And having saluted after the dignified Zulu fashion, Mazook departed to tie up his split trousers with a bit of string. There was something utterly incongruous between his present appearance and his melodious and poetical words, instinct as they were with qualities which in some respects make the savage Zulu a gentleman, and put him above the white Christian, who for the most part regards the "nigger" as a creature beneath contempt. For there are lessons to be learned even from Zulu "niggers," and among them we may reckon those taught by a courage which laughs at death; an absolute fidelity to those who have the right to command it, or the qualities necessary to win it; and, in their raw and unconverted state, perfect honesty and truthfulness.[45]

As in Kenyatta's tale, Haggard (or Quatermain) with sly cynicism is perfectly ready to extend to his own civilized compatriots the pejorative animal imagery unfailingly reserved for natives. Thus in *King Solomon's Mines* a hunted herd of elephants stumbles down into a dried water bed, "struggling in wild confusion to get up the other bank, and filling the air with their screams, and trumpeting as they pushed one another aside in their selfish panic, just like so many human beings."[46]

Like all paradigm shifts, the transition from Victorian romanticism to *fin-de-siècle* modernism was by no means an auspicious victory of the new over the old. Modernity dissolved religious tradition and intensified moral anarchy in thought and act. Even in the earlier age of Victoria's empire, where hands and face were washed daily and feet and neck fortnightly, life had not achieved spiritual serenity and security; and by the time Haggard's romances first appeared, moral confusion pervaded both the intelligentsia and the workers, industrial and agricultural alike. Friedreich Nietzsche in *The Gay Science* (1882, 1887) proclaimed his touchstone "Parable of the Madman" in which a visionary hysterically cries, "God is dead. God remains dead. And we have killed him." Given the mocking response of "those who did not believe in God" to Nietzsche's prophetic madman, the oracle infers: "I have come too early ... my time is not yet. This tremendous event is still on its way, still wandering; it has not yet reached the ears of men. Lightning and thunder require time; the light of the stars requires time; deeds, though done, still require time to be seen and heard. This deed is still more distant from them than the most distant stars—and yet they have done it themselves."[47] This parable of lost transcendental access to a sustaining life reiterates the lament of the old Greek Pausanias: "Pan is dead" and "They come no longer!... These things happen no longer!" And in Plutarch's "The Obsolescence of Oracles," a divine voice had imparted the news of Pan's death to a sailor: "Thamus, are you there? When you reach Palodes, take care to proclaim that the great god Pan is dead."[48] And in Haggard's day Elizabeth Browning's poem "Pan is Dead" cites Plutarch's work, according to which a cry of "Great Pan is dead!" swept across the sea at the hour of Christ's crucifixion, and the oracles ceased. Yet for Haggard, Nietzsche's madman was wrong if he supposed that any collective human logos or heroic individual could or should replace divinity: the time had come, as Haggard and others of his generation felt, for a reaffirmation not of Great Pan but of the mysticism at the roots of Christianity, if not an outright recognition of sin, grace, redemption, and the sacraments as a living truth.

Perhaps this resistance to a death-of-God ideology in transitioning from nineteenth-century romanticism to an emerging twentieth-century skepticism finds one of its most deliberate embodiments in Haggard's novel *The Ivory Child* (1916) in which Quatermain is persuaded to travel to the far interior of Africa in search of ivory. There he encounters the Manichaean country of the Kendah controlled by two antagonistic powers, namely light or goodness identified with an Ivory

Child fetish and darkness, chaos, and evil embodied in the elephant-god Jana:

> "Lord, Jana among us Kendah represents the evil in the world, as the Child represents the good. Jana is he whom the Mohammedans call Shaitan and the Christians call Satan, and our forefathers, the old Egyptians, called Set."
>
> "Ah!" thought I to myself, "now we have got it. Horus the Divine Child, and Set the evil monster, with whom it strives everlastingly."
>
> "Always," went on Marut, "there has been war between the Child and Jana, that is, between Good and Evil, and we know that in the end one of them must conquer the other."49

Quatermain is told his role in this country is to banish the darkness and to restore it to light, an amalgamation of Christian theology with Egyptian and Babylonian nature-worship. But whereas Allan does rescue the abducted Lady Ragnall, an Isis figure with a white crescent-moon birthmark on her "breast"—or, as she demurely locates it, on her "neck"50—it turns out that it is not Allan who fulfills the salvific role, but the Hottentot Hans. After the ivory Child had been dashed to pieces by the mortally wounded and demonic Jana, the theurgic dirge of Nietzsche's madman arises: "A voice called: 'The god is dead!...' From every side was this wail echoed: 'Fly, People of the Black Kendah, for the gods are dead!'"51 If Haggard allows the death of a god, it is an idolatrous divinity whose mandates enslave. What takes its place is Elizabeth Browning's new Christian mysticism. Quatermain like Haggard may have believed only obliquely in these African gods; but in that great desolation Allan feels at the loss of his faithful servant Hans, he fathoms the power of a self-sacrificing love: "in all the world there is but one real thing, and its name is Love, which if it be but strong enough, the stars themselves must obey."52 Thus unforeseen but indisputably, the "little Yellow Dog"53 Hans incarnates the power of the ivory Child, the son of Isis.

When, in Conrad's *Heart of Darkness*, Charlie Marlow pronounced Kurtz, after he whispered "the horror! the horror!" to be "a remarkable man,"54 Marlow did so for precisely the same reasons that T. S. Eliot found Baudelaire's *Fleurs du mal* to be such a relief from the *ennui* of contemporary civilization—if damnation is possible, then salvation is also.55 This discovery by the lost of a universe with a moral compass is what Haggard's literal Africa—its dangers, its longings, its temptations, its losses, its joys—represents for his readers. On the figurative level, the journeys, the characters, the natural landscape, represent (though in no dogmatic terms) the eternal strife of the forces of good with the forces of evil, in each single soul and within society as a whole. In this, Haggard has profound affinities with an occultism that owed much to the romantic desire for transcendence.

The romantic author characteristically had desired to break free from dreary daily reality in order to attain a more intense consciousness of what Coleridge in "The Eolian Harp" called "the one Life within us and abroad." When theorizing, romantic writers appear to define their symbols as unproblematic avenues of transcendence promising an escape from painful self-confrontation; but in practice, these dream-fantasies frequently portray the writer or protagonist as ironically encountering a darker double. Romantic symbols of metaphysical plenitude, promising access to some angelic beauty and power, waver, dissolve, and turn the seeker back upon a corrupted image of self. In "Resolution and Independence," Wordsworth laments: "By our own spirits are we deified:/ We Poets in our youth begin in gladness;/ But thereof come in the end despondency and madness."[56] Though Wordsworth's pattern might be typically schizoid or manic-depressive, his replacement of transcendence with the irrational or diabolic is a key signature of romantic dreaming. This romanticism ambiguously straddled the *mar si crudele* of Dante's *Inferno* and the blinding radiancy of his *Paradiso*, an irresolute synthesis always coming into being, never yet there. Ayesha in *She* terminates a philosophical monologue (like Schreiner's Lyndall, she is a great talker) with this peroration:

> "Good and evil, love and hate, night and day, sweet and bitter, man and woman, heaven above and the earth beneath—all these things are necessary, one to the other, and who knows the end of each? I tell thee that there is a hand of Fate that twines them up to bear the burden of its purpose, and all things are gathered in that great rope to which all things are needful. Therefore doeth it not become us to say this thing is evil and this good, or the dark is hateful and the light lovely; for to other eyes than ours the evil may be the good and the darkness more beautiful than the day, or all alike be fair. Hearest thou, my Holly?"[57]

In one form or another, the "great rope" is Haggard's romantic symbol of an interwoven reality, the mysterious coming into being of a *totum simul* in which the self transcends its solipsistic fragmentation and blindness.

Among the most famous nineteenth-century definitions of the romantic symbol's capacity to empower the self are those of Coleridge in *The Statesman's Manual* (1815)—"A symbol is characterized by ... the translucence of the Eternal through and in the Temporal"[58]—and of Thomas Carlyle in the chapter of *Sartor Resartus* (1836) entitled "Symbols": "In the Symbol ... the Infinite is made to blend itself with the Finite, to stand visible, and as it were, attainable there."[59] These definitions are consistent with one of British literature's most explicitly mystical passages in which Wordsworth defines symbolic vision in "Tintern Abbey" as:

> ... that blessed mood,
> In which the affections gently lead us on,—
> Until, the breath of this corporeal frame
> And even the motion of our human blood
> Almost suspended, we are laid asleep
> In body, and become a living soul:
> While with an eye made quiet by the power
> Of harmony, and the deep power of joy,
> We see into the life of things ...[60]

Probably the oldest use of the word *symbol* is "traceable to Cyprian, Bishop of Carthage (circa 250), who applies L. *symbolum* to the baptismal creed" (*Oxford English Dictionary*, "Symbol") as a "mark" or "sign" separating the Christian from the pagan. As a sacrament signifying purification and spiritual rebirth, baptism as the original use of symbol is highly significant, insofar as it is a response to the fall, a reintegration of that unity lost by division—in this case the division between the self and God. Interestingly, the late Latin *symbolum* derives from the Greek *symballein*, *sym/n-* ("with," "together," "similarly," "alike") + *ballein* ("to throw"). For the romantics, the symbol is what unifies reality, it enables the self to see the external world as no longer foreign but as that in which its own life consists—to discern Coleridge's "one Life" or what Wordsworth in "Tintern Abbey" called "A motion and a spirit, that impels/ All thinking things, all objects of all thought,/ And rolls through all things."[61]

To speak figuratively, the symbol appeared when Satan fell from heaven and is a "throwing together" of that which the devil first threw apart. *Devil*, according to such standard etymologies as the *Oxford English Dictionary*, is a specific derivation from the Greek *diabolos*, the radical of which is *ballein* and the prefix of which derives from the Greek root *dyo* ("two")—*dyo* being an alteration of the Indo-European *dis-* meaning "apart," "asunder," "twice," "in different directions." Thus *devil* in its most literal, basal sense means "to throw apart, to divide."

What gives the romantic symbol its problematic status is that like Milton's fallen angels "in wandering mazes lost,"[62] it can never quite extricate itself from this diabolic discord.

In *The Ivory Child*, Haggard uses Egyptian mythology to dramatize this lost unity. The child of the fertility figures, Osiris and his sister-consort Isis, god and goddess of sun and moon, is Horus who is represented in the effigy of the ivory child. Horus himself combines the powers of both his divine progenitors in a *concordia discours*. But in Haggard's story, Horus is absent, veiled even more than his mother Isis, because the forces of darkness and discord are still at war with the powers of light and harmony. Again and again in Haggard this relationship—the moral suitor against the selfish one; the good tribe against the diabolic one; the holy ground against the profane place; white enchantment against black magic—is the basis of the action, and a glimpse of its reconciliation is the denouement.

Turning the diabolic condition of loss and mortality back upon itself, the romantic cries out from the depths of his self-contradiction and names the "Life" outside his power to control. This "grace" appears in the blessing of the water-snakes by Coleridge's Ancient Mariner, a transformation of "slimy things" (DeQuincey's exact phrase in the *Confessions* also) to "golden fire."[63] Understood in terms of its earliest applicability to the ancient Christian baptismal rite, as the "mark" or "sign" healing a diabolic separation of mortals from the divine, the ontology of the romantic "symbol" has precedent in theological history. But though Romanticism has an explicit theology of sin, it typically attains, even figuratively in dreams, only an incomplete theology of grace. Celestial perfection becomes for the romantic a function of time and dependent upon imperfection for its temporal expression; mundane life is all-important as the only manifestation of a truth, a beauty, and a strength that the symbol descries but never directly embodies. Although the romantics persist in speaking of the symbol's "translucence" or define it as "transparent," what the evolving practice of the century implies is that whatever we know of truth is not transcendent to life or is so deep as to be fathomless; rather, the temporal and historical—that is, the diabolic in its root sense—becomes itself the site where meaning resides, not the ecstasies of a timeless eternity but the meaningfulness of temporal reality despite its catastrophic nature.

But though early modernism and popular taste still took Romanticism as its foundation in the 1880s, literature either flirted with mild realism, the everyday life of genteel society, or with naturalism, everyday degeneration. As noted, Haggard's "About Fiction" (1887) attacked both the politely moral (what one might stigmatize as the diminished legacy of Mrs. Gore's seventy novels) and the new naturalistic depiction, without moral judgment, of the ugly crimes and passions of drunks and prostitutes on urban streets and in barrooms and tenements. If laws of nature, heredity, and environment ruled out moral freedom, then romantic vision and supernaturalism were passé. Insofar as Haggard confronted the elusiveness of genuine spiritual affirmation—a social crisis not just in his home of Britain but in the new cross-Atlantic culture also—he seems to anticipate that reaction to the sterile wasteland of modern urban civilization as reflected in the poetry of T. S. Eliot and Eliot's Harvard professor, Irving Babbitt: a beginning in disgust with the disintegration of faith and dissolution of tradition and an ending in reaffirmation of faith in *something* felt to be above man. Haggard's themes are like those of Eliot in *Ash Wednesday*: temptation, doubt, the tensions of good and evil in the human heart. This undoubtedly is why the Christian apologist, C. S. Lewis, embraces Haggard's use of myth as backdrop for his adventure tales. Haggard, like Eliot or Lewis, is venturing to return large symbols of hope to a modern life devoid of spiritual meaning. He finds them not in the biblical tradition *per se*, but in Africa and the Zulu's ritual and magic, "in all their superstitious madness and bloodstained grandeur,"[64] as well as in those common scenes of singing and dancing natives, as Selous and, notoriously afterwards, Conrad pictured them. Selous describes "their naked figures and wild gestures, now brought into strong relief against the dark background, and anon but dimly seen in the uncertain light of the large log fires."[65] And Conrad renders "a burst of yells, a whirl of black limbs, a mass of hands clapping, of feet stamping, of bodies swaying, of eyes rolling, under the droop of heavy and motionless foliage.... They howled, and leaped, and spun, and made horrid faces but what thrilled you was just the thought of their humanity—like yours—the thought of your remote kinship with this wild and passionate uproar."[66] Selous and Conrad may be assessing the tribal dances of Africa somewhat too hastily in terms of the European conventions of the cotillion.

What Haggard has done is to dramatize mankind's deepest psychological conflict—that *agonia* between flesh and spirit, the horror of mortality and the even more awesome recognition of one's quasi-divinity. C. S. Lewis defines the significance of *She* as just this thematic accomplishment. It reveals

> our irreconcilable reluctance to die, our craving for an immortality in the flesh, our empirical knowledge that this is impossible, our intermittent awareness that it is not even really desirable, and (octaves deeper than all these) a very primitive feeling that the attempt, if it could be made, would be unlawful and would call down the vengeance of the gods. In [*She*] the wild, transporting, and (we feel) forbidden hope is aroused. When fruition seems almost in sight, horrifying disaster shatters our dream.[67]

Haggard, like his colleague Andrew Lang, is an important folklorist and an important investigator of African totemism, magic and religion. In this capacity he is a forerunner of Sir James Frazer and his landmark study of social anthropology, *The Golden Bough* (1890–1915). And like a master storyteller, he is able to blend his firsthand experiences in Africa with the principal elements of romance plot—figures of mythic dimension, the heroic quest, the "lost civilization," and the supernatural. In the telling of his story he is able to suppress the inessential, condensing massive quantities of scene, image, and action into a few select phrases, yet the resultant narrative is almost always more complex and ironic—passing beyond his quirky and lovable sense of humor—than has yet been realized. As to that humor, it can rise to the level of Evelyn Waugh. In *The Ivory Child*, the oh-so-proper British servant is named Savage; and we have that marvellous moment recounted by Quatermain in which the infatuated Scroope tells Miss Manners that "she was looking beautiful, and stared at her with such affection that I fell back a step or two and contemplated a picture of Judith vigorously engaged in cutting off the head of Holofernes."[68]

It is time for literary historians to recover Haggard's accomplishments. It is time to consign to the junkyard of critical misconceptions his image as a writer of mere potboilers, deficient in polished literary style or delineation of character. Haggard's style has been criticized as prosaic, unremarkable in every way. One might assert this as a positive quality—it doesn't get in the way of his story. Critics decry that he was not a "careful craftsman or an accomplished man of letters," while simultaneously praising his "virtues of raciness and vividness."[69] Indisputably Haggard's details, powerful and prolific, underpin his mythopoeic gift. What novels open with greater promise and end with more horrifying disaster? And to his credit, Haggard swaps the elitism of self-conscious artistry—that urbane belle-lettres formalism of the gilded age he was stepping away from—for a more spontaneous, unadorned and colloquial narration, purging his prose of Paterian preciousness except when, sensitive to mood and purpose, he pursues a calculated poetic effect.

C. S. Lewis complains that Haggard can't be bothered to write: "hence the *cliches*, jocosities, frothy eloquence. When he speaks through the mouth of Quatermain he makes some play with the unliterary character of the simple hunter. It never dawned on him that what he wrote in his own person was a great deal worse—'literary' in the most damning sense of the word."[70] Lewis is undoubtedly too much the Oxford don in his prose values here. Whereas Haggard usually avoided eloquence and rhetoric and sought concreteness, simplicity, intensity, the real speech of contemporary life, on occasion Haggard's style can be highly wrought. The drawn-out "*a*'s" and "*m/n*'s" that communicate stress ("I considered the matter with an earnestness that almost amounted to mental agony"[71]) are worthy of Alexander Pope. At times his style is not unrelated to new poetic trends, perhaps drawing inspiration from French symbolism of the late nineteenth century. When in 1936 England's greatest poet of that century, William Butler Yeats, edited *The Oxford Book of Modern Verse*, he introduced his modernist collection with a passage in *vers libre* from Water Pater's prose on Leonardo da Vinci's Mona Lisa. Yeats's purpose was to show the "revolutionary importance" of "this passage which dominated a generation." For all the criticism of Haggard's style as rough and ready, like Pater he too is able, in Yeats's phrase, to empower prose "to arise out of its own rhythm."[72]

Haggard's description of Umkulunkulu, the Zulu Queen of Heaven and of the Dead, is as poetically intense as the visionary images of Pater's imaginative reinterpretation. Both Fatal Ladies are vehicles of magic, passion, and the ceaselessly interacting antinomies of generation and decay. Haggard's speaker is the old Zulu Mopo, traditional blind seer and poet. Not unlike the old Norse or Anglo-Saxon scop, Mopo is most clearly the bard of the African praise-poem. Following Yeats's audacious overture to the modernism of his cohorts, this is Haggard presented verbatim but in *vers libre*—in the line of vision forward to Eliot, Pound, Auden, and Yeats himself:

Umkulunkulu

The sun sank redly,
  flooding the land with blood;
      it was as though all the blood that Chaka had shed
      flowed about the land which Chaka ruled.

Then from the womb of the night
great shapes of cloud rose up
    and stood before the sun,
    and he crowned them with his glory,
    and in their hearts the lightning quivered
        like a blood of fire.

The shadow of their wings
fell upon the mountain and the plains,
    and beneath their wings was silence.
Slowly the sun sank,
    and the shapes of cloud gathered together
        like a host at the word of its captain,
    and the flicker of the lightning
        was as the flash of the spears of a host.

I looked,
and my heart grew afraid.
The lightning died away,
the silence deepened
    and deepened till I could hear it,
        no leaf moved,
        no bird called,
the world seemed dead—
I alone lived in the dead world.

Now, of a sudden, my father,
a bright star fell from the height of heaven
    and lit upon the crest of the storm,
    and as it lit the storm burst.

The grey air shivered,
a moan ran about the rocks
    and died away,
then an icy breath burst from the lips of the tempest
    and rushed across the earth.

It caught the falling star
    and drove it on toward me,
        a rushing globe of fire,
    and as it came the star grew and took shape,
    and the shape it took was the shape of a woman.

I know her now, my father;
> while she was yet far off
I know her
> —the Inkosazana who came as she had promised,
> riding down the storm.

On she swept,
borne forward by the blast,
and oh! she was terrible to see,
> for her garment was the lightning,
> lightnings shone from her wide eyes
> and lightnings were in her streaming hair,
while in her hand was a spear of fire,
> and she shook it as she came.

Now she was at the mouth of the pass;
> before her was stillness,
> behind her beat the wings of the storm,
>> the thunder roared,
>> the rain hissed like snakes;
she rushed on past me, and as she passed
she turned her awful eyes upon me,
> withering me.

She was there!
She was gone!
> but she spoke no word,
> only shook her flaming spear.

Yet it seemed to me
> that the storm spoke,
> that the rocks cried aloud,
> that the rain hissed out a word in my ear,
>> and the word was:—
"Smite, Mopo!"

I heard in my heart,
or with my ears,
what does it matter?

Then I turned to look;
> through the rush of the tempest
> and the reek of the rain,
still I could see her sweeping forward high in air.

> Now the kraal Duguza was beneath her feet,
> and the flaming spear fell from her hand upon the kraal
> and fire leaped up in answer.
>
> Then she passed on
> over the edge of the world,
> seeking her own place.[73]

For direct picture-making and the sonorous ascent and fall of clauses, this is surely no less a feat of creation than that occasion in *King Solomon's Mines* when Umbopa breaks into his chant of victory, a passage that Haggard himself considered the high-water mark of his literary skill. Ignosi's chant of renewal, which Quatermain describes as "in a language as beautiful and sonorous as the old Greek,"[74] denotes just this organic rhythm of free-verse prose.

Haggard's delineation of character also has been criticized. His characters are static and not complex, his heroes less successful than his heroines, especially the semi- or wholly supernatural women. But one might note that the older Allan Quatermain has Haggard's own personality—simple, visionary, amiable—and Haggard's creation of strong, faithful, humorous servants is often successful. In "A Tale of Three Lions" Quatermain orders his brawny Swazi named Pharaoh to punish the careless Jim-Jim:

> to give him a beating for letting the oxen stray, which Pharaoh did with the greatest gusto, although he was by way of being very fond of Jim-Jim. Indeed, I saw him consoling Jim-Jim afterwards with a pinch of snuff from his own ear-box, whilst he explained to him that the next time it came in the way of duty to flog him, he meant to thrash him with the other hand, so as to cross the old cuts and make a "pretty pattern" on his back.[75]

In the cheerful performance of his duty, Pharaoh's sympathy neither tempers his severity towards Jim-Jim nor provokes the least racial resentment against his "baas." This incongruous toughness and tenderness of the manly Swazi rises way beyond the comedy of caricature both to define a native friendliness of disposition and to epitomize an ideal of Anglo-African consensus. One random and obscure example from *The Ivory Child* will testify to Haggard's ability to catch a world of meaning in two sentences. This is Lady Longden, gathering with the rest before going into dinner: "She was an ample and, to my mind, rather awful-looking person, clad in black satin—she was a widow—and very large diamonds. Her hair was white, her nose was hooked, her dark eyes were penetrating, and she had a bad cold in her head."76 Try reading these two sentences omitting the last phrase in each, and one has a cliché of the dreariest sort. But the *size* of her ostentatious diamonds contrasting with the misery of the common head cold ironizes this thumbnail sketch.

Graham Greene, the novelist and dramatist, testifies to Haggard's mythic, visionary impact on his imagination:

> If it had not been for that romantic tale of Allan Quatermain, Sir Henry Curtis, Captain Good, and, above all, the ancient witch Gagool, would I at nineteen have studied the appointments list of the Colonial Office and very nearly picked on the Nigerian Navy for a career? And later, when surely I ought to have known better, the odd African fixation remained. In 1935 I found myself sick with fever on a camp bed in a Liberian native's hut with a candle going out in an empty whisky bottle and a rat moving in the shadows. Wasn't it the incurable fascination of Gagool with her bare yellow skull, the wrinkled scalp that moved and contracted like the hood of a cobra, that led me to work all through 1942 in a little stuffy office in Freetown, Sierra Leone?... Yes, Gagool has remained a permanent part of the imagination, but Quatermain and Curtis—weren't they, even when I was only ten years old, a little too good to be true?... Sir Henry Curtis perched upon a rock bleeding from a dozen wounds but fighting on with the remnant of the Greys against the hordes of Twala was too heroic. These men were like Platonic ideas: they were not life as one had already begun to know it.77

But were Homeric heroes any less ideal? Realism of characterization is not the point in romance; rather, truth to an inner vision, the consistency of a self-contained *mythos*, is the measure. In Haggard's world of physical and moral courage, brave and noble deeds (or their opposite), characters do come alive, are visualized in act and speech, and do generate the story action. It was precisely that mythic dimension of the plot—including those "too heroic" archetypes—that fed the imaginations of young Greene and his generation and made *King Solomon's Mines* and the subsequent novels of Africa profound works of literature.

Though Haggard claims to have borrowed his hero's fictional name from a quondam Norfolk neighbor, its function as a charcternym is its key: "Allan" derives from the Celtic and means "comely" or "fair"; "Quater-" comes from the Latin *quater* meaning "four times"; and "-main" originates in the Old English *maegen*, meaning "strength," as used in the phrase "with might and main." Thus Allan Quatermain is handsome and strong, a lesser sort of Tennysonian Sir Galahad:

> My good blade carves the casques of men,
> My tough lance thrusteth sure,
> My strength is as the strength of ten,
> Because my heart is pure.[78]

Sir Galahad in the *Idylls* aids those in need, but his quest for the Grail is a lonely ordeal that requires sacrifice of domestic ties. Quatermain too has great loves, allegedly stronger than death, but none outlasts the slings and arrows here below. This connection of Quatermain with the heroic questor extends to that more ancient but similar Tennysonian paladin, Ulysses, who is presented leaving Ithaca for further wanderings that have no explicitly envisioned goal, unless it be to meet once more "the great Achilles whom we knew." Yet in their quest for "the great Achilles" or the Grail, a mysterious inner strength and vision sustain both Ulysses and Galahad through terrestrial hardships, their outer achievements shadowed by dream and magic. Actually, in *The World's Desire* (1890), the coauthors Haggard and Lang envisioned Ulysses dying for love of Helen of Troy, a death that culminates a lifelong search for "Beauty's self."[79] Like Ulysses, Quatermain's unending pursuit of adventure is the mark of his devotion to imagination, spirit, and the wilderness—stormy, savage, bestial, passionate, uncontrolled, unknown, magical, and deadly.

But Quatermain's character is also importantly nuanced by nineteenth-century preoccupations, including definitions of manhood. Haggard's hero may fulfill many of the "great white hunter" stereotypes (only once in the range of Haggard's fiction is Quatermain so designated, in *Maiwa's Revenge*[80]) but his "greatness" is in neither of those popularly expected traits, physical stature and bravado. He is unimpressively smallish and again and again Quatermain says he is timid—his joke on what the newspapers considered essential for the fulfillment of a masculine identity—because foolishly incautious elephant hunters did not live long lives. Yet rejecting narrow definitions of manhood, Quatermain knows that only on the fine edge of life poised against sudden death is he truly alive. His experience of terrain and wild beasts, his knowledge of firearms, his awareness of his limitations, and his willingness to absorb native tradecraft become the pragmatic tools of his survival. Haggard's African romances do not neglect the intricate social and historical trappings of past times, but in Quatermain Haggard personalizes the dry historical facts in a visceral, combustible yet contemporaneous way.

King Solomon's Mines and later novels were derided for their violence, certainly in part because Haggard was so effective at crafting an uncanny aura of dread to heighten the banality of evil. His "history-as-it-happens" style of writing draws his readers emotionally into the scenes as a living spectacle. If his novels cannot be as vivid as cinematic "docudramas," nevertheless even his "savage" characters, speaking in their own words, take the reader right into their minds and hearts. Yet he surpasses the historical novel's strong sense of place and event, not only by constituting Quatermain as an actual eyewitness "embedded" in the scenes but also by holding him accountable in a major way for the outcome of history as it has transpired in his presence and afterwards is inscribed. Had Quatermain as a direct participant and agent of change, known, guessed, or seen more clearly, had he understood the implications for the future better, perhaps documented history as in some measure the product of his witting or unwitting choices might have turned out better. This allows Haggard to contemplate a possible rewriting of Zulu history from the point of view of what might have been and to make thinly disguised rebuttals to the British agenda for control of Zululand. Once the door is opened to alternative outcomes, the "impossible" idealism of the mystic is at least imaginatively conceivable. In that world, empire and colony become a Utopia found.

Undeniably, a hundred years of social evolution have given Quatermain's "heroic" code of conduct a certain quaintness to contemporary eyes, barely less antiquarian than that to which the Red Cross Knight pledged his honor. In *King Solomon's Mines* or *Nada the Lily* masculine bonding is so forthright, post-Freudian readers would suspect homoeroticism, were it not based on a connection to the feminine rooted in prehistoric myth. By the end of two world wars in a very brutal and disillusioning century, not only was Victoria's empire unraveling into a postcolonial vacuum of moral leadership, but belief in the chivalric virtues clearly had become artificial and unreal. The Haggard hero, as a candle that shines like "a good deed in a naughty world," had mimicked "the greater glory" of an imperial optimism magnitudes brighter than any twenty-first-century Western interloper, such as Elmore Leonard's protagonist in *Pagan Babies* (2000), ever could achieve. Already even in 1899 Conrad's Kurtz had engaged in an imperial "horror" only approximated by such freebooters in Haggard as Philip Hadden (*Black Heart and White Heart*, 1900). By the enchanted distance fallacy, his fiction deliberately harked back to a more intense and exceptional, a more grotesque and macabre, bygone world, finding its themes in the free play of strength and love in savage life. Haggard is now known as "the greatest adventure fantasist of all time" because his romance elements anticipated later commercial successes: Quatermain is the prototype for such popular adventurers as Indiana Jones, Bilbo Baggins, Tarzan, and John Carter of Mars. Even the description of the Zulu Queen of Heaven in Haggard's poetic and free-flowing *Nada* anticipates a "new age" exoticism. But none of this diminishes the original mythopoeic power of narratives. Both a romantic and an antinomian, Haggard gives his readers something malign in the beauty of his queenly women and the fatalism of his warriors, their enchantment and heroism reaped from intense passions, grotesque even in the insanity of their expression, yet permeated with loveliness, pathos, rapture, and mystery. Haggard's new sort of fantasy, those tales of lost lands and races, may thus be thought of as emblematizing the lost mystery and romantic spirit of the African continent itself.

❦ THREE

Diamonds and Deities: The Spoils of Imperialism

The site of *King Solomon's Mines* (1885) is suggested by nineteenth-century maps showing stone ruins near Victoria in Mashonaland, called Great Zimbabwe, discovered and explored between 1868 and 1871 by Renders and Mauch. Of course, contemporary exploration and the politics of diamond mining were not the only formative influences on Haggard's romance. Set in a strange land where the marvelous abounds, its plot embraces elements of folklore and myth. Every reader now knows that the trio went to Solomon's mines for its diamonds; the rescue of Sir Henry's brother served only as a convenient pretext for recovering its ancient treasures, the objective of the lost George Curtis in the first place. The wisest and richest of biblical rulers, Solomon would have provided the strongest moral sanction for the Victorian resumption, as it were, of mineral extraction on the dark continent. When Haggard's adventurers arrive at "a vast circular hole with sloping sides, three hundred feet or more in depth, and quite half a mile round," Quatermain asks:

> "Can't you guess what this is?" I said to Sir Henry and Good, who were staring in astonishment down into the awful pit before us.
>
> They shook their heads.
>
> "Then it is clear that you have never seen the diamond mines at Kimberley. You may depend on it that this is Solomon's Diamond Mine; look there," I said, pointing to the stiff blue clay which was yet to be seen among the grass and bushes which clothed the sides of the pit, "the formation is the same."[1]

His allusion to the Kimberley "Big Hole" connects mining activities in southern Africa in the 1870s-1880s to a biblical antecedent in the mythopoeic Africa of Solomon's legend.

In 1867 diamonds had been discovered in the alluvial deposits of the Orange and Vaal rivers. From that moment on, the area to the north underwent a rapid transformation, part of the inglorious European "scramble for Africa" that engulfed the whole continent. As a dreamy, vocationally clueless youth, solidly immured in a gentrified Victorian family, Haggard, undoubtedly to everyone's great relief, discovered his capacities in this imperial venture, his passage from hearth-rug to adulthood guided by the rhetoric of the era. When John Ruskin in his Inaugural Lecture at Oxford called upon the "youths of England" to make their country preeminent, one might imagine that Haggard, despite never having attended the university, harkened no less than Cecil Rhodes to Ruskin's adjuration. Certainly Haggard's personal participation in the diamonds-and-gold politics of the Transvaal formed the ideological matrix for his romances. At the very moment Haggard was employed there, Anthony Trollope visited and described diamond-mining in *South Africa* (1878). Haggard later remarked that Trollope rushed through South Africa in a post-cart, and, as a result, published his impressions of that country: "My first introduction to him was amusing. I had been sent away on some mission ... and returned to Government House late one night. On going into the room where I was then sleeping I began to search for matches, and was surprised to hear a gruff voice, proceeding from my bed, asking who the deuce I was. I gave my name and asked who the deuce the speaker might be. 'Anthony Trollope,' replied the gruff voice, 'Anthony Trollope.'"[2] Trollope describes "the first known finding of a diamond" by a Boer child, then recounts the origin of the Kimberley mine.[3] Except for his reference to Kimberley as "the largest and most complete hole ever made by human agency,"[4] Trollope's account of one of the world's greatest capitalistic booms is a dry, factual recital without fictional flair.

The first report in Europe to link modern mining operations such as Kimberley to the legend of Solomon's diamonds and the ancient gold-mines in Mashonaland (now Zimbabwe, formerly Rhodesia) was an anonymous notice, "The Ophir of Scripture," in the *Illustrated London News* (11 January 1873):

> Strange stories have been told of late about the Ophir of Solomon having been discovered. The recently-opened diamond mines of South Africa led to explorations further north, which resulted in the revelation of extensive gold-mines. Mr. Hartley, the lion-hunter, and Mr. Mauch, the German explorer, went further, and made known a more northern auriferous district. It is in the last-discovered gold-field that the real Ophir is supposed to have been seen.[5]

Haggard more directly benefitted from at least one prior tale of ancient diamond mining. Based on Zimbabwe's gold-mining history, a fictional account of Egyptians, Solomon, and the lost city of Ophir by Hugh Mulleneux Walmsley, *The Ruined Cities of Zulu Land* (1869), provided the thematic background for Haggard's adventure into the unknown African interior. It contained details of a stalactite cave, a sorcerer's dance, a sinister chieftain (the historic Mozelkatse), and even at the chief's kraal a sorcerer-prototype for Gagool. Walmsley's description of the Ophir ruins definitely suggests features also in Haggard's Kukuanaland.

Slightly more than a decade after he had transposed these ruins northwards in *King Solomon's Mines*, Haggard summarized their significance in a preface to A. Wilmot's *Monomotapa* (1896):

> Baines, and other travellers now dead, reported the existence of great ruins in the territories known as Matabele and Mashona Lands, and on the banks of tributaries of the Zambesi River, which from their construction must have been built by a race of civilised men; and in 1871 Herr Mauch re-discovered the fortress-temple of Zimbabwe, that now, as in the time of the early Portuguese, was said to be nothing less than the site of one of the ancient Ophirs.[6]

Thomas Baines was an explorer, artist, and author of the posthumous *The Gold Regions of South-Eastern Africa*. Known for its Victoria Falls, the Zambezi flows 1,600 miles into the Indian Ocean. Pushing north of the Zambezi, the hunter F. C. Selous reflected on Christmas Day, 1877, that "we were in a country never before trodden upon by even the wandering feet of a subject of Queen Victoria."[7] The ruins Haggard describes are considerably south of the Zambezi, which marked the extreme frontier in Haggard's day. He continues:

> In 1891, after the occupation of Mashonaland by the Chartered Company of British South Africa, Mr. Bent, the learned explorer, visited the ruins of Zimbabwe and proved to the satisfaction of most archaeologists that they are undoubtedly of Phoenician origin. There are the massive and familiar Phoenician walls, there the sacred birds, figured, however, not as the dove of Cypris but as the vulture of her Sidonian representative, Astarte, and there, in plenty, the primitive and unpleasing objects of Nature-worship, which in this shape or that are present wherever the Phoenician reared his shrines. There also stands the great building, half temple, half fortress, containing the sacred cone in its inner court, as at Paphos, Byblos, and Emesus. It is now ascertained moreover that within the walls of this temple men did not only celebrate their cruel and licentious rites, they also carried on their trade of gold-smelting.[8]

Later scientific investigations have shown these conjectures, as found also in James Bent's *The Ruined Cities of Mashonaland* (1893), to be incorrect; they are native African ruins dating from several centuries earlier, possibly connected with the gold traffic carried on between central Africa and Arabs on the coast. But Haggard's incorporation in his story of Astarte, the moon-goddess and chief female deity of the ancient Syro-Phoenician nations, clearly derives from similar early speculations. Haggard concluded his preface with the characteristic sentiment that "it is legitimate to hope, it seems probable even, that in centuries to come a town will once more nestle beneath these grey and ancient ruins, trading in gold as did that of the Phoenicians, but peopled by men of the Anglo-Saxon race."[9]

In "The Starlight Night"—composed in 1877, the same year as Shepstone's annexation of the Transvaal—G. M. Hopkins likened stars to the mine pits of Kimberley, "the diamond delves!" But whereas Hopkins's stars are instinct with the divine life of Christ, who is "the bright and morning star" (Revelation 22:16), the imperialist's star is ironically no more than the clichéd diamond in the sky. This diminishment becomes explicit in the writing of Olive Schreiner, Haggard's co-Africanist. In her *Story of an African Farm* (1883), Schreiner goes back to a pastoral moment that is about to vanish forever, an afternoon in the dry summer of 1862, five years before the little Boer farm girl found that first rough nugget of crystalline carbon on the banks of the Orange River. Schreiner's opening scenes are contextualized by what her readers knew only too well was about to occur, yet of which her young protagonists were blithely unaware. But already they have swallowed the poisonous seeds of the coming capitalistic rush, are tainted with socially constructed values and have lost sight of nature's intrinsic worth. Their turn away from a mystic life in nature and toward value as a function of the material economic structure of society is also the offense in Haggard's *King Solomon's Mines*—this, signified by Quatermain's ingrained impulse to stuff his pockets with Solomon's booty. Thus in Schreiner's novel the boy Waldo fails to see the sun as the miraculous fire for which he prays, and Lyndall fails to see nature's ice-plant as better than "real" diamonds. Lyndall "took up the ice-plant leaf and fastened it on to the front of her blue pinafore with a pin. 'Diamonds must look as these drops do,' she said, carefully bending over the leaf, and crushing one crystal drop with her delicate little nail. 'When I,' she said, 'am grown up, I shall wear real diamonds, exactly like these, in my hair.'"[10] Twelve-year-old Lyndall supposes she must leave the farm to get her diamonds. This is very similar to Schreiner's eponymous heroine, Undine, wondering "if the dew lying on the English grass were really as lovely as the great drops that used to stand trembling on the bushes and silvery ice-plants among the stones of the koppie."[11] The genteel British landscape, as Schreiner knows, is never as pristine or powerful as the African wilderness. What Lyndall fails to see is that the "drops"—either Undine's dew or the large glittering *papillae* which give the African plant its appearance of ice—are the very prototypes that name her desire, diamond "drops." Only at the novel's end does Waldo recognize the preciousness of nature's ice-plant, "and it thrilled him."[12]

Schreiner has been criticized for focusing only on the white, colonial world of South Africa, leaving the natives far in the background. Haggard, on the other hand, has been excoriated for presenting Zulus as heartless, wild savages who need to be governed by civilized Europeans for their own future well-being. But although a neo-Hegelian, idealist and organic vision of social organization links both writers in a sympathetic, ameliorative ideology that does not question the right of Europeans to colonize native land, Schreiner and Haggard outflank the dominant popular imperialism of newspapers, schools and, often, missions. As the young daughter of a bankrupt missionary, Schreiner in 1872 had joined her brothers as their housekeeper (though the "house" was a tent) in the rush to the diamond fields. She vividly described the "Big Hole," first in her juvenile *Undine* and then later in "Diamond Fields" (1882):

> Up and down upon the thousand shining wires run the iron buckets.... Standing on the edge, and looking down, the mine is a large, oval basin with precipitous rocky sides, so deep that the men at work in the claims below seem mere moving specks, as they peck at the hard, blue soil. Around the edge of the whole mine is the whirl and rush and tumult of many thousand shouts and voices. An eager, hungry, struggling passionate life animates the whole scene. Every man, every wheel, every implement is in motion. At the wheels upon the staging that rises tier above tier along the edge of the craterlike hollow, niggers are turning ceaselessly at iron handles drawing up and letting down the shining buckets which glint in the hot afternoon sunshine. As the blue stuff is landed on the staging, it is quickly thrown down, and in Scotch carts or barrows is carried away to the gravel mounds where the sorters sit. A very din of machinery and babel of tongues truly, for in the crowd are representatives of every humanity under heaven.... On the top and sides of the gravel heaps that tower like little hills about the mine, sit the sorters; generally white men, for the master does not like to see his nigger at the sorting table. He sits

on a campstool or a turned-up bucket, and as he scrapes the gravel off the table with a piece of tin, watches eagerly for the sparkle of the coveted white stones; and yet keeps all the while half an eye on the black men who rock the sieve or break the blue clonts with the heavy sticks.[13]

The ungrammatical dangler in the second sentence quoted here suggests this is an unrevised, certainly incomplete, narrative of her firsthand experiences a decade earlier.

As material embodiments of value, diamonds serve as metaphors of the African colonies. David Leslie had called Natal colony "the brightest jewel in the British crown."[14] And later when Haggard described the impending annexation of the Transvaal in 1877, he declared that Queen Victoria "will add a jewel to her crown which, though it be unpolished, is still a jewel of price," poeticizing the economic motivation for intervention, its prize of gold and diamonds hidden decorously in his understated locution "mineral resources."[15] But if diamonds are a metaphor of the imperial enterprise, they are equally symbolic of a higher value that the material derives from language. Schreiner had dreamed of replacing the forced use of a colonial language controlling the construction of indigenous identity with a new nineteenth-century English lingua franca, of getting the "empire" out of the language—those disturbing effects or the political static of control—to reach an almost neo-Hegelian homogeneity of speech as large as the heterogeneity of human "thought and knowledge." Schreiner sees the possibility of constructing a better idiom liberated of racial or sexist oppression, a universal and international English:

> We do not dream of our language that it shall forcibly destroy the world's speeches and all they contain, reigning in solitary grandeur, but, as gold in a ring binds into one circle rare gems of every kind and some of infinitely greater beauty than itself, so we dream that our speech being common may bind together and bring into one those treasures of thought and knowledge which the peoples of earth have produced, its highest function being that of making the treasures of all accessible to all.[16]

In Schreiner's allegory, "The Sunlight Lay Across My Bed," Leslie's and Haggard's image of the jewels in the British crown is given the intensely visionary form of a heavenly cirque of gems—gems mined in heaven, one realizes with something of a shock, like the diamonds at Kimberley—that epitomizes a regenerate Cape Colony. The song sung by the miners is the gold binding the gems of human diversity into a unity very like her ideal of a super-imperial language: "And the crown was wrought according to a marvellous pattern; one pattern ran through all, yet each part was different."17 English is the golden song of unity that binds the gems of the world's tongues into the ring, cirque, or crown of a new global *imperium*. Is this a cultural hegemony or an echo of what in *Nada* Haggard called the "great pattern" of the Queen of Heaven: "All things are a great pattern, my father, drawn by the hand of the Umkulunkulu ... how can we build who are but pebbles in a wall? how can we give life who are babes in the womb of fate? or how can we slay who are but spears in the hands of the slayer?"18

§ §

Not only did Haggard value works of "spiritual intensity" but also in *The Days of My Life* Haggard described *King Solomon's Mines* as "a work of pure imagination" because in its time "very little was known of the regions wherein its scenes were laid."19 Among "purely romantic fiction," he implicitly included his own recently published romance. Haggard sought to blame a British ethos of gentility for turning him away from the novel of "life as life is, and men and women as they are" and towards romance.20 This attack on contemporary fiction produced a backlash that inflicted lasting damage on his reputation; for a century, he was ostracized by the literary establishment as little more than a writer of juvenile action-fantasy who got his start imitating *Treasure Island*. Certainly Haggard's dedication of *King Solomon's Mines* ("to all the big and little boys who read it") suggests an obvious marketing strategy to piggyback on Stevenson's success; but dark and bloody adventure also released Haggard's imagination in ways that were neither puerile nor prurient.

Haggard's earlier attempts at realistic fiction had aspired to something like Schreiner's entangled, tragic relationships. One of his early novels with an African setting, *The Witch's Head*, though artistically interesting, had modest sales. Only in romance was he able to capitalize on mythic and visionary patterns to give full rein to the longing of unrequited desire and "the soul and the fate of man" in a modern, hellish world.21 Though Haggard's (and on this occasion also Rudyard Kipling's) sense of the hellishness of modern existence may be partly the infirmities of two old men intensified by the mood of the First World War, Haggard's despairing vision was also for Andrew Lang a key trait: "Men brood on buried loves, and unforgot, / Or break themselves on some divine decree, / Or would o'erleap the limits of their lot"—as Lang phrased it in "*She*," his poetic tribute to Haggard's second romance.22

What Haggard needed to do was harness the tremendous potential of African gold, diamonds, natives, warfare, magic and ritual in an exciting adventure narrative. In the wake of Gladstone's "betrayal," Haggard turned to romance—a myth-making that in *King Solomon's Mines* offered a utopian alternative to the British bungling of African settlement. Haggard really wanted to be a statesman (a Shepstonian white chief, perhaps) and the success of *King Solomon's Mines* was a "sad thing" because it induced him to support his family afterwards by serializing what perhaps have been unfairly called formula-written romances. As he said in his speech: "I came home ... and then a sad thing happened to me—I wrote a successful book.... So it was gentlemen, I took to fiction."23 He really meant this—the political ferment and excitement of those years now could only be relived, at secondhand, in his new authorial calling. Roger Lancelyn Green describes this turning point best:

> Stevenson's *Treasure Island*, recently published, was attracting considerable attention, and to while away dull evenings in London lodgings, Haggard wrote *King Solomon's Mines*: "it was written out of a bet with his brother. The bet was made casually, to prove it possible for someone, not at all known in authorship, to do a 'thriller' as successful as *Treasure Island*." The book was a complete novelty, and publisher after publisher refused to undertake it. Finally it came into the hands of W. E. Henley, who showed it to Andrew Lang, between whom and Haggard a firm friendship soon sprang up. Either Henley or Lang recommended it to Cassells, who agreed to publish it on a small copyright basis. On the eve of publication, so Sir Max Pemberton recalls, he was sitting next to a well-known London publisher at a dinner table, who remarked to him: "There's a silly story of a diamond mine published today. It's by a man named Rider Haggard. They offered me this book six months ago, and I declined it. Some fool has bought it as you will see—and I'm sorry for him." "I have often wondered," Sir Max goes on, "how sorry he remained when Cassells were at their wits' end to bring the book out fast enough and it remained easily the best seller of the year."24

King Solomon's Mines was published in September 1885 by Cassell & Company in a binding designed to make it look like a companion volume to Stevenson's *Treasure Island*. With a flair for advertising, Cassell's plastered large posters all over London announcing "King Solomon's Mines—The Most Amazing Book Ever Written." Richard Dalby notes that

> in spite of this apparent confidence in the book's potential, Cassell's printed only a modest 2000 copies of the first edition, of which only one thousand were bound up in September (the first issue with a catalogue at the

rear dated 5G.8.85). Five hundred more were bound up in October with a catalogue at the end dated 5G.10.85 (the second issue), and the remaining five hundred were shipped to New York and bound up there in November.[25]

The cover was in red cloth on which was imprinted its title and author's name, with a design, called a "trophy" by bibliographers, of a Zulu shield, weapons, and elephant tusk. The first edition also has a splendid frontispiece, a fold-out treasure map drawn by Agnes Barber, a friend of Haggard's wife:

> Haggard's favourite anecdote concerning Agnes Barber's entrancing and cryptic map took place on the day he took it to be bound with the manuscript of *King Solomon's Mines*, and travelled on the London Underground. An old lady sitting opposite him in the carriage was earnestly studying a copy of the same map, printed at the beginning of the newly published volume which rested on her knees. Unable to resist the temptation, Haggard took the real map out of his pocket, placed it on his knee and began to study it with equally rapt attention. This naturally caught the old lady's eye, and caused her complete bafflement as she looked back and forth from her copy to the genuine original, "written in blood upon a dirty piece of torn linen—the shirt-tail of Don Jose da Silvestra." Neither of them spoke, but as the train was about to leave the next station, the lady sprang up and leapt from the carriage, the book and unfolded map still in her hand![26]

The popularity of Haggard's tale quickly eclipsed even that of *Treasure Island*. Because Haggard's romance spoke of the reassertion of British masculinity, of exploits utterly absent from nineteenth-century drawing rooms, the novel sold 31,000 copies in its first year, an enormous number for that era.

All of Haggard's fictional characters contain much of him in them, and *King Solomon's Mines* is no exception. Someone once said that Quatermain is what Haggard thinks he could have become; Good is what he is thankful for not having become; and Sir Henry what he would like to be—in an age of Berserker warriors, perhaps. Umbopa, of course, is simply Sir Henry born Zulu, as we see after the spectacle of Khiva's death when the two bond with Umbopa's observation of his and Sir Henry's stature: "we are men, you and I."[27] Umbopa, we know, is modeled on the exploits of M'hlopekazi, son of M'Swazi, king of Swaziland, whom Haggard met in Pietermaritzburg in the later 1870s. M'hlopekazi, by then sixty years old, originally had arrived in Natal in 1859, perhaps because he was too close to the Swazi throne for safety. At his death at the age of eighty (24 October 1897), obituaries in the

Natal Mercury and the *Natal Witness* noted that as a young man he had fought in the Nyati Regiment, "the crack corps of the country," and that at Pietermaritzburg, "being a 'Prince of the Blood' and a warrior of some renown, Umhlopekazi appears to have commanded a considerable amount of respect from the first; and shortly after his arrival he was taken into the service of the late Sir Theophilus Shepstone, accompanying that gentleman as a kind of aide-de-camp in his travels and mission through the Cape Colony, Basutoland and the Transvaal."[28] Haggard, of course, changed not only his name but also his nationality from Swazi to Kukuana-Zulu. Later in *Allan Quatermain* (1887), *Nada the Lily* (1892), and *She and Allan* (1921) Umhlopekazi also reappears as Umslopogaas. As Quatermain tells Umslopogaas at the outset of their expedition to the land of the Zu-Vendi in *Allan Quatermain*: "Once before we three journeyed thus, in search of adventure, and we took with us a man such as thou—one Umbopa; and, behold, we left him the king of a great country."[29] M'hlopekazi may have been dimly aware of the dawning incentive for Chief Buthelezi to reestablish the Zulu national consciousness. Asked if he was proud to be in Haggard's novels, M'hlopekazi replied: "to me it is nothing. Yet I am glad that Indanda [Haggard] has set my name in writings that will not be forgotten, so that when my people are no more a people, one of them at least, will be remembered."[30]

Despite Haggard's disclaimers, F. C. Selous was popularly supposed to have been the prototype for Allan Quatermain.[31] Certainly Selous's prose, as straightforward as Haggard's, brings the reader face to face with the aboriginal Africa with which Haggard was fascinated. Selous described himself as "a professional elephant-hunter";[32] and as Teddy Roosevelt aptly commented in his foreword to Selous's *African Nature Notes and Reminiscences* (1908): he "is much more than a mere big-game hunter, however; he is by instinct a keen field naturalist, an observer with a power of seeing, and remembering what he has seen; and finally he is a writer who possesses to a very marked and unusual degree the power vividly and accurately to put on paper his observations."[33] Selous several decades later encounters Livingstone's harassed convert Sechele. This bizarre scene is played out deep in the wilderness of Bechuanaland, "four months' continuous travelling by bullock waggon"[34] from the coast:

> he is a tall, portly old Kafir, and to me, a stranger, he appeared to be a very pleasant old fellow. He was living in a large well-built house, over the dining-room mantelpiece of which stood a handsome good-sized mir-

ror; above the doorway was a large clock, while in the bedroom I caught a glimpse of a fine iron bedstead. We had tea with him, and I was surprised to see it served in a silver tea-pot and a handsome set of china tea-things. Altogether, judging only from outward and visible signs, old Secheli appeared to me to be the most completely civilised Kafir that I had yet seen. I have since heard that although a most diligent student of the Old Testament (for he can read the Sechuana translation), he is not thought, by those who consider themselves capable of judging, to be a particularly good and sound Christian. He was very anxious about Queen Victoria's health, and seemed much concerned to hear of the recent illness of the Prince of Wales.35

Apparently, Livingstone's mission of civilization had proceeded slightly better than his work of conversion; nevertheless, if Sechele didn't speak English with a Scots burr, as indeed many products of the mission schools did, he seems to have been one of the Queen's loyalist subjects there on the fringes of the Kalahari.

Undoubtedly Khiva's death in *King Solomon's Mines* is indebted to Selous's account of the fate of one Quabeet, who had not returned to camp after a day's hunting. The dry, matter-of-fact voice might almost be Quatermain speaking:

> I give the story of this mishap as I heard it from Clarkson's own lips.... "At break of day I left camp, and riding straight to where I had shot the first elephant, took up the spoor of the tuskless bull, and had followed it for maybe two miles when I came to a place where he had stood under a tree amongst some dense underwood. From this place he had spun suddenly round, as the spoor showed, and made a rush through the bush, breaking and smashing everything before him. Fifty yards farther on we found Quabeet's gun, a little beyond this a few odds and ends of skin that he had worn round his waist, and then what remained of the poor fellow himself. He had been torn in three pieces; the chest, with head and arms attached, which had been wrenched from the trunk just below the breastbone, lying in one place, one leg and thigh that had been torn off at the pelvis in another, and the remainder in a third. The right arm had been broken in two places and the hand crushed; one of the thighs was also broken, but otherwise the fragments had not been trampled on." There is little doubt that the infuriated elephant must have pressed the unfortunate man down with his foot or knee, and then twisting his trunk round his body wrenched him asunder.36

Finally, when Quatermain crosses the dry desert, his prose descriptions have their origins at least partially in the May 29–June 2 entries of Selous's hunting season of 1879.37

Haggard described his method of romance-writing as "swift, clear, and direct," purged of "dark allusions": "such work should be written rapidly and, if possible, not rewritten, since wine of this character loses its bouquet when it is poured from glass to glass."38 In his *Private Diaries,* Haggard remarks, however, a propos of Kipling's appreciation of *Yva* (*When the World Shook*), still in manuscript, that "he [Kipling] has imagination, vision and can *understand,* amongst other things that Romance may be the vehicle of much that does not appear to the casual reader."39 Haggard may be referring either generally to figurative meanings beneath the literal or specifically to nineteenth-century spiritualism that flourished in such groups as the Order of the Golden Dawn or the Society for Psychical Research. The Victorian and Haggardian mind was perfectly able to combine the empirical methods of science with a spiritualism beyond scientific verification: "notwithstanding a thousand explanations, what is more mysterious than a telephone wire, except a telephone without one?"40 If Haggard had gone on for another sentence or two about this irreducible mystery at the heart of physics, he might almost have begun to anticipate Pierre Duhem in *The Aim and Structure of Physical Theory* (1908). In his fiction, Haggard has Allan Quatermain use common sense to explain away uncanny powers and second sight—never wholly succeeding. This is a tactic whereby the occult can be examined empirically; then, escaping definitive explanation, emerge validated.

Haggard's spontaneous imagistic "bouquet" has powerful affinities with dreams or with such early psychoanalytic devices, even, as Rorschach tests, tapping lapsed memories and subliminal impressions. At the climactic moment in *King Solomon's Mines,* the trio is illuminated in the dimming lamp: "Presently it flared up and showed the whole scene in strong relief, the great mass of white tusks, the boxes full of gold, the corpse of poor Foulata stretched before them, the goat-skin full of treasure, the dim glimmer of the diamonds, and the wild, wan faces of us three white men seated there awaiting death by starvation." Quatermain observes that "wealth, which men spend all their lives in acquiring, is a valueless thing at the last."41 Despite Haggard's predilection for "grip" in romance writing, one cannot dismiss this "scene" as simply the climactic moment of suspense before the escape. Nor is Quatermain's sudden insight into the valuelessness of London diamonds merely melodramatic depression. In his Canadian speech, Haggard cited this specific passage to assert that the commercial and technological wealth of urban life is valueless apart from an Antaeus-like contact with the land and its fertility. Like the native, the European must go to the land, must discover the natives' wealth, not in the form of diamonds but as a power of rebirth, renewal. This is the fundamental mythopoeic hook on which Haggard hangs his heroic quest.

In recent decades, interpretations of *King Solomon's Mines* characterize it either as an adventure across psychological terrain into unknown and tabooed frontiers of the unconscious or as a journey of exploration, capitalist conquest, and the establishment of a colonial patriarchy. Without discarding psychological and cultural readings, an interpretation that combines diamonds and deities—Victorian imperial politics with the world of magic and religion—best explains the relevance and context of this novel. Sitanda's Kraal with its encompassing rivers, the trio's last outpost before the desert, is on old maps of Rhodesia, located in present-day central Zambia; but beyond this point Haggard's topography becomes mythopoeic—or, as others somewhat too hastily conclude, reflects the stereotypes of imperialist romanticism. At the time Haggard wrote *King Solomon's Mines*, what are now Zambia's central and northern provinces were still outside the area of imperial expansion. In F. C. Selous's *A Hunter's Wanderings in Africa*, we are told this greatest African hunter of all time nearly dies of fever and starvation at the kraal of Sitanda, the chief of that country:

> Eight wretched little Kafir fowls, about the size of a bantam, and just mere skin and bone, and a little Kafir corn and bad water, was absolutely all we had to eat and drink; and if we had not got sufficiently well to have moved out of this accursed pestilential spot before our slender allowance was finished, it would have been a poor look-out indeed. Taking a straight line as the crow flies, we were more than four hundred miles from Inyati, the farthest trading outpost and missionary station in the Matabele country, which was the nearest point where we could hope to get anything like food for a sick man.[42]

Haggard's imperceptible segue from similar facts to fantasy, from history to fabrication, is one of the strongest features in all his novels.

"The rifle must replace, and, indeed, actually has replaced, the assegai and the shield," observed Haggard.[43] In describing the outfitting of Quatermain's expedition into the interior, he supplies a torrent of firearms detail. It was remarked that one could tear this leaf out of the novel,[44] hand it to the outfitters, and then head into the heart of darkness. Not, of course, without danger: when Mary Kingsley arrived in *Allan Quatermain* territory, she was ominously advised to "get some introductions to the Wesleyans; they are the only people on the Coast who have got a hearse with feathers."45 This outfitting climaxes with an amazingly detailed list of firearms: three of each (one for each adventurer)—elephant guns, expresses, Winchesters and Colts. Firearms were the preeminent symbol of imperial power; and the two named gun makers are, interestingly, American. Just as the scramble for Africa got underway, a parallel push across the great plains and mountains of the United States gave rise to a new post-Civil War generation of firearms. Did technology precede and make possible the opening of new frontiers or did the need to open those frontiers call forth the new technological inventions? Whichever, the role of firearms gave their owners temporal, if not spiritual, powers. Only Conrad in *Heart of Darkness* questions the Winchesters' efficacy. His passengers on the riverboat stand "with Winchesters at 'ready' in their hands." Then, says Marlow, "A fusillade burst out under my feet. The pilgrims had opened with their Winchesters, and were simply squirting lead into that bush. A deuce of a lot of smoke came up and drove slowly forward."46 If the fusillade was no more effective than the frigate shelling the wilderness earlier, the firepower at least was its own excuse for being. Actually, Oliver Winchester's technology clearly was an asset in more uncanny struggles, such as with the wolves commanded by a vampire in Bram Stoker's *Dracula*, a human-animal alliance that may owe something to Umslopogaas and Galazi in *Nada the Lily*. Quincey Morris says in chapter twenty-four: "'I propose that we add Winchesters to our armament. I have a kind of belief in a Winchester when there is any trouble of that sort around' ... 'Good!' said Van Helsing, 'Winchesters it shall be.'"47 Allan's favorite rifle, however, was a single-shot Purdy that reappears in the adventure tales with regularity.48

In *King Solomon's Mines* the trio shoots a buck with the "magic tube that speaks"—another proof the "wizards" "do not speak empty words"49—and then inquires, a not-so-subtle form of intimidation, if any native still doubts and wishes to volunteer as object of the next demonstration. In contrast to the natives' awareness of mortality, Quatermain proclaims "we do not die."50 The trio then is introduced to Twala, who was first *bonga*-ed (praised) as "husband of a thousand wives, chief and lord paramount of the Kukuanas, keeper of the great road, terror of his enemies, student of the Black Arts, leader of an hundred thousand warriors, Twala the One-eyed, the Black, the Terrible."51 Against this figure, Solomonic in sexual potency, demonic in magic, the trio must disguise the fact they are "impostors."52 Twala tries to turn back upon the trio their own psychology of intimidation. He has his son spear a loyal soldier as proof of his power and suggests he could make the adventurers "as him whom they bear away."[53] When the king then demands they too kill a human as proof of their powers, they shoot another animal and say "Thou hast seen. Now know we come in peace, not in war."[54] After presenting Twala with a gift of one of their Winchesters (which the king has no idea how to use), Quatermain fires on the flat side of a spear blade at forty paces—"the bullet struck the flat of the spear, and broke the blade in fragments."[55] This is the definitive demonstration of the superiority of the white man's weapons over those of the African; one senses in its cleverness that this was once an actual demonstration about which Haggard had been told.

At mid-century, the study of early man in comparative mythology owed much to F. Max Müller, a linguistic ethnologist, who hypothesized the origin of culture as lying in a "mythopoeic age" in which the diurnal and seasonal "solar drama" was reenacted by a young hero whose death is "suggested by the Sun, dying in all his youthful vigor, either at the end of a day, conquered by the powers of darkness, or at the end of the sunny season, stung by the thorn of winter."[56] And Brian Street[57] asserts Sir Henry's speculation on Ashtoreth[58] derives from Max Müller's *Introduction to the Science of Religion* (1870). Among the most influential of Müller's successors in systematizing ritual and myth was E. B. Tylor, whose *Primitive Culture* (1871) became for its day the standard in cultural anthropology. Scheick's and DeMoor's essays hint that Haggard's narrative can be approached from the avenue of J. G. Frazer's investigations;[59] but, of course, Frazer's *The Golden Bough* (1890–1915) is not an influence on the romance, only a belated affinity. However, not only were the gods and heroes of myth already established for Haggard as solar or vegetation figures, but even the sort of literary relevance that T. S. Eliot, W. B. Yeats and James Joyce later found in Frazer's work had been anticipated by the liberal bishop of Natal, J. W. Colenso. A friend of Haggard's father, Colenso was an African luminary that the young Haggard "cannot but admire, with his intellect written on his face;... he recognized my name the first time I saw him."[60] The crucial anthropological implication of Colenso's biblical scholarship "was the relevance of so-called uncivilized thought and lower cultures to the most cultivated and sophisticated theological, philosophical, and historical viewpoints. Thus, in a modest and oblique way he adumbrated the shattering implications later thinkers were to find in *The Golden Bough*."[61] Haggard does not acknowledge specific anthropological indebtednesses, but the names that crisscross Tylor's references to travellers, historians, and missionaries amply document a plethora of contemporary observations of primitive myth and ritual. Further, an emergent friendship with Andrew Lang indicates Haggard's parallel preoccupations and knowledgeability. By envisioning Tylor's savage "survivals" as able to reanimate contemporary society, Haggard's novel appears both to have anticipated the modernist's fantasy of Africa as the locale for a recovery of spiritual vitality and to have foreshadowed Eliot's interpretation of modernism's handling of myth as "a continuous parallel between contemporaneity and antiquity."62 The young Haggard had attended London spiritualist séances with nearly the same credulity as the youthful Yeats a generation later.

From youth, years before his discussions of comparative mythology with Andrew Lang, Haggard had been a deeply interested student of ancient Egyptian and Teutonic customs and religion: "From a boy ancient Egypt had fascinated me, and I had read everything concerning it on which I could lay hands.... I love the Norse people of the saga and pre-saga times.... I have a respect for Thor and Odin, I venerate Isis, and always feel inclined to bow to the moon!"63 Haggard began his lifelong personal acquaintance with Lang when he was seeking a publisher for *King Solomon's Mines*. At that time, Haggard might have been familiar with Lang's earliest work on myth in the periodicals (*Frazer's, Fortnightly, Academy*) or, possibly, in his first book on the subject, *Custom and Myth* (1884); but most likely their instant bonding was based on common personal interests in folklore, dreams, and ghosts. In the 1870s, Lang undertook to refute Müller's narrowly based philological explanations and argued that survivals from savage myths still persist in modern life, their basic themes and symbols refined variously in differing cultures; in later years, Lang also responded to Frazer's work. As a young man preoccupied with thoughts of death and toying with religious skepticism, Haggard had been drawn to pagan notions of reincarnation as an alternative to orthodox belief. This was perfectly in tune with an agrarian, Romantic mythopoesis and with Haggard's instinctive rejection of the social values emerging from the shift to an industrial base. Thus when Quatermain announces that he is "going to tell the strangest story that I know of,"64 Haggard may well be hinting at a narrative that replaces tea in the British drawing-room with the worship of ancient deities and their rites of death and rebirth. Quatermain begins his account of Solomon's treasure by pretending to ignore Sheba and claiming that his story has "no woman in it—except Foulata. Stop, though! there is Gagoola, if she was a woman and not a fiend. But she was a hundred at least, and therefore not marriageable, so I don't count her. At any rate, I can safely say that there is not a *petticoat* in the whole history."65 Quatermain is quite right about the missing petticoat (colloquially and metonymically, a nubile young woman whose clothing defines her as non-African) since Foulata does not wear petticoats and, of course, is "not marriageable" to an Englishmen—on this Quatermain is culturally resolute. Of course, the fabled Zulu maiden, Umkxakaza-wakogingqwayo, is described "*e bincile umuntsha wezindondo*"—but as a chief's daughter (thus unlike Foulata, who is not quite the "Kukuana Pocahontas" of Andrew Lang's phrase) one might expect to see Umkxakaza on festive occasions in a brass-beaded "petticoat."66 Also in Haggard's *The Ghost Kings* (1908) Zulu maidens are "dressed in bead petticoats."67 As to Solomon's Sheba, Bunn, McClintock, and Scheick have pointed out that the landscape the adventurers cross is visualized as the female body, in which the treasure map read upside down limns Sheba's nippled breasts, navel, and pudendum.68

Haggard expands this image of Sheba into an icon of the African landscape in its fertility and death. The "big and little boys" to whom Haggard's narrative is dedicated undoubtedly were titillated by "Sheba's breasts,"69 if not by dawn blushing "like the cheek of a girl";70 but Victorian schoolboys probably did not notice any extended pattern of sexual imagery. What Haggard draws upon for his legend of Solomon and the Queen of Sheba comes from sacred sources, both 1 Kings 10:1 *et seq.* and chapters twenty-seven and thirty-four of the Qur'an (Koran), "The Ant" and "Sheba," as well as later Islamic tales and medieval European art. The tradition of Sheba as African (the country and, metonymically, the woman) is at least as old as the historian Flavius Josephus (37–100 AD) who calls her the "Queen of Egypt and Ethiopia." She is a Moorish, mythopoeic figure from the city of Ophir, to whom in the Song of Solomon the words "I am black but comely" traditionally are ascribed (1:5). In the language of sculpted torsos and art-studio nudes, Quatermain suggests an ideal of Sheba's physical perfection between life and myth. Phrases such as "fleecy envelope," "gauzy mist," and "cloud-clad privacy"71 describe the envelopment of her erogenous zones like a graceful nineteenth-century figure: "The mountains we had crossed now loomed high above us, and Sheba's breasts were modestly veiled in diaphanous wreaths of mist."72 But though Sheba is even more draped than Antonio Canova's well-known *Pauline Borghese as Venus* (1808), her sexuality is indeed palpable, only disguised by the upside-down map and momentarily veiled by a summertime raiment befitting a maiden-goddess not unlike a Kore. One is reminded of the disguised reality, in contrast to Holly's banal conjectures, of the gauzy Ayesha in *She* (1887): "At length the curtain began to move. Who could be behind it?—some naked savage queen, a languishing Oriental beauty, or a nineteenth-century young lady drinking afternoon tea?"[73]

Did Haggard's readers perceive Sheba as one of Holly's figures, with (chaste) or without (carnal) petticoats? Current criticism highlights her as a gender victim. But "Sheba's breasts" are not narrowly indicative of the rapist-imperialist's sexual oppression of women, native or otherwise; and the patriarchal connections within modernist expressions of the primitive—the landscape as female, sexual, and deadly—would have been seen by Haggard and Victorian anthropologists as a "survival" from ancient myth. Haggard understands human identity and its relation to nature in terms of a mother/mistress analogue in which birth and death are expressed by a female landscape, both generative and fatal. Within this mythic drama, Sheba and Solomon are mutually restorative figures, whose union is productive of the interval in which life supplants death. A mythic potency flickers across the form of Sheba because, like the animistic Venus, she too expresses the procreative force. The novel's earthy allusiveness to breasts and pudendum is a strike at Mrs. Grundy's strait-laced abhorrence of the natural and erotic, Haggard's assertion that neither social conventions nor literary art can or should suppress passion and beauty. The Victorian urge, in the genteel, mid-century tradition of Thomas Bulfinch or Charles Kingsley, to refine and classicize away the violence and sexuality of myth in contrast to the anthropological realism of Tylor's shocking accounts of primitive behavior, trivialized and cheated myth of its power. Both Haggard and the major modernists deplored the disruption of a primal connection between man and nature, the impoverishment of mystery and wonder; but whereas Frazer, the Cambridge Anthropologists, and Jung (writing on racial memory) all are seen as contributing to the modernists' mythic imagination, Haggard in 1885 had only Tylor and Lang to inspire his fictional use of elemental and regenerative archetypes.

The Solomon-Sheba legend is Haggard's literary presentation of those primal interrelations of love, pain and death; and his trio of nineteenth-century adventurers themselves confront this mythic fertility pattern in the witch hunt, in the battle, and in their entrance into the place of death. Haggard explicitly opens the door to such an anthropological interpretation when he describes the austere goddess of the Silent Ones, manifestly a feminine double of Sheba, as having on her head "the points of a crescent."[74] She and her companions are "'Ashtoreth the goddess of the Zidonians, Chemosh the god of the Moabites, and Milcom the god of the children of Ammon'"—heathen or biblically "false divinities."[75] Their silence signifies an archaic fatality and is rooted in such biblical passages as Jeremiah 8:14 and Psalms 94:17, 115:17. Solomon, doubtless under the influence of his thousand wives, had built a high-place for Ashtoreth at Jerusalem (1 Kings 11:5; 2 Kings 23:13). Ashtoreth-Astarte is the Mesopotamian mother-goddess, the personification of life itself, the female principle of fertility, both of the reproduction and growth of plants and trees and of sexual love. She is the female counterpart of the sun-god Baal; and because she was represented with horns, she was formerly assumed to be a lunar goddess. In the Mesopotamian astral-theological system, not only the moon but the planet Venus was identified with Ashtoreth in her variant guises: "Now Astarte, the divine mistress of Adonis, was identified with the planet Venus, and her changes from a morning to an evening star were carefully noted by the Babylonian astronomers, who drew omens from her alternate appearance and disappearance. Hence we may conjecture that the festival of Adonis was regularly timed to coincide with the appearance of Venus as the Morning or Evening Star."[76] Thus when the trio announce they are from the "biggest star," they align themselves, dishonestly and ominously, with this goddess since after the sun and moon, Venus, the morning and evening star, is the most brilliant body in the sky.

In Greek mythology, Demeter gives birth, fertilizes the fields and clothes nature; but she is also a grim goddess, cruel and destructive, who revokes her life-giving power and brings barrenness and death. Demeter, as Walter Pater describes her, is "the wrinkled woman," who "grows young again every spring yet is of great age."[77] Gagool, the "Mother, old mother,"[78] is Demeter in her cruel phase who slays her child but is concurrently mourning her loss; thus, as Pater describes her, she is the "mistress and manager of men's shades."[79] Her cyclic pattern was personified by her twinned daughter(s), Kore the goddess of summer and Persephone the goddess of winter. Hades, seeing Kore-Persephone gathering flowers, abducts her to his gloomy palace under the earth; only when she returns to the sunshine do flowers spring up again. In the Mesopotamian variant, as midsummer approaches—Haggard's adventurers predict the eclipse in June, a date that coincides with the Kukuana ritual of sacrifice—the springtime consort of the goddess is slain. She then enters the nether world to rescue him; and at each of the seven gates through which she passes, some of her clothing and adornments are removed until she passes through the last gate naked. The earth continues infertile until the goddess reemerges, arrayed again like nature in her full splendor. The strikingly different phases of the summer and winter Venus reflect this cyclic aspect of the goddess.

In Haggard's text, Ashtoreth as astral-lunar goddess finds her counterpart in Milcom and Chemosh, aspects of Baal the sun-god. Here, too, the "silent ones" represent not only a mythic pattern of thesis-antithesis (moon-death-nakedness in strife with sun-life-raiment) but also a synthesis, the mother-goddess personifying all of nature's life forces—moon against sun and, taken together, earth's ceaselessly interacting antinomies of generation and decay: "'What is the lot of man born of woman?' Back came the answer rolling out from every throat in that vast company—'Death!'"[80] This chorus swells to recount "various phases of human passions, fears, and joys. Now it seemed to be a love song, now a majestic swelling war chant, and last of all a death-dirge ending suddenly in one heartbreaking wail that went echoing and rolling away in a volume of blood-curdling sound."[81] When we first encounter Foulata she is like Kore, the fairest maiden gathering flowers, "flower-crowned."[82] As the summer goddess, she nurses Good, her consort, back to health. Foulata, marked out to be killed by the Gagool-Twala-Scragga cohort, embodies with her antagonist, Gagool, the darker aspect of the earth-mother's cycle of death that precedes renewal. Gagool's origins, as an intensified version of the "witch-finder," initially were historical, as Haggard himself had observed:

> Suddenly there stood before us a creature, a woman, who, save for the colour of her skin, might have been the original of any one of Macbeth's "weird sisters." Little, withered, and bent nearly double by age, her activity was yet past comprehension. Clad in a strange jumble of snake-skins, feathers, furs, and bones, a forked wand in her outstretched hand, she rushed to and fro before the little group of white men. Her eyes gleamed like those of a hawk through her matted hair, and the genuineness of her frantic excitement was evident by the quivering flesh and working face, and the wild, spasmodic words she spoke. The spirit at least of her rapid utterances may thus be rendered:—
>
> "Ou, ou, ou, ai, ai, ai. Oh, ye warriors that shall dance before the great ones of the earth, come! Oh, ye dyers of spears, ye plumed suckers of blood, come! I, the Isanusi, I, the witch-finder, I, the wise woman, I, the seer of

strange sights, I, the reader of dark thoughts, call ye! Come, ye fierce ones; come, ye brave ones, come, and do honour to the white lords! Ah, I hear ye! Ah, I smell ye! Ah, I see ye; ye come, ye come!"[83]

Fred Fynney, a Natal border agent and inspector of native schools, is worth quoting at length from *Zululand and the Zulus* (1880), "Our Native Tribes: Their Customs, Superstitions and Beliefs," because he also demonstrates the basis of Haggard's fantasy in reality:

> There are among the natives a class known as the *Izanusi* or *Abangoma*, who profess to have direct intercourse with the spirit-world, and to practice divination. Their influence is invoked in the "smelling-out" or finding out of the *abatakati* [wizards or witches, singular: *umtakati*]. In Natal, they have been forbidden to practice their dark arts, but they do so secretly, all the same, and cause a deal of mischief; for though no one, within the boundaries of this colony, dare openly accuse another of witchcraft, still there are many heart-burnings and much bitter feeling caused by their hints and innuendoes.
>
> In Zululand, where these *abangoma* are unrestrained, the influence they exercise is something awful, for during the last sixty years they have been the means of causing the death of hundreds of thousands of innocent creatures, through their minor "smellings out" and the more fearful *Ingomboco*—which means, within the circle, or surrounded. When I refer to the minor "smellings out," I mean that of individuals; but the *Ingomboco* is a tribal affair, which I can, perhaps, best explain by relating an incident that happened within my own knowledge in the year 1856. During that year, I went to Zululand, accompanied by a staff of carriers, for the purpose of hunting and trading. We formed a large party, and it was therefore necessary, in looking out for a resting place at night, to secure the most commodious kraals along our line of travel. After a weary day's march, on one occasion, I noticed a large kraal some two miles ahead, in a beautiful valley, which seemed to give promise of rest to our weary bodies, and furnish the necessary food for the party; we therefore decided upon staying there for the night. On arriving at the gate, however, we discovered that the kraal was unoccupied, and there was altogether an uninviting weirdness about the place which the glorious rays of a setting sun could not dispel; so, with one accord, we decided to move onward, late though it was. I had noticed crowds of vultures in the valley below the kraal, and altogether the appearances of the place were an enigma to me. We had not gone far down the valley before we came upon another kraal, of much larger dimensions than that just quitted, and which, I soon found out, belonged to Nobeta, a cousin of Umpande, who was then king. As in courtesy bound, I reported myself to the chief, with the intention of at once passing on, as I had heard that Nobeta was not one of the most amiable magnates of Zululand. The old chief, however, would not hear of my going past him, and he gave instructions that quarters were to be prepared for us.... I mentioned incidentally that it was by mere chance that we had got

THREE: Diamonds and Deities

that far, as we had purposed staying at a kraal farther back, only we had found it deserted. The old reptile thereupon callously observed, "Oh, yes; I wiped them all out two days ago. They were all *abatakatis;* they killed my mother, or assisted in doing so; but there are more *abatakatis* to be smelt out yet."

We were treated most hospitably the night we stayed at Nobeta's kraal, and next morning, on my proceeding to bid the chief good-bye, I was surprised to find that he would not hear of my going just then. He wanted my presence at his kraal that morning, he said, as they had a great piece of business on, and I must see how he punished evil-doers. I pleaded the urgent necessity of our getting forward on our journey, but all to no purpose, so we made a virtue of necessity and remained with the chief, as requested.

I noticed, about 10 o'clock that morning, that batches of natives began to arrive outside the kraal, from all directions. They came with sullen, downcast looks, and observed an ominous silence; each enveloped in a blanket, and carrying only a short stick. After some little time a bevy of girls came out of the kraal, and began a sort of chant, to the music of which they kept time by clapping their hands; young men, armed with knob kerries, next came upon the scene; and last of all, five of the fearful *abangoma* advanced toward where the sable throng was seated. The appearance of these fearful creatures, enveloped as they were in everything which tended to make them hideous, in the shape of snake skins and portions of reptiles and other animals, would baffle description. Reluctant observer of such a scene as I was, they inspired me with a feeling of awe and disgust, for I then realized what their presence foreboded. Each carried in his left hand a bundle of small assegais and shield, whilst in the right hand was the tail of a gnu,—their gaunt forms according well with their panther-like actions. The young warriors drew round the terror-stricken lines of defenceless natives. The chant was struck up, and the smelling out began. Victim after victim was revealed by the aid of the spirits as an *umtakati*, upon which, the *umgoma*, bounding over each, switched him with the Gnu's tail; this was the signal for his being seized upon the spot and dragged away, as food for the ever-ready vultures and wolves. No sooner were the different victims disposed of, than a band of warriors were dispatched to the several kraals to continue the work of destruction, and seize the cattle. I do not know the number of those killed, but I believe there were seventeen, all kraal owners, together with their families, which constituted a total, in one day, that makes one's very heart revolt at the thought of it.

Whilst compelled to sit by Nobeta in the kraal, I observed a lot of vultures settled on a tree above our heads, and I was so disgusted with the old fellow's mercilessness, that I indiscreetly remarked that he had not yet satisfied his friends the vultures, asking if he could not find another *umtakati*. He flew into a fearful rage, charged me with ingratitude, and bade me begone. I obeyed at once.[84]

When Odysseus tells Polyphemus that he is "no man," he effectively disguises his threat as colonizer. But in *King Solomon's Mines* Gagool doesn't see the announced intentions of the adventurers as peaceable. She foretells bloodshed because of imperial incursions. Repulsive, Gagool nevertheless correctly sees an imminent bloody cataclysm and warns of a new colonialism in pursuit of diamonds. In this, she picks up Shaka's famous dying words about "the running of the feet of a great white people which shall stamp out the children of the Zulus."[85] One also wonders if at the end, with an audible *"crunch"*[86] under thirty tons of rock, Gagool may not be in some subliminal way a casualty of imperial silencing. Perhaps the savage Polyphemus tricked by wily Odysseus may have a subliminal connection with one-eyed Twala, making him a Cyclops-victim. No less than the broken promises of the British government in the Transvaal, the trio's misrepresentations of their motives and identities in Haggard's tale corrupts the wisdom of Solomon, a king who speaks to birds and animals and commands demons and jinn. The colonial script allowed the adventurers to establish control over the natives by framing their imperial presence with deceit. Thus when the natives beg to be pardoned for mistaking the trio as merely mortal, fearing they might be killed, Quatermain's "imperial smile" is so self-aware that Haggard must have been conscious of the implications of his scene:

> "It is granted," I said, with an imperial smile. "Nay, ye shall know the truth. We come from another world, though we are men such as ye; we come," I went on, "from the biggest star that shines at night."
>
> "Oh! oh!" groaned the chorus of astonished aborigines.
>
> "Yes," I went on, "we do indeed;" and I again smiled benignly as I uttered that amazing lie. "We come to stay with you a little while, and bless you by our sojourn."[87]

Here their assertion of truth-telling is a most outrageous prevarication. Just before, Good hoodwinks the natives with the prediction of an eclipse and Quatermain calls out: "'Look, chiefs and people and women, and see if the white men from the stars keep their word, or if they be but empty liars!'"[88] Ignosi declares with merely the barest soupçon of skepticism that "'English "gentlemen" tell no lies.'"[89]

In creating their own eclipse myth (Tylor, incidentally, inventories eclipse myths in *Primitive Culture*[90]), the trio's imperial ambition is symbolized in recurrent images of the moon eaten or swallowed. This devouring motif is given resonant concreteness in Haggard's maiden foray into print on Zulu war-dancing (an essay assuredly "of quality and fabric" even if banalities swarm around its noetic moments) by the European's depletion of the native's herds of game. In "A Zulu War-Dance," if one gets past Haggard's clichés, one realizes that his remarkable detail of the silence owing to over-hunting[91] is a form of Gagool's prediction that the "white people ... shall eat ye up"—an eventuality as yet unrealized in the panoramic scene-painting from Kukuanaland which includes "countless herds of game or cattle" and "groups of dome-shaped huts ... whilst over all was the glad sunlight and the wide breath of Nature's happy life."[92] Yet however expedient and lifesaving their prevarications may be, the trio pursues Solomon's diamonds with lies that manipulate and nullify the truth of nature.

Haggard based his description of the Kukuana civil war on his friend Fynney's and Sir Melmoth Osborn's firsthand accounts of a Zulu battle at the Tugela River. This anecdote (told circa 1876) is from Haggard's *The Days of My Life* (1926):

> I heard many a story of savage Africa from Sir Theophilus [Shepstone] himself, from [Sir Melmoth] Osborn and from [Fred] Fynney.... Osborn actually saw the battle of the Tugela, which took place between the rival princes Cetewayo and Umbelazi in 1856. With the temerity of a young man he swam his horse across the river and hid himself in a wooded kopje in the middle of the battlefield. He saw Umbelazi's host driven back and the veteran regiment, nearly three thousand strong, that Panda had sent to aid his favourite son, move up to its support. He described to me the frightful fray that followed. Cetewayo sent out a regiment against it. They met, and he said that the roll of the shields as they came together was like to that of deepest thunder. Then the Greys passed over Cetewayo's regiment as a wave passes over a sunken ridge of rock, and left it dead. Another regiment came against them and the scene repeated itself, only more slowly, for many of the veterans were down. Now the six hundred of them who remained formed themselves in a ring upon the hillock and fought on till they were buried beneath the heaps of the slain....
>
> It is wonderful that Osborn should have escaped with his life. This he did by hiding close and tying his coat over his horse's head to prevent it from neighing. When darkness fell he rode back to the Tugela and swam its corpse-crowded waters.[93]

Cetewayo (or Ketshewayo), son of Panda, defeated his brother Umbelazi to become King of the Zulus.

In Haggard's mythic potpourri, Sir Henry, not Umbopa, defeats Twala in single combat to win the kingdom, suggesting that Sir Henry is the double of Ignosi. When Umbopa arises as Ignosi, Sir Henry goes into exile like the yearly wounded vegetation god Adonis-Tammuz. As winter goddess, Gagool brings her slain consort Twala to the Place of Death, like a Valkyrie to Valhalla. Her hall is a sort of Westminster Abbey in Kukuanaland where the famous dead are enshrined not in marble but in calcium carbonate—since Haggard condoned "a little crudeness" in characterization for effect (Twala is "native beer" and Umbopa was the name of Chaka's assassin), why not also a bit of high kitsch in the visual setting?94 In his *Private Diaries,* Haggard mentions an old explorer who told the story of a ring found in an Inca burial chamber "wherein, round a stone table, sat a dead and mummified man at the head and about a dozen other persons ranged round the table....The tale made a deep impression on my youthful mind and, in fact, first turned it towards Romance. I used it in *King Solomon's Mines* when I depicted the White Dead sitting round the stone board under the presidency of the White Death."95 In life, Twala is honored as "the One-eyed, the Black, the Terrible" and is a student of Gagool's "black arts," a necromancer whose malevolent magic discloses the future by consulting the dead. He is allied to the one-eyed Norse deity Odin, god of the dead—his single eye is the sun, his lost eye the moon, according to Tylor's *Primitive Culture.*96 But in death, Twala becomes the vassal of the huge skeleton who presides, like Odin, over the banquets of slain heroes. Gagool's and Twala's cruelty has placed the land under a curse, in "trouble" and "darkness," until the king, "languishing in exile," restores fertility: "So, O king! then is a curse taken from the land."97

Umbopa's birthright, proven by his secret snake tatoo, is confirmed by the transfer of the great uncut diamond from Twala's decapitated head to his, marking a national regeneration linked to the vegetation cycle: "The winter is overpast, the summer is at hand."98 Like Jacob-Israel, who wrestled with the angel and was renamed because he had "striven with God and with men, and ... prevailed" (Genesis 32:29), Umbopa becomes Ignosi. But unlike Ignosi, the adventurers are not mythically reborn from this shadowland. To explicate the narrative's sexual innuendo further, one may observe that "Kukuanaland," parsed as low slang, becomes "cuckoo" (the cuckoo lays its eggs in other bird's nests; thus, in slang usage the cuckoo is the penis and the cuckoo's nest the female pudendum) followed by "anal" with the copula "and." This crude pun of "cuckoo-anal-and" is less indicative of schoolboy prurience than of the biological-mythic structure that the adventurers enter at the mine-pit and the political question: will the British rehatch them-

| THREE: Diamonds and Deities |

selves in Africa's nest; will they fulfill Haggard's aborted Anglo-African ideal for the Transvaal of 1877? In the romance, their entry into the chamber of the mine-pit may be a sexual penetration, Boccaccio's gates of hell or the devouring female pudenda; but the trio's exit is certainly of the earth, earthy. Haggard's phallic and anal amalgamation, together with his multiple references to the "bowels" of the earth,[99] clearly indicate that whatever sort of symbolic engendering their entrance into the cave may be, the trio is sexually devoured and shat out like lumps of excrement. This is an ironic rebirth at best, a parody of renewal.

Haggard's essay on the Zulu war-dance had described the warrior who served as a model for Sir Henry as a lordly general. But the warrior in Haggard's essay was emasculated and did not know it. In Zululand, the imperialist had annihilated the native's game and rendered his primitive weapons obsolete. But in Kukuanaland Sir Henry's hand-to-hand combat implicitly restores the potency of the chieftain's weapons at the climatic moment and so suggests a different native-foreign power balance in Kukuanaland from that of the Boers and English in the land of the Basutos and Zulus. Unlike the Transvaal, governed by ambitious Europeans, and unlike Zululand, partitioned among British puppets, Kukuanaland will be ruled by an ancient-modern African chieftain who holds his ground not on "sufferance," war-dancing for entertainment, but as the "rightful lord" of a region closed to the enterprise of European settlers. Here the native ways of life and African herds of game survive untouched by capitalist development. Clearly, Haggard's blueprint for a restored Kukuanaland repudiated the Victorian imperial stereotype of subjugated tribes, especially notions of wealth created by trade. Umbopa-Ignosi is the new Solomon, an African ruler whose principles of kingship are British—up to a point, they double Sir Theophilus Shepstone's Zulu reforms[100]—but whose religion is mythic, and whose foreign policy is isolationist: Ignosi decrees a Kukuanaland uncontaminated by the socioeconomic structures of the West; "traders" and "praying-men" who "make a path for the white men who follow to run on" will be repulsed, and total demolition of the quarry will greet those who "come for the shining stones."[101]

Haggard wants to meld the best of Anglo culture, its justice and mercy, with the best in Zulu culture, its spirituality and courage. But this cross-cultural influence takes place at the level of abstract utopian synthesis, not in the arena of real men and women represented by contact with the missionaries and traders. Unfortunately, such abstractions of cultural intermixing are frustrated or "backlashed" by the practicalities of life as lived. Plaatje opens *Mhudi*, his tale of the injurious Barolong-Boer alliance, with a parable from life in pre-Matabele Zimbabwe: "Barolong cattlemen at times attempted to create a new species of animal by cross-breeding between an eland and an ox. One cattle-owner, named Motonosi, not very far from Kunana, raised two dozen calves all sired by a buffalo. The result proved so disastrous that Barolong tradition still holds up his achievement as a masterpiece of folly, and attempts at cross-breeding thereafter became taboo."[102] That cultures cannot intermingle with impunity is true, but perhaps not the whole truth. Unlike the intermixed Solomon with Sheba, the trio achieves no mystical interplay of sun and moon, and thus no cure attends their ordeal and escape. When Ignosi invites the trio to remain and marry native wives, repeating Twala's offer, they choose the recovered diamonds; so Ignosi curses the stones that have bereaved him. And he announces that the trio "'will be as dead to me ... your names, Incubu, Macumazahn, and Bougwan [their Zulu agnomens] shall be as the names of dead kings, and he who speaks them shall die.'"[103] Haggard footnotes this Zulu custom of tabooing names of the dead, later explicitly documented by Frazer,[104] not just for reasons of anthropological curiosity but to emphasize that the trio has entered a ghostly existence, like the calcified kings who guard Solomon's treasure. Tylor had noted that the natives, impressed with the white man's "'pallid deathly hue combined with powers that seem those of superhuman spiritual beings, have determined that the manes of their dead must have come back in this wondrous shape.'"[105]

Very much like Haggard's untouched African landscape—fascinating, willing to be taken over—Foulata is the helpless virginal maiden who awaits heroic rescue by the chivalric male. Dying, Foulata had asked Quatermain to tell Good that "'I love him, and that I am glad to die because I know that he cannot cumber his life with such as me, for the sun cannot mate with the darkness, nor the white with the black.'" She then imagines a reunion in the afterlife "in the stars," an impossibility because the cosmic interplay between black and white, moon and sun remains arrested: "'I will search them all, though perchance I should there still be black and he would—still be white.'"[106] On the mythic level, Haggard implies that Foulata is forever separated from her revitalizing consort because, owing to the trio's return to England with the diamonds, Good will not pursue her from the underworld to the stars. Quatermain priggishly considers her death "a fortunate occurrence" that avoids the complications of racial miscegenation;

and Foulata's corpse is borne into the treasure chamber of the underworld, thenceforth always to be associated with its attendant diamonds like the pomegranate seeds that seal Persephone's presence in Hades. Years later, Haggard singled out this scene in the infernal halls of the kingdom of the dead to condemn the choice of wealth by trade rather than an adoption of the land's mystic plenitude.

Although the adventurers claim to be gods, all have been injured in the leg—before, during, and after their quest: Allan Quatermain has been mauled by a lion and his leg continues to pain him; Good's leg has been badly wounded by a native tolla; and Sir Henry is accidentally shot in the leg by Quatermain's son while hunting. Even the leg of the lost George Curtis has been crushed by a boulder. The dandaical Good with monocle, false teeth, gutta-percha collars and all, quickly is established, by virtue of his "beautiful white legs," as the most unlikely of sex objects, contributing his quota of humor to the plot. Indeed, an episode similar to Good's seems to have occurred to the naked-legged Selous among the natives on the lower Chobe river:

> On my walking amongst them, clad solely in a coloured cotton shirt and an old felt hat, there was a wild stampede amongst the women, who, catching up their dusky offspring, rushed away, shrieking with fear, from the fair-skinned, bearded apparition.... Curiosity before long conquered all other feelings in the minds of the fair sex, and I was soon surrounded by the entire female and juvenile population of the encampment, who kept staring at me in the most embarrassing manner, laughing and pointing at me all the time.[107]

The nearly idolatrous farewell to Good's legs by "a pretty young girl, with some beautiful lilies in her hand"—Foulata rejuvenated for the Kukuanas but not for the English—suggests a phallic significance, as in nineteenth-century slang of "leg-business," "leg-lifting" meaning sexual intercourse: "'Let my lord show his servant his beautiful white legs, that his servant may look on them, and remember them all her days, and tell of them to her children; his servant has travelled four days' journey to see them, for the fame of them has gone throughout the land.'"[108] The lame white gods become the nineteenth-century version of Frazer's sexually impotent deities. But the wounded leg that leaves its stigmata of mortality upon Sir Henry and his companions, and even upon Ignosi's name-changing prototype Jacob, does not emasculate the Kukuana or their new king. Ignosi is the regenerative consort of Kukuanaland-as-Sheba. In Solomon's legend in the Koran and medieval art, Sheba is lame in one foot or suffers from hairy legs or ass's hooves and undergoes a conversion and cure by Solomon. In the final analysis, Sheba is one of those ambiguous females who attempts, like Gagool, to subvert masculine power; she is Solomon's dark double, at first challenging and impeding the king's claim to power and freedom, but finally rejoicing in his revitalization of the sacred cosmic (and patriarchal) order. In a strange and surreal way, the goddess-queen-sorceress, appearing to do evil, ends by doing good.

Though a "Lady" is the suspected cause of the quarrel over the inheritance between Sir Henry and his brother George, and thus at the root of the adventure, by narrative's end the brothers are reunited while the contested "Lady" is, like Foulata or Sheba-as-Africa, abandoned—or, rather, replaced by the diamonds. Although Quatermain will arrive just at Christmas to publish his novel, how vital is a drizzly London Christmas in comparison to the *dies natalis solis invicti* or the seasonal rituals of Kukuanaland? Good himself becomes the laughing-stock of society papers, a most unheroic apotheosis, and cannot find among the petticoats a mate as attractive as Foulata. George, after his rescue and reconciliation, discards his alias Neville to resume his rightful identify, a feeble echo of Ignosi retaking his kingly name. And how meaningful is the wounding and healing of Sir Henry precipitated by Quatermain's son, the future doctor, compared to the wounds of native battle and Foulata's mythic ministrations? The quest that began over a "Lady" and a contested inheritance, paralleled in Twala's and Umbopa's disputed kingdom, ends with riches in London but, in contrast to the national restoration of Kukuanaland, with no recovery by modern man of his original birthright in nature. The trio's diamonds embody what the Marxists call "commodity fetishism," in which, separated from their base in human labor, they are endowed with an economic power, yet, in contrast to nature, diminished to the status of a mere salable, monetary commodity. "'The world is a great mart, my Holly, where all things are for sale to him who bids the highest in the currency of our desires,'"[109] says Ayesha in *She*, portraying, much to Holly's moral consternation, a proto-capitalistic consumerism in Kor.

For some in England, mass consumerism had emasculated culture, since lavishing money to acquire genteel objects frequently imbued with exotic or useless qualities was seen as morally debilitating to the fabric of English domestic life. This loss of the heroic in England, including the truth of human destiny, and its replacement with the material comforts of a spiritually arid society became, of course, Haggard's target in "About Fiction." Perhaps Haggard's trio of social misfits has not escaped from Valhalla but has arrived in London at Hela's moldering realm of the unheroic, spiritually dead. In *Allan Quatermain*, the continuation of this saga, the burial of Quatermain's son opens the narrative; seeking heroic closure, Quatermain there decides to return to Africa to "die as I had lived, among the wild game and the savages."[110]

❧ FOUR

Zululand: Native Auto/Biography

Haggard's saga of the rise and fall of the Zulu empire begins with *Nada the Lily* (1892), set in the 1820s and dealing with Shaka, the founder of the Zulu nation. Originally serialized by the *London Illustrated News*, January through May 1892, it was first published at the end of April 1892 by Longmans in New York and then, nine days later in May, by the same publisher in London. The figure of Allan Quatermain links *Nada* with several later Zulu romances, most notably a historically ordered Zulu trilogy that Haggard described both as "the autobiography of Allan Quatermain" and as "the epic of the vengeance of Zikali ... and of the fall of the House of Senzangakona."[1] Those narratives are: first, *Marie* (1912) set in the 1830s and concluding with Dingaan's massacre of the Boers; next, *Child of Storm* (1913) set in the 1850s and culminating in the battle of Tugela; and finally, *Finished* (1917) set in the 1870s and climaxing with the pyrrhic victory of the Zulus at Isandhlwana. The plotting and sweep of this action, with an abundance of magical wizardry, ends with the necromancer Zikali terrifying the dying king Cetywayo with apocalyptic visions of the dead. Haggard noted that this trilogy "tells the secret story of the causes of the defeat of Cetywayo and his armies by the English in 1879, which happened not long before Quatermain met Sir Henry Curtis and Captain Good" in *King Solomon's Mines*.[2] However, the linkage between these romances, other than that of historical chronology and Quatermain, is nominal; and the Zulus, of course, appear in numerous other of Haggard's novels as well—*The Witch's Head* (1884), *Swallow* (1899), and *The Ghost Kings* (1908), also in several short stories.

FOUR: Zululand

Articulating the significance of African life before missionary conversions, imperial trade, technology, and annexation had effaced mystery and heroic romance, Haggard's *Nada the Lily* enthralled Victorians with striking episodes from the precolonial empire of Zululand. Currently emerging as a controversial text of imperialism—recently, even more problematic than *King Solomon's Mines* (1885) or *She* (1887)—Haggard's saga recounted the bloody reign, assassination, and aftermath of Shaka KaSenzangakona (otherwise in colonial orthography: Chaka, Tyaka, T'shaka, 1780s–1828), the greatest African ruler of the nineteenth century. Here also Haggard devised a fictional "prequel" for his near-mythical warrior from *Allan Quatermain* (1888), Umslopogaas, son of Shaka, who in this narrative is entangled in a doomed love for Nada, a visionary figure of quasi-mystical purity and the "lily" of the Zulus. Fred Fynney, Haggard's campfire buddy from his Natal period, had noted in *Zululand and the Zulus* (1880), two lectures published a dozen years prior to *Nada*, that in the popular press in the wake of the Zulu War (1879) "the word 'Zulu' has become almost a household word" but "though we have heard so much of the Zulus, as a matter of fact, little is actually known of their history."[3] Although Bertram Mitford's notable *Gun-Runner* (1882) was set in the turmoil of the Zulu War, Haggard's *Nada the Lily* was the first popular account of the early Zulu kingdom—that is, before the British partitioning of Zululand in the wake of the Zulu War—and the novel had an immense impact on British perceptions of the native peoples.

If the conduct or culture of one civilization cannot be impartially judged by the standards or intellectual criteria of another, then history must be shaped to confirm the practices and hopes of whoever tells or writes it. Such histories validate or condemn customs and beliefs by means of documentarily constructed mythologies. Nineteenth-century British chroniclers assumed an evolutionary scale that placed English culture at the pinnacle; Zulu culture was considered both more static and more primitive, the living relic of a European past. Thus the "civilizing" mission that Conrad mocked in the opening pages of *Heart of Darkness* (1899) was certainly an outgrowth of this sort of anthropological thinking. Shaka, the bloody monster and his out-of-control Zulu *impis* (war battalions), were necessarily wiped out for the common good of Africa and England. But there is another Shakan history as well. In the twentieth century the Zulus have interpreted their own past. Donald Burness in *Shaka: King of the Zulus* confirms that Shaka became "a mythic figure" in far-flung areas of African society, "a symbol of protest against exploitation and acculturation." Moreover, Mazisi Kunene in "South African Oral Traditions" maintains that the lyrical poetry of Zulu oral literature prior to Shaka lacked strength and vigor but during the Shakan period its dominant theme became the expression and interpretation of a transformed and unified national and, ultimately to some degree, continental consciousness.[4] In the hearing of this present writer, Shaka has been called the "Abraham Lincoln of the Zulus." According to this Zulu academic, only a semantic difference exists between Lincoln's "preserving" national unity and Shaka's "creating" a union, since to preserve with force what had originally been a voluntary affiliation is to establish through coercion an involuntary union. Both leaders, according to this apologist, "waded through the blood of their soldiers" to realize the higher ideal of national unity. Perhaps these lines from *King Solomon's Mines* were on his mind:

> "The ways of black people are not as the ways of white men, Incubu, nor do we hold life so high as ye." ... I remarked that Ignosi had swum to the throne through blood. The old chief shrugged his shoulders. "Yes," he answered; "but the Kukuana people can only be kept cool by letting the blood flow sometimes. Many were killed indeed, but the women were left, and others would soon grow up to take the places of the fallen. After this the land would be quiet for awhile."[5]

In dramatizing Shaka and the rise and fall of the Zulu empire, Haggard followed the historical interpretation of the forgotten Fred Fynney, who according to his title page was "Inspector of Native Schools, Natal (Late Border Agent)." Although Haggard's vision of Shaka's cruelty and despotism probably derives generically from Nathaniel Isaac's *Travels and Adventures in Eastern Africa* (1836), Haggard specifically relied upon Fynney, who had noted that Shaka's "good qualities" balanced his "dark side." Fynney in *Zululand* notes Shaka's "loyalty" to mentors, his openness to "white" European culture, "to civilizing influences, for he had a great mind."[6] Fynney stressed that "whilst dreaded, he was said to have a liberal hand, and to be a benefactor to those with small kraals.... He never allowed a brave man to go unrewarded or a coward to go unpunished, and the surest way to find favour with Tyaka was to be a dauntless warrior."[7] Of Shaka, Haggard footnotes both genius and wickedness: "The Zulu Napoleon, one of the greatest geniuses and most wicked men who ever lived. He was killed in the year 1828, having slaughtered more than a million human beings."[8] Haggard does not so much mitigate Isaac's image of a despotic monster as present Shaka in a considerably more complex political and anthropological context, though certainly not with Kunene's veneration. Haggard's best biographer, Morton Cohen, interestingly asserts that Haggard's Zulu fiction early on played an important role in presenting to the Zulus their own national history,[9] although more recently Doris Sommer's *Foundational Fictions: The National Romances of Latin America* (1991) has brought the underlying premises of such an assumption into question.

In the writing of *Nada*, Haggard also drew extensively on Fynney's pamphlet for events and scenes that characterized Shaka; particularly, the material in Fynney's first lecture, "The Rise and Fall of the Zulu Nation," became the dramatic content of Haggard's novel, though this was undoubtedly supplemented with an account by his mentor, Theophilus Shepstone, "Early History of the Zulu-Kafir Race,"[10] in John Bird's *Annals of Natal* (1888). Laura Chrisman asserts that "Haggard's portrayal of Shaka is strikingly unlike that of F. B. Fynney."[11] It is difficult to follow her distinction of Haggard's Shaka as "metaphysical" and "outside of history" whereas the Shaka of Fynney's account is "political" and productive of history. Given the need to dramatize expository materials through Mopo's interpretative eye, *Nada* remains, *mutatis mutandis*, a fictional recasting but essentially a reproduction of Fynney's data. Also in his preface to *Nada*, Haggard cites the works of Bishop Henry Callaway and David Leslie as principal sources. From Callaway's *The Religious System of the Amazulu* (1870) Haggard took material on native weapons, on Mopo's powers as a "diviner," and on Zulu religion, particularly Zulu cosmogonic myths and the *deus ex machina* figure of Umkulunkulu, Queen of Heaven.[12] From Leslie's *Among the Zulus and Amatongas* (1875), he took the concept of Nada herself ("a Zulu Venus"), material on native "doctors," and borrowed from two Zulu narratives, one literally true ("the artifice by which Umslopogaas obtained admission to the Swazi stronghold") and one fictional ("the fate of the two lovers at the mouth of the cave") which he combined to create the love-story subplot.[13] Umslopogaas himself was modeled on a Swazi camp assistant of Shepstone who had told Haggard stories of his people.[14] For Shaka's successor, Dingaan, Haggard repeats a sinister anecdote: "Of the incident of the Missionary and the furnace of logs, it is impossible to speak so certainly. It came to the writer from the lips of an old traveller in 'the Zulu'; but he cannot discover any confirmation of it. Still, these kings undoubtedly put their soldiers to many tests of equal severity."[15] Since it epitomizes the Zulu ethos and comes directly "from the lips of an old traveller in 'the Zulu,'"[16] it stays true to the narrative's own standards of historical interpretation.

Probably the proximate origin of *Nada* lay in the remark of Haggard's friend and collaborator on *The Word's Desire* (1890), the anthropologist Andrew Lang, two years before its serial publication: "How delicious a novel *all* Zulu, without a white face in it, would be!"[17] Not long after Lang's comment on an "all Zulu" story, Haggard in *Allan's Wife and Other Tales* (1889) described "a record of events wherein Mr. Quatermain was not personally concerned—a Zulu novel, the story of which was told to him by the hero many years after the tragedy had occurred."[18] Accordingly, Haggard produced a fictional biography of Shaka by a Zulu narrator with no white face except Haggard's outer-frame chronicler, the unnamed Allan Quatermain from *King Solomon's Mines*, who observes that he himself "plays no part in this story."[19] Haggard's "double-I" narrative device possibly looks forward to Conrad's *Heart of Darkness*. But of course the white trader who publishes Shaka's history hears it not from a Charlie Marlow-type adventurer but from a native witchdoctor, a prosopographic (because historical data are so scant) Mopo living under the alias of Zweete near Shaka's grave. Mopo is a contraction of Umbopo, the historical assassin of Shaka, not to be confused with Umbopa of *King Solomon's Mines,* although in *The Ghost Kings* Rachel asks Mopo: "'By what name shall I name you, O Slayer of a king? Will you be called Mopo or Umbopa, who have borne them both?'"[20] This suggests that the *King Solomon's Mines* figure was originally envisioned by Haggard as a princely alternative to the Zulu tyrants much as Umslopogaas was: the lost ideal, like Cetywayo's brother Umbelazi defeated at the Tugela. Though Umslopogaas had been at the Tugela with "Macumazahn" in 1856,[21] Mopo is blind and has never met Quatermain, who has operated as a trader in the 1870s.[22]

Haggard describes *Nada* as a "romance" or a "tale,"[23] implying poetic feelings and strange or legendary happenings, what the early missionaries and British functionaries called "dark superstitions,"[24] not the realistic novel's unremitting emphasis upon things as they "really" are—as, for example, in Victorian drawing rooms or as reported in the *Annals of Natal*. According to numerous critics of the previous generation, this novel "is generally considered to be Haggard's finest work, a sustained, tragic story. While Nada is a sop to the romantic market, the remainder of the book is powerful, imaginative, filled with cultural detail."[25] Actually, the figure of Nada is much more than a "sop to the romantic market," as my late friend Ian Fletcher notes: "rather like the Angelica of Ariosto's *Orlando Furioso* she becomes the emblem of man's need to project unity and meaning into his world."26 Roger Green, a scholar and critic who was a close friend of later fantasists C. S. Lewis and J. R. R. Tolkien, described *Nada* as "a masterpiece in which is no serious flaw": "There is a superb and epic grandeur in the unrelieved gloom and the relentless feeling of fate that characterize the whole book. Haggard understood the Zulus as probably few white men have ever done, and not one of his characters seems ever to be out of place, or lacking in harmony with the whole conception."27 Perhaps readers from Lang to Green did not consider it necessary to note that a Zulu biography of Shaka, within a fictionalized autobiography of the historically shadowy Umbopo, could be criticized for lacking cultural authority if its author is a white colonial and not of Africa and African. Who but a civilized white man, these earlier critics seem to assume, could write those Zulu life stories? Indeed, the colonial origin of Haggard's narrative is currently seen as such a "serious flaw" that its integrity, other than as colonial exculpation for the destruction of Zulu nationality, is in need of substantial rehabilitation.

How could a white colonial writer choose to place himself in the mind of the most iconic of African heroes and expect to go unchallenged? Contemporary Zulus feel that when their history is not in their own hands, transmission of a distorted view to posterity is likely. Thus social expectations about who should be the authority in a given subject-domain often constrain and nullify freedom of investigation. *Nada*, and Haggard's other novels, are appraised as distorting mirrors inasmuch as they reflect a political history divergent from the ideologies of current militants, theorists, and critics. The argument is that Haggard's is not the voice of the Zulu but the voice of the white imperialist, an apologist for colonialism, and that by portraying a maniacal Shaka Haggard stole a people's collective response to national consciousness-building. Rather than pointing to Shaka's character flaws, Haggard should have considered those of the subsequent imperialists. Moreover, though it is human to have rage at enemies, Haggard reduces the revolt against Boer imperialism of Dingaan, Shaka's successor, to superstition and erotomania.28 In *Nada* and *Marie*, for example, Dingaan lusts for sex with the eponymous women—one light-skinned, the other white.29 Haggard thus problematizes these Zulu chieftains, adding layers of fallacious psycho-history to their motives. Indeed, the nearly articulated premise is that only a black writer could and should undertake Haggard's topic; only someone culturally tribal can "know" the native mind.

Though filled with interesting and fruitful aperçus, recent criticism of *Nada*, centered on Haggard's interpretation of Shaka and on the deconstruction of his imperialist ideology, too often seems to jump from premise to conclusion with overly determined readings derived from programmatically selective citations. A native biographer of Shaka like Kunene or of Mzilikazi like Plaatje is extraordinarily positioned "to interpret to the reading public one phase of 'the back of the Native mind.'"[30] But English as written by black authors is almost entirely a twentieth-century phenomenon since class considerations, even more than race or color, excluded nineteenth-century Africans from white schools. In that era a few native authors produced *translations* from English into their indigenous languages, such as Tiyo Soga's of Bunyan's *Pilgrim's Progress*, or sporadic *original productions*—most notably Thomas Mofolo's *Chaka*, actually written in Sesotho in the first decades of the twentieth century but influenced stylistically by missionary standards of English. At the risk of appearing caustic, one may say the take on Haggard in recent years by Armstrong, Chrisman, Hamilton, Katz, Kunene, Low, McClintock, Wylie, and others seems to be that since he was not a Zulu he could not write their history honestly; that *Nada* contains "glaring contradictions and incoherence"; that he should have used indigenous "Zulu oral sources"; that he should have kept closer to the "empirical facts"; that he should have known (or at least it is to be deplored that he did not know) "what we know currently"; that he should not have been in Africa to begin with, given "the injuriousness or immorality of colonization"; that *Nada* is a product of "historiographical misprison"; that he never confronted his colonial "guilt" or his sense of "superiority"; that his interpretive sources were unreliably "derivative"; that he did not approach "racial and economic issues" from a materialist perspective; that he was an Anglo-Christian naively "transcoding Zulu belief systems in the language of the colonial power"; that he deployed Mopo and Nada merely as "neo-colonial proxies"; and that he "cannibalized" Zulu qualities for British "dreams of empowered masculinity."[31]

To compress somewhat this recent debunking of Haggard's novel, one may say that *Nada* is found to mix hearsay facts with fantasy so as to portray Shaka as evil incarnate and that the persuasiveness of this demonizing is not its empirical truth but its covert white colonial construction of Zulu culture. Thus the twentieth-century nationalist Zulu poet of Shakan oral history, Mazisi Kunene, would describe any reliance of Haggard's sort upon documentary materials as "the thick forest of propaganda and misrepresentation that have been submitted by colonial reports and historians."[32] And Dan Wylie asserts that the Shakan tales of Fynney, so often repeated in other early accounts, lack not only empirical evidence but, even, portray Shaka's behavior as outside his own Zulu customs or belief systems—as defined, of course, by twenty-first-century anthropological analyses.[33] Citing a climactic scene of atrocity in *Nada*,[34] even the error-prone E. A. Ritter, whose own initial manuscript was itself judged too predisposed to stress Shaka's "tortures and other horrors" writes: "Shaka was never a fool, whatever else he may have been, and for popular-fiction writers to assert that he marched the whole E-Langeni tribe—man, woman and child—over a precipice to their destruction—a tribe, be it noted, who as a whole acclaimed him as their hero—is not only nonsense, but cheap sensationalism."[35] Haggard here is combining two incidents from Fynney: the unnamed tribe whose bodies were butchered to fill the donga and, in the next paragraph, Shaka's revenge on Makedama, chief of the E-Langeni.[36] Undoubtedly one man's "cheap sensationalism" may be another man's shocking but illustrative atrocity. Perhaps the images of human sacrifice in *Heart of Darkness* are less sensational, but what about descriptions of the near-extermination of the Barolong by Mzilikazi's Zulu in Sol Plaatje's *Mhudi*?[37]

As fiction, *Nada*'s sacrifice of detail and factual accuracy is less important than its interpretation of events and historical processes, a principle that recent biographers who value the "imaginative sense of fact" often defend.[38] To judge the interpretive authority of *Nada* in terms of its divergence from the objective truth of Shakan history, and this is what recent discussions of *Nada* center around, is impossible given the insurmountable disagreements between and within indigenous and colonial accounts that skew interpretations. Wylie himself confesses that historians are "locked into an infinite regress of interpretative subjectivities."[39] Even setting aside the main issue of whether Shaka was a gifted but moral monster (Haggard) or a noble and consummate leader (Kunene), significant aspects of the historical record of the Zulu empire before and after Shaka will always remain problematic. Was, for example, the rise of the Zulu empire inspired by external European example or initiated by internal factors? How extensively did black informants—avowed enemies of Shaka or collaborating subjects?—cross-fertilize the atrocity stories disseminated by the white observers? Were the British missionaries, hunters, and administrators entirely exploitative and opportunistic or, as Conrad so ironically described the politics of Marlow's aunt, might not at least an exceptional imperialist have been "something like an emissary of light, something like a lower sort of apostle"?[40] Few today could entertain this last alternative without its irony, yet in Haggard's time the example of David Livingstone seemed almost to justify the simile.

Since every biographer and historian transforms the fragmental facts of the past through the filters of his own affiliations, interpretive artifices, and rhetoric, Haggard's paraphrase of historical events unarguably must have mirrored a nineteenth-century intellectual's comprehension of an African way of life and culture, even by then already vanished. But does this mean—it seems almost too brazen to ask—that in 1892 an educated and literary ex-colonial would have been fated to misconstrue "primitive" experience? If so, how does this impact upon or vitiate his aesthetic achievement? Might a negative judgment also mean that Frazer's *Golden Bough* in 1890 was thus equally unreliable? Not many years after *Nada*, Lang had suggested that Haggard should "read the opening chapter of Frazer's *Golden Bough*."[41] Was that chapter then or is it now intellectually bankrupt? But if we impute to both Haggard and Frazer a priori bad faith, how do we exempt Shakespeare when he presents Calaban as a savage man, vicious and vengeful, conniving yet naive? Was the Bard a bigot and is *The Tempest* fatally flawed on some deep moral level?

Haggard's *Nada* did not dishonestly distort Shakan history nor was it meant to exonerate the white colonialism that followed, in which Haggard himself played a part. Setting the narrative frame of his novel on the brink of the Zulu War, Haggard seems to ask if the soul's journey to spiritual wealth can be through imperial expansion and its allied material productive forces. Or, rather, will pale, homesick Victorians, "wandering"—in Matthew Arnold's image in "Stanzas from the Grande Chartreuse"—"between two worlds, one dead, / The other powerless to be born" bring their lives into contact with the dark and passionate myths of Africa's body, engendering thereby new symbols for their lost primordial identity?

Haggard's novel is an elegy for the loss of that possibility. Just as at the conclusion of *King Solomon's Mines* the trio of adventurers fails to achieve a rebirth into a more-vital mythopoeic primal unity with the land, so the collapse of Shaka's Zulu empire signals the loss of any mystical Anglo-African selfhood as a nobler alternative to the mercantile colonial model. In *King Solomon's Mines* the incursions of trade and missionary conversions were not permitted to destroy the fertility, beauty, and mystical power of the land. More pessimistically, Haggard's *Nada* signals the coming into being of that other "heart of darkness" known so well to those who experienced Africa after the Zulu War—namely, the failure of the Gladstone government to live up to its obligations in Africa, the retrocession of the Transvaal, and the despotism of a commerce blind to the spiritual power of the Zulus' Queen of Heaven. Here the parallel that Plaatje draws may be instructive for Haggard's position: as the native chief Mzilikazi's imperial dreams crumbled with the advent of the Europeans, so the power of these new imperialists in time may falter also. Haggard's Zulu narrator serves as a way of talking about not only the lost national identity of the Zulus but also about what the British have lost. *Nada*'s importance in the twenty-first century is not its empirical truth to Zulu history; neither is it primarily to be seen as an imperialist's *apologia pro vita sua*; rather, it must be read first for its implicit self-critique of British culture, then for what has been recognized as the "disquieting vitality" of its "mythopoeic" vision,[42] the tangible attainment of which in secular life was obliterated in the aftermath of the Zulu War.

Though unavoidably embedded in the political framework of colonialism, the major organizing aesthetic of *Nada* is indebted in innovative and influential ways to emerging anthropological theories of "the primitive." In the introduction to *Allan Quatermain* cited in chapter two, Quatermain completes his excursus on kinship with this thesis:

> supposing for the sake of argument we divide ourselves into twenty parts, nineteen savage and one civilised, we must look to the nineteen savage portions of our nature, if we would really understand ourselves, and not to the twentieth, which, though so insignificant in reality, is spread all over the other nineteen, making them appear quite different from what they really are, as the blacking does a boot, or the veneer a table. It is on the nineteen rough serviceable savage portions that we fall back in emergencies, not on the polished but unsubstantial twentieth. Civilisation should wipe away our tears, and yet we weep and cannot be comforted. Warfare is abhorrent to her, and yet we strike out for hearth and home, for honour and fair fame, and can glory in the blow.[43]

The most influential writer on ritual and myth in the nineteenth century was E. B. Tylor, whose *Primitive Culture* (1871) became for its day the standard in cultural anthropology. Tylor, for example, had described the Zulu deity Umkulunkulu introduced in *Nada*. Haggard's novel can be appreciated as part of the intellectual context to which

Tylor's investigations belonged and to which, later, those of the just-published *Golden Bough* of Frazer also contributed. Thus Haggard fictionally portrayed a return to Tylor's savage "survivals" as able to reanimate contemporary society: "The fact that we, in these latter days, have as it were macadamized all the roads of life does not make the world softer to the feet of those who travel through it"—adding years later that there probably are "many roads to the gate of Life; but ... it can scarcely be reached by the faint and wandering path of a materialised and eviscerated Christianity."[44] Haggard might have been thinking (perhaps unfairly) of Alfred Tennyson's "lame hands of faith" in *In Memoriam*. There, too, Tennyson had urged his readers to "Move upward, working out the beast, / And let the ape and tiger die" (Canto 55; see also 118). Haggard not only believed the shedding of blood is in man's savage roots, but he embraced this animalistic wildness.

Not unlike many another work, *Nada* becomes a parable of a world in which good and evil struggle, in which justice and mercy are provisionally asserted by an enlightened Christianity, but in which ultimately European greed, Wordsworth's "getting and spending," lays nature and spirit to waste. Mopo notes how a new and better city, Stanger, rose from the ashes of Shaka's Dukuza:

> Where the gate of the kraal was built there is a house; it is the place where the white man gives out justice; that is the place of the gate of the kraal, through which Justice never walked. Behind is another house, where the white men who have sinned against Him pray to the King of Heaven for forgiveness; there on that spot have I seen many a one who had done no wrong pray to a king of men for mercy, but I have never seen but one who found it.[45]

Haggard turns this Zulu-British correlation from Fynney into symbolic significance. As at the end of *King Solomon's Mines*, so at Dukuza too the British bring justice and mercy; and the place of loss and evil becomes the place of life and salvation. But to allege that this amelioration of Shakan rule reveals a smug British pride adds to the question of Haggard's imperialism an overpacked, underdelimited category of deadly sin. Justice here means "the rule of law," a phrase that A. V. Dicey had coined about this time to describe an ideal of political sovereignty based on the consent of the governed (Haggard knew full well that an effective domestic government could not be imposed by an external authority); and "mercy" is neither more nor less than the first of the "virtues of delight" that Blake had defined in "The Divine Image":

> And all must love the human form,
> In heathen, turk or jew.
> Where Mercy, Love & Pity dwell
> There God is dwelling too.[46]

Are these terms so debased in *Nada* as to be read as racial or nationalistic superiority?

What is at stake here is Haggard's moral-theological vision of the necessary interrelation of evil and good, an epistemological principle of substantial relevance to his politics. In Haggard's nearly allegorical novel, *The Wizard* (1896), there is a hill "and on that mount stands a tree; it is called the Tree of Death, and it stretches a thousand hands to Heaven, praying for mercy that does not come, and from its boughs there hangs fruit, a fruit of dead men—yes, twenty of them hang there this day."[47] This Tree of Death becomes the Tree of Life, the Cross of Calvary, when the wizard is crucified upon it. So too even Zikali echoes this pattern of the diabolic within the holy when Allan reproaches him as evil for creating war:

> "Oho! Macumazahn, you think that, do you, who cannot understand that what seems to be evil is often good. I wished to bring about war and brought it about, and maybe what bred the wish was all that I have suffered in the past. But say you, who have seen what the Zulu Power means, who have seen men, women and children killed by the thousand to feed that Power, and who have seen, too, what the English Power means, is it evil that I should wish to destroy the House of the Zulu kings that the English House may take its place and that in a time to come the Black people may be free?"[48]

Thus in *Marie* Allan puzzles:

> I recollect ... wondering how the Almighty could have permitted such a deed as I had seen done. How could it be reconciled with any theory of a loving and merciful Father?... In the end, however, reflection and education, of which I had a certain amount, thanks to my father, came to my aid. I recalled that such massacres, often on an infinitely larger scale, had happened a thousand times in history, and that still through them, often, indeed, by means of them, civilisation has marched forward, and mercy and peace have kissed each other over the bloody graves of the victims.[49]

This is more than the discredited rationalization that the end justifies the means, despite Haggard's phrase "by means." Evil is part of a wider good, as a discord may form part of a larger musical harmony.

Finally, in *The World's Desire* the son of Circe kills his father, Odysseus. He lies dying at the feet of Meriamun and Helen, the rivals to his love. In an echo of Ayesha in *She* (v.i. chapter seven), they vow to meet him again where they soon shall be reincarnated. Then Odysseus responds:

> "there or otherwhere shall we meet again, and there and otherwhere love and hate shall lose and win, and die to arise again. But not yet is the struggle ended that began in other worlds than this, and shall endure till evil is lost in good, and darkness swallowed up in light. Bethink thee, Meriamun, of that vision of thy bridal night, and read its riddle. Lo I will answer it with my last breath as the Gods have given me wisdom. When we three are once more twain, then shall our sin be purged and peace be won, and the veil be drawn from the face of Truth."[50]

That is, when the rivals coalesce and together become the consort to an Apollonian god of Truth, then the ceaselessly interacting antinomies of time are at rest in eternity. As the wicked Meriamun says of the flawless Helen: "'Perchance she and I are *one* Odysseus.'"[51] Yet precisely because the presence of the manifold within time (the finite and imperfect) constitutes the related whole of eternity, evil is a foundational element within a comprehensive "pattern" that neither is rendered evil nor is, even partially, contaminated by it.

One can never respond to every imputation of Haggard's colonial misprison; but Gail Low's allegation of flawed anthropology in Haggard's endeavor in *Nada* to "think with the mind and speak with the voice of a Zulu of the old *régime*"[52] epitomizes both the method and thrust of recent objections:

> Where the continuity between the white mythology and black history is achieved, Haggard's task of narrating Zulu history becomes not merely an anthropological task of cultural translation and interpretation but of transparency and appropriation: "the author's aim, moreover, has been to convey in narrative form, some idea of the remarkable spirit which animated these kings and their subjects, and to make accessible, in popular shape, incidents of African history" [*Nada*, Preface]. As Eric Cheyfitz writes of Fenimore Cooper's *Pioneers*, the "activity of colonization as translation" is "precisely not to understand the other that is the original inhabitants.... [but is] to understand that other all too easily, that is, as if there were no question of translation"; such an act marks the point "where the other becomes usable fiction."[53]

However, *Nada* manifestly presents native history with attentiveness to observed detail and an understanding of native customs in terms of multiple and historical tethers. It transcends popular preconceptions and generalized frameworks of post-Darwinian armchair anthropologists, such notions as a superiority based on racial evolution or, as alleged above, the presentation of Zulu culture "as if there were no question of translation." As a primitive or folk epic in prose, *Nada* is ostensibly narrated in Zulu by Mopo and translated into a high-heroic archaic English by the "white man."

Contemporary historians love to stress the self-evident: that translation is often interpretation; and that translations from the local tongue into the colonial language may reinforce hegemonic images of the colonized. At first sight Haggard's "translation" may seem an ersatz English of unremitting archaisms reminiscent of the biblical King James Version—"And, lo!" "skinned the buck and ate of it," and so on—and in places an out-of-fashion polyphonic or poetic prose like the Psalms and the Song of Solomon, much rarer now than in the nineteenth century. And yet David Leslie, cited in the preface of *Nada*, describes the Zulu style of speaking as "very sententious," "epigrammatic," and "much more copious and minute, as well as concise, than our own, in terms relating to things material."[54] When Leslie retells a "story of Kaffir life" (the episode of the Swasi caves that Haggard borrowed for Mopo's tale), he says "the incidents of romance ... lose nothing in the narrative by a native of high class.... I have endeavoured to give it in Zulu translated into English. It is a genuine native narrative; it pretends to nothing more"; and then, as he begins his tale he feels it necessary to interpolate in brackets that his use of the phrase "all ... gathered together" as a "mode of expression is not plagiarised from Scripture."[55] Indeed, that most famous of Zulu phrases that Leslie, Haggard, and so many other translators use, to "eat up" meaning to "destroy," is as native to the Pentateuch as to Zululand.

This comparative gesture by Leslie and Haggard, given the prestige of "Scripture" for unequalled euphony, is a calculated assertion of the power of the original Zulu. This is very unlike the kind of cultural imperialism that fills the supposed void of native oral cultures with Bibles to replace native superstitions, newspapers to interpret colonial behavior, and action-adventure tales to praise heroic British soldiers. Elsewhere, as in *Marie*, Haggard describes Hans's Hottentot narration as "the simple, dramatic style characteristic of his race"[56] and Quatermain's proficiency in Zulu as a "beautiful but difficult tongue";[57] similarly, Mitford in *The Gun-Runner* writes of Cetywayo's messenger:

> to the white listener there was something more than impressive in the force and graphic emphasis of the speaker, who, seated there on the floor

in the lamplight, rolled forth his well-turned phrases in his sonorous and liquid native tongue. He had heard some of the best orators that his own country could produce, but among them not one could touch the grace of gesture which came easy and natural, and as a matter of course, to this savage diplomatist.58

In *King Solomon's Mines*, Quatermain describes Ignosi's "chant" of renewal as "in a language as beautiful and sonorous as the old Greek."59 When one considers what Greek language and culture signified in the 1880s for British intellectuals, this comparison foils possibilities of Western ethnocentricity. That old Oxford classicist, Walter Pater, would have been startled by any comparison of the power of Homeric language to the alliteration, the cadences of an African praise-poem. Moreover, because both Leslie and Haggard regarded Western textuality as incomplete in comparison to African orality, they seem to anticipate more recent contemporary anthropological discussions on the polarization of oral and literate cultures.60 Leslie praised the "extraordinary descriptive powers ... and expressive action" of the native storyteller before an audience that is lost in any written "recital at second-hand."61 Haggard's persona also says his "written pages" omit "portions" of the story that have been "forgotten" or are "irrelevant" (the former the translator's failing; the latter perhaps a self-confessed white cultural failing), lose "the full force of the Zulu idiom," and give no indication of how Mopo "acted rather than told his story;... he had many voices, one for each of the actors in his tale."62

Nada appeared long before Thomas Mofolo's *Chaka* (1925), which was first published in Sesotho and then translated into English in 1931 by F. H. Dutton, before Rolfes Dhlomo's fictionalized history, *UShaka* (1937), and nearly forty years before the first English-language novel by an indigenous author, Sol Plaatje's *Mhudi* (1930), also set in this period of precolonial decline. *Mhudi* is an authentic native historical narrative; but Plaatje's mother tongue is refracted through his colonial mission-English, revealing a tension between the English vehicle and his African tenor, which he defined remarkably akin to Haggard: to interpret "'the back of the Native mind.'"63 Plaatje uses phrases such as "eligible swains," "thought nought," "pastoral duties," "uttering a dread imprecation," and so on. Certainly more than Haggard, Plaatje replaces the terminology of the imperial oppressor: "hut," for example, is alternatively rendered in places as "home" or "dwelling"; and one certainly doesn't find the pejorative noun "savage" for "man." However, the "interference" of Plaatje's African oral tradition with his "classic" English from the King James Bible and canonical works from the Elizabethans to the Victorians (especially moralistic writers such as Bunyan) produced an Africanized English that reflected the colonial circumstances of the natives, yet supported an emergent indigenous self-definition.

Not until Chinua Achebe's *Things Fall Apart* (1958) is the imperial tongue purged of overt colonial terms and traits, reflected in his opening paragraphs that brilliantly reproduce native orality within textual English. Achebe has remarked that

> For an African, writing in English is not without its serious set-backs. He often finds himself describing situations or modes of thought which have no direct equivalent in the English way of life. Caught in that situation he can do one of two things. He can try to contain what he wants to say within the limits of conventional English or he can try to push back those limits to accommodate his ideas. The first method produced competent, uninspired and rather flat works. The second method can produce something new and valuable to the English language as well as to the material he is trying to put over. But it can also get out of hand. It can lead to simply bad English being accepted and defended as African or Nigerian. I submit that those who can do the work of extending the frontiers of English so as to accommodate African thought patterns must do it through their mastery of English and not out of innocence.[64]

Eras being what they were, among those initiating an international or African English not subservient to empire is Haggard. While utilizing the language of colonial occupation to tell Mopo's story, Haggard, like Plaatje and Achebe, melds English with indigenous African words, idiomatic turns of phrase, songs, proverbs, and even changes of the meanings of words to match localized African concepts (as for example Mopo's "My father" idiom, a form of respectful address among natives or by blacks to whites, authentic for the colonial era and its class relationships) as well as supplying narrative verisimilitude in details of African manners, dress, speech and customs of the country.

One of Haggard's most adroit uses of a putative Zulu proverb occurs in his story "Magepa the Buck." When Magepa boasts "'I am swifter of foot than any man in Zululand,'" Quatermain remonstrates: "Still, remember the saying of your people, 'At last the strong swimmer goes with the stream and the swift runner is run down.'""[65] At the story's end this runner is run down and would have gone with the stream but for Quatermain's outstretched hand. The native proverb thus becomes the narrative hook for the incident's unfolding emotional and dramatic crisis. Haggard, like Quatermain, may be the "white man," but if native and colonial ideas cross-fertilized each other from the first, then his personal interactions with the Zulus and the secondary Zulu voices in Callaway's, Leslie's, and Fynney's accounts, as enumerated in his preface, allow him to construct, if not empirically to *re*construct, a past Zulu context that is narratively plausible and imaginatively faithful to past events. In this Haggard is like a modern anthropologist who, having lived in South Africa and studied Zulu society, tries to look at native culture through native eyes, applying a relativistic and "internationalized" set of interpretations and norms. Of course, he was not modern, so the less anachronistic comparison may be to the progressive Bishop of Natal, J. W. Colenso, an acquaintance of Haggard's father and of Haggard himself.66

How successful does Haggard's stance seem to be in the sweep of history? Kurtz's faith in the progressivist, modernist values of bourgeois capitalism sustained and legitimated a European hegemony. But Conrad knew that the project of modernity not only remained uncompleted but was increasingly incompletable, destined to fail as a result of an unrealistic desire to foster reproductions of itself in a non-European context. Schreiner's ideal of an international English may not be a conscious form of cultural imperialism, taking on the white man's burden by speaking for the African "other," but unless her vision of a new *lingua franca* also cherishes the smaller, more particular cultural "others" in a dialogic way, itself standing alongside the African tongues, her "assimilationist" goals of progress and freedom are illusory and will evaporate before they are achieved. The test of time suggests that any imperfect integration of an "other" into an adopted cultural language creates psychological handicaps, alienating native speakers from their origins. It has been observed by one postcolonial commentator that "in time, more and more Africans can be expected to share Sékou Touré's opinion that 'To be ourselves once again, to be in harmony with ourselves, it is essential that we express ourselves in our own languages.'"67 Exploring the tragedy of having forfeited one's mother tongue for a new language, Gustavo Firmat writes in "The Facts of Life on the Hyphen," that "one of the most disabling forms of low self-esteem arises from the conviction that one cannot speak one's native language well enough, the shattering sense of inferiority that arises, not when words fail you, but when you fail them."68 Haggard appears to have dealt with these linguistic and cultural pitfalls by the astonishing expedient of embracing an almost-incompatible dual religious-cultural vision both European-Christian and African-animistic. By this expedient his texts and politics survive.

※ ※

In his autobiography, Haggard wrote: "What we behold is but a few threads, apparently so tangled, that go to weave the Sphinx's seamless veil, or some stupendous tapestry that enwraps the whole Universe of Creation which, when seen at last, will picture forth the Truth in all its splendour, and with it the wondrous story and the meaning of our lives."[69] C. S. Lewis, an impassioned Christian apologetic, amusingly, though somewhat unfairly, labels Haggard's theology "an eclectic outfit of vaguely Christian, theosophical and spiritualistic notions, trying to say something profound about that fatal subject, 'Life'"—to which Haggard already had given a reply: "I am not a theologian."[70] The "great pattern" phrase is found in numerous of Haggard's other novels, such as *Finished*,[71] and ultimately embodies the same romantic trope of divine Life that runs from the Ancient Mariner's interweaving water-snakes, through the "web" of the Spirits and Hours in Shelley's *Prometheus Unbound*, and down to C. S. Lewis's own "Great Dance" at the conclusion of *Perelandra*. Haggard's most extended passage on cosmic patterning is in *The Ghost Kings*:

> a new song began, the song of the rushing worlds. Far away she could hear it, that ineffable music, far in the utter depths of space. Nearer it would come and nearer, a ringing, glorious sound, a sound and yet a voice, one mighty voice that sang and was answered by other voices as sun crossed the path of sun, and caught up and re-echoed by the innumerable choir of the constellations....[72]

The shattering of bodies and souls in the ceaselessly interacting antinomies of good and evil, light and dark, becomes in Mopo's eerie vision of the Queen of Heaven, among the century's most mystically powerful passages, a harmony of musical notes in mutation and opposition, the divine voice as "a sound of singing," a song "of the making of Things, and of the beginning and the end of Peoples."[73] Mopo's own "song" is "of a people that is doomed."[74]

Before one dismisses Haggard's vision of the supernatural as theosophical claptrap, one may do well to place his ideas in their historical contexts, both anthropological and literary. Haggard's leitmotif of pattern and reincarnation coincides with the Victorian anthropological concept of the continuance of souls through the ever-sustained process of totem-transmigration. In *Nada* "the wolf-brethren" episode of Galazi and Umslopogaas is the only major interpolated cluster of events in what is otherwise a fabric of wholly African incidents and lore. Haggard's reference in the preface to these happenings, sandwiched among his carefully cited historical sources, explains:

> As for the wilder and more romantic incidents of this story, such as the hunting of Umslopogaas and Galazi with the wolves, or rather with the hyaenas,—for there are no true wolves in Zululand,—the author can only say that they seem to him of a sort that might well have been mythically connected with the names of those heroes. Similar beliefs and traditions are common in the records of primitive peoples.[75]

Apart from the Völsunga Sagas, Haggard's likely source was Sabine Baring-Gould's *Book of Were-Wolves: Being an Account of a Terrible Superstition* (1880), especially the third chapter: "The Were-wolf in the North." But far from being the "diversionary episode" as labeled by Wylie,[76] this interlude of the two noble heroes carries both an ancient allegorical and a romantic anthropological significance. Fynney's account had first given Haggard the suggestion of werewolf transmigration: "Tyaka's character appears to have been one which was an enigma even to the Zulus themselves, for, as one of his old indunas once explained to me.... 'He was a strange man; nay, a *silwana* (a wild animal), but we Zulus loved him for all that.'"[77] This quotation of the "old induna" reappears dramatized in *Nada* when Umslopogaas learns that he is the son of Shaka: "'*Wow*! who would have guessed that I was the son of that *Silwana*, of that hyaena man? Perhaps it is for this reason that, like Galazi, I love the company of wolves, though no love grows in my heart for my father or any of his house.'"[78]

Though Umslopogaas is a heroic Zulu, and Shaka an evil, both alike express a wolfish primitive power. *Silwana* or *isilwane* (*isi-* or *izi-* as singular or plural prefix + its stem *-ilwane*) means wolf, beast, animal, creature, and loosely hyena. When Haggard dedicated *Nada* to his mentor in Natal, Sir Theophilus Shepstone, he hailed Shepstone both as "my father," the Zulu "*Baba, Nkosi ya makosi*" (Father, Chief of Chiefs), and he affirmed "in you dwelt the spirit of Chaka."[79] By virtue of this indwelling spirit, Shepstone was acknowledged by the Zulus as having the right to install Cetywayo as their next chief. This heredity of the "wild animal" also descends to Haggard from Shepstone his "father." If Haggard is being accused of "regurgitating" Shaka stories, certainly recent critics one after the other have repeatedly interpreted this Shaka/Shepstone/Haggard "father" affinity since it was first proposed, somewhere back in the mists of 1980s speculation (at least as far back as McClintock's "Maidens"80), as Haggard's *soi-disant* effort to endow himself through Shepstone with a lineal authority as Zulu "interpreter," though literally he was sort of an interpreter, as Fynney had been on Shepstone's diplomatic staff: the "Chief Interpreter of the Colony." But this observation is never linked to its all-important anthropological source in totem-transmigration. That the British administrator of native affairs should be, as he himself proudly assented, the "holder of the spirit of Chaka"81 is a significant utilization in colonial policy of totem-transmigration according to Victorian anthropological insights into Zulu customs and beliefs. But in Haggard, as will be seen, it becomes primarily a personal and mystical-anthropological ideal of renewal, not a practical and political device. As repugnant as slaughter is to the Western mentality, blood as renewal belongs as much to Christian ritual as to the wolf-brethren or, even, to Shaka's haematomania.

As *doppelgängers*, Galazi and Umslopogaas have a classic model of friendship in the half-earthly, half-celestial brothers, the Dioscuri, who had an important cult in Sparta. Although the twins Polydeuces and Castor live and die interchangeably, presaging Galazi's sacrifice of life for Umslopogaas, the more applicable *doppelgänger* may be Romulus and Remus, brethren suckled by a she-wolf and fed by a woodpecker (Umslopogaas's alternate *nom de guerre*). Leader of a warlike band, Romulus, sired by Mars the god of war, is the legendary eponymous founder and first king of Rome; Remus dies by his hand. But unlike their classical prototypes, the empire these dispossessed Zulu princes might have founded died with Nada. Umslopogaas wins his axe and the title of "Slaughterer" by killing in combat Jikiza the Unconquered "on the first day of the new moon of the summer season."82 As the fifty-second challenger for "Groanmaker," and the first to succeed, he and his weapon epitomize the deadly forces of nature as prelude to renewal. And Galazi the Wolf wins his fabulous club "Watcher" by reclaiming from the wolves' cave the shrivelled body of the Dead One.83 According to Frazer this "carrying out death," to which a life-giving potency is ascribed, brings the divine spirit to life in a fresher form, engendering spring-summer.84 This cave, its rocky hymen opened, is the "lap" of the ghostly woman of the mountain. Galazi wins the "lap of her who sits in stone forever" by killing the king and queen of wolves; their failure of vital energy is replaced by the Zulu brothers wearing their skins as leaders of these "grey people," who are the reincarnations of cannibals in their former human lives.85 Frazer cites the devouring of

Sir Charles M'Carthy by the Ashantes in 1824 as among well-known instances of empowerment or fertility sacrifices (chapters 51–52) related to this practice.[86] Closely associated with the soul-animal that is the vehicle of the spirit of a dead human is the wer-animal, the alternative form or double of a living human. Lycanthropy, the belief that one has become a werewolf (*wer-* man + wolf), is based on the more-general totemic wearing of the hides or plumage of bird or beast or by putting on a mask resembling its face, each initiate finding a mystical rapport with his special animal, his totem. Certainly Haggard's use of totem-transmigration and its associated bloodshed—the nearly diabolical possession of the heroes and cannibals-become-wolves—is initially rooted in the Platonic doctrine of metempsychosis or preexistence and transmigration. Plato had theorized that birth is never the creation of a soul, but only a transmigration from one living creature, man, animal, or even plant, to another.

This shape-shifting also reflected the current anthropological interests of Frazer and Haggard's close friend, Andrew Lang, in totemism as an aboriginal answer to how man has an indwelling spirit.[87] In the fourth chapter of *The Golden Bough* (1890), Frazer had discussed totemism, the "exchange of life or souls between the man and his totem," the "infusion into him of fresh life drawn from the totem," and the treatment of "the bears or the wolves, etc., as his brethren, since in these animals are lodged the souls of himself and his kindred"; and he described such practices as dressing in wolf skins to "be born anew as a wolf."[88] According to Frazer, the clan springs from its totem, each clansman at death resuming totemic form—as did Haggard's wolf-cannibals. In a vision, the Dead One tells Galazi: "'Gird the black skin upon thy shoulders, and the wolves shall follow thee; all the three hundred and sixty and three of them that are left, and let him who shall be brought to thee gird on the skin of grey.'"[89] Galazi wears the black and is followed by the dog-wolves; Umslopogaas wears the she-wolf's grey. Originally there were 365 wolves, the same number as days in the year, suggesting that Galazi and Umslopogaas function as sun and earth, animal-daimons representing the male principle by which the earth or female principle is fertilized.

Like ancient warrior friendships, Haggard's duo loves fighting more than women, until Umslopogaas's yearning for Nada splits them apart.[90] Kipling's Mowgli in the *Jungle Book* (1894), who is raised by wolves and can turn himself into a beast at will, was indebted to *Nada*.[91] Thus Mowgli, like Umslopogaas, is attracted to a woman at puberty and leaves the brotherhood. In antiquity the Spartans most closely approximated Plato's ideal of public life, an ethos both military and monastic, and in the nineteenth century, Haggard is aware, Shaka's military regimentation attained this ideal. The Zulu rule of continence protects against contamination by feminine weakness, assures victory in war, and symbolically redirects male reproductive energy into bloodshed-as-renewal. Although the superiority of the Winchester 44-40 to Zulu spears is made explicit in *King Solomon's Mines* when Quatermain shoots at an assegai "and broke the blade into fragments,"[92] in heroic battle the Zulu-Viking Sir Henry Curtis dressed himself as a Zulu general and reverted to native weapons, swinging a battle axe. Haggard's readers were thrilled by this image of British masculinity transposed from Scandinavian mythology to a nineteenth-century Zulu battle. Ever since the Roman legions had been hacked to carrion at Cannae, the white-skinned northerner with dirty beard and tangled blond hair became, according to Livy, the most terrifying emblem of savage blood-lust.[93] Though in later centuries the disciplined Roman legions exacted a terrible revenge on these northern tribesmen, they were true spiritual sons of the Old Norse hero Berserk. Clad only in the shirt (*serkr*) "sark" or skin of bear (*bjorn*), these "berserks" in their reputedly magical bear- or wolf-hooded shirts were intoxicated with bloodshed and famed for reckless bravery in combat. Alleged shape-shifters, these warriors found their strength in an animalistic blood-awareness, howling like wolves in battle madness with an almost diabolical possession; they appeared to grow huge, their eyes flashed, snarling or roaring they charged wildly believing themselves proof against pain and wounds. Such totemic transformations had been depicted earlier in Homer and legends such as the founding of Rome and again later, as when Beowulf strips off his battle gear to meet Grendle and even in Shakespeare's *Henry V* when the king describes the physical transformation that should turn his men into "beasts."[94] One of Tennyson's early commentators singled out this image of battle intoxication from "Ulysses" as the finest, or among the finest, lines written in that century: "And drunk delight of battle with my peers, / Far on the ringing plains of windy Troy."[95] Haggard's most magnificent image is in *The World's Desire* where Odysseus

> saw the golden head, unhelmeted, of a man taller than the tallest there from the shoulders upwards. Unhelmeted he came and unshielded, with no body armour. His flesh was very fair and white, and on it were figures pricked in blue, figures of men and horses, snakes and sea-beasts. The skin of a white bear was buckled above his shoulder with a golden clasp,

fashioned in the semblance of a boar. His eyes were blue, fierce and shining, and in his hand he held for a weapon the trunk of a young pine-tree, in which was hafted a weighty axe-head of rough unpolished stone.[96]

Mitford's *Gun-Runner* applies this directly to the Zulus and their captain, Ngavuma:

> "*Usutu! 'Sutu!* We see red!" howl the infuriated savages, maddened with the taste of blood, tossing the reeking blades of their assegais aloft, crashing their knob-kerries on their shields, and roaring with the semi-frenzy of wild beasts.... Thundering the sonorous war-cry, he waves the black leopard-skin aloft; leaping, bounding like the savage beast who once wore it, he hurls himself forward with lightning irresistibility.[97]

Even Mopo in *Nada* becomes a momentary berserker, seeing a red cloth descending before his eyes in his fury.[98]

That Haggard is not implying that Zulus are completely demented fighters is perfectly clear in numerous scenes, such as the climactic battle in *Maiwa's Revenge* (1888). In *Allan Quatermain* Umslopogaas is described as "*in his own savage fashion,* the finest general I ever knew."[99] Street finds in this phrase and in the native "faithfulness" of Umslopogaas an instance of "patronising condescension."[100] But before one begins to hear in Haggard something like Ernest Dowson's ironic refrain, "I have been faithful to thee, Cynara! in my fashion," one must recognize that precisely *because* Umslopogaas is not the "very model of a modern major general," whose white superiority lies *only* in technical innovations, his "savage" sagacity produces a plan that under the exigencies of the Masai attack is accepted as "the best chance of success": "'Ah, old lion!' I said to Umslopogaas, 'thou knowest how to lie in wait as well as how to bite, where to seize as well as where to hang on.'"[101]

※ ※

If a feigned translation of Mopo's Zulu life story is the vehicle for Haggard's historiography, then the novel's tenor is the more-figurative "translation" of shape-shifting and the continuance of souls through totem-transmigration. Putting on the wolf or bear skin becomes a complex translational event in which outer surfaces have symbolic import—the bare/bear skin, as it were, bespeaking the inheritance of an inner self. But not all exterior transformations are virile. Some are just virulent. In *Nada*, the snow lies on Natal in the opening scene in which Allan Quatermain goes to hear the story of the Lily of the Zulus. Similarly, in *King Solomon's Mines* the female body of Africa, the "breasts of Sheba," had been covered with the snow; and unlike the nurturant quality of the maternal breast, this is a whiteness that nearly kills all the adventurers and, indeed, does kill Ventvögel. *Nada*'s "landscape blind with snow" has an uncanny resemblance to Mopo's "sightless eyes, and one hand—his left—white and shrivelled":[102] "'Look at it now, my father; you can see, though my eyes are blind. The hand is white, like yours—it is white and dead and shrivelled.'"[103] Unlike the empowering wolf skin, the hand that Shaka had demanded Mopo hold in the flame as proof of his loyalty becomes a shrivelled, impotent white skin acquired by fiery pain. Mopo's white hand testifies to his claim of revenge upon Shaka and Dingaan, for its whiteness is very much akin to the whiteness of "colossal Death" in *King Solomon's Mines*, who presides over the slain or otherwise dead calcified kings. Death is also the whiteness that shrouds the imperialist's tenure in Africa, a false purity that has much in common with Marlow's vision of Brussels, the metropolitan center of empire, as "a whited sepulcher."[104] Similarly Haggard jokes in *Marie* that the seasick Hottentot Hans "declared that all these evils had fallen upon him because he had been fool enough to forsake the religion of his people (what was that, I wonder), and allow himself to be 'washed white,' that is, be baptised, by my father."[105] Whitewashing and washing white are an imperial, impotent shape-shifting or transmutation.

The basic black-white antithesis of the African-European encounter is the product of socially constructed notions of forbidden miscegenation, of a whiteness perpetually antithetical to the darkness of Africa. In Tennyson's "Locksley Hall" the hysterical young man who lost his cousin Amy is tempted to "take some savage woman" but recoils at the bestiality of being "mated with a squalid savage," siring offspring "with narrow foreheads, vacant of our glorious gains."[106] The native heroines Foulata in *King Solomon's Mines* and Mameena in *Child of Storm* are somehow instinctively aware of the imperialist's fear of miscegenation. Dying, Foulata had asked Quatermain to tell Good that "'I love him, and that I am glad to die because I know that he cannot cumber his life with such as me, for the sun cannot mate with the darkness, nor the white with the black.'" She then imagines seeking him in the afterlife "'in the stars,'" though she is still black and he white.[107] On the mythic level Haggard implies that Good is forever separated from his revitalizing consort because, since the trio intends to return with their diamonds to England, Good will not pursue her beyond the underworld to the stars.

But if Mopo's eyes and hand resemble the snow-white curse of sterility and physical impotence on the land, they may also be a prelude to knowledge. Though wounded, Mopo becomes a blind seer and, as a historian, becomes a male Zulu version of Mnemosyne, goddess of memory, offspring of Heaven and Earth, mother of the muses. His other hand is "red and strong—red with the blood of two kings."[108] But until the bloody-handed slayer, embodying the deadly forces of nature, flings wide the red gates of renewal, dark and light, outer skins and inner hearts and souls remain unmixed, sterile, mere dry bones mocking life. Mameena, too, says:

> "I know well enough what you mean—that you are white as snow and I am black as soot, and that snow and soot don't mix well together."
>
> "No," I answered gravely, "snow is good to look at, and so is soot, but mingled they make an ugly colour. Not that you are like soot," I added hastily, fearing to hurt her feelings. "That is your hue"—and I touched a copper bangle she was wearing—"a very lovely hue, Mameena, like everything else about you."[109]

Like Mameena's "hue," Nada's white-black heritage (the in-mixing of a Portuguese grandfather) results in her special tone: "her skin was lighter—more of the colour of pure copper."[110] Copper or "Venus" (so designated by alchemists, perhaps from copper mirrors) is reddish in hue and brings together the fatal red vitality Africa with "the whitenesses of soul,/That Virgil had."[111] The sanguine coloring of both women betokens a miscegenation (by heredity or desire) of black and white, a forbidden knowledge paradoxically instrumental to, indeed the necessary precondition for, finding heaven's unsullied purity. As a matter of fact, Nada seemingly may be the priestess or earthly incarnation of the female deity Umkulunkulu, much as Lady Ragnall in *The Ivory Child* was the expression of Isis: the flash of Umkulunkulu's arms and breast "were like the driven snow, when it glows in the sunset,"[112] the copper color of glowing snow in the light of the setting sun.

Precisely this duality is discerned in the African *agapanthus umbellatus* or "Goya" lily in *Allan Quatermain*, a striking foreshadowing of the as-yet unwritten *Nada the Lily*:

> This lily, which the natives say blooms only once in ten years, flourishes in the most arid soil.... I know not how to describe its beauty and splendour, or the indescribable sweetness of its perfume. The flower—for it only has one bloom—rises from the crown of the bulb on a thick fleshy and flat-sided stem, the specimen that I saw measured fourteen inches in diameter.... First there is the green sheath, which in its early stage is not unlike

that of a water-lily, but which as the bloom opens splits into four portions and curls back gracefully towards the stem. Then comes the bloom itself, a single dazzling arch of white enclosing another cup of richest velvety crimson, from the heart of which rises a golden-coloured pistil.[113]

In the next century, Georgia O'Keefe certainly would have understood the sheath-crimson-pistil sexuality of this botanical excursus. As white, Nada is indicative of heavenly purity, her aloof beauty paradoxically warmed by the red rose of Aphrodite, the enclosed cup of "crimson." Haggard's own unrequited passion for Lilly ("Lilith") Jackson may well play into this imagery. The serpent is the instrument of Lilith's vengeance, according to Rossetti and others, and the lily itself sprung from the repentant tears of Eve as she went forth from Paradise.

Mopo's reddened hand mediates his own white-hand, black-hand schizoid allegiances, red bespeaking his temptation, fall, and mortality. As Haggard looking back on his African experience later wrote to one of his siblings in Kenya—he found the world a very red apple, observing a tad cynically that even if women sometimes have a rotten heart, the outside of the apple is no less red and women are not less beautiful because they are false![114] Most circumspect on any personal escapades with native women, Haggard in Africa undoubtedly enjoyed the apple's erotic flavors; and the fatal kiss of Mameena and Allan Quatermain doubtless sprang from more than mere fancy. Years later, in an amazingly confessional passage only posthumously published, Haggard connects red with the femme fatale, both as erotic passion and death:

> When we rode the wild horses of our youthful sins, the red blood coursing through our veins like wine, who was it that seized the reins and again and yet again delivered us from the last disaster?... Nature, "red in tooth and claw," is not begotten of God alone. Surely the powers called Satan and Death have had a hand in its makings. Thus Nature says to Everyman who is a man: "See where She stands with longing arms and lips that murmur love. Hark to what She says who would be the mother of your child: 'Seek! Seek for heaven hid in these dark eyes of mine and find all Earth's desire....'" "Touch not, taste not, handle not," answers the cold stern Law. "Pass on, she is not thine." Often enough it is Nature that prevails and, having eaten of the apple that She, our Mother, gives us, we desire no other fruit.... Shame comes, sorrow comes; come death and separations. And, greater than all of these, remorse rises in the after years and stands over us at night, since, when our eyes are no longer clouded with the mists of passion, we see and bewail our wickedness.[115]

In *Areopagitica* Milton alluded to how from "one apple tasted ... the knowledge of good and evil ... together leapt forth into the World. And perhaps this is the doom which Adam fell into of ... knowing good by evil."[116]

This allegorizing of the Fall illuminates the apparent contradiction between Haggard's evident admiration of civilization's justice and mercy (virtue) and man's necessary return to the destructive and chaotic qualities of nature (evil). As Milton would say, "that which purifies us is trial, and trial is by what is contrary."[117] This fallen sensory vitality and the blood-awareness of animals is represented in *Allan Quatermain* by a red robin on the coffin of Quatermain's son, sending him back to Africa:

> It was a dreary December afternoon, and the sky was heavy with snow, but not much was falling. The coffin was put down by the grave, and a few big flakes lit upon it. They looked very white upon the black cloth!... A robin redbreast came as bold as could be and lit upon the coffin and began to sing.... The thirst for the wilderness was on me; I could tolerate this place no more; I would go and die as I had lived, among the wild game and the savages.[118]

One thinks of Thomas Hardy's thrush presiding over the century's corpse outleant; but the red of Haggard's robin mixes death with a restoration of "wild" and "savage" life. Haggard's and Milton's red apples are essentially the same.

Nada herself is at first glance an uncomplicated icon of Victorian neo-Platonic romanticism, as much at home in the London of Dante Rossetti and Walter Pater as in the Renaissance Italy of Ariosto. Often Haggard's fiction contains an allegorical, Endymion-like quest of hero and goddess for each other, seeking the perfect love that is a perfect vision. One has only to think of Solomon and Sheba in *King Solomon's Mines* or Ayesha and Kallikrates in *She*. Nada the Lily, even more than Sheba, is a kingly prize beyond Solomon's magnitude: "Consider the lilies of the field, how they grow; they toil not, neither do they spin: And yet I say unto you, that even Solomon in all his glory was not arrayed like one of these" (Matthew 6:28–29). Closer to Anglo-African literature was Olive Schreiner's neo-Platonic allegory of a Hunter who glimpses in the water the "shadow" of "a vast white bird, with silver wings outstretched, sailing in the everlasting blue." Dying, he is rewarded with a single feather—a handsel of the elusive Ultimate Reality.[119] Socrates in his palinode on love says that before the highest class of soul had fallen from its preincarnate phase into a body, it had accompanied a deity to the rim of the heavens and seen beauty "standing with modesty upon a pedestal of chastity."[120] Nada, a new virgin Venus of supreme, flawless beauty, is the primordial Platonic vision of the *Phaedrus* glimpsed anew. Indeed, Haggard had described truth in art as like "some perfect Grecian statue ... cold but naked, and looking thereon men should be led to think of naught but beauty."[121]

Yet in *Nada*, men who want to possess this fairest of all women do so at their risk and may be paralyzed by the vision, like Keats's knight-at-arms. Haggard's phrase, "naught but beauty," suggests that Nada's true ontological status is nonmaterial, as in Spanish/Portuguese (ironic legacy of her grandfather?) *nada* is "nothing" or "not at all"; interestingly, the Zulu *nada-nada* denotes a person in a daze. Of course in Russian *nada* is the "hope" of the three holy virtues of faith, hope, and charity. Perhaps its Slavonic overtones play off against its Iberian origin to suggest an intrinsic doubleness. Only the knight Umslopogaas momentarily reifies this impalpable ideal; and, like the visionary Lamia of another allegory of Keats, Nada then is lost. Hiding from enemies in the wolf-cave of Galazi and Umslopogaas, she rolls the closing rock beyond its pivotal point and, following Leslie's Zulu tale, fatally seals her doom. Only the mythic or divine escape into an ideal realm. Perhaps as Keats's Hermes and the nymph fled in "Lamia," so too have Solomon and Sheba long ages ago escaped into legend? This desire of the lover to grasp a perfection more than mortal is a pervasive theme, as typical of Keats's Lamia or Hawthorne's birthmarked Georgiana as of Nada, who had correctly predicted that Umslopogaas's love would destroy both her and the Zulus' best hope for national continuance: "when Nada died," Mopo observes of Umslopogaas, "he lost his desire to be great."[122] More comically, in *King Solomon's Mines*, Good becomes the wandering hero bereft of his native love. Haggard's philosophy is a neo-Platonic, romantic *thanatos*, in which life has corrupted the universal One into many flawed particulars; but Death, releasing the buried divinity within, permits man to merge again with the ideal world beyond temporality. Thus Shelley in "Adonais" declares: "Die, If thou wouldst be with that which thou dost seek." If Death tramples to fragments the colors that stain "the white radiance of Eternity," then "No more let Life divide what Death can join together."[123] So congruent is the death scene of Nada with Shelley's lament for his "Adonis," the *adonai* or "lord" of the reproductive energies of nature, that one could easily imagine Umslopogaas uttering lines 469–77 with the simple substitution of Nada's name for that of Adonais.[124]

While the ultimate distinction of evil and purity abides as very real, in this life the two are strangely intermixed. Thus the radiantly white

Umkulunkulu, Queen of Heaven and the Eve-like mother of mankind, manifests herself under another guise as the Goddess of the Dead, the Witch of the Mountain beneath whose visage and in whose cave as tomb-and-womb the young heroes wallow like wolves in blood-lust and raw animality.[125] Although this may seem a Manichaean universe of distinct good and evil, man's fallenness is integral to his redemption. As Olive Schreiner's dream, "The Sunlight Lay Across my Bed," declares: "Hell is the seed ground from which Heaven springs."[126] And in *The World's Desire* the light and dark female rivals, Helen and Meriamun, both cause men's deaths; Odysseus is "beguiled"[127] by the snake of Meriamun, as was Eve (Genesis 3:13; 2 Corinthians 11:3); and Argive Helen dwells with death,[128] yet like Nada she is "Beauty's self."[129] Just as Umkulunkulu is counterbalanced by the Witch of the Mountain, so in *King Solomon's Mines*, Foulata/Sheba and Gagool as witch embody the Earth-mother's cycle of life, death, and rebirth. And so too Nada, no less Circean than Ayesha in enticing men to reify the dream, is a cause of misfortunes and a goddess of death: "all men, white and black, seek that which is beautiful, and when at last they find it, then it passes swiftly away, or, perchance, it is their death."[130] But within a neo-Platonic duality of good and evil, spirit and body, light and dark, one contrary has its origin in the other. Thus injustice and cruelty are a necessary diabolic precondition for their symbolic antithesis in Stanger's new structures. But in a typical pattern of thesis and antithesis, the last stage of synthesis, though adumbrated in the new hall and church, cannot be definitively achieved, not any more than Nada as an ideal can be captured this side of death. In that epic struggle on the site of Dukuza, metonymic of the world itself, the diabolic (Gk *dyo* two > *dia-* across, apart + *ballein* to throw) and the symbolic (*syn* together + *ballein*) perpetually break, heal, and break again until Umkulunkulu's rods of ivory and ebony end the discord of history and apportion souls between "the gates of light" or "the gates of blackness."[131] Until then, the only way to approach the flawless beauty of Nada is to lie down where all the ladders start, to return to the embeddedness of one's own primitive self in the blood of earth, in its processes of generation and decay. Both Quatermain and Umslopogaas are thus perpetual wanderers, incessantly searching for this elusive ideal, glimpsed and loved, but never to be found till death.

✥ FIVE

From the Cape to the Zambezi: Boer and British

Three novels, three romances and several stories by Haggard—mainly *affaires de coeur* with suitors virtuous or evil—utilize the historic region of the Matabeles (amaNdebele) as the scene of their action: *The Witch's Head* (1884), *Jess* (1887), and *Swallow* (1899) are novels; *Marie* (1911), *Allan's Wife* (1889), and *Maiwa's Revenge* (1888) are romances that chronicle Allan Quatermain's love affairs and hunting adventures. Several short tales also are set in this region between the Vaal and the Zambezi that came to be called the Transvaal (*trans*, across + Vaal River). The Vaal River (its name means "foul" because of its murky water) rises in the Drakensberg Mountains and flows west to join the Orange River. These rivers drain much of the South African interior tableland that, in the early nineteenth century, had been invaded by tribes forced from their land by the *impis* of Shaka. Led by the Zulu chief Mzilikazi, they exterminated or absorbed most of the earlier indigenous Sotho-Tswana-speaking inhabitants.

The Boers, dissatisfied with British rule around the Cape, had begun to move northwards under the pressure of successive British annexations, initially settling north of the Orange River, then pushing further north "across the Vaal," ultimately by the end of the century all the way to the Zambezi. Sol Plaatje's novel *Mhudi* is set in this land of Mzilikazi's Matabeles, against whom Plaatje's ancestral Barolongs, allied with the Boers, fought. Distrust and loathing between the British government and its Dutch subjects produced these trek-Boers: "who hated and traduced missionaries, loathed and abominated British rule and permanent officials, loved slavery and killed Kaffirs whenever they got the chance."[1] The Boers not only felt the magistrates and missionaries coddled and favored the natives but that in their dealings with Dingaan "those English missionaries have poisoned the king's mind against us Boers."[2] A massacre of these *Voortrekers* in 1836 by the Zulu chief Dingaan was revenged in 1838 by the battle of Blood River, so renamed because it ran red with Zulu blood.

In "The Transvaal," Haggard had envisioned a rejuvenation for the British in Africa akin to that of Kukuanaland. But after the Zulu War, intervention to establish British ideals of justice did not include an indigenous ruler of the land. Later, in *Cetywayo* Haggard criticizes the British balkanizing of Zululand into more than a dozen suzerainties overseen by an ineffectual British "resident." One suspects a *quid pro quo* between Haggard's ceremonial flag-raising over Pretoria in 1877 and his piece of domestic propaganda the same month, inasmuch as the essay's rhetoric had culminated with a vision of the British flag about to be unfurled:

> The Transvaal is a magnificent corn-producing country, with great mineral resources which only require development. Left in the hands of the Boers these resources will never be developed, but once in the hands of the English they may repay the enterprise of thousands.... It is our mission to conquer and hold in subjection, not from thirst of conquest, but for the sake of law, justice, and order.... Decidedly, the day when the British flag—a flag that has always brought blessings in its train—is first unfurled there should be a glad day for the Transvaal, Republic no more— for the South African colonies, who will welcome a new and beautiful sister, and for England, who will add another lusty child to her splendid progeny.[3]

Haggard probably downplayed the economic motivation of gold and diamonds ("mineral resources") because for him diamonds were less precious than the powers in the land itself. Though the land belongs by "birthright" to the "natives" (the root *nasci*, to be born, grounds that principle), the unfurling of the Union Jack allows the British colonists to be naturalized in the Transvaal by giving birth or rebirth to themselves as Anglo-African "progeny" (*pro-* forth + *gignere* to beget)—the last word in Haggard's essay.

After the Zulu War but before the Anglo-Boer War, Haggard voiced for the younger British reader, undoubtedly thinking of Cecil Rhodes and a future Union of South Africa, the following jingoistic prediction:

> The Zulus as a nation are dead, and never again will a great Impi, such as swept away our troops at Isandhlwana, be seen rushing down to war. Their story is but one scene in the vast drama which is being enacted in this generation, and which some of you who read these lines may live

to see, not accomplished, indeed, but in the way of accomplishment—the drama of the building up of a great Anglo-Saxon empire in Africa—an empire that within the next few centuries may well become one of the mightiest in the world. We have made many and many a mistake, but still that empire grows; in spite of the errors of the Home Government, the obstinacy of the Boers, the power of native chiefs, and the hatred of Portuguese, still it grows. Already it is about as big as Europe, and it is only a baby yet, a baby begotten by the genius and courage of individual Englishmen.[4]

The excuse for this propaganda of empire was a volume edited by his friend Andrew Lang "in the shape of a Christmas book"[5] for young boys in which British heroism, synonymous with patriotism, was a required sentiment. But already for Haggard, the possibility of rebirth into a more vital mythopoeic primal unity with the land faltered when the Transvaal was returned to the Boers in 1881[6] and died completely after his return visit to the vassal kingdom of Zululand in 1912.

Not many other successful novelists of empire, apart from Kipling, Stevenson, and Conrad, usually come to mind when comparing Haggard with his contemporaries. Undoubtedly his affinities were not only with Mitford but also with the South African realist and allegorist Olive Schreiner. Like Haggard, Schreiner at first was indisputably involved in the politics and economics of what Anthony Trollope had called the "demoralizing quest" of the diamond boom in the vicinity of the Vaal, the pursuit of that new industrial wealth conditioning social, political and intellectual life. And like Haggard, Schreiner soon surmised that a technologically aggressive enterprise was ravaging the redemptive power of the African landscape. Although known primarily for *The Story of an African Farm*, Schreiner may have been more celebrated during the last decades of her life as the author of *Dreams* (1890), a slim and now only academically appreciated collection of eleven allegories. Haggard's mythic affinities lie with Schreiner's brief allegories, surreal and fugue-like word-paintings that once were felt to be only just this side of poetry. Arthur Symons, a leading exponent of advanced aesthetic theories, implicitly connected Schreiner's allegorical "poems in prose" with the French Symbolists' mystical correspondences and visionary ideals, their desire to go above or beyond the rationalism and materialism of the nineteenth-century temper.[7] Later popular standards of low-mimetic "formal realism" have devalued the oracular and moralistic, but Schreiner's allegories received an enthusiastic reception when they were collected and published. This vogue for Schreiner's *Dreams* owed much to its compatibility with Platonic myth, with

Swedenborgian and German Romanticism (Goethe, Novalis), as well as with British Romanticism from Blake and Carlyle to the visionary art of the Pre-Raphaelites and the lyricism of the *fin-de-siècle* Yeats.

The daughter of missionary parents in South Africa, Schreiner early on, however, had noticed that the Sermon on the Mount's social message was not a constituent of the overt behavioral or cultural activity within the colony or empire. This from *The Story of an African Farm*:

> One day, a notable one, we read on the "kopje," and discover the fifth chapter of Matthew, and read it all through. It is a new gold-mine. Then we tuck the Bible under our arm and rush home.... We are quite breathless when we get to the house; we tell them we have discovered a chapter they never heard of; we tell them what it says. The old wise people tell us they knew all about it. Our discovery is a mare's-nest to them; but to us it is very real.[8]

Which "gold-mine" will define society—the commercial enterprise, imperial and patriarchal, or a nonimperial and innocent coming of the kingdom and the doing of the will of that other power who fathers forth? In the morality of the Sermon on the Mount, the child has made what she supposes to be a great discovery; but the "old wise people" disparage it as tedious nonsense. They implicitly offer instead an alternative biblical text for colonial practice, more agreeable with the sort of paradigm depicted by Homer. In *Thoughts on South Africa* (1923) Schreiner pointed to biblical accounts of the Israelites' conquest of the Promised Land to explain the subjugation of South Africa by the Huguenot ancestors of the nineteenth-century Boers, thereby supplementing the ancient European-Homeric literary pattern with a religious model of equal cultural influence:

> To these homeless fugitives the Europe that they had left was as the "house of bondage." The ships which bore them to South Africa were the Ark of the Covenant of the Lord their God, in which He bore His chosen to the Land of His Promise. As the Huguenot paced the deck of his ship and saw the strange stars of the Southern Hemisphere come out above him, like Abraham of old he read in them the promise of his covenant-keeping God:—"To thee and to thy seed shall the land be given and they shall inherit it. Look up and see the stars of heaven if thou canst count them: so shall thy seed be for multitude; like sand, like fine sand on the seashore. And when thou comest to the land that I shall give thee, thou shalt drive out the heathen from before thee."[9]

Earlier, David Livingstone's popular *Missionary Travels* (1858) also had made just this observation on the Boers' claim: "They being the chosen people of God, the heathen are given to them for an inheritance, and they are the rod of divine vengeance on the heathen, as were the Jews of old."[10] The Zeus of Odysseus was simply supplanted by the Jehovah of the Afrikaners when the ancient Greek paradigm of social aggression was naturalized, indeed fetishized, in the authority of that ultimate *Ur*-text, the Bible, and became the canonical story of Anglo-African settlement.

Schreiner drew a distinction, however, between Boer and British cultural interaction with the natives. According to Schreiner who lived among the Boers as a governess while writing *The Story of an African Farm*, these Dutch-Huguenot settlers were seventeenth-century anachronisms: simple, ritualistic, and with a sense of divine immanence that would do credit to the Psalmist. Schreiner saw the earliest Boer-native massacres not as imperialistic, since they involved neither a superior technology against an inferior—the struggle between flintlock and poison arrow was only slightly less than even-handed—nor the enhancement of wealth for absentee investors, but as undertaken for survival, brutal but inevitable. In *Thoughts on South Africa*, Schreiner describes these early settlers trekking with "their flint-lock guns" into the veld, their "rhinoceros-hide whips their only scepter of rule":

> Those were the days of hard living and hard fighting.... The plains were not wide enough for both, and the new-come children of the desert fought with the old. We have all sat listening in our childhood to the story of the fighting in those old days. How sometimes the Boer coming suddenly on a group of Bushmen round their fire at night, fired and killed all he could. If in the flight a baby were dropped and left behind, he said, "Shoot that too, if it lives it will be a Bushman or bear Bushmen." On the other hand, when the little Bushman saw his chance and found the Boer's wagon unprotected, the Boer sometimes saw a light across the plain, which was his blazing property; and when he came back would find the wagon cinders, and only the charred remains of his murdered wife and children. It was a bitter, merciless fight, the little poisoned arrow shot from behind the rocks, as opposed to the great flint-lock gun. The victory was inevitably with the flint-lock, but there may have been times when it almost seemed to lie with the arrow; it was a merciless primitive fight, but it seems to have been on the whole, compared to many modern battles, fair and even, and in the end the little Bushman vanished.[11]

Though the Boer's "gold-untouched ideals"[12] were less corrupt than nineteenth-century imperial ambitions, his pragmatic agenda and incipient pantheism did not often embrace the mystical vision of the land redeemed from evil.

Despite her use of such adjectives as "bitter" and "merciless," the objective tone of Schreiner's portrait of the Boer's manners and customs derives from the sense of herself as an innocent outsider to this bloodshed. With much the same ethnographic detachment, for example, Livingstone had observed the internecine slaughter among African tribes: "they had a curious taste," he remarks coolly of one tribe, "for ornamenting their villages with the skulls of strangers."[13] But when discussing the British, Schreiner's tone is considerably more caustic. This was her patriarchal heritage, and it betokened her group involvement in a land-grab more capitalistic and deviously exploitative than that of the Boers, trader and missionary ominously abetting each other:

> St. Francis of Assisi preached to the little fishes: we eat them. But the man who eats fish can hardly be blamed, seeing that the eating of fishes is all but universal among the human race!—if only he does not pretend that while he eats he preaches to them! That has never been the Boer's attitude towards any aboriginal race. He may consume it off the face of the earth, but he has never told it he does it for its benefit.[14]

In *The Story of an African Farm* the Boer's propensity for "consuming" the land and its people is burlesqued in the satiric figure of Tant' Sannie, whose analogous consumption of sheep's trotters—no less than of husbands—leaves her so obese by the novel's end as nearly to abandon bodily locomotion. Just as Odysseus, eating the Cyclopes's "sweet cousin ram" is exposed as a more egregious double of the despised Polyphemus, that "damned cannibal" devouring Odysseus's shipmates,[15] so the British also are paralleled with the stereotypical cannibals in Schreiner's caricature of "John Bull seated astride of the earth, his huge belly distended with the people he has devoured and his teeth growing out yet more than ever with all the meat he has bitten and looking around on a depeopled earth and laughing."[16] "'You say that, with your guns shooting so many shots a minute, you can destroy any race of men armed only with spears,'" Rebekah observes in Schreiner's posthumous novel *From Man to Man* (1927), "'but how does that prove your superiority, except as the superiority of the crocodile is proved when it eats a human baby, because it has long teeth and baby has none?'"[17]

Schreiner's stature owes much to her reputation as a fiction writer who embodied an unusual combination of feminism and colonial Victorianism; yet in an age of notable life stories, she never attempted to record in any comprehensive way her autobiography. At times she seems to suggest as strongly as Dinesen, Haggard, and Mitford the oxymoronic possibility of an innocent imperialist. She defines the greatness and goodness of Sir George Grey, to whom she dedicated her political novella of protest against Rhodes's territorial ambition, *Trooper Peter Halket of Mashonaland* (1897), in terms of Sir George's "uncorruptible justice" and "broad humanity," unproblematically linked to a noble "Imperial Rule"—all summed up in lines from Robert Browning's "Grammarian's Funeral."[18] But Browning's verse can be read ironically, not as lauding the Grammarian's life but as mocking it. In Schreiner's eulogistic dedication, as in the tribute to the Grammarian by his students, ironic innuendo is unintentional. Yet might not that which is implicit and unintentional rise up to trouble the writer in other contexts—even in the telling of Schreiner's own life story, say? Of all the quotations that she could have chosen, isn't it odd that she should have fastened on one from such a master of irony to describe the achievement of a Governor who, like the Grammarian, can never quite evade our sense of his well-intentioned but possibly naive or misguided expectations? Reliving her anguished childhood sense of this contradiction, the adult Schreiner recalls:

> I had grown up in a land where wars were common. From my earliest years I had heard of bloodshed and battles and hair-breadth escapes; I had heard them told of by those who had seen and taken part in them. In my native country dark men were killed and their lands taken from them by white men armed with superior weapons; even near to me such things happened ... and I had seen how white men used the dark as beasts of labor, often without any thought for their good or happiness. Three times I had seen an ox striving to pull a heavily loaded waggon up a hill, the blood and foam streaming from its mouth and nostrils as it struggled, and I had seen it fall dead, under the lash.... Why did we hate and kill and torture?[19]

The "we" reflects Schreiner's awareness of her firsthand participation—she "had heard," "had seen"—in an ongoing colonial enterprise that was programmatically blind to its moral failings. Usually sooner than later child and native discover "European light"[20] for what it really is. Whipping becomes for Schreiner's characters (for Waldo, for Jannita), as it had been in her own upbringing, the patriarchal compulsion behind the "loving hand": "There is as little inconsistency in loving through thrashing your nigger as there is in birching a child of your own flesh and blood," proclaimed an editorial in the journal *Rhodesia*,[21] adding that this was a lesson of "practical colonial experience." It is no anomaly that the whip is equally suitable for oxen; Dinesen makes an observation very similar to Schreiner's: "The oxen in Africa have carried the heavy load of the advance of European civilization.... The whips have marked their sides, and you will often see oxen that have had an eye, or both of them, taken away by the long cutting whip-lashes."[22] Bloodshed by assagai, firearm or whip; hatred, torture, death, or escape; the advance of European civilization: this was Haggard's context for his tales of Boer and British.

Haggard's first fictional treatment of Africa was in *The Witch's Head* (1884), a novel that begins and ends in England but the central chapters of which are set in Pretoria. And although the English episodes and images are effective, such as the eroding coastal cemetery which would be worthy of Thomas Hardy, it only takes Haggard two paragraphs after his hero flees to Africa before his narrative jumps into life-and-death suspense. Haggard made good use of his personal experiences in *The Witch's Head*, as testified to by such autobiographical reminiscences as "Lost on the Veld"[23] repeated in *Days of My Life*, in which Ernest thinks he sees "the white cap of a wagon"[24] in the distance only to be sadly deceived. And in "An Incident of African History," Haggard describes his command in the Pretoria Light Horse during the Zulu crisis which parallels that of Ernest.[25] Finally, almost in the manner of life imitating art, the death of Alston in the novel undoubtedly drew Haggard to his account of "Major Wilson's Last Fight" in which the death of the major and his patrol fighting Lobengula in December 1893 so closely resembled Ernest's near-fatal encounter with the Zulus at Isandhlwana.

Haggard's hero is named Ernest—a full decade before Oscar Wilde in *The Importance of Being Ernest* (1895) famously burlesqued that "earnestness" in thought and deed to which Thomas Carlyle had urged his countrymen. In *The Way of All Flesh* (1903) Ernest Pontifex, Samuel Butler's principal character, also has such a morally confused earnestness that it lands him in jail. Tennyson had employed yet another dimension of its meaning—as a down payment or pledge—when in "Lockesley Hall" he prophesies a future Utopia: "Men, my brothers, men the workers, ever reaping something new; / That which they have done but *earnest* of the things that they shall do."[26] Optimism in such progress at home gave the British the moral right, they believed, to turn their attention to "the white man's burden" in the rest of the world. Longfellow echoed that temper in his "wall-motto" poem, "A Psalm of Life": "Life is real! Life is earnest!"[27] Already in 1877 Gilbert and Sullivan had produced a sentimental farce, *Engaged*, about two men in love with Belinda: the first man points a pistol to his head; the second man desperately offers to give her up; then: "First man. If I only thought you were in earnest; but no—(*Putting the pistol to his head again*). Second man. In earnest? Of course I'm in earnest!"[28] Of course, he isn't.

Haggard's Ernest is a lover jilted and disillusioned, possibly not unlike Haggard's experience with Lilly Jackson five years earlier right at the time of this novel's climactic Zulu War. Ernest's downfall is Florence's female jealousy, a force anarchic and destructive for the male the woman professes to love. The witch's head that the beautiful and innocent Eva finds in the sea, which so much resembles her evil sister Florence, is very clearly a "terrible" but "fascinating" Anglo-Saxon Medusa:

> Let the reader imagine the face and head of a lovely woman of some thirty years of age, the latter covered with rippling brown locks of great length.... Let him imagine this face, all but the lips, which were coloured red, pale with the bloodless pallor of death, and the flesh so firm and fresh-looking that it might have been that of a corpse not a day old.... Then let him imagine the crowning horror of this weird sight. The eyes of a corpse are shut, but the eyes in this head were wide open, and the long black lashes, as perfect now as on the day of death, hung over what appeared, when the light struck them, to be two balls of trembling fire, that glittered and rolled and fixed themselves upon the face of the observer like living human eyes.[29]

With more than just a soupçon of high kitsch, we are told her eyes "were balls of crystal fitted, probably with the aid of slender springs, into the eye-sockets with such infernal art that they shook and trembled to the slightest sound, and even on occasion rolled about."[30] The witch's head seems to have been silicified, as perfectly pickled as the body of old Silvestra had been preserved by the cold in *King Solomon's Mines*.

Medusa, according to Ovid's *Metamorphoses*, was once a beautiful maiden whose golden hair was her supreme glory, but having dared to vie in beauty with Athena, the goddess changed her ringlets into hissing serpents. Though many classical writers suggested her hideousness turned men to stone, others maintained it was her stunning beauty. Thus later ancient art, such as the Rondanini Medusa (a Roman copy of a work by Phidias or Kresilas in the Munich Glyptotek), often depicts her with the face of a beautiful, perhaps deeply sorrowful, maiden. Goethe described the Rondanini Medusa as "a wonderful work which, expressing the discord between death and life, between pain and pleasure, exerts an inexplicable fascination over us as no other ambiguous figure does."31 If Haggard had not seen the famed marble by Canova in the Vatican based on the antique Rondanini Medusa, *Perseus with the Head of Medusa*, first shown in 1801, he may have read Shelley's seminal fragment *On the Medusa of Leonardo da Vinci in the Florentine Gallery* (1819). As in romantic iconography, so for Haggard the witch's head represented an equivocal beauty, that intrinsic doubleness in which life and death, beauty and horror, good and evil, spring and winter, tyranny and freedom, ceaselessly pass into each other. Haggard's wholesome heroine Dorothy wants it cast back into the sea. She echoes what Goethe's Mephistopheles says to Faust when he sees an image of his Margaret: "'Let it be—pass on—no good can come of it—it is not well to meet it—it is an enchanted phantom, a lifeless idol; with its numbing look, it freezes up the blood of man; and they who meet its ghastly stare are turned to stone, like those who saw Medusa.'"32

When Reginald Cardus has the witch's head hung in a case on a bracket "that jutted from the oak panelling at the end of the room,"33 Haggard is creating a visual arrangement just a bit less complex than the *pinacotheca* of the Roman villa in Walter Pater's *Marius the Epicurean* (1885). Pater's Medusa, "drawn up in a fisherman's net, with the fine golden *laminae* still clinging here and there to the bronze"34 also embodies the malevolent spirit of the waves. But the curious form of Pater's room, oddly oval, suggests binary foci with the head of Medusa perhaps positioned at one focus and with the beholder standing at the other interchangeable focus—a sinister arrangement. This exactly symbolizes the intrinsic doubleness and diabolic polarization of her ambiguous roles as preserver and destroyer. Like Foulata and Gagool in *King Solomon's Mines*, the two sisters, Eva (originally the Graeco-Roman form of Eve, "life," the mother of us all) and Florence (from Flora, the Roman goddess of spring and flowers) play out the ancient fertility cycle of Kore and Persephone. Here love and life in its innocence are destroyed by the treacherous jealousy of Florence—the Medusa of Leonardo in the gallery at Florence, if you will. Ernest's perilous obsession with Eva and, by extension, her Medusan alter ego, could certainly have been consciously connected by Haggard to African ritual masks—ancestral spirits, spells and taboos—but he may have also intended a psychosexual meaning. Not only Goethe, but Dante earlier had construed Medusa as a seductive temptress. She is that which is primordial and subversive within the erotic, including the subliminal threat of a devouring female sexuality.

When, at the end of Haggard's novel, Ernest returns from the slaughter of Isandhlwana, blinded by lightning, his theurgic cicatrix is really the hero's mark of triumph and renewal.35 In *The Witch's Head* Haggard had introduced the parodic figure of an insane wandering German, Hans, who like Bunyan's pilgrim seeks the Celestial City of Rustenberg and the Tree of Life.36 Hans's visionary Tree of Life is not unlike the tree of the cross in Schreiner's *Trooper Peter* and *The Wizard*, to be discussed in chapter six. And protected by his insanity because the Zulus consider the mad to be inspired,37 Hans partakes in the occult like their wizards. Hans describes his cart, built as a hearse, as his wife. Thus, married to his coffin, Hans on the "middle veldt" ironizes as a fallen Eden Fred Fynney's horticultural reference to the Rustenberg district as "the Garden of the Transvaal."38 When Ernest is rescued on the veldt by Hans, he sleeps inside this coffin-wife, "buried alive," but is awakened by its collapse in a parodic "resurrection."39 Like the nomadic Hans, Ernest after Eva jilted him had been roaming southern Africa in disillusionment with multiple "love affairs" and, in search of death, leading a frustratingly charmed existence.40 Hans's rescue of Ernest on the Rustenberg Road has the allegorical significance of a divine intervention in satiric disguise. If we consider Hans a sort of missionary-to-one, with his prophetic warning to Ernest of the trial from heaven in the form of his blindness by lightning,41 then Ernest becomes a Saul of Tarsus to Hans's Stephen. Hans is not violently and heroically martyred, nor does Ernest miraculously receive again his sight; but as Hans like Stephen "fell asleep" (Acts 7:60) in vision, so Ernest recovers not sight but love in the person of Dorothy back in England. As on the road to Damascus, so in nineteenth-century Africa, the miracles of the early church transpire for those who have "eyes to see."

At the conclusion, Medusa's case is knocked open by a falling gauntlet and old Atterleigh, Cardus's scrivener, looks into her crystal eyes, as at the beginning Florence had gazed into those eyes "seeking an inspiration";42 and so, like the swine suddenly possessed with devils (Matthew 8:3), he plunges into the quicksand with Ernest's African stallion "Devil" and the broken assegai from Isandhlwana:

> On at whirlwind speed towards the shuddering quicksand two hundred yards away!
>
> *Splash!* Horse and man are in it, making the moist mass shake and tremble for twenty yards round. The bright moonlight shows it all. The horse

shrieks in fear and agony, as only a horse can; the man on its back waves the spear.

The horse vanishes, the man vanishes; the spear glitters an instant longer in the moonlight, and then vanishes too.[43]

Medusa's evil spirit is exorcized and returned to the marshes and quicksand. The reason why the witch's curse fell upon Ernest is as mysterious as why Dorothy's love should finally save him; given a sufficient explanation, the myth vanishes.

Among Haggard's shorter fictions examining plighted troth, as a variation on the disloyalty of Eva, is "The Blue Curtains." Set in Natal and London during the "Basuto wars in the Cape Colony,"[44] a period more or less bracketing the Zulu War of 1879, and ranging as far north as the Zambezi falls, "The Blue Curtains" first appeared in the *Cornhill Magazine* in 1886 and then was collected in *Smith and the Pharaohs and Other Tales* in 1920–1921. Its subject is Haggard's personal preoccupation with betrayal in love. Bottles is a British trooper jilted by his London fiancée, Madeline, who succumbs to family pressure and marries a much older, wealthier and titled suitor. Bottles is magnanimous in forgiving and carries a perpetual torch for her. One recalls Lovelace's lines "To Lucasta": "I could not love thee, Dear, so much, / Loved I not Honor more." Like his gentleman's and military honor, this "beautiful delusion"[45] becomes necessary to his existence. The motifs of red camellias and blue curtains suggest the wounds of love and his compensatory holy-heavenly ideal.

The denouement has Bottles's former fiancée, now widowed and again available, asking if he had known the officer—Bottles himself—whose "mad or inspired"[46] act of military bravery was so widely admired. Without his knowledge and against all honor his soldiers had fired on a flag of truce, and Bottles had then ridden to the enemy kraal to apologize to the chief. The outcome was that when several of Bottles's troopers were captured they were not tortured to death but returned by the chief "with a message to the effect that he would show the English officer that he was not the only man who could behave 'like a gentleman.'"[47] Bottles's "mad or inspired" battlefield gesture suggests that insanity and inspiration may be more alike than one would believe. Whereas Bottles's gesture of honor had been reciprocated by the chief, his fidelity to Madeline has not been and will not be. She lacks the integrity of a savage African. And unlike Kurtz's Intended, Bottles is not spared the modern horror. Thus when he stoops to spy on Madeline from behind her blue curtains and his brother shows how truly mercenary she is, Bottles discovers not only that he has lost her but that he has now also forfeited his honor. He takes his life with a sleeping potion. Shallow and selfish, Madeline has no inkling: "To this day she tells the story as a frightful warning against the careless use of chloral."48

༺ ༻

Coinciding with the fracas over "About Fiction," *Jess* (1887) was critically eclipsed and has never received the acclaim it deserves as one of the great novels of South Africa's tragic, blood stained history. In the same year he praised Olive Schreiner's *The Story of an African Farm* in "About Fiction," Haggard broke with his defense of romance to write his own realistic story of an African farm. Similarities between these works proliferate owing in large part to each author's awareness of the other's work in the presentation of life as it actually was in rural colonial Africa. Jess—the diminutive of Jessica—looks back both to Schreiner's strong-willed heroine Lyndall and forward to her figure of Rebecca in *From Man to Man*. Jess is not as obviously beautiful as Lyndall, but Haggard's stress on her eyes as windows of an independent and superb spirit, her depth of intellect, and her yearning for an ideal love fated to be frustrated by social codes, nature, and war—all these qualities hark back to Lyndall. Haggard's images and speculative phraseology (as in the transition from chapter eighteen through the first pages of chapter nineteen) as well as his reflections on love and the life of nature are powerfully reminiscent of Schreiner. In all but the more classic causality of plot events in *Jess*, the two works are comparable explorations of colonial feminine psychology. If Schreiner pushed the novelistic envelope by creating a pregnant, unmarried heroine whom the reader is expected to admire, not patronize with fashionable pity, Haggard's Jess is no less socially singular. In the moment when the crisis reaches its greatest intensity, Jess creeps silently into the tent of the sleeping Boer commander, the villainous Frank Muller, and like Jael in the book of Judges bloodily kills him with a Kaffir hunting knife. Perhaps because the plots of High Victorian novels had not yet visualized any way to fulfill the spiritual aspirations of such socially vivid, transgressive women, both must die—physically, if not spiritually—to resolve the plot action. One is tempted to observe that later Schreiner's *From Man to Man* borrows the structure of Jess's sibling relationships in creating an older intellectual heroine and a younger more beautiful but conventional sister—Bessie in *Jess* and Bertie in *From Man to Man*.

Coming hard on the heels of *King Solomon's Mines* and *She, Jess* appears to be Haggard's final bid to achieve recognition in the dominant mode of the realistic novel. Set on an ostrich-farm in the Transvaal, and climaxing with the events of the retrocession in 1880–1881, the autobiographical echoes of Haggard's own experiences in those years are inescapable. As much as *Jess* owes to *The Story of an African Farm* it may owe more to contemporary political events—if not necessarily more to Haggard's own ostrich farming. Captain John Neil has left the army to buy a share of Silas Croft's farm, Mooifontain, in the Transvaal near the border with Natal. (Neil retired much as had Good from the navy, Haggard perhaps suggesting that the military too often discharges as supernumerary its most worthy warriors.) As Schreiner's novel had been a polemic against a narrow patriarchal religion and women's subjugation, so Haggard's is an assault on the political establishment in England. Written only a half dozen years after the retrocession, the novel opens with a killer-ostrich attack that establishes character and foreshadows the larger political turmoil to come. Old Silas Croft's English patriotism and brutal treatment at the hands of the Boers clearly conveys Haggard's overt anger at what he sees as the British betrayal of the English colonists and British soldiers in the Transvaal: "But, after all, what does it matter?—a little square of neglected graves at Bronker's Spruit, a few more widows, and a hundred or so of orphans. England, by her government, answered the question plainly—it matters very little."[49]

Haggard is even willing to have the Boers throw back at the British the contemptuous characterization of them by Napoleon as "a nation of shopkeepers." Paul Kruger (unnamed here because he was still a potent political figure in 1887) says of the Englishman:

> "He knows nothing—nothing. He understands his shop, he is buried in his shop, and can think of nothing else. Sometimes he goes away and starts his shop in other places, and buries himself in it, and makes it a big shop, because he understands shops. But it is all a question of shops, and if the shops abroad interfere with the shops at home, or if it is thought that they do, which comes to the same thing, then the shops at home put an end to the shops abroad. Bah! they talk a great deal there in England, but, at the bottom of it, it is shop, shop, shop. They talk of honor and patriotism too, but they both give way to the shop."[50]

"Oom Paulus" clearly serves as the mouthpiece for the author on this issue of British hypocrisy and political opportunism; and Haggard knows the truth always stings most when uttered by those one scorns. But though the Boers are presented as violent and uncultivated (compare, for example, the amusing description in chapter ten with that of Schreiner in part two, chapters five and six of *The Story of an African Farm*) they are not entirely without conscience or pity.[51] It is no coincidence that the opportunistic villain of the novel is himself racially half British, half Boer.

Engaged to the beautiful younger sister Bessie, John travels during the Boer uprising to Pretoria to bring Jess back to the farm. Because of the hostilities, they are ordered "into laager." Occupying a safe and idyllic cottage during this threat of attack, Jess and John fall into unspoken love. Muller arranges a safe-conduct pass out of Pretoria for the two, intending them to die by drowning in fording the Vaal. Caught in their floating cart and supposing themselves about to die, John and Jess are now free to confess their mutual passion. Surviving, the two reproach themselves so totally that the reader may be impelled to go back in the narrative to find the missed scene of passion—did two pages get turned at once? But their intercourse was purely of the nineteenth-century variety, verbal and social. "Operatic melodrama" is one's first reaction until one recollects the river boating expedition in George Eliot's *Mill on the Floss* (1860) in which Maggie and Stephen are innocent but irremediably disgraced. Those socially constructed codes were not stopgap theatrical props for the faltering imagination of the storyteller but were as tangible in social relationships as a laager's barricade was to military tactics. Muller, supposing the two dead, goes to arrest and condemn Silas for treason, intending to use the danger of her uncle's death to force Bessie to marry him. Separated by the Boers from John, Jess returns to Mooifontain and secretly dispatches Muller, after which she and John by chance meet in a secluded kloof-cave. She dies of exhaustion and not even John suspects her role in Muller's death, which is widely assumed to be revenge by one or another native servant. Her death allows the novel to conclude with John and Bessie united, much like Gregory and Em in Schreiner's story; but like Gregory's love for Lyndall, John's prosaic marriage to Bessie will always remain shadowed by his greater love of his lost soul mate, Jess. This certainly is an echo of Ernest's earlier predicament in being unable to shake off the influence of Florence because "what we are now passing through is but a single phase of interwoven existence." Dorothy answers:

> "Ernest, I daresay your belief is a true one, at any rate for you who believe it, for it seems probable that as we sow so shall we reap, as we spiritually imagine so shall we spiritually inherit, since causes must in time produce effects. These beliefs are not implanted in our hearts for nothing, and surely in the wide heavens there is room for the realisation of them all.

But I too have my beliefs, and one of them is, that in God's great hereafter every loving and desiring soul will be with the soul thus loved and desired. For him or her, at any rate, the other will be there, forming a part of his or her life, though, perhaps, it may elsewhere and with others also be pursuing its own desires and satisfying its own aspirations. So you see, Ernest, your beliefs will not interfere with mine, nor shall I be afraid of losing you in another place."[52]

Haggard's saga of the Transvaal, *Swallow, A Tale of the Great Trek* (1899), is less an adventure fantasy than a historical novel, serialized in the *Graphic* from July through October 1898 and issued in book form by Longmans, Green in New York and London, February–March 1899. Set during the Boers' Great Trek of 1836–1838, its timing could not have been worse from the point of British sales, appearing barely six months before the outbreak of the Anglo-Boer War. Even its proofreading seems unusually negligent, although its transposition of a whole line[53] is not wholly unique. One might assume that anti-Boer sympathies would bubble to its surface, since it was composed during the rising tensions between the Boer republics and the British *Uitlanders* who were soliciting full political rights. But Haggard's dedication to Marshal Clarke suggests otherwise:

> You, as I know, entertain both for Dutchman and Bantu that regard tempered by a sense of respectful superiority which we are apt to feel for those who on sundry occasions have but just failed in bringing our earthly career to an end.... I hope that the dour but not unkindly character of Vrouw Botmar will prove to you, time softens a man's judgment. Nor have I ever questioned, as the worthy Vrouw tells us, that in the beginning of the trouble the Boers met with much of which to complain at the hands of English Governments. Their maltreatment was not intentional indeed, but rather a result of the systematic neglect—to use a mild word—of colonies and their inhabitants.... At the least, allowance should always be made for the susceptibilities of a race that finds its individuality and national life sinking slowly, but without hope of resurrection, beneath an invading flood of Anglo-Saxons.[54]

Ralph, the castaway Scottish boy adopted by the Boers who becomes Suzanne's beloved, is almost Haggard's justification for a European solidarity that recognizes the best in a Boer upbringing.

The *Bookman* compared *Swallow* to *Jess* in its closeness to real life that made it more convincing than sensational. Indeed, it was rated by one early reviewer, Katharine Woods, as superior to Schreiner's *The*

Story of an African Farm.[55] Clearly the emphasis in both novels on characterization and common life might suggest a likeness. And both novels have an amusingly masculinized Boer farm wife; Haggard's *vrouw* loves her husband resolutely yet pronounces him "stupid."[56] The apter comparison of *Swallow*, however, is with Haggard's earlier *Jess*. In both Haggard presents the Boers as flawed and refractory but with a code of honor; in this novel Suzanne is pursued by the villainous Black Piet whereas in *Jess* Jess is pursued by Frank Muller. But Haggard's empathetic strategy of putting his story into the mouth of the ancient *vrouw* falters. Carried along on the flow of his narrative, he ignores his first-person observer and doesn't really capitalize on her ethnic quiddity, though her dogmatic mistakenness about scientific facts is surely right on target as is her desire to hang "the accursed missionaries of the London Society,"[57] which reflects a historical anger at what the Boers considered their cynical manipulation of the British government with accusations of Boer cruelty. But because the old *vrouw* is more observer than participant, the characteristic first-person immediacy is largely dissipated.

Once again, the villain of the piece is stock, though his mixed Boer-African heritage reflects a more extreme combination than in other Haggard tales, such as Frank in *Jess* who had been Boer-British. The advantageousness of national and racial mixing is by no means explicit in Haggard's opinion. Quatermain, on the one hand, speaks for conventional British standards of racial purity, the greatness of "untainted" British blood,[58] when he suggests that Good's love of Foulata is socially undesirable; on the other, the reader's sympathies are fully enlisted in this British-African romance, as they are time and again with the incipient possibilities represented by Mameena (*Child of Storm*), Sabeela (*Heu-Heu*), Nobela (*Finished*) or Shadow (*Treasure of the Lake*). Moreover, Nada's or Nanea's mixed heritages (in *Nada* and *Black Heart*) are certainly advantageous to their beauty. However, describing an English-French Creole heritage, Haggard's Leonard asserts that "crossbred dogs are fierce";[59] similarly in *Jess*, Haggard comments on Frank Muller that "you can deal with a Boer and you can deal with an Englishman, but cross-bred dogs are bad to handle."[60] Elsewhere Quatermain observes that a band of "mixed-bloods,"[61] the children of a Scotsman and native women, are "demoralized" by conflict; and in his own prefatory comments to "Elissa" Haggard describes the gold trading empire of Zimbabwe as "weakened by luxury and the mixture of races."[62] As Olive Schreiner had observed, crossbreeding in domestic animals produces a reversion "to that original parent stock from which both varieties have descended." So also "there is a danger, and we are inclined to believe a very great danger, of reversion to the lower primitive type where two widely severed varieties cross, that humanity may in that process lose the results of hundreds of years of slow evolution.... When from under the beetling eyebrows in a dark face something of the white man's eye looks out at us, is not the curious shrinking and aversion we feel somewhat of a consciousness of a national disgrace and sin?"[63]

Perhaps what alarmed Haggard about miscegenation was not genetic as much as it was environmental. One need hardly observe that in the colonies mixed blood both carried a social stigma and blocked career opportunities. More complexly, analyzing the Boer-British character of Frank Muller in *Jess*, Haggard like Conrad in *Heart of Darkness* comments on civilization's restraints upon man's innately sinful self:

> Left to ourselves ... we become outwardly that which the spirit within would fashion us to, but, placed among our fellows, shackled by custom, restrained by law, pruned and bent by the force of public opinion, we grow as like one to another as the fruit-bushes on a garden wall.... The place of a man like Frank Muller is at the junction of the waters of civilization and barbarism. Too civilized to possess those savage virtues which, such as they are, represent the *quantum* of innate good Nature has thought fit to allow in the mixture man, and too barbarous to be subject to the tenderer restraints of cultivated society, he is at once strong in the strength of both and weak in their weaknesses.[64]

But if mixing is environmentally a weakness, perhaps on occasion it may be genetically a strength—after all, Smut in *She and Allan* and Stump in *Treasure Lake*[65] were crossbred dogs, fierce because they were loyal to the death. Thus the wizard Noie, a mixed breed (half dwarf-folk and half Zulu), loves Rachel,[66] saves her life at the cost of her own life, and like the witch doctoress Sihamba in *Swallow*, facilitates the heroine's marriage to her soul mate. In *Allan's Wife*, Haggard actually gives us the missing link in the baboon-woman Hendrika, almost as human as a Bushman.[67] Hendrika, too, was preternaturally powerful; her loyalty and love for her mistress absolute, but also ungovernable and destructive. And in the opening pages of Sol Plaatje's *Mhudi* the crossbreeding experiment of a Bechuana tribesman proved so disastrous that "attempts at cross-breeding thereafter became taboo."[68] While Plaatje's incident may prefigure the ill-advised political cross-alliance of Boer and native against Mzilikazi, it also suggests that such mixing unleashed an uncontrollable power. But when the dynamic qualities of wildness, passion, and terror invest the formal values of refinement, breeding, and tradition, then social exhaustion is repaired. Even without racial mixing the "second sight" of Rachel in *Ghost Kings* and the telepathy of Suzanne in *Swallow*[69] are primitive powers that enhance the "effete Caucasian."[70] In *Swallow* Ralph is Scottish whereas his "Intended," Suzanne, is Dutch-French—might not the cultural obstacles between these young lovers resemble for Haggard the feared genetic consequences of racial mixing, both fostered by fear of breaking the manacles of nationality, language, religion?

※ ※

Among Haggard's numerous imitators of African romance, possibly the first and among the best was Bertram Mitford—although since Mitford's *The Gun-Runner* was published in 1882, who imitated whom is rather ambiguous. As presented to the readers of the *Eastern Daily Press*, Mitford, like Haggard, "is a quick writer.... Twenty-three years ago he went to South Africa, and during his long stay there became personally acquainted with Cetewayo and all the prominent Zulu chiefs and leading men who engineered the Kaffir war of 1877, on the Cape border."[71] In 1894 Mitford published *The King's Assegai*, set in the western Transvaal, the first romance in an "all Zulu" quartet, doubtless inspired by Haggard's *Nada the Lily*. Mitford's narrative like *Nada* is an elegy on the loss of Zulu Matabele nationality. Though its outer-frame narration is pointedly set overlooking Ulundi after 1879,[72] his storyteller Untúswa focuses not on Shaka's empire building, but on Mzilikazi's hacking out "a new nation"[73] between the Vaal and Zambezi. Among Mitford's indubitable talents is writing rousing scenes of native battles. *The King's Assegai* opens with an internecine fight,[74] and from there on the forward momentum of the plot is largely fueled by further warfare interspersed with the hero's lovemaking[75]—his relations are carnal, but so bowdlerized that the term "courtship" is descriptively more applicable. Like Umslopogaas, Mitford's Zulu is a youthful running and fighting machine; and like Mopo, he has a familiar relationship with the king, whose "dark handled assegai," like Shaka's small red-wood assegai, he now owns.[76] Despite a finely depicted Zulu witch doctor, an excellently morbid scene of cannibal prisoners, and arresting descriptions of Zulu tactics and other military details, Mitford's greatest achievement is heuristic, inasmuch as the novel's traits clarify or substantiate Haggard's achievements. *The King's Assegai* lacks the chillingly powerful imagery and mythic action of *Nada*, and there is less emphasis upon psychology. Mzilikazi as king is much less complex than Shaka, and Untúswa has a simpler motivation than Umslopogaas—that is, to get the girl, to rise in social station. His goal is Victorian social advancement, enjoyed as valuable in its own right; and neither comedy nor tragedy plays into his rise. Indeed, in this tale all turns out "happily ever after"—well, maybe the girl was not the wife he'd envisioned, but hearts here are never broken. Only later in Mitford's quartet of novels do love and misfortune grow in emotional intensity. Here there is no consideration of the Zulu human condition, unless it is the warriors' willingness to die fighting—that is, nothing existential since the hero does not suspect an incompatibility between human desire and its fulfillment. Mitford does incorporate praise poems/songs and Zulu terms and customs, and this ethnographic detail is certainly integral to the action and to the establishment of character and motive. It has been said, most inaccurately, that since Zulu history, religion, and poetic lore are not specifically part of Untúswa's psychological matrix, the novel seems more like a purely white-invented fiction, all Mitford in black face.[77] But that is certainly too narrow a judgment, similar to those leveled at Haggard for being an imperialist.

Haggard's *Marie* was originally serialized in *Cassell's Magazine* from September 1911 through the following February and published in London by Cassell (January 1912) and in New York by Longmans (in March) with the added subtitle: *An Episode in the Life of the Late Allan Quatermain*. It was the first of a trilogy on Zulu history following *Nada* and may owe much to the concept of Mitford's four linked Matabele novels written between 1894 and 1902, the first of which had been *The King's Assegai*. Set against the backdrop of the Boer's Great Trek in the 1830s, *Marie* opens in the era of the Kaffir War of 1835, alternatively called the Sixth Border War,[78] and moves to the Retief massacre and its aftermath in February 1838. Whereas *Nada* and the later *Child of Storm* (1913) are focused entirely on Zulu history, *Marie* omits native magic and ritual—i.e., the mythopoeic, except for a telepathic voice[79]—and dwells on Boer society and the historical Boer-Zulu clashes. As an instance of early-twentieth-century colonial historiography, Haggard's *Marie* might well earn respect as an alternative to the racist paradigm at the core of antiblack historiography in which the invaders disguise or misrepresent their predatory expansion by denying that they are destroying anything of value, defining the natives' oral traditions and their land as an emptiness waiting to be filled either with a European spiritual message in the Bible Society's innumerable translations or with gold and diamond mining, not to mention Mistah Kurtz's dark-hearted ivory trading. George McCall Theal's eleven-volume *History of South Africa* (1910) and its pro-colonial celebration of the Boer's trek still awaited its popularization in the early twentieth century. Haggard's retelling of the Great Trek differs substantially from the principal myth that it became in twentieth-century white South Africa in which the natives with "no God, no morality, no history"[80] struggled against the forces of civilization and were conquered.

Marie is a tale of how Allan Quatermain met his first wife, Marie Marais, and the historical events linked to her tragic history. This earliest chronicle of his life begins just past childhood. The two villains, both of whom desire Marie, are the Zulu chief, Dingaan, Shaka's brother (who had a lecherous desire for Nada also), and a Portuguese cad, Hernan Pereira, who not only is trying to rob Allan of Marie but plots to kill him if necessary. Haggard's clunky overuse of coincidences and close calls;[81] the worthy but disadvantaged (poor, English) lover Allan, who both is and is not like Saduko in *Child of Storm*; the cartoonish stage villain Pereira;[82] the failure of the romantic heroine, Marie, to rise above a sterile stereotype of beautiful innocence; and the star-crossed fate of the lovers, anticipated by Foulata and Nada—all here are the failings of formulaic romance writing in the period. Then, too, Haggard trots out several stock situations specific to his fiction: an attack on the homestead,[83] as earlier in *Allan Quatermain*;[84] a shooting match,[85] as occurs again later in *The Ivory Child*;[86] a prophetic pronouncement[87] of Gagool's sort in *King Solomon's Mines*,[88] and so forth. And yet for all this situational reiteration, the novel holds the reader's interest. There is a reason for such recurrence that does not involve a failure of imagination. All artists invoke personal archetypes and conventional situations—and whether the devil or God is in the details, such particulars endow the recurring patterns and stereotypes with permanent appeal.

Haggard, like Milton describing Satan, writes more effectively of evil women than of the nobly feminine; but if Marie as romantic heroine is a stock figure, she is very effectively visualized as a young child. In this, Haggard may well have learned much from Schreiner about the double alienation of a European in Africa and of a woman in a colonial patriarchy. Of course, Marie was a Boer and Schreiner's Lyndall was Anglo-African, but both were pawns in the three-way tension between the British, Boer and African cultural forces, as well as victims of societal tensions between children and adults, males and females. As a female child on the frontier and as a young adult, Marie expresses a feminist will.[89] In this, she rises above the stereotyped female so outrageously satirized by Oscar Wilde in *The Importance of Being Earnest*. Marie is not unlike Mitford's Nidia Commerell in *John Ames, Native Commissioner* (1900)—both could be incipient types of Gwendolyn and Cecily, except for their presence on the imperial frontier. Mitford's Nidia's face "had a way of lighting up—a sudden lifting of the eyelashes, the breaking into a half smile, revealing a row of teeth beautifully even and white. She had blue eyes, and her hair, which was neither brown nor golden, but something between, curled in soft natural waves along the brow"[90]—and so on for many more words. But on a visit to Matabeleland, unfortunately timed to coincide with the 1893 rising, she returns from a pleasant walk to encounter: "On the couch beneath the window aforesaid lay the form of Hollingworth—the form, for little else about the wretched man was distinguishable but his clothing. His skull had been battered in, and his features smashed to a pulp.... In one corner lay the corpse of his wife—and, in a row, four children, all with their skulls smashed, and nailed to the ground with assegais."[91] Take a beautiful girl, put her in a world of "hideous butchery," and if she doesn't faint (or even if she does) she will improve characterologically. Suddenly, not only her circumstances but for the reader she herself becomes much more absorbing.

In *Marie* the violence begins with a similar attack on the homestead to which Marie offers sturdy resistance. The theme of carnage culminates when Allan accompanies the ill-fated Pieter Retief and the Boer Commission on their historical embassy to Dingaan that ends in a blood-curdling massacre. In Haggard's account, the half-breed Portuguese Pereira instigates this massacre, although the Boers suppose it to be "through the treachery of the English, who arranged with Dingaan that he should kill them."[92] Haggard is concerned here to repudiate the misapprehension of British complicity, in part because although English and Afrikaners had been mortal enemies in the Anglo-Boer War, after Union in 1910 this more-brotherly version of the Afrikaner myth might serve to promote white reconciliation and nation building—at the expense of a black nationalism that, in light of the Matabele rising of 1893, foreshadowed the possibility of becoming increasingly confrontational. Although Haggard supports the Afrikaner struggle against hostile international British capitalism, he only hints at native slavery as an issue underlying the Trek and casts Dingaan as a superstitious and vicious despot, not a leader whose land is being invaded by a people of unprecedented power. *Marie* does not consciously ignore the issue of land rights; rather, the novel applies the dominant historical parameters of the last two centuries, particularly the Anglo-European prerogative of a benevolent and just colonization.

Haggard and Schreiner did not believe in a benevolent imperialism simply because they were patriarchal colonists blinded by beams in their eyes. But neither Haggard nor Schreiner can match Mitford in a pro-Zulu explanation of the Retief massacre. In *The Induna's Wife* (1898) Untúswa explains:

> It is said by you white people, *Nkose* [lit. "chief," Zulu address of respect] that Dingane acted a cruel and treacherous part in thus causing the leaders of the Amabuna [Boers, fr. *ama* people of + *buna*, alt. *booma* "boom," the roar of their guns] to be slain. That may be, when seen with a white man's eyes. But seen with ours the thing is different. These Amabuna had come to take a large portion of the Zulu country from the Zulu people, and, had they done so, how long would it have been before they had taken the whole? They made a show of asking the land from the King, but had Dingane refused to listen to them, would they have gone back the way they came? Is that the manner of the Amabuna, I would ask you, *Nkose*? Again, if their hearts were good, and free from deceit, why did they not send messengers to Nkunkundhlovu ["trumpeting elephant," Dingaan's kraal] before they entered the land as they did, to obtain the answer of the King and the Zulu people? But instead of doing this, they came over Kwahlamba [the border river] in great numbers, with their horses and their guns, their waggons and their oxen, their cattle and their women, falling upon the land like a vast swarm of devouring locusts. Whether they obtained leave or not, they had come to stay, and that we did not wish; and further, by thus entering the Zulu country in armed force without the King's permission, they had deserved death.[93]

One is reminded of the Ibo's response to nature's "devouring locusts" in Achebe's *Things Fall Apart* (1958)—the pestilential insects are roasted and eaten as a delicacy. If Dingaan's was an overreaction by European standards, Mitford's implication here and in a following paragraph is that by Zulu custom it was not. Even by modern international standards an *ex post facto* exchange with the sovereign after an invasion has taken place does not mitigate the aggression. Later in Mitford's narrative a Boer kangaroo court executes Dingaan's emissaries with less debate than Dingaan had devoted to Retief's party.

Unlike Haggard, who isolates a dastardly Portuguese half-breed and a crazed wizard as instigators of the massacre, Mitford lays the blame squarely on the Boers themselves. Of course, the British "take" on the Boers in 1898 facilitated this interpretation; Haggard, on the other hand, remained sufficiently pro-Boer through the events of the Anglo-

Boer war and after so as to allow a mainly Afrikaner explanation to dominate. An explanation similar to Haggard's is proffered in the early film *Die Voortrekers / Winning a Continent* (1916), scripted by the historian Gustav Preller, a champion of the as-yet-unofficial Afrikaans language. The film's dual language intertitles make clear that two Portuguese traders, resenting the fair "trade valuations" of the Boers, foment the massacre by poisoning the king's mind. By contrast, just prior to the above-quoted passage, Mitford's Boers had begun their discussion with Dingaan by outrageously declaring that the Zulu land they desired "was little used, if at all,"[94] a provocative assertion that echoes John Ruskin's ethnocentric concept of "fruitful waste ground."[95] Possibly what Mitford tells us is less effective than what Haggard shows us, but surely Mitford's narrator (very much the author's mouthpiece) has taken a principled stand unusual for the nineteenth century. He denounces

> the senselessness of deciding offhand the morality of this or that deed which helpeth to make history from one hard-and-fast point of view, and that point of view the British; or of stigmatising even a savage potentate as a treacherous and cruel monster, because he is not particular as to his methods when it becomes a question of preserving his nation's rights and his nation's greatness, what time such are threatened and invaded by Christians, whom subsequent events show to be the reverse of models of uprightness or fair dealing themselves.[96]

Haggard certainly seems vastly more pro-European. Dingaan is a "black-hearted villain"[97] and Quatermain meditates this eulogy: "Those poor Boers, whatever their faults, and they had many, like the rest of us, were in the main good and honest men according to their lights. Yet they had been doomed to be thus brutally butchered at the nod of a savage despot, their wives widowed, their children left fatherless, or, as it proved in the end, in most cases murdered or orphaned!"[98] Whereas Mitford claims the Boers were "the reverse of models of uprightness or fair dealing," Haggard says that they were "in the main good and honest men." Ultimately the full extent of the Trek's underlying problems of slavery and land rights is not again after Mitford directly addressed in a major novel until Sol Plaatje's *Mhudi* (1930).

Spencer Blackett issued *Allan's Wife and Other Tales* in December 1889 with thirty-four in-text vignettes and illustration plates by Maurice Grieffenhagen and Charles Kerr, "printed in a superior manner on good paper, and tastefully bound"[99]—in every way a deluxe edition very different from the lackluster uniform volumes of the twentieth century. Its title novella appeared here for the first time; the three other tales were all previously published African hunting stories about Quatermain's close escapes from misadventure: "Hunter Quatermain's Story" (published 1885), "A Tale of Three Lions" (1887; a variant, possibly its original version for younger readers appeared in 1898 under the title "Allan the Hunter"), and "Long Odds" (1886, revised for this 1889 collection). Not unlike so many other tales of Quatermain purported to have been written by him and then edited by H. Rider Haggard for publication, these also are retrospective narratives ostensibly told to Haggard and his companions Good and Sir Henry in the oak-paneled trophy room of Quatermain's comfortable Yorkshire manor. This took place during the three years after Allan's adventures in Kukuanaland (which occurred in the wake of the Zulu War, as dated in the "Editor's Note" to *Marie*) and not long before his death in the Zu-Vendis country of central Africa as narrated in *Allan Quatermain*.[100] Plainly, these tales are set many years earlier than their 1881–1884 telling. The story of Stella, Allan's second wife, belongs to the early 1840s, and the three hunting tales more or less to the decade and a half after the Zulu battle of the Tugela (1856).

Because "Hunter Quatermain's Story" appeared in June 1885, some three months before *King Solomon's Mines*, it is actually the first Quatermain story published, and it advertises the forthcoming novel by alluding to "strange rumours that are flying about to the effect that Sir Henry Curtis and his friend Captain Good, R.N., recently found a vast treasure of diamonds out in the heart of Africa, supposed to have been hidden by the Egyptians, or King Solomon, or some other antique person."[101] "Three Lions," which begins with a stint by Allan as an unsuccessful gold miner, is narrated in the archetypal form of later Ernest Hemingway safari tales. Son Harry, now fourteen, accompanied his father on this expedition[102] and nearly brings the hunt to disaster by prematurely firing at the lions, a hint that Harry has not inherited his father's skill or caution, especially given that later, not long before the telling of this story, he accidentally shoots Sir Henry in the leg.[103] The final story in the volume, "Long Odds," is a tale of Quatermain's mauling by a lion which occurred in 1869.[104] Since Quatermain makes reference to the mauling of David Livingstone whom he "knew very well,"[105] one suspects Haggard modeled Quatermain's limp on Livingstone's originative account, brilliantly positioned by author or publisher at the very outset of *Missionary Travels*, an anecdote that Selous also distinctly recollects.106 Haggard's opening scene of a kraal emptied by fever,107 both epidemiological and uncanny by turns, is in its way as unforgettably dramatic as Livingstone's narrative vignette.

The burden of all these tales, and of Haggard's fiction generally, is the intensity and delight of a life poised against death, the life and death of both the hunter and the hunted. In the title story, Haggard describes the morning mist on the veldt from which

> come strange sounds—snorts, gruntings, bellows, and the thunder of countless hoofs. Presently this great curtain would grow thinner, then it would melt, as the smoke from a pipe melts into the air, and for miles on miles the wide rolling country interspersed with bush opened to the view. But it was not tenantless as it is now, for as far as the eye could reach it would be literally black with game.108

Suddenly a tired buck, chased by hyenas, appears and "looks wildly round and sees the waggon. He seems to hesitate a moment, then in his despair rushes up to it, and falls exhausted among the oxen." Quatermain kills the hyenas with a shotgun loaded with loopers (slugs) and saves the buck. Then without transition he comments: "Ah, how beautiful is nature before man comes to spoil it! Such a sight as this have I seen many a hundred times, and I hope to see it again before I die."109 Killing the predators, saving the buck, sharpens his love of this panorama with its herds of vilderbeestes, springbok, giraffes, and blesbock and, indeed, allows him to contemplate his own demise as a component of the rolling country's vista. Even in *King Solomon's Mines* the beauty-danger motif crops up on the desert in the purple prose of Haggard's description of a breathtakingly beautiful dawn that may well bring to the adventurers their hot death by thirst. This indispensable closeness of life and death, the beauty of nature and its lethality, is a leitmotif in Haggard that later writers of hunting tales, particularly Hemingway, assimilated and reproduced as their personal credo. Game in Haggard's time was, certainly, more of a renewable resource than at present, although in "A Zulu War-Dance" and elsewhere Haggard deplores the over-hunting that occurs. And at least by 1908 Haggard describes, forgivingly yet regretfully, a young hunter's bloodlust:

> About thirty yards away to the right, looming very large through the dense fog, stood the fat reed buck. Richard wriggled towards it, for he wanted to make sure of his shot, while Rachel crouched behind a stone. The buck becoming alarmed, turned its head, and began to sniff at the air, whereon he lifted the gun and just as it was about to spring away, aimed and fired. Down it went dead, whereon, rejoicing in his triumph like any other young hunter who thinks not of the wonderful and happy

life that he has destroyed, Richard sprang upon it exultantly, drawing his knife as he came, while Rachel, who always shrank from such sights, retreated to the cave. Half an hour later, however, being healthy and hungry, she had no objection to eating venison toasted upon sticks in the red embers of their fire.110

More typically, as in *King Solomon's Mines*, hunger blots quite out all humane reflections: "the smoke cleared, and revealed—oh, joy!—a great buck lying on its back and kicking furiously in its death agony. We gave a yell of triumph—we were saved, we should not starve."111

One very curious exception to Haggard's carefully organized outline of Quatermain's life occurs in this volume. As with Kiva in *King Solomon's Mines*, so in "Hunter Quatermain's Story" the faithful Hottentot retainer Hans is killed and mutilated by an angry beast:

> fixed in a stout fork of the tree some eight feet from the ground was Hans himself, or rather his dead body, evidently tossed there by the furious buffalo. One leg was twisted round the fork, probably in a dying convulsion. In the side, just beneath the ribs, was a great hole, from which the entrails protruded. But this was not all. The other leg hung down to within five feet of the ground. The skin and most of the flesh were gone from it. For a moment we stood aghast, and gazed at this horrifying sight. Then I understood what had happened. The buffalo, with that devilish cruelty which distinguishes the animal, had, after his enemy was dead, stood underneath his body, and licked the flesh off the pendant leg with his file-like tongue.112

This, however, is the same Hottentot Hans who about 1874 in *The Ivory Child* (1916) undergoes a second death, this time by the enraged bull elephant, Jana:

> I heard a Dutch curse and saw a little yellow form; saw Hans, for it was he, thrust the barrels of my second elephant rifle almost into that red cave of a mouth, which however they could not reach, and fire, first one barrel, then the other.
>
> Another moment, and the mighty trunk had wrapped itself about Hans and hurled him through the air to fall on to his head and arms thirty or forty feet away.... I staggered off to look for Hans and found him lying senseless near the north wall of the temple. Evidently he was beyond human help, for Jana seemed to have crushed most of his ribs in his iron trunk. We carried him to one of the priest's cells and there I watched him till the end, which came at sundown.113

Shakespeare said the brave man dies but once, the coward many times; but Haggard's poor brave Hans had to die horribly twice.

Not only does Hans die in "Hunter Quatermain," so also does the warrior-tracker Mashune; and in "Three Lions" the voorlooper Jim-Jim is killed, and what remains uneaten by the lioness is buried in a bread bag. The sharp edge of war and love's lethality is analogously a theme in *Allan's Wife*. There the love is never so intense as when the dangers of jealousy, revenge or combat color its sensations. The country so beautiful in morning mist has also its horrors of war:

> Not very long before Mosilikatze the Lion, Chaka's General had swept across it in his progress towards what is now Matabeleland. His footsteps were evident enough. Time upon time I trekked up to what had evidently been the sites of Kaffir kraals. Now the kraals were ashes and piles of tumbled stones, and strewn about among the rank grass were the bones of hundreds of men, women, and children, all of whom had kissed the Zulu assegai. I remember that in one of these desolate places I found the skull of a child in which a ground-lark had built its nest. It was the twittering of the young birds inside that first called my attention to it.[114]

Clearly the juxtaposition of the child's skull supporting the young birds becomes a morbidly fine vignette of new life nurtured by the cruel death of a similarly young nursling. One is inclined to add that for the innocent child it was a random, senseless demise except, of course, that its meaning lies in nature's recreative, fertile response.

In the ceaselessly interacting antinomies of war and love, the horror of the Boer massacre by a Zulu *impi* intent on revenge for the battle of Blood River leaves Quatermain the protector of little Tota, just as his love for Stella produces their child Harry. Stella, whose astral name gives her the mythic resonance of the morning and evening star, rescues Quatermain from death by dehydration and he, in turn, rescues her from a half-crazed companion and chaperon, Hendrika, who seems to bridge the gap between humans and the anthropoid apes.[115] Haggard certainly had Wordsworth's Lucy cycle of poems in mind, especially those lines "And beauty born of murmuring sound / Shall pass into her face" from "Three years she grew" in describing Stella's "long years of communing with Nature.... Had she caught that murmuring voice from the sound of the streams which fall continually about her rocky home?"[116] But nature, in the form of Hendrika's inarticulate worship, challenges Allan's love for Stella in a death struggle; and Allan's pyrrhic battle with this incarnation of the hypothetical "missing link" ultimately forces him to relinquish his beloved to death in childbirth. Years later he walks to her grave "through the ruined garden. There it was a mass of weeds, but over my darling's grave grew a self-sown orange bush, of which the scented petals fell in showers on to the mound beneath."[117] Ruined gardens always bespeak the loss of paradise; yet in a prelapsarian world no tree of knowledge could ever be so poignant as this self-sown orange bush, the scented petals of which fall like a benediction upon the mortal remains of Allan's fallen star. This image turns back upon Allan's first encounter with his earlier wife, Marie, who as a child in a peach orchard, "which just then was a mass of lovely pink blossom," was "clad in a frock which exactly matched the colour of the peach bloom."[118] Here this first innocence is lost through the larger hostilities of ethnic struggle. Allan's life "will always be shadowed by memories"[119] of her, and his love is itself intensified by the death of the beloved.

Maiwa's Revenge; or, The War of the Little Hand was published first in New York by Harper (23 July 1888) and just after by Longmans in London (3 August 1888), with the different subtitle of *A Novel*. The "Three Lions" had concluded with a promise to tell the story of Maiwa at another time,[120] and so Quatermain does one evening not long after. Set about 1858, four months after the previous tale of the lions, during which time Allan was an unsuccessful shopkeeper, the novella splits exactly halfway between hunting stories (woodcock in England; buffalo, rhinoceros, and elephant in Africa) and human fighting. One suspects Haggard is here opportunistically cobbling together two shorter pieces of material for a book-length publication, though Haggard's expediency would be any lesser writer's exceptional act of inspiration. The shooting episodes are problem stories of dangers rising by levels as Allan moves skillfully and, given that he lives to tell the tale, providentially, towards his shot, first identifying the quarry, then disposing of metastasizing complications that forestall the kill. This may be the only time Quatermain is described, quite unironically by Maiwa, with the cliché "great white hunter,"[121] although elsewhere he is the "mighty white hunter" and the "great white man."[122] Haggard's novel exaggerates neither the excitement and danger of the pursuit of ivory nor its end-use value for which native life itself is sacrificed and the "immortal soul" is risked.[123] So in the *Ivory Child* Quatermain plans to carry his tusks to "a good road to facilitate their subsequent transport to a land where they would be made into billiard balls and the back of ladies' hairbrushes,"[124] perhaps recalling the vestal virgin social goddess Belinda's toilet in "The Rape of the Lock": "The tortoise here and elephant unite, / Transform'd to combs, the speckled and the white."[125]

As a somewhat more bashful hunter of women to love, Quatermain had caught both Marie and Stella; but after the latter's death he hunted love no more, at least of the European petticoat kind. Allan, however, still can be a knight-errant for an attractive Zulu demoiselle, rescuing or revenging her against a cruel lord. After the feat of shooting three elephants with three shots, the second half of the narrative, told on the following evening, concerns Allan's backing of Maiwa's revenge because of the murder of her infant by the chief Wambe, a type of Shaka who will not permit any heir to the leopard-skin seat to live. Wambe is the sadistic owner of a lion trap used as a human torture engine, which the natives personify as "the Thing that bites." Returned to England at the end of the tale, this "Thing" is another instance of European civilization bestowing a greater harm than benefit upon Africa. *Maiwa* is also in its second half a rescue mission similar to *King Solomon's Mines*; and we have an internecine war of good and bad tribes with a Zulu Queen of battle, like Sorais in *Allan Quatermain*. The themes of ivory and professional elephant hunting link the first and second halves of the story since, in revenging Maiwa by destroying Wambe, Quatermain also captures the ivory at Wambe's kraal and rescues from there John Every, another white hunter and original owner of "the Thing that bites." But the pattern of moral law in which good triumphs over evil is not broken by any monstrous resolution for, and unholy joy in, revenge as in traditional revenge dramas. Although when Allan shoots the captain of the escort in the final battle, he does say that it is the only time he didn't feel remorse for taking a life:[126] "He had caught sight of me, and making a vicious dig at my stomach with a spear (which I successfully dodged) shouted out, or rather began to shout out, one of his unpleasant allusions to the 'Thing that—' He never got as far as 'bites,' because I shot him after 'that.'"[127]

Maiwa, fighting and victorious, possibly may suggest the Greek warrior-goddess Athena; but in the taking of the fortress that emblematized royal misrule, she is even more an African reincarnation of Eugene Delacroix's polemical *Liberty Leading the People* (1830): "There too on the wall stood Maiwa, a white garment streaming from her shoulders, an assegai in her hand, her breast heaving, her eyes flashing. Above all the din of battle I could catch the tones of her clear voice as she urged the soldiers on to victory.... All along their line swept the wild desperate charge; and there, straight in the forefront of the battle, still waved the white robe of Maiwa."[128] Since Wambe is a tyrannical ruler, Maiwa becomes the allegoric personification of freedom and civic emancipation. In the last line of the story, Haggard, the second "I"-narrator to whom Quatermain tells this tale, confesses: "I dreamed that I had married Maiwa, and was much afraid of that attractive but determined lady."[129] This dream receives its emphatic concluding position because it involves the desire for a socially forbidden miscegenation as well as a psychosexual fear of Maiwa's emasculating femininity. Quatermain relates: "The woman, who, as I have said, was quite young and very handsome, put her hand into a kind of little pouch made of antelope hide which she wore fastened round the waist, and to my horror drew from it the withered hand of a child, which had evidently been carefully dried in the smoke."[130] It is possible to construe this as the symbolic phallus of her castrated child. She tells Quatermain that Wambe discovered some soldiers who "passing the hut saw the child and saluted him, calling him the 'chief who soon shall be.'" The distrustful chief kills his child:

> "'Among the things that he had stolen from the white men who he slew is a trap that will hold lions. So strong is the trap that four men must stand on it, two on either side, before it can be opened.'"
>
> Here old Quatermain broke off suddenly.
>
> "Look here, you fellows," he said, "I can't bear to go on with this part of the story because I never could stand either seeing or talking of the sufferings of children. You can guess what that devil did, and what the poor mother was forced to witness."[131]

If this is a symbolic castration, clearly Wambe did the deed with this trap in his torture-cave: "the 'Thing that bites' lives in the dark ... edged with sharp and grinning teeth."[132] But in the murky world of Freudian projections and transferences, the antelope hide pouch of the mother is an analogous cave-womb that engulfs and threatens the child's masculine identity by her appropriation of his disjointed member, a dismembered joint in the *vagina dentata* of the devouring Mother. Any procreative attraction to Maiwa would inevitably be counterbalanced, analogous to the inversely complementary figures of Foulata and Gagool, by its antithesis of blood, castration, death.

Haggard here may be revealing the archetypal structures of his own anxieties, representing a death-fear transformed into sex-fear, or playing on the culturally constructed subconscious fears of his readership. As the product of a patriarchal society in which women have "no teeth," no power to effect their wills, readers may have been especially susceptible to the fantasy that those teeth might emerge as the *vagina dentata* to revenge upon the male the social castration of the female. In particular the semicircular stockade of ivory tusks that surrounds the mouth of the cave appears to be composed of hundreds of erect severed native phalluses—very few "soft,"[133] Quatermain later notes:

> "The smallest ones, though none were small, were placed nearest to the cliff on either side, but they gradually increased in size till they culminated in two enormous tusks, which set up so that their points met, something in the shape of an inverted V, formed the gateway to the hut. I was dumbfounded with delight; and indeed, where is the elephant-hunter who would not be, if he suddenly saw five or six hundred picked tusks set up in a row, and only waiting for him to take them away? Of course the stuff was what is known as 'black' ivory; that is, the exterior of the tusks had become black from years or perhaps centuries of exposure to wind and weather."[134]

Quatermain draws his knife and scratches it: "there beneath the black covering gleamed the pure white ivory. I could have capered for joy, for I fear that I am very mercenary at heart."[135] John Every, the great white hunter-surrogate for his friend Allan Quatermain, is rescued in the nick of time from being forced into the "Thing" by Wambe's women; and at the end he becomes the successful shopkeeper that Allan wasn't. What "Oom Paulus" says about shopkeepers in *Jess* has its significance here. Quatermain thus conquers Every's "Thing"—i.e., "everything" that threatens him—and becomes its possessor. He eventually banishes it to England and it ends up in "some museum or other."[136] Like Selous and other great white hunters who send their arsenic-embalmed zoological specimens to the British Museum or sell their kill for "hairbrushes,"[137] Quatermain has vanquished wild nature and rendered it a harmless trophy in London.

SIX

From Zululand to the Far Interior: Natives and Missionaries

Child of Storm was published in London by Cassell, January 1913, and a few weeks later in February by Longmans in New York. Haggard claimed that this, of all his novels, gave him the most literary pleasure; like *She*, it was "written quite easily, dictated straight away and except for a few Zulu details not altered at all, also more or less invented as I went along."[1] This comment suggests a spontaneity of invention that taps subconscious patterns of thought. Whereas the white goddess Ayesha is Haggard's best-known *femme fatale*, Mameena in *Child of Storm* is Quatermain's most striking native temptress. Mameena is more elementally natural, and therein lies her greatness and her evil. "Child of storm" is the meaning of Mameena's Zulu name because she was born in the howling wind; she is both the product and cause of the serious disturbance of elemental powers, its "child," in the sense of one who raises the "storm" of war. Although *Child of Storm* is the middle volume in the Zulu "trilogy," it was written before *Marie* which is the first in historical order. Next to *Nada the Lily*, *Child of Storm* is Haggard's most important Zulu novel, imaginatively the finest narrative of the "trilogy." Set in the early Zulu kingdom between 1854 and 1856, with an epilogue placed five years later, it climaxes with "the great battle of the Tugela,"[2] fought between Cetywayo and Umbelazi for the succession to the Zulu empire.

Once again, Haggard drew upon Fred Fynney for his essential historical background interpretation:

> The latter days of the old King Umpande were made miserable by the conduct of his two sons, Cetchwayo and Umbulazi—half-brothers—who,

> as soon as they grew up to man's estate, commenced a feud as to who was to succeed the old King.
>
> Ungumbazi, Cetchwayo's mother, was the *Inkosikazi* or chief wife, and, according to Zulu law, her son must be the heir.... Umpande appears, however, during his latter years, to have formed a strong attachment to Umbulazi's mother, who was of a kindly disposition, from all accounts, but who, nevertheless, used all her influence to get the old King to nominate her son and so displace Cetchwayo; and there is no doubt that she did manage to influence Umpande in her son's favour, for, when repeatedly urged openly to proclaim his successor and so set at rest the dispute—which was likely to assume a serious aspect,—he would not do so.... and finally said, on being once more referred to, "You squabble about the succession before I am dead, therefore the best way to settle it will be to fight it out." Unfortunately, this idea met with a ready response from the disputants.3

The novel moves on two interconnected levels: Fynney's large historical scale of the Zulu struggle for succession and the tempestuous personal scale of Mameena's intrigues. Manipulating the interconnections between them is Zikali, the witch doctor sworn to destroy the house of Shaka, his grief nourished with the hope of vengeance. Today this name Zikali or Zikhali still exists as a tribal authority area on the fringes of the old Zulu kingdom. Haggard's Zikali presumably is not primarily indebted to any notable locale but conceivably is an echo of Gasitye the Wizard in Bertram Mitford's *The Induna's Wife* (1898).

When Quatermain visits the kraal of the chief Umbezi, he learns that the noble young Saduko is infatuated with Mameena, the chief's daughter, a "Zulu Helen" who is not only "an extremely beautiful" woman but also "the most able, the most wicked, and the most ambitious."4 Saduko is the protégé of the old wizard Zikali, "the thing-that-should-never-have-been-born" as Shaka had named him. And Zikali intends to use Saduko's obsession for Mameena to undermine the royal house of Senzangakona. Haggard draws a telling contrast to the king's daughter, Nandi. Lacking Mameena's irresistible beauty, she is nonetheless the embodiment of Victorian wholesomeness: she is fertile whereas Mameena is barren; is self-sacrificial, not selfish; loyal not faithless; noble, not a sorceress. And yet, of course, Nandi doesn't beguile, doesn't captivate Saduko who can never give Nandi his ultimate allegiance. Although socially Saduko's first wife, Nandi bears the humiliation of being relegated to secondary status emotionally. We like Nandi more, but we feel an intenser primitive stirring contemplating Mameena, who uses her body to advantage even in the public "smelling-out":

"Friends," she said, with a little laugh, "there is no need to touch me," and, rising, she stepped forward to the centre of the ring. Here, with a few swift motions of her hands, she flung off first the cloak she wore, then the mooch about her middle, and lastly the fillet that bound her long hair, and stood before that audience in all her naked beauty—a wondrous and lovely sight.5

Quatermain had earlier described her figure as "absolutely perfect— that of a Greek statue indeed. On this point I had an opportunity of forming an opinion, since, except for her little bead apron and a single string of large blue beads about her throat, her costume was—well, that of a Greek statue."6 The image of Sheba, her snowy breasts surmounting the landscape, and the passage on the naked beauty of art in "About Fiction" are certainly relevant to Mameena; but again the factual original of the naked maiden is, at least partly, to be found in Haggard's very first essay, in which he observed at Pagadi's kraal:

> In front of the hut were grouped a dozen or so of women clad in that airiest of costumes, a string of beads. They were Pagadi's wives, ranged from the first shrivelled-up wife of his youth to the plump young damsel bought last month. The spokeswoman of the party, however, was not one of the wives, but a daughter of Pagadi's, a handsome girl, tall, and splendidly formed, with a finely-cut face. This prepossessing young lady entreated her lords to enter, which they did, in a very unlordly way, on their hands and knees.7

Of course, beautiful naked African girls may have been an unspoken dimension of Haggard's more intimate experiences in Natal as well, given current disclosures about his own liaison with a native *intombe.*

With both his wives deceased several decades previously, Quatermain, very much in spite of his better judgment, is dazzled by the irresistible beauty of this Zulu siren as surely as Good had been by the more innocent Foulata. To Allan and Allan alone she declares her love and ambition: "'Forget your pale white women and wed yourself to that fire which burns in me, and it shall eat up all that stands between you and the Crown, as flame eats up dry grass.'"8 And then: "She glided up to me, she threw her arms about me and kissed me on the lips, and I think I kissed her back, but really I am not sure what I did or said, for my head swam."9 In *Marie* Quatermain recalls uncomfortably the "native wives"10 of the early settlers in Durban and also fends off the "pretty young woman, Naya" who in vain "suggested naïvely that I might do worse than marry her."11 Although powerfully drawn to Mameena, Quatermain, ever the social puritan and prudish about racial mixing, only partially reciprocates, ultimately resisting her feminine wiles. Conrad (before he deleted the manuscript passage) has Marlow explain in *Heart of Darkness* the cultural structure that keeps the Englishman from going native: "There's very few places on earth where you haven't a man next door to you or something of him, the merest trace, his footprint—that's enough. You heard the yells and saw the dance and there was the man next door to call you names if you felt an impulse to yell and dance yourself."[12] Quatermain even in Zululand heeded the "footprint" (an amusing echo of Robinson Crusoe's discovery he was not alone); Kurtz in the Congo apparently did not. Of course, when it came to imprinting that European footprint in Africa, one truly admires Mary Kingsley's moment deep in the jungle in the upper reaches of the Niger. Separated from her party, alone but fully clothed as always in black hightop shoes, multiple skirts, laced bodice, dress hat and parasol, she encounters an armed and painted native hunting party that has never seen a white man, much less a woman dressed like Queen Victoria. They file past her, eyes averted, no salutation, no backward glances: she was, of course, taken for an ancestral ghost, taboo and protected. Mary was the "footprint" of Britannia in the jungle; she herself had no need of reminders from Mrs. Grundy.

For Quatermain, even if the flesh is willing the spirit flinched before the touchstone of such as the ghostly Mary Kingsley. Certainly Allan's disapproval of the blossoming relationship between Foulata and Good in *King Solomon's Mines* is proof enough. Yet more than his romance with two tragically dead wives and Platonic interludes with other women, Allan's contretemps with Mameena is literally undying. Mameena's spirit warns and protects Quatermain in his crises and quests; and when, in *She and Allan*, Ayesha allows him to behold once again the women he has loved and lost, they have all forgotten him save for Mameena—and his old dog. Haggard would not have known the phrase "multicultural agenda," but it seems appropriate when one considers that the reader's sympathies, always manipulated by the author, lie more with Quatermain's yearnings than with his Victorian discretion. For that transitional era 1880–1920, his treatment of male desire and feminine eroticism is graphic, indeed no less frank than many works of literary naturalism. And despite the apparent stigma of miscegenation, Haggard and his readers are all in favor of passion's taint. The humanizing side of such fallen love makes rebellion against an overly controlled, too rational, and racist morality a virtue. Quatermain's tragedy is to resist nature and to accept the social taboo on running away with Mameena.

| SIX: From Zululand to the Far Interior |

At the Tugela, jealous of Umbelazi's affair with Mameena, Saduko deserts him for Cetywayo, thereby giving the Zulus their last, disastrous king. There is, of course, nothing historical about Saduko's treachery in Fynney's account:

> The ground selected by Umbulazi upon which to give his brother battle was that known as the Indondakusuka, within about six miles of the border [with the British colony of Natal]. He may have selected this ground from the knowledge that his force was inferior to that of his brother's, and hoping to get over into Natal in the event of a defeat. That he had misgivings as to the result is shown by the fact of Umbulazi's crossing over into Natal two days before the fight to solicit aid from Mr Walmsley, the then Border Agent. This gentleman could not grant such a request, but agreed to send John Dunn over with a small force consisting of about thirty constables (natives) and some kraal kafirs. His mission was to make peace if he could, and smooth over the difficulty; but those who know what Zulus are, when the war spirit is aroused within them, and how thoroughly deaf to reason they become under such circumstances, will readily understand that Mr Dunn's mission was a failure. He crossed over with Umbulazi, or soon after; and on the morning which heralded one of the most sanguinary fights ever known to natives of late years, went with his handful of men to meet Cetchwayo's advancing host and tried to parley, but the only answer he got was a bullet at his head—which came too close to be pleasant—followed by another. Dunn, seeing that all chance of mediation was vain, called upon his men to charge up, and they dashed on to meet fearful odds, but, nevertheless, managed to turn the flank twice or three times. Both he and his men fought with the most dogged determination, and his conduct upon that day won him lasting admiration, even from the side against which he fought. Had all the rest of Umbulazi's followers shown the bravery exhibited by Dunn's little band, there is no doubt but that Cetchwayo would have been defeated.
>
> After Dunn engaged the right wing of Cetchwayo's force, the fight became general, for the left pushed on with the view of surrounding entirely that of Umbulazi's, whose followers appear to have fought in a half-hearted way, for they entirely failed to sustain the fight and broke in all directions, the bulk making for the Tugela river, which was swollen at the time and unfordable. Dunn, seeing that all was lost, and being wounded, made for the river, and managed to get across by swimming his horse. His little band perished fighting bravely back to back. The victors now became the pursuers, and the fugitives were driven back upon their women and children, whom they had unfortunately secreted between the battle field and the river Tugela. The orders were—'Slay, and spare not.' In this case, old family feuds aroused a spirit of vindictiveness in many instances, so there was no mercy. A teaming throng of pursued and pursuers came pouring down the slopes leading down to the Tugela, hundreds falling by the way;

mothers dragging their helpless offspring were mercilessly slaughtered, despite their cries for mercy; thousands poured into the water, to be either drowned or assegaied, a very small proportion reaching the Natal side. Umbulazi, seeing all lost, fled in a northerly direction, and is supposed to have been assegaied near the Inyoni river. His brothers, or half-brothers—Tyankweni, Dabulezinye, Mantantatyela and three others—fell that day, whilst it is estimated that upwards of one hundred thousand of the people—men, women and children—were slain....

After this fearful slaughter of Umbulazi's people, Cetchwayo's victorious followers retraced their steps homewards from the border river, looting all cattle as they went, together with everything else of value that they came across, and butchering such of the defeated chief's followers as they fell in with.[13]

This incredible battle, so little regarded in England, becomes in Haggard rightly no less epic than landmark battles in the rise of Western power, from Thermopylae to the last ghastly thrusts at Isandhlwana.

This frequently mentioned "epic" quality of Haggard's Zulu narratives is especially evident in *Child of Storm*. Kipling told Haggard not only that this novel was "the best thing that you have done" but his observation that it was "as terse and strong as a Greek play" is right on target, although his description of Mameena as "a nice little bitch, though dusky" is over the top.[14] Haggard's depiction of the Zulu war of succession has inescapable connections with the *Iliad*, though the parallelisms with Homer's epic are as loose as James Joyce's more ironic adaptation of the same author's *Odyssey*. Mameena, we have been told, is the "Zulu Helen."[15] According to ancient Greek legend, Helen was the most beautiful woman of her age, daughter of Zeus, as Mameena is Zikali's adopted daughter. Alexander Pope writes of her: "She moves a goddess and she looks a queen."[16] First carried off by Theseus, who corresponds to Mameena's Masapo, Helen was returned by her brothers and chose Menelaus, king of Sparta, who in the novel is Saduko. Finally she is seduced by Paris, son of Priam, king of Troy, who is Umbelazi, son of Panda. Andrew Lang's poem, "Helen of Troy," alleges that Helen was not Paris's reluctant and innocent prisoner, but an adultress, even though she protests that Aphrodite transported her to Troy for an undeserving man. Helen was the favorite of "the orgiastic Moon-goddess Aphrodite—whose sacred bird is the sparrow, and whose priestesses cared nothing for the patriarchal view that women were the property of their father and husbands"[17]—and Mameena's vicissitudes also suggest a close association with her moon-protectress, Aphrodite. Menelaus-Saduko assembled the Greek princes, those who were her former suitors, to make war on Troy, a prototype for the Zulu war of succession. Haggard simplifies somewhat Homer's multitude of personalities by conflating Paris with Hector, the handsome, most loved warrior, and Menelaus with Achilles, whose proud anger and withdrawal from battle models that of Saduko's. As Hector is killed by Achilles, so Saduko's outright treason against Umbelazi destroys that prince. In this shadow play, Allan Quatermain is, of course, the crafty, resourceful Ulysses, never reckless but with courage when essential; and he always rises to the occasion—more modest than the splendid tragic heroes, his judgment, unlike that of Achilles, is never clouded by passion, so he survives both the dangers of war and the pitfalls of female charms. At their conclusions the narratives of Homer and Haggard diverge. After the fall of Umbelazi, Mameena ceases to be Helen, who returns with Menelaus to a wholly prosaic life; Mameena, by contrast, is adjudged by a witch hunt and must take poison.

One can never quite tell how much belief Homer himself invested in his anthropomorphic gods and goddess—are they merely opportune ornamentation for his tales or are they indeed forces operative in human affairs? As to Quatermain's belief or skepticism that Zulu history is governed by the plans and desires of the gods, his anguished and conflicted "philosophical" speculation on historical causality is nearly at the center of the novel:

> as Saduko and the others were Mameena's tools, and as all of them and their passions were Zikali's tools, so he himself was the tool of some unseen Power that used him and us to accomplish its design. Which, I suppose, is fatalism, or, in other words, all these things happened because they must happen. A poor conclusion to reach after so much thought and striving, and not complimentary to man and his boasted powers of free will; still, one to which many of us are often driven, especially if we have lived among savages, where such dreams work themselves out openly and swiftly, unhidden from our eyes by the veils and subterfuges of civilisation. At least, there is this comfort about it—that, if we are but feathers blown by the wind, how can the individual feather be blamed because it did not travel against, turn or keep back the wind?[18]

Unequivocal in Kipling's *Jungle Book* (1894) had been the central emphasis upon accord with "the Law" by which civilized society defines the rights and duties of its members. Allan's despondent fatalism is at odds with a moral causality that he would prefer. On the one hand, if historical occurrences are fixed in advance for all time and humans are powerless to change them, then Anglo-Zulu history is not defined by the morality of individual or political behavior. On that hypothesis there is only an explanatory causality within history, a Darwinian force and struggle. But, on the other, if human destiny is produced by free choices for or against the true, the good, and the beautiful, then history is regulated by principles of moral causality and social justice. Because the spirit world exists, Haggard knows Quatermain and the others *must* make fateful choices until evil is lost in good.

John Ruskin had quoted a passage in Dante that presents three moral possibilities: *ribelli,* rebellious; *fedeli,* faithful; and *per se,* for self: "*Mischiate sono a quel cattivo coro/ de li angeli che on furon ribelli/ ne fur fedeli a Dio, ma per se fuoro.*"19 Those who are *per se,* neither for nor against, those that Christ will spew out of his mouth (Revelation 3:16), are remanded by Dante to the vaguely defined vestibule of hell (*Inferno*, canto 3). T. S. Eliot had in mind these melancholy Dantesque souls "who lived without infamy or praise and are mingled with that cowardly company of Angels, who have been neither rebellious nor faithful to God, but were for self" when he described Baudelaire as one who welcomed "the reality of Sin" like a *vita nouva*; "and the possibility of damnation is so immense a relief in a world of electoral reform, plebiscites, sex reform and dress reform, that damnation itself is an immediate form of salvation—of salvation from the ennui of modern life, because it at least gives some significance to living." To be human, "what we do must be either evil or good; so far as we do evil or good, we are human; and it is better, in a paradoxical way, to do evil than to do nothing; at least we exist."20 This also is why Conrad's Marlow in *Heart of Darkness,* sensing all the "inefficiency," the paralysis and disconnections, the hypocritical talk of "unsound methods," finds Kurtz "remarkable." Like Baudelaire—but unlike Marlow living "in a sickly atmosphere of tepid skepticism, without much belief in your own right, and still less in that of your adversary"—Kurtz has plumbed "the horror,"21 an awareness of his transgression of moral codes and of his damnation. Marlow must come to terms with his condition of *per se,* without infamy or praise, in the imperial enterprise; and although he hates lies as much as Quatermain, he must now tell his tale anew to account to himself for lying to Kurtz's Intended. Consequently, the old seaman Marlow becomes an ironic image of Coleridge's ancient mariner, telling to his indifferent or impatient auditors a tale of moral blindness, not of his sins against a sacramental nature but of his bewildered impotence. Quatermain, too, retelling his adventures, likewise describes a quest of spiritual perplexity, a descent if not into the hell of Homer, Virgil, or Dante, then certainly into the primitive and subconscious—and he too must deal with the responsibility for the dark knowledge that might render void any idea of civilizing progress.

In Haggard's novels, Mameena like Kurtz is the ultimate overreacher, the remarkable woman whose dying kiss could have been described in Marlow's summation of Kurtz's last words: "this was the expression of some sort of belief; it had candor, it had conviction, it had a vibrating note of revolt in its whisper, it had the appalling face of a glimpsed truth—the strange commingling of desire and hate."[22] In a history governed by explanatory causality, Mameena is little more than an epiphenomenon of history, a merely noncausal by-product; in a world of moral value she becomes tragically heroic. A true flower of evil, Mameena symbolized "something," said Quatermain, "which reminded me of a flower breaking into bloom, that one does not associate with youth and innocence."[23] Faithless to her lovers, she is yet true to Quatermain. She maps her own, and Quatermain's, damnation; and it is just here that Mameena becomes so fascinating. Haggard's sirens always choose love or revenge, no middle way. But Haggard, along with Bishop Colenso and Dean F. W. Farrar, unmistakably rejects the teaching of eternal punishment. Though Haggard's universe is no less supernatural than that of the Evangelicals, in the place of damnation he puts reincarnation. If Homer's Helen is not punished in the *Iliad*, neither in her afterlife is Haggard's Mameena.

Dante's word *ribelli* is the epitome of the adventures of Mameena's "unrepentant"[24] soul on earth, but Quatermain is *per se*, attracted to yet afraid of her heart of darkness. Though fearing the path of Zikali and damnation that Mameena offers, Quatermain cannot entirely make the choice for crown and Christianity either. One tradition about the angels who chose to remain neutral relates that God gives them a second chance as humans. But they become exiles to a passion and energy experienced by both faithful and fallen angels alike, perpetually saddened by the shadow of all they have lost. Quatermain, with or without companions like Sir Henry and Umslopogaas, thus lingers an exile and wanderer, always seeking the next adventure that may perhaps validate his life. If the lion trap of *Maiwa* embodies the fearsome procreative fecundity of Africa that becomes only a harmless, dusty museum relic in England, so too the elephant's ivory and the diamonds of Solomon acquire salable value in the international commodities market at the sacrifice of their living connections to nature. Similarly Good looks back to Africa's mystical interplay of sun, moon, and stars for a lost love; and, poignantly, Quatermain's son born in Africa will soon lie buried in an English village churchyard. So at the end of *King Solomon's Mines* London seems the vestibule of hell; and, of course, this is why Quatermain and his *confrères* flee the bleakness, dullness, and emptiness of England to return to Africa—not to damnation but to an eternal transmigration of souls. They will flee back to Africa, to its "wild game and the savages,"[25] to the intensity and delight of life lived in the face of death, into the lion trap of the *Magna Mater*. Unlike Ulysses arriving home, Allan never finds his Ithaca or Penelope. Indeed, his luck with women is so bad that one wit has been moved to point out that for any woman to fall in love with Allan is tantamount to a death sentence.[26]

In the 1880s new ideas of female independence emerged—the New Woman who worked at an untraditionally female job, explored sex without marriage, or dressed and acted in masculine ways. In 1895 Gwendolen Fairfax, the comic figure in Oscar Wilde's *The Importance of Being Earnest*, had told her beloved Jack that although her mother "'may prevent us from becoming man and wife, and I may marry someone else, and marry often, nothing that she can possibly do can alter my eternal devotion to you.'"[27] Wilde, of course, ruthlessly undermines Gwendolen's cliché of "eternal devotion" so as to ridicule such Victorian ideals as those expressed by Elizabeth Barrett Browning's famous love sonnet: "I love thee with the breath,/ Smiles, tears, of all my life; and, if God choose,/ I shall but love thee better after death."[28] By the early twentieth century such idealistic faith in love and marriage had worn more than a bit thin; nevertheless, Haggard insists upon the cliché of "eternal devotion" but he avoids naiveté by transposing gender issues to Africa and putting into Mameena's mouth a statement that would have been comically ironic had it been uttered by that unintentional feminist Gwendolen. His African setting allows him to revitalize stale Victorian social clichés, to examine "eternal devotion" without its modern cultural static of laughter. But given the figure of Mameena, does Haggard display a nostalgia for the old aristocratic patriarchal values in the face of the urbanized New Woman? Does he desire to drive the energetic New Woman, no longer submissive to church, society or husband, back into her place as Victorian wife and mother? Or perhaps his male fear of domination sees her like Ayesha's ambiguous pillar of fire, both sustaining and consuming? In a society that stifles ambitious women, that considers them chattel and condemns them to the role of biological reproduction, Mameena's determination to resist the paradigm and to wield power is nothing less than her would-be liberation from bondage. She fails, but just barely. Mameena is Victorian literature's first "dusky" feminist—perhaps this is why Kipling found the derogatory epithet "bitch" a proper descriptor for her.

※ ※

Essentially *Finished* is a romance about who or what makes or controls the unfolding of historical events. And a triple pun in the novel's title suggests this quandary: "Finished" is the name of the dying king's kraal,29 an actual place; it also describes the final vengeance of Zikali upon the House of Senzangakona;30 and it is Haggard-the-author's culminating novel in his ambitious trilogy. *Finished* appeared in August 1917, published by Ward Lock in London and Longmans in the United States. When *Punch* reviewed it in September 1917, the magazine missed the significance of Haggard's sociological run-up to epic adventure; namely, that dealing in stolen stones points to a criminality hidden beneath what might be an innocent and beautiful setting:31

> The matter is, to begin with, an affair of a shady doctor, of I.D.B. [Illicit Diamond Buying] and an abduction, none of it, I admit, any too absorbing. But about halfway through the author, as though sharing my own views upon this part of the plot, exchanges (so to speak) the Shady for the Black, and transports us all to Zululand. And if you need reminding of what H.R.H. can do with that delectable country, I can only say I am sorry for you. Incidentally there are some stirring scenes from certain pages of history that the glare of these later days has rather faded—Isandhlwana and Rorke's Drift among them; as well as the human drama of the feud between Cetewayo (terror of my nursery!) and the witch-doctor Zikali."32

Such lootable natural resources as diamonds destabalize colonial law and order and form a counterplot to the primary conflict of the Zulu War and the downfall of the empire.

Haggard uses Fred Fynney's account to give a Zulu background to the British efforts to establish tranquility in the kingdom:

> The death of Umbulazi occasioned the deepest grief to Umpanda; in fact, he never got over it, for the writer has known the old King, years afterwards, to give way to bitter wailing on account of this son's death. Umbulazi must, for all accounts, have been a King Saul among the Zulus, for it is said that his bulky form could be distinguished a long way off, towering head and shoulders above the assembled warriors. He was a man possessed of great personal attractions as well as of splendid physique, and the Zulus invariably speak of him as "Umbulazi the handsome." He was also of a much milder disposition than his brother, if we may credit the opinion of the Zulus, who, in making comparisons between the two, are wont to say that Cetchwayo had more of the Tyaka in his composition.33

Quatermain himself makes no secret of his preference for this brother.[34] Fynney continues:

> The old King Umpanda, though a confirmed invalid from gout, lingered on till 1873, when, unlike his immediate predecessors on the throne of Zululand, he passed peacefully away. The event was formally reported to the Governor of Natal, as representing the British Nation, with the request that his Excellency would be pleased to send representatives to Zululand with a view of installing Cetchwayo in the kingship thus rendered vacant. This request was complied with, and Sir (then Mr) Theophilus Shepstone proceeded to Zululand, with an imposing retinue, to represent the English Government at the ceremony.
>
> At his installation as king, Cetchwayo was required to enter into certain obligations, which he most willingly did; among them being one by which he agreed that no Zulu should be put to death without a fair and open trial; another, that he would not make war upon his neighbours without first obtaining the sanction of the Government of Natal; and a third, that he would permit the work of Christian missions to be carried out without opposition or interference.... No longer, it was now felt, would the people live in dread of being cut off at a moment's notice, without the slightest chance of vindication. The cruel practice of "smelling out" would now cease. The wanton war-spirit would now be quenched, and its concomitant horrors and injustices would cease to prevail.[35]

When the British invaded Zululand, their reasons were that Zulus had violated Shepstone's conditions of installation.[36] In reality, the British undertook a preemptive strike against Cetywayo's *impis* from which they feared attack.

In *Finished* Maurice Anscombe (handsome, wealthy, and naive) and Heda Marnham (beautiful, pure, talented) are young lovers whose romance is set against Zikali's destruction of the house of Senzangakona. Not only does Haggard present a proper Victorian courtship played out on the imperial frontier, but he contrasts with it the infatuation of Nombe for Heda,[37] a socially improper lesbian love that nevertheless rises to heroic levels. This is very much like Mameena's unsuitable passion for Quatermain or Foulata's for Good. The kiss of Mameena is so often cited in the course of the narrative in *Finished* that it becomes a sort of leitmotif for the refusal of Quatermain, like Good, to embrace the possibilities of self-determination, to create a personal paradigm outside the givens of social propriety. On this issue of Victorian standards, one thinks especially of the reply of Mitford's eponymous hero in *John Ames, Native Commissioner* (1900) to his subinspector in charge of the Matabele Police:

"I say, old chap, why don't you chip in for some of old Madúla's daughters—marry 'em, don't you know? He has some spanking fine ones, anyway."...

"Because I hope to make a better thing of life, Inglefield. But that sort of thing is rather apt to stick to a man, and crop up just when least convenient. I'm no prig or puritan, so putting it on that ground alone, it's better not touched."38

Liberal that he is and "no prig," John Ames nevertheless recognizes the social practicalities that orchestrate behavior. He conforms, albeit he hasn't Quatermain's considerably greater temptation to kick off the traces of social propriety. Quatermain prefers to content himself with sardonic witticisms, observing here and elsewhere that the most dangerous quarry for the hunter, in ascending order, are lions, elephants, buffaloes, and girls.39 (Selous, less frivolously, nominates lions as most dangerous because they are sly.40) But Allan's mulish emotional detachment and prudery (or is it simply "the horror, the horror" of unconstrained lust?) are turned back upon him in the delicious revenge of the press when the horribly ugly Kaatje is publicly identified as one of his polygamous wives: "Within a few days there appeared in one of the Natal papers and, for aught I know, all over the earth, an announcement that Mr. Allan Quatermain, a well-known hunter in Zululand, after many adventures, had escaped from that country, 'together with his favourite native wife, the only survivor of his extensive domestic establishment.'"41 In this fictional account of garbled journalism one can almost glimpse Haggard's chagrin at the newspaper's misspelling of his name upon his arrival in Natal with Bulwer—misidentified, he must have felt himself an inauthentic, would-be notable in the drama about to unfold.

In the course of the action, Anscombe and Heda experience history almost as a play orchestrated by Zikali, as at "The Great Council"; and at the end these lovers disappear entirely from the historical matrix in which Quatermain remains. Quatermain himself is only a player in a pantomime of history, never one of its dispositive authors. Zikali, like Gagool, would orchestrate that historic tragedy; at one point he is compared to a London medium,42 a type Haggard knew so well. But Zikali may not be the writer of the historic script—perhaps Umkulunkulu is the author, or perhaps not. When Olive Schreiner defended her technique of assembling diverse fragments in *The Story of an African Farm*, she described it in her preface as

> the method of the life we all lead. Here nothing can be prophesied. There is a strange coming and going of feet. Men appear, act and re-act upon

each other, and pass away. When the crisis comes the man who would fit it does not return. When the curtain falls no one is ready. When the footlights are brightest they are blown out; and what the name of the play is no one knows. If there sits a spectator who knows, he sits so high that the players in the gaslight cannot hear his breathing.43

Is the history that we know the product of tangible but impersonal events, of God's mercy or God's holy wrath, or of an author's literary vision and interpretation? And what, anyway, do we know when we "know" history? This critique of realism has recently been taken up in Nancy Armstrong's theorizing about the images of mass culture that get between the viewer and his/her direct grasp of the "real" world.44

Olive Schreiner has a figure who says to a young artist: "'Whosoever should portray truly the life and death of a little flower—its birth, sucking in of nourishment, reproduction of its kind, withering and vanishing—would have shaped a symbol of all existence.'"45 One supposes Schreiner is borrowing her image from Tennyson's "Flower in a Crannied Wall." But the impossibility of total understanding, "all in all," both leaves Quatermain in a quandary and allows some critics of Haggard to charge that he did not tell the true Zulu "story" that we know today. One is tempted to invoke that line from Bacon's essay: "What is Truth? said jesting Pilate, and would not stay for an answer."46 However, Schreiner's speaker continues: "'all true art ... is a little door that opens into an infinite hall where you may find what you please.... All true facts of nature or the mind are related. Your little carving represents some mental facts as they really are, therefore fifty different true stories might be read from it.'"47 Since we never have direct access to "the object as in itself it really is," ethnographic or sociological descriptions of the world at best represent a connection to the objective reality of persons, places, or things that is a contingent construction of truth; but as nineteenth-century aesthetic theory posits, the mythic dimension of the aesthetic image, marked by an infinite multiplicity of meanings, provides a polysemous way of seeing or understanding those hidden "things-in-themselves" that we call "reality." The heterogeneity of meanings offered by the aesthetic image validates its fidelity to experience. Thus in his trilogy Haggard need make no claim to reconstruct history in itself, merely to construct a past Zulu world that is narratively plausible and imaginatively faithful to his "mental facts."

"Magepa the Buck" (1912) is an Allan Quatermain tale originally published in *Pear's Christmas Annual*, reprinted in *Princess Mary's Gift Book* in 1914 and again in *Smith and the Pharaohs and Other Tales*.[48] Its scene is Zululand, just before the battles of Isandhlwana and Rorke's Drift. (A "drift" is a ford, here located on the Buffalo River that separated Zululand from the Colony of Natal.) The story offers itself as a slice of life, a realistic account of how Magepa, known as the "buck" because of his fleetness of foot, ran to the Buffalo River with his grandson on his back, eluding pursuing soldiers of the Natal Native contingent (an indigenous British unit). Just before leaping into the Buffalo, from which he is pulled by his old comrade in arms, Quatermain, he turns to take a tolla in his chest from one of the pursuers. Dying, he extracts a promise from Allan to deliver the child safe to Natal.

Among the ironies of the incident are that Magepa was a British sympathizer who had given Quatermain intelligence as to Cetywayo's intentions, that the Natal Natives pursuing Magepa comprised a reconnaissance unit on the side of the British against Cetywayo, and that Quatermain "wrote a beautiful report of all that I had learned, of which report, I may add, no one took the slightest notice."[49] Magepa's fate is perhaps a foreshadowing of the ill luck about to be visited upon the British. The invaders of Zululand were surprised and overrun at Isandhlwana, their preemptive strike turned into the greatest defeat in British colonial history, though something of Tennyson's "Charge of the Light Brigade" also infuses this moment of British magnificence and defeat. In *Finished* Haggard attributes the defeat "to lack of generalship"; and though Colonel Durnford, Haggard's friend, is thoroughly exculpated here,[50] many years earlier in "Isandhlwana" (1893) Haggard is more candid about Durnford's tactical choices.[51]

When, at the opening of "Magepa," Haggard the "editor" of Quatermain's account quotes Allan's note that he found in "a book, much soiled and worn, that evidently its owner had carried about with him for years"—probably the *Ingoldsby Legends*—the implicit allusion to the British soldiers' awards for valor is significant:

> "I wonder whether in the 'Land Beyond' any recognition is granted for acts of great courage and unselfish devotion—a kind of spiritual Victoria Cross. If so I think it ought to be accorded to that poor old savage, Magepa, at least it would be if I had any voice in the matter. Upon my word he has made me feel proud of humanity. And yet he was nothing but a 'nigger,' as so many call the Kaffirs."[52]

Quatermain's "nothing but a 'nigger'" recalls his protest against use of the epithet in *King Solomon's Mines*, with its suggestion of smug Anglo superiority. Yet if anyone showed human endurance, love, and courage, it was Magepa.

Near Isandhlwana, at the brave defense of Rorke's Drift, where fewer than one hundred and fifty British soldiers defended a supply station against four thousand Zulus, the largest number of Victoria Crosses for "conspicuous bravery" ever awarded in British history to any regiment for a single battle was given. Haggard seems to say that a Zulu too may deserve the highest honor and regard. The Victoria Cross, which takes precedence over every other military decoration, is imagined awarded to Magepa not for devotion to country but for a mighty and selfless effort to save his grandson. Pursued like the tired buck that Quatermain shields from the hyenas in *Allan's Wife*, here Magepa's heroic run is recompensed by Quatermain's seeing to his grandson's mission-education as an interpreter, a position of respect and one that Haggard himself had filled.

Another short story, "Black Heart and White Heart," is not an Allan Quatermain tale, but supposedly was communicated directly to Haggard by a Zulu bride, Nanea,[53] and retold by him in the third person. Its setting is also Isandhlwana at the time of the opening hostilities of the Zulu War (1878–1879). It appeared in *Black Heart and White Heart and Other Stories*, one of Haggard's lesser-known titles published by Longmans in May 1900, during the Anglo-Boer War, in a deluxe edition with heavy bevelled boards. The volume contained two other stories that originally had appeared also just prior to the war. The title story had been published in the *African Review* (January 1896); the other two tales were "Elissa," set in Rhodesia in the time of the Phoenicians, and first serialized in the *Long Bow* (February–June 1898); and "The Wizard," serialized in the *African Review* (as early as July–November 1896). Subtitled "A Zulu Idyll," this is a short picturesque piece about Zulu life and love in which the happy innocence of an idealized romance is almost destroyed by a culturally insensitive, dishonest transport-rider and trader in "the Zulu," Philip Hadden. Reminiscent of Nada, the "bronze-hued" Nanea is described in the "crimson glow" of sunset, a beauty of partly "ancestral Arabian or Semitic blood."[54] In the background to the romantic triangle of Philip Hadden and the Zulu lovers, Nanea and Nahoon, is the larger conflict of Cetywayo and the British invasion of Zululand. One suspects that Philip's fate, in its similarity to the battle's outcome at Isandhlwana, may serve as a covert comment on imperial British pride and overconfidence: "he disliked Nahoon; at times he even hated him. Their natures were antagonistic, and he knew that the great Zulu distrusted and looked down upon him, and to be looked down upon by a savage 'nigger' was more than his pride could stomach."55 Philip underestimates the power of native cultural forces, natural emotional attachments, occult Zulu vision, and military loyalty and courage. Nahoon, the Zulu warrior, has the white heart of innocence; Philip, whose desire for Nanea casually dismisses the betrothal of Nahoon to Nanea and Cetywayo's alternative intent for her of royal concubinage, has the black heart of selfish, racial pride. Haggard points the moral of Philip's opportunistic life with didactic gusto: "it was a law of Hadden's existence never to deny himself anything that he desired if it lay within his power to take it—a law which had led him always deeper into sin."56 In a sense, Haggard is exploring the same heart of imperial darkness that Conrad presented a year previously in Kurtz and the Belgian operations in the Congo. If Philip comes off as the universal villain of literature and if Cetywayo plays the bully and despot, both are very likely transcripts from reality. The important political statement here lies in the pro-native figure of Nahoon, who at the end "is one of the Indunas of the English Government in Zululand."57 One of several chiefs subject to the control of the British resident magistrate, Nahoon clearly represents Haggard's Umbopa-Ignosi ideal of what could have been the best in Zulu self-rule after Cetywayo's death in 1884. Subsequent to the story's first publication, the British allowed Cetywayo's son Dinizulu to return in 1898 to become a "government induna"; and he was regarded during the Boer War by most of the Zulus as their national leader.

Possibly the finest "romancette" or "romancella" by Haggard, somehow disregarded from the time of its publication in 1896 to the present, is *The Wizard*. With high imagination, this powerfully "symbolic-diabolic" native tale of the fantastic and occult captures an early black-white encounter with razor-sharp drama. It is a missionary story of the wealthy English cleric Thomas Owen who gave up not only his comfortable "living" but the girl of his dreams for the "savagery and death" (Dedication) of his new calling. Sold for one shilling in October 1896 in J. W. Arrowsmith's *Christmas Annual*, with black-and-red-lettered paper wraps, this tale is set loosely in the south central African region north of the Zambezi, in what was then known as British Central Africa, some years after the Zulu War—a reference to the Salvation Army's work early in the narrative makes it probable its events occurred not many years prior to its publication in 1896. In *The Wizard* Haggard's use of fantasy takes the form of miracle against magic—the necromantic Hokosa challenged by Owen's recuperation of the extraordinary providences of the Hebraic prophets and of Christ and the Apostolic age. Owen uses the name Messenger that derives from the prophecy in Malachi 3:1 and that the gospels of Matthew, Mark and Luke apply to John the Baptist, patron saint of missionaries because he was sent to "prepare the way of the Lord." Quite possibly Bertram Mitford's missionary among the Matabele in *The White Shield* (1895) may have been an evocative precursor, since here the gospel of Christian peace is pitted against the Zulu culture of war.[58] Mitford organizes his tale around three battles of increasing intensity and ferocity, reflecting an ethos of bloodshed against which Christianity seems nearly irrelevant. In anticipation of Haggard's character, Mitford's white *"isanusi"* offers himself in substitution for several of Umzilikazi's subjects, though ultimately he dies at his post of a fever.[59] The essential difference is that Mitford's Father among the Zulus is secondary to the principal characters and their climactic battle against Mhlangana's and Dingane's *impi*, whereas Haggard's narrative is centered on Owen's mission. The tribal war of succession in which Owen is caught, not unlike that which Panda had caused in Zululand, is the counterplot. And finally, Mitford's world is one of physical forces tinctured with magic; mythic patterns, hidden powers beyond the scope of human manipulation, are barely evident.

Amusingly, the Reverend Thomas Owen is one of several clergymen in Haggard's fiction whom the Anglo world deems mad,[60] but whose noble insanity, admired by Haggard, is that of the Holy Fool. Owen's God is pitted against the native god, "a meteoric stone of unusual size" with "a peculiar resemblance to a seated human being holding up one arm towards the sky."[61] Haggard undoubtedly is alluding to such black meteoric stones as that at Mecca, which supposedly fell from Paradise with Adam and was as white as milk but turned black on account of man's sins, or the meteoric stones worshiped by the ancient Greeks or Romans, in particular the rough black meteoric effigy of the Great Mother brought to Rome by Elagabalus. Owen's efforts to convert the tribe, especially its dying king and his favorite son, are resisted by the wizard Hokosa in league with the evil heir, Hafela. The two claimants to the throne look back to the good-bad of Umbopa-Twala or the sister-queens in *Allan Quatermain*, as well as forward to the warring forces in the *The Holy Flower* and *The Ivory Child*. By the grace of God, Owen is given telepathic vision and divine protection in the lightning-contest,[62] not unlike the putative powers of the witch doctor. Although the dramatic contest of trial by lightning previously played out in *Allan's Wife*[63] is here repeated in the contest between the wizard Hokosa and the missionary Owen,[64] Haggard's descriptive powers are so inventive this recycled situation does not in the least trouble the enthusiastic reader. Haggard pinpoints Owen's identical erosion of native authority that the unworldly Livingstone unsuspectingly described as besetting Sechele upon his baptism—including insult, military desertions, and the stumbling block of monogamy.[65] Quite possibly this romancette is the source for Achebe's incident of the killing of the sacred python in *Things Fall Apart*, given the very similar scandal created by Christian preachments in *The Wizard*.[66]

Whereas Owen renounced though never forgot the woman he desired, who would not accompany him on his "mission,"[67] Hokosa the wizard could barely renounce his mistress Noma, a "bronze-hued"[68] beauty whose ambitions parallel those of Mameena. In the first instance love of the flesh is overcome by love of the spirit; in the latter Hokosa's desire for Noma proves too strong and ultimately brings about his downfall: "She hated him, and he worshipped her with a half-inhuman passion—a passion so unnatural, indeed, that it suggested the horrid and insatiable longings of the damned—and yet their souls were naked to each other. It was their fate that they could hide nothing each from each—they were cursed with the awful necessity of candour."[69] Biblically, wizardry was the power to converse with spirits of the dead (Isaiah 29:4), an offense punished with death (Leviticus 20:27). As the impetus and tool of Hokosa's witchcraft, Noma in one splendid scene, reminiscent of Saul and the witch of Endor (I Samuel 28:7), awakes from her vision of the spirits of the dead:

> "Take me hence," she cried, "or I shall go mad; for I have seen and heard things too terrible to be spoken!"
>
> "What have you seen and heard?..."
>
> "I do not know," Noma answered weeping; "the vision of them passes from me; but all the distances of death were open to my sight; yes, I travelled through the distances of death. In them I met him who was the king, and he lay cold within me, speaking to my heart; and as he passed from me he looked upon the child which I shall bear and cursed it, and surely accursed it shall be. Take me hence, O you most evil man, for of your magic I have had enough, and from this day forth I am haunted!"[70]

Even C. S. Lewis himself never conjured up a better scene of necromancy than this, though the opening pages of *Out of the Silent Planet* come close.

Ultimately, Owen's example belatedly converts the witch doctor Hokosa, but not before his betraying Owen and Nodwengo into a trap proposed to Hafela and also not before his poisoning the missionary rather than having to endure the scourge of Noma's tongue. In the process of Hokosa's conversion, Haggard transposes to Africa the paradigm of Christ's redemptive act. Hokosa ponders:

> Given the position of a universe torn and groaning beneath the dual rule of Good and Evil, two powers of well-nigh equal potency, he found no great difficulty in accepting this tale of the self-sacrifice of the God of Good that He might wring the race He loved out of the conquering grasp of the god of Ill. There was a simple majesty about this scheme of redemption which appealed to one side of his nature. Indeed, Hokosa felt that under certain conditions and in a more limited fashion he would have been capable of attempting as much himself.[71]

Like the "universe," the tribe is literally torn between the good king and the bad. And by an act of self-sacrifice in the climactic scene, Hokosa wrings his people out of the grasp of the evil claimant to the kingship.

One suspects a direct influence of Haggard's culminating spectacle of Hokosa's tree-crucifixion in 1896 upon a similar scene in Olive Schreiner's romancette, *Trooper Peter Halket of Mashonaland* in 1897. Their settings are contiguous—Haggard's north of the Zambezi and Schreiner's just to the south. The narratives of both authors center on a conversion to Christianity that demands self-sacrifice to achieve justice. And both foreground the binding of an African to a cross, in both instances an iconology as dramatic and Christological as that of C. S. Lewis. The iconic similarity of these climactic images of crucified blacks, the texts' near dates of publication, and the narratives' romancette lengths—all this, if not a direct borrowing, is certainly a remarkably similar response in the light of Rhodes's and Leopold III's territorial acquisitions to what Christianity must mean for an Africa freshly opened to European penetration. Haggard's English missionary not only converts Hokosa to the Christian principles for which the wizard is crucified but also dies, both because of his poison and for the sake of his redemption as well. Analogously, Schreiner's British trooper, converted by a vision of Christ, liberates the black Christ-figure and substitutes himself, dying in his stead.

Both writers utilize a tree as an emblematic Christian cross: Haggard's is a "great tree," "the bark on its great bole was leprous white."72 Owen's vision tells him

> "it is called the Tree of Death, and it stretches a thousand hands to Heaven, praying for mercy that does not come, and from its boughs there hangs fruit, a fruit of dead men—yes, twenty of them hang there this day.... I tell you that this Tree of Death shall become the Tree of Life for all the children of your people." ... High up upon the tree, and standing clear of all the other branches, was one straight, dead limb, and from this dead limb two arms projected at right angles, also dead and snapped off short. Had a carpenter fashioned a cross of wood and set it there, its proportions could not have been more proper and exact.73

Just as Haggard described in *Allan Quatermain* the primitive self that underlies the civilized man or as in *Nada* the fall of diabolic Dukuza engenders the rise of Christian Stanger, here also there is a more-specifically iconic religious complementarity, best illuminated in the quaint allegorizing of John Donne's "Hymn to God, My God, in My Sickness" in which he observes "We think that Paradise and Calvary, / Christ's Cross, and Adam's tree, stood in one place."74 Because the cross was made from wood that grew from the seed of the forbidden tree and its foot rested in Adam's grave, so according to the principle of the *dia+* and *syn+ballein*, moral failure becomes the seedbed of righteousness.75 William James in *Varieties of Religious Experience* (1902) explains that "the monistic philosopher finds himself more or less bound to say, as Hegel said, that everything actual is rational, and that evil, as an element dialectically required, must be pinned in and kept and consecrated and have a function awarded to it in the final system of truth."76

On this tree Hokosa is crucified: "Now the moon sank, but in the darkness men were found who dared to climb the tree, taking with them strips of raw hide.... Little by little the soldiers drew him up and in the darkness they bound him fast there upon the lofty cross."77 The tree in Schreiner is "a short stunted tree; its thick white stem gnarled and knotted; while two stunted misshapen branches, like arms, stretched out on either side."78 The native is tied to the tree "with riems [rawhide strips] round his legs, and riems round his waist, and a riem round his neck.... The black man hung against the white stem, so closely bound to it that they seemed one."79 The white Halket, who was supposed to execute the prisoner, releases him and is himself shot at the tree's foot in summary execution. Schreiner offers the vivid image of Peter Halket "lying under the little tree, with the red sand trodden down over him, in which a black man and a white man's blood were mingled";[80] and Haggard's Hokosa, the man who murdered Owen, dies with an affirmation of trust in the missionary on his lips.

In both narratives, the Christians have New Testament namesakes: doubting Thomas (John 21:25) and denying Peter (Matthew 26:34–35, 75), initially weak but ultimately, according to the Apocrypha and tradition, both heroic missionaries. Francis Owen was a missionary at Umgungundlovu encamped on a hill overlooking Dingaan's massacre of Piet Retief's party, which he describes in *The Diary of the Reverend F. Owen* (1926). Rather than warn the Voortrekker camp, just a few hours' ride distant, of Dingaan's war of extermination, Owen fled to Port Natal (Durban). Thomas Owen's less-than-heroic surname may incorporate motifs of his predecessor in the mission field, a faltering "spiritual Sisyphus,"[81] or it may suggest the last remnants of Owen's own self-regard that he must renounce. Although both whites die for the blacks, in Haggard's story the Christian convert is a native witch doctor, whereas in Schreiner's the conversion befalls the white trooper himself. It could be argued that Schreiner saw a greater need for a British conversion than an African. However, Haggard's focus here is not imperial abuse, as it had been in Schreiner's explicit attack on Cecil Rhodes, but modern miracle. Haggard effectively divorces the task of Christianizing the natives from any immediate military and economic conquest because the Sons of Fire live in the far interior: "Until that people is conquered—which very likely will not be for generations, seeing that they live in Central Africa, occupying a territory that white men do not desire—no missionary will dare again to visit them."[82] What is at stake in Haggard's narrative is the nature of modern belief, the ability of civilized man to recapture through his religious convictions the occult powers to which his eviscerated faith offers only lip service: "the Christian who of a truth believes the promises of our religion should trust to them and go."[83] Only if the British missionary can find the miraculous grace of God in his own life to overcome Thomas's doubt can he bring spiritual rebirth to the African. Thus Hokosa's conversion actually encompasses both races, for salvation is constituted by a mutuality of grace—i.e., by those miracles that redeem sinner and saint alike.

The translation of the Gospel of John on which Owen steadily labors[84] owes its selection to the purpose set forth in its prologue: the deity of Christ and the manifestations of faith and unbelief. The Gospel is filled with "signs" given by Jesus (John 20:30–31), including both the raising of Lazarus and his own resurrection, after which he appeared to Mary, to the disciples when he gave them the power to forgive sins, and again to the disciples in the presence of doubting Thomas Didymus (John 20: 11–29)—Owen's Christian name. John's preoccupation with a Christ whose mystical and divine nature transcends earthly experience and his emphasis upon the "new commandment" (John 13:34, 15:12; I John 2:7–8, 2 John 1:5) of Christian love—both on God's part, as in John 3:16, and on man's part—are the result of his desire to establish the fundamental principles of Christianity and to prepare the way for the future of the Church on earth. Jerome has given us the familiar story of the elderly Apostle John at Ephesus who, so weak and aged that it was necessary to carry him to worship, nevertheless could summon enough strength to repeat over and over: "Little children, love one another." Clearly Owen's final sermon[85] echoes the deed and message of the Apostle. The circumstances of Owen's translation of the Gospel of John emulate those of the Venerable Bede, who worked on his gospel translation until literally his last breath, completing the work on the very day of his death.

A second missionary romancette by Haggard, "Little Flower," first appeared in the collection *Smith and the Pharaohs* (1920). Set in the domain of the old Zulu empire that after 1879 became part of the Portuguese territory across the border from partitioned Zululand, its title is the Zulu name given to Tabatha, the daughter of the missionary Thomas Bull. Reminiscent somewhat of Rachel's missionary father in *The Ghost Kings*, the splendidly ironic pen-portrait of Bull is among the very best of Haggard's comic male characters. But if this story is a comedy, it is a profound comedy in which the innocence of youth, set against the poison of a religious-cultural imperialism, triumphs. The contestation of the Christian missionary with the heathen witch doctor is identical to that of *The Wizard*; but out of the same circumstances, Haggard—perhaps more mellow in the late autumn of life—shows how Tabatha's innocence leads the Zulu-Basutos from heathenism to faith. An example *in minimis* of Haggard's sly comedy lies in the mother's and daughter's names: Dorcas and Tabatha. Acts 9:36 tells of "a certain disciple named Tabatha, which by interpretation is called Dorcas: this woman was full of good works and alms-deeds which she did." The mother Dorcas and her daughter Tabitha (their Aramaic names denote the graceful gazelle and signify beauty) are two sides of the same coin: while the mother's inherited money is lavished by her husband Thomas on building projects, she uses it quietly for charitable assistance;

and the power or beauty of the daughter's innocence converts the witch doctor and his adherents to a radical Christianity.

Unlike Thomas Bull's doctrinal prejudices that even his bishop does not share, Tabatha's life and faith assimilate indigenous ways. She became "impregnated with the native atmosphere. She who ought to be at a Christian school now talked more Zulu than she did English, and was beginning to look at things from the Zulu point of view and to use their idioms and metaphors."[86] In telling the native children Bible stories, she did so "with embellishments and in their own poetic and metaphorical fashion."[87] Since Britishness signified imperial power, Tabatha was courting social stigma. But Haggard means his readers to understand that she is both the "little child" of Isaiah (11:1–9, though when she puts her hand on the "hole of the asp" and is bitten, it requires the witch-doctor to heal her) and one of the Sermon on the Mount's "lilies of the field."[88] As the natives perceived their "little flower," she was "one adored of dead and living, one to be cherished even in her dreams, one whom 'Heaven Above,' together with those who had 'gone below,' built round with a wall of spells."[89] Written after the Great War had bled Britannia white, this story came too late to be more than a postmortem on the fading of an empire on which the sun never set; its collapse is perhaps emblematized by Thomas Bull's new church undercut by the Zambezi in flood: "As the tower collapsed the clock sounded the first stroke of the hour, then suddenly became silent for ever and vanished beneath the water, a mass of broken metal."[90] But the witch doctor is fatally wounded by the debris of the bell's clapper. In his last act he endows Tabatha with his "Spirit" and accepts baptism, "led by his love of a little child whither he never wished to go; not for his own soul's sake, but just because of that little child."[91] This death is Haggard's clearest fictional exposition of radical Christianity, as he turns his heritage of Anglicanism back upon his deference to African animism.

If the code of colonial values was ostensibly the Bible, in the politicization of religion scripture was used to manage cultural interaction by hiding exploitative intent behind benevolent utterances. Perhaps for this reason Schreiner also consistently distanced herself from her pietistic heritage, remarking in a letter that her husband somewhat flamboyantly described as her only religious disclosure: "Personally I owe nothing to the teaching of Jesus: except the 5th and 6th chapters of Matthew no part of his teaching morally ever touched me as a child, and from the time I was 14 when I ceased to read the Bible or go to church Christianity has been almost non-existent for me."[92] One could, however, remark that the Sermon on the Mount in Matthew's gospel is more than enough to make anyone a saint, let alone an average Christian in the Cape Colony; and that ceasing to read the Bible at fourteen is vastly different from not having read the Bible at all. Both Schreiner and Haggard were "radical Christians" (from the Latin, *radix*, root) in their dismissal of the institutionalized church as they encountered it. Perhaps more truly than many of their spiritually comfortable contemporaries they followed the example of Christ who broke bread with the unclean and railed at the religious hypocrisy of his generation. Schreiner rejects not only the imperialist's "story" but also the missionary's "story" as she knew it in her household—the former because it was exploitative, the latter because it was paternalistic.

However much Haggard's or Schreiner's Anglo-African society may have imagined that the English missionary's Bible provided a mandate for colonial occupation, the inability of the "old wise people" to cope with the morality of the Sermon on the Mount undercut the myth of a univocal biblical entitlement by the Europeans to the land. The Sermon on the Mount can be understood as the voice of the oppressed Other, replacing the cultural myth of Europe's Protestant imperial identity with a code of values that will heal. As artist and social crusader, Schreiner embodied the same devoted earnestness as her missionary parents; but assimilating the very part of the Gospel to which her society merely paid lip service, she situated herself in a subversive or antagonistic posture vis-à-vis this dominant imperial and patriarchal social configuration. Haggard's or Schreiner's antagonism to cultural standards recasts the object of the conversion narrative. The child or woman or native victimized by colonial patriarchy and imperial power now functions as a reverse missionary sent from some non-European and aboriginal mount of mystical vision to challenge the dominant culture. As opposed to the colony's fraudulent manipulation of the missionary's "story" of spiritual worth, their stories rearticulate the religious and social morality of equality. Their insight is that society cannot have just one "story," that of the colonial master, but must listen to many stories told by the voices of children, women, and by extension the land and all of its inhabitants. Both Boer and Britisher, missionary and trader, were complicitous in creating the canonical "story" of imperialism resistant to the alternative stories that embrace the cries and songs of the indigenous peoples. Haggard and Schreiner, however, persist in desiring a national script liberated of doubleness and deceit, a universal and perfected language. They proposed a rectification of the master-servant, male-female, empire-colony hierarchy that was not a role reversal in which the disempowered seize control, but a radical role dissolution in which the mystical power of the land is in harmony with the material power of technology.

In a fascinating exchange between Christ and Peter Halket, which was Schreiner's South African updating of the Sermon on the Mount (the "kopje" on which they sit is a small hillock or "little head"), Christ gives Peter a story to tell Rhodes and the British:

Suddenly he felt the stranger's eyes were fixed on him.

"Who gave you your land?" the stranger asked.

"Mine! Why, the Chartered Company," said Peter.

The stranger looked back into the fire. "And who gave it to them?" he asked softly.

"Why, England, of course. She gave them the land to far beyond the Zambesi to do what they liked with, and make as much money out of as they could, and she'd back 'em."

"Who gave the land to the men and women of England?" asked the stranger softly.

"Why, the devil! They said it was theirs, and of course it was," said Peter.

"And the people of the land: did England give you the people also?"

Peter looked.... at him and was half afeared. "Well, what could she do with a lot of miserable niggers, if she didn't give them to us? A lot of good-for-nothing rebels they are, too," said Peter.

"What is a rebel?" asked the stranger.

"My Gawd!" said Peter, "You must have lived out of the world if you don't know what a rebel is! A rebel is a man who fights against his king and his country. These bloody niggers here are rebels because they are fighting against us. They don't want the Chartered Company to have them. But they'll have to. We'll teach them a lesson."[93]

Trooper Peter simply repeats as gospel the story that disguises the guilt of those who enact it: the natives are rebels because the land is England's. Who gave the land to England? "'Why, the devil,'" says Peter, hiding in a mere profane cliché the diabolic basis of colonialism.

Christ charges Peter to deliver a counter-story to Rhodes and the English that originates in the regenerate heart, a mystical vision that expands outward from the heart to the farm, the colony, the empire, and the world. Though he dies a martyr, Trooper Peter had failed, not without a hint of his namesake, to carry the message of the Sermon to the British on any national level. The opening verses of the Sermon spiritually empower precisely those whom a patriarchal society would suppress—the meek, the merciful, the pure in heart, the peacemakers, the persecuted. Indeed the noun "peacemaker" appears only once here in the King James and Revised Versions; and the arms dealer who christened the famous Peacemaker revolver—side arm of the U.S. cavalry and Indians, of British and Boer alike—must have been deliberately mocking the Sermon's morality: on the frontier technological superiority, not spiritual values, made the peace of imperialism. Thus when in the Kikuyu tale of the "Gentlemen of the Jungle" the Lion of Great Britain wants "peace and tranquility" in his kingdom, his failure to mention the justice that must underlie any peace clearly suggests a self-serving agenda of agricultural and mercantile exploitation, the Sermon's sowing and reaping, toiling and spinning, rather than a spiritual vision of the landscape—the Sermon's celebration of birds, grass, and lilies—and of its people delivered from evil (Matthew 6:13, 26–30).

An instructive comparison with Haggard's novel also exists in Mitford's *John Ames, Native Commissioner* (1900), described on the title page as "a romance of the Matabele rising." Like Schreiner's Trooper Peter, Ames is an employee of Rhodes's Chartered Company; but he resigns his post entirely because he unavoidably has pledged his word not to reveal the source of the natives' leadership, a lunatic white man impersonating their god and out to revenge himself on the colonial system. Mitford's literary strengths lie in genre painting—the Cape resorts, the frontier homestead and trading post, a sorcerer's cave—and in his narration of military engagements. Secondarily, his sharp sense of the complex social etiquette of courtship, so bizarre to contemporary experience—the hesitant use of given names, an obsessive sense of social respectability, emotional reticence, hyper-awareness of modesty in dress and gesture—all have an antiquarian appeal. But Mrs. Bateman's all-but-lesbian jealousy of John's closeness to Nidia surely would have been more candidly expressed in Haggard. And Mitford's wilderness landscapes sometimes just escape theatrical artificiality. His doting couple in the "uninhabited fastnesses of the Matopo" mountains[94] might be contrasted with the graphic local color of Haggard's similar stranding of Rachel and her companion in the opening scenes of *The Ghost Kings*. Finally, on the political issue of the Chartered Company and its injustices, Mitford avoids Schreiner's fierce indictment. Early in the narrative his heroine Nidia addresses Ames:

> "I don't wonder you pioneers are proud of the part you took in extending the Empire. Isn't that the correct newspaper phrase? At any rate, it sounds something big."
>
> John Ames smiled queerly. He was not especially proud of the extension of the Empire; he had seen a few things incidental to that process which had killed within him any such incipient inflation.
>
> "Oh yes; there's a good deal of sound about most of the doings of 'the Empire,' but there—I must not get cynical on that hand, because the said extension is finding me in bread and cheese just now, and I must endeavour to be 'proud of' that."[95]

What "few things" Ames saw we never discover; at the end Ames is enriched by a windfall from the lunatic Matabele *führer*, married into the wealthy family of Nidia. In short, he has become an unemployed squire back in England. His curiously passive way of protesting the "extension of Empire" is by smiling "queerly" and choosing withdrawal. In the last chapter he savors "the outlook from the library window of the beautiful and sumptuous home," enjoying with Nidia the "golden August, with the whirr of the reaping-machine, as the yellow wheat falls to the harvest, blending with the cooing of wood-pigeons among the leafy shades of the park."[96] The stuttering of Schreiner's Maxims haunts our encounter with Mitford's so very unironic scene of "happily-ever-after." But Mitford's, Schreiner's, and Haggard's narratives do assume another sort of interest in historical hindsight: the commonwealth they envisioned, a great Anglo-Saxon empire in Africa, is so very different from the one that actually emerged and that continues to define itself today in the land of Cecil Rhodes's nineteenth-century British *imperium*.

SEVEN

Romances of the Lakes Region: Tales of Terror and the Occult

The geographical background of Haggard's occult romances, including an Allan Quatermain subseries, is here no longer as directly based on the locale that Haggard himself observed in the 1870s and 1880s; rather, the journals of Richard Burton and other travel writers come into play. Nominally set in the 1870s in central Africa, inclusive of those present-day "heart of darkness" countries, Rwanda and Burundi, or in eastern Africa, the "great lakes region" of Kivu, Tanganyika, and Victoria bordered by today's Kenya, Uganda, and Tanzania, these fantasies were written, with the exception of *She* (1887), in the second half of Haggard's career. The adventures occur in a nonexistent world of incredible characters, embracing themes of magic, human sacrifice, monster-gods, lost races, and kidnaped white women. Haggard's loss of his only son and the death of his mother may have suppressed bleak reality and focused his range of motifs; but on the other hand, his end-of-century themes of magic and reincarnation may owe their strange power, their intensity and conviction, to the heart-mysteries of his personal griefs.

One may say of these "darkest Africa" adventures that as a rule they have less character development than earlier romances, probably for the very reason Olive Schreiner cites in the preface to her second edition of *African Farm*: namely, that wild adventures and hairbreadth escapes "are best written in Piccadilly or in the Strand: there the gifts of the creative imagination, untrammeled by contact with any fact, may spread their wings."[1] Fewer restraints of realism were in place when Haggard wrote of the unexplored interior, but Schreiner's disdain for such romances—or the disdain of the Victorian intelligentsia—does not, of course, mean that Haggard's trademark of popular romances remains unworthy of serious consideration in our postmodern age. Someone once said that writers of speculative fiction are the hounds of hell: they raise their shaggy black heads and sniff the wind, and feel the future coming. And then they howl. Perhaps Haggard's tales of terror and the occult achieve a more perfect fusion of vision and design when the politics and religion of his own time and place ripen conceptually beyond prosaic minutiae. The quest to heal the fragmentation or failure of wholeness, beginning in romantic thought, escalates towards crisis in the literature of transition between 1880 and 1920. The relations of the seasons in the annual cycle, good and evil, birth and death, reason and intuition, or the sacred and profane are incommensurable, capable only of a perpetual turning back of the one upon the other—a restlessness that this side of death never can be tamed. Certainly these eleven novels of the uncanny or occult are among Haggard's most explicit presentations of his romantic preoccupation with unity, division, and sought-after reintegration.

Analysis will begin with the most famous of all Haggard's novels, *She: A History of Adventure* (1887), and a group of five other fantasies that also do not feature Allan Quatermain: *The People of the Mist* (1894), *Benita* (1906), *The Ghost Kings* (1908), *The Yellow God* (1908) and *Queen Sheba's Ring* (1910). Next, I will examine the belated "prequel" to *She* and four other Quatermain tales written from about 1915 to the end of Haggard's life. Arranged in the approximate chronological order of Allan's adventures, these are: *She and Allan* (1921) set in the early 1870s; *The Holy Flower* or in the U.S. *Allan and the Holy Flower* (1915) occurring around 1870–1871; and three loosely linked sequels taking place between 1871 and 1874, *The Ivory Child* (1916), *Heu-Heu, or The Monster* (1924), and *The Treasure of the Lake* (posthumously 1926; composed circa 1916). Several other Allan Quatermain tales do not have an African venue. *The Ancient Allan* (1920) is a sequel to *The Ivory Child* but involves an earlier Babylonian-Egyptian incarnation; its ensuing story, *Allan and the Ice Gods* (posthumously published, 1927), presents Allan incarnated as an ice age caveman.

Haggard's *She: A History of Adventure* was published by Longmans, Green on 1 January 1887 in Prussian-blue bevel-edge boards. Though written in six weeks, its success, borne out by continuous reprints and movie adaptations, unequivocally confirms it the literary masterpiece of fantasy. Three later novels have the same eponymous *femme fatale*, Ayesha, but only *She and Allan* has its setting in the same sub-

Saharan region; and arranged not by original dates of publication but according to a chronological story of the queen herself, the order within this so-called "Ayesha Quartet" would be: *Wisdom's Daughter, The Life and Love Story of She-Who-Must-Be-Obeyed* (1923); *She and Allan* (1920); *She: A History of Adventure* (1887); and *Ayesha, The Return of She* (1905). In each of these novels Ayesha as erstwhile high priestess of Isis, moon goddess of the Egyptians, plays out the eternal love triangle. In *She and Allan*, Ayesha's original adversary in *Wisdom's Daughter*, Amenartes, has been replaced by Inez, forced by Rezu the villain to challenge Ayesha's power. Inez, rescued by Quatermain, ultimately becomes the mother superior of a convent in Natal. Her spiritual "marriage" as a nun removes her as Ayesha's rival in political dominion and in earthly love. Quatermain who falls under Ayesha's spell nonetheless is rebuffed.[2] Then in *She*, Ayesha's first adversary is reincarnated in Ustane, the native girl who loves Leo. Ustane is killed by the jealous Ayesha. And finally in *Ayesha, The Return of She*, the original Amenartes figure is reembodied in Atene who contests Ayesha for Leo's love—and loses, once again. Haggard's Ayesha as first portrayed in *She* owes several artistic debts: to Homer's Circe, to the Medusa myth from his earlier novel, *The Witch's Head*, and to the old legend of Tannhäuser's enchantment.

That Haggard as a "mere romance writer" was fully aware of the late-nineteenth-century intellectual *gestalt* has not been fully acknowleged; but his literary affinities hurdle genre lines in strikingly audacious ways: in images, vocabulary, sources, and structural design. The concept of a *Zeitgeist* may help explain these unanticipated textual interweavings, given our incomplete knowledge of what Haggard read. Ayesha as "She-who-must-be-obeyed" rules "far across the Zambesi"[3] in her mountain fastnesses as a White Goddess over a primitive lost race who slavishly worship her. This germ of Haggard's plot, whether by direct borrowing or cultural osmosis, belongs in part to the story of Venus and Tannhäuser's "strange idolatry." In "Two Early French Stories" (1872) and in "Pico Della Mirandola" (1871), Walter Pater drew on Henrich Heine's romantic concept of the return of the pagan gods to define this early idea of bondage to love in the Tannhäuser fable:

> In their search after the pleasures of the senses and the imagination, in their care for beauty, in their worship of the body, people were impelled beyond the bounds of the Christian ideal; and their love became sometimes a strange idolatry, a strange rival religion. It was the return of that ancient Venus, not dead, but only hidden for a time in the caves of the Venusberg, of those old pagan gods still going to and fro on the earth,

under all sorts of disguises. And ... this rebellious and antinomian element ... has made the delineation of the middle age by the writers of the Romantic school in France ... so suggestive and exciting.[4]

Precisely this godlike refusal to subject her passion to moral law endows Haggard's Ayesha with dread and splendor.

The syncretic Ayesha is also an echo of Medusa, the innocent beauty fallen. Raped by Neptune in Minerva's temple and punished for no fault of hers with a hideous transformation, Medusa had become the victim of an evil *force majeure*, an established tyranny—as depicted, for example, in Shelley's poem on Leonardo DaVinci's drawing of her. Leonardo's fascination with Medusa also had been examined by both Pater and, later, Freud, suggesting that during the period of transition into modernism she had become something of a cultural icon. In Haggard's novel, one form of Leo's name that had mutated over the centuries from Vindex to Vincey had been De Vincey—clearly related to DaVinci. Thus the female whom Leo/Leonardo pursues should be construed as the half-mortal, half-divine Medusa of the Florentine gallery described in Shelley's fragment or in A. C. Swinburne's interpretation of Leonardo's drawing: "beautiful always beyond desire and cruel beyond words; fairer than heaven and more terrible than hell; pale with pride and weary with wrong-doing; a silent anger against God and man burns, white and repressed, through her clear features.... She is the deadlier Venus incarnate ... for upon earth also many names might be found for her."[5] And one of them is Ayesha. But she is not an irredeemable figure of evil because, as we are told in *She and Allan*, like Medusa Ayesha was betrayed by Aphrodite and cursed by Isis. And like Medusa, she too embodies a subversive power for social transformation. On the one hand she epitomizes the fallenness of man and nature; but on the other she energizes the ideality and creative power glimpsed within corruption: "Death has met life, but there is life in death."[6] Her mating with the phallic pillar of fire in the cave-womb enacts nature's perpetual renewal of beauty, spring after spring, dawn by dawn: "it seemed to take the shape of a mighty man,... blood-red, splendid arms that stretched themselves toward me as though to clasp me to that burning breast.... I longed to lose myself in that embrace of fire."[7]

Finally, Haggard explicitly compares Ayesha to Circe several times, and Ayesha herself uses animal names for her British visitors: baboon for Holly, lion for Leo, pig for Job. A popular allegorical figure in the lusty Renaissance—George Chapman's Homeric translation and commentary was everywhere echoed—Circe masqueraded in many different guises: Spenser's Acrasia and Milton's Eve are surely her echoes or doubles, no less than her son Comus. Though Circe appeared in the visual art of the Victorians, the era's imaginative works tended not to cite her by name—with the exceptions of Matthew Arnold's "The Strayed Reveller," Walter Pater's *Gaston de Latour*, and, less notably, Ruskin's 1863 comment on Burne-Jones's painting of Circe and Augusta Webster's poem "Circe"—possibly because she too blatantly personified a decadent sensuality. But from John Keats's "Endymion," where Circe does appear in Book III, as well as in his "Lamia" and "La Belle Dame sans Merci" through to Oscar Wilde's *Salomé*, the century dramatized Circe's body-spirit dualism. Ayesha is Circe to Holly's Ulysses, and Circe's magic island, bower, or grotto that trapped Ulysses is central to the nineteenth century. Haggard, like Holly, admires Ayesha; and Ayesha-as-Circe, taken as psychobiography, represents Holly-Haggard's fascination with morbid beauty, both tempting and repellent, a dazzling carnality that perhaps defines Haggard's own fundamental desire for and uneasiness with human sexual activity but which certainly undermines the Victorian paragon of the asexual "angel" with her attending acolyte, Repression, all but mummified in a habitat "faint and delicate, and suggesting the essence of white rose."[8] As *paterfamilias*, Haggard platonically reined in his unruly horses of passion except when he unbridled them in romance writing. When Haggard in "About Fiction" used the image of naked beauty, he was initiating a new Victorian chapter in the history of the very ancient idea of Eros. The idea of the soul mate, noble or sinister, had earlier been explored by Haggard's influential precursor Stevenson in *The Strange Case of Dr. Jekyll and Mr. Hyde* and by Pater in the tale of Cupid and Psyche in *Marius the Epicurean*, both in 1885. But in 1887 in *She* Haggard not only incorporated the doppelgänger of Leo and Kallikrates but also linked this theme to the idea of a Platonic soul mate by means of Ayesha's deathless desire. Almost like Ulysses who carries a divine countercharm against Circe, Holly and Leo become obscurely but indubitably the beneficiary of Ayesha's patronage.

Haggard's immersion in the mystical life of London as a young man is ample warrant for his belief in the soul mate. Many of the ideas current were a mishmash of Eastern and Western arcana, but occultism's closest affinity to legitimate speculation would have been Plato and neo-Platonic theorizing. Ayesha defines the influence of beauty and love in terms of Plato's *Phaedrus*: that is, according to the innate inclinations of the beholder, not beauty's intrinsic morality as such. The Platonic theory that the lover's search for his own best self takes place through his idealization of the beloved—i.e., that the beloved's "counterlove" (*anterota*) is a reflected image (*eidolon*) of the lover's desire (*eros*) for him—is veiled in the "mythological fantasies" of the *Phaedrus*, in the Great Speech or "palinode" of Socrates on love and beauty. Socrates says that before the highest class of soul had fallen from its preincarnate phase into a body, it had accompanied a deity to the rim of the heavens and seen wisdom and goodness. For Plato, as for the Platonizing Wordsworth, birth was "but a sleep and a forgetting." Afterwards, this "lover and philosopher" adorns, honors and worships the beloved as if he were a reflected image of this deity or a statue of that primordial and imperfectly remembered Platonic beauty "standing with modesty upon a pedestal of chastity."9

The Platonic "effluence of beauty" wording appears twice in the *Phaedrus,* initially at 251b and also at 255c. In Plato this "stream" of beauty "called 'desire'" flows from its source in the beautiful one (Ganymede) toward the lover (Zeus), filling him, overflowing and rebounding back to the beloved:

> The stream of that fountain, which Zeus when he was in love with Ganymede called "desire," flows copiously upon the lover; and some of it flows into him, and some, when he is filled, overflows from him; and just as the wind or an echo rebounds from smooth, hard surfaces and returns to the place from which it came, so the stream of beauty passes back into the beautiful one through his eyes ... where it reanimates ... the soul of the loved one with love.... He sees himself in his lover as in a mirror without knowing who it is that he sees.... And in the lover's presence ... love's reflected image, love returned, dwells within him.10

From the beautiful one, the lover's soul catches and reflects back a glimpse of primordial beauty, to which the beloved conforms himself. Because the proper object of love is always the primordial beauty within and behind earthly beauty, the true lover becomes a mirror in which the merely physical is reflected as spiritual, inspiring the beautiful one's idealizing "counterlove." Socrates implies by his praise of the soul's beauty that love is more a passion for the Absolute than a desire for the beautiful one. In *She*, Ayesha's speech to Holly echoes just this Platonic passage: "For deep love unsatisfied is the hell of noble hearts and a portion for the accursed, but love that is mirrored back more perfect from the soul of our desired doth fashion wings to lift us above ourselves, and make us what we might be.'"11 Whereas Plato's effluence of beauty depicts Greek love, Victorian editors such as W. H. Thompson and Benjamin Jowett virtually purged the phrase of its original homoerotic overtones. The alert reader may observe that the adventures of Holly and Leo began at Cambridge, with Holly, a bachelor long since destroyed by a woman's selfishness, and Leo superficially very like, but emphatically not, the master's younger lover. Given that the nineteenth century's Hellenism and sexual politics were epitomized by the ancient universities of Cambridge and Oxford, Holly and Leo's terminus *a quo* and *a quem* is by no means irrelevant: in a world of romantic friendships surpassing the love of women, these two pursue a vision of both spirit and body, a beauty flourishing as an inner vision of flawless perfection yet rooted in the palpable earth.

Plato's ideal of a celestial love was ignored by Greek and Roman poetry but was embraced in medieval–Renaissance philosophy and art by the neo-Platonists of Florence and north Italy, such as Marsilio Ficino, Pico Della Mirandola, Michelangelo, Giordano Bruno and others. Haggard's use of the myth of Ayesha-as-Circe reflects this neo-Platonic allegorizing by the *dolce stil nuovo* of Plato's panegyric in the *Phaedrus* on the "inspired lover" and the noble and base impulses of the soul in love.[12] Broadly influenced by the commentary of Marsilio Ficino on Plato's doctrine of love, Bruno's *De gli eroici furori*,[13] published in England and dedicated to Sir Philip Sidney, takes its title specifically from the *Phaedrus*.[14] Bruno defines "Circean enchantment" as erotic, heroic and noble, and divinely inspired. Circe's love madness entails not only the voluptuousness that enslaves the soul but also the soul's quest for the divine light of reason. Bruno's mystical interpretation of Circe mitigates her fatality by integrating her into the background of the Platonic *trattati d'amore* and the *stilnovisti*.[15] The progress of Circe's lovers is from carnal desire through affliction to spiritual grace. Particularly significant is the suitors' recognition of Circe's chastening role in their rehabilitation: "Oh steps spent for good fortune, oh goddess Circe, oh glorious afflictions! Oh, how the pains of so many months and years are so many divine graces, if this is our recompense after so much torment and misery!"[16]

Bruno's chastening goddess of the spiritual quest, rather than the fatal goddess of brutish desire, is the key to Haggard's presentation of Ayesha as Circe. The ethical issues of good and evil expressed in the Victorian antithesis of sense to spirit and the contrasting, more-ancient ideal of perfection hidden within a fallen physical love reached something of a crisis in late-nineteenth-century intellectual-literary circles. Ontologically, Haggard's position is very like Browning's affirmation of the validity of the world and the temporal process in "Fra Lippo Lippi."

The Prior's folly in urging Lippo to paint pure soul is answered by Lippo's insistence that the world, though a snare, is for the artist a symbol of the glory of God. Though bourgeois Victorians defined body and spirit as contraries, Bruno and the *stilnovisti* had sought to bring them into harmony by a dialectical process: "For the most brilliant and the most obscure, the beginning and the end, the greatest light and the most profound darkness, infinite potency and infinite act coincide."[17] By virtue of Bruno's "coincidence of contraries,"[18] Circe, daughter of the sun, reappears as Diana at the moment when the chastened suitors come to appreciate the spirituality of material reality. As Bruno explains: "It is impossible for anyone to see the sun, the universal Apollo and absolute light as the supreme and most excellent species; but very possible to see its shadow, its Diana, the world, the universe, the nature which is in things, the light shining through the obscurity of matter and so resplendent in the darkness." If the lover does not directly apprehend divinity's "true essence," he nevertheless "sees it in its germination which is similar to it and is its image [alternatively, "will see her offspring, her image similar to herself"],... where it is contemplated and gazed upon as the sun is through the moon, which is illuminated by it."[19] For Haggard, too, this vision of a morally regenerate humanity ultimately originates within the diabolic discords of sexuality and death, modes made whole in the symbols of love. For nineteenth-century theists as for the neo-Platonists, the symbol heals the dissonance of strange calamity by throwing back together what had been thrown apart, enabling the idealizing mind to see the external world as no longer foreign but as that in which its own life consists.

In Plato's *Symposium* man is described as a whole divided by Zeus into two half-beings, male and female, who are impelled by love to reunite once again into the perfect whole. Socrates adds that love is not the happiness of possession but the insatiable yearning to possess. Who needs whom, who serves whom, who is the prey of whom and who the hunter—the answer is each by turns. Ayesha is blamed, burned, resurrected, redeemed and doomed, but ultimately her quest, like Tannhäuser's in the Venusberg, is for absolution and salvation. Ayesha is the mystical *totum simul*: "'Know that I, Ayesha, am but a magic wraith, foul when thou seest me foul, fair when thou seest me fair; a spirit-bubble reflecting a thousand lights in the sunshine of thy smile, grey as dust and gone in the shadow of thy frown.... Think of the hideous, withered Thing thou sawest naked on the rock, and flee away, for that is I. Or keep me lovely, and adore, knowing all evil centred in my spirit, for that is I.'"[20] But the conflagration of their consummate kiss destroys Leo's love; Ayesha vanishes as entirely as Lycius's beloved in Keats's "Lamia."

In a little-known and uniquely revelatory response to a reviewer, Haggard professes in the *Pall Mall Gazette* that his novel traces

> the probable effects of immortality working upon the known and ascertained substance of the mortal.... [T]he legend is built up upon the hypothesis that deep affection is in itself an immortal thing. Therefore, when Ayesha in the course of ages grows hard, cynical, and regardless of that which stands between her and her ends, her love yet endures, true and holy, changeless amidst change. Therefore, too, when at last the reward is in her sight, and passion utterly possesses her, it gives her strength to cast away the evil, and ... even to do homage to "the majesty of virtue." For love is to her a saving grace and a gate of redemption, her hardened nature melts in the heats of passion, and, as has happened to many other worldly-minded people, through the sacred agency of love, she once more became (or at the moment imagined that she would become) what she had been before disillusion, disappointment, and two thousand wretched years of loneliness had turned her heart to stone.
>
> Lastly, it occurred to me that in She herself some readers might find a type of the spirit of intellectual Paganism, or perhaps even of our own modern Agnosticism: of the spirit, at any rate, which looks to earth, and earth alone for its comfort and rewards. All through the book, although Ayesha's wisdom tells her that there is some ultimate fate appointed for man which is unconnected with the world (pp. 187 and 237), it is to this world only and its passions that she clings. Even in the moment of her awful end, she speaks of a future *earthly* meeting with the lover whom in the past she had feared to follow into death. When Holly, the Christian, refuses her gift of life, and tells her of his own hopes of immortality she mocks him. To her, all religion is but "a subtler form of selfishness and terror for the end." In the insolence of her strength and loveliness, she lifts herself up against the Omnipotent. Therefore, at the appointed time she is swept away by It with every circumstance of "shame and hideous mockery." Vengeance, more heavy because more long-delayed, strikes her in her proudest part—her beauty; and in her lover's very presence she is made to learn the thing she really is, and what is the end of earthly wisdom and of the loveliness she prized so highly....
>
> If any reader of the book is but half as much in love with She as I confess to being, he will understand how necessary I thought her fate to the moral, before I could steel myself to bring her to such an end.... Knowing that allegory if obtrusive is bad art, I was anxious not to bring it too much to the fore, with the result that this side of the story has evidently become almost imperceptible.[21]

Although Haggard's public comments do not probe the depths of his cultural mythology, the key to Holly and Leo's escape from their prolonged dalliance with Ayesha is the Platonic "law" enunciated in the *Phaedrus* and elsewhere that the carnal cannot obliterate the spiritual.22 When the unruly horses of passion seduce the souls of young men, says Plato, "the madness of love brings them no small reward; for there is a law that the paths of darkness beneath the earth shall never again be trodden by those who have so much as set their foot on the heavenward road, but shall live a happy life in the light as they journey together, and because of their love shall be alike in their plumage when they receive their wings."23 Haggard agrees with Bruno that the "decree and destiny of a new metamorphosis ... is ... said to be offered ... by Circe herself,"24 inasmuch as she is prototypically of the flux in its mutation, opposition, and latent reconciliation. Plato's transcendental theory of love in the *Phaedrus* is linked to the theory of the healing symbol; the primordial vision of beauty and the fallenness of external reality are interconnected and react with each other to make a whole. Thus the symbol is less a self-effacing window on the infinite, as suggested by Coleridge and Carlyle, than a self-reflexive mirror in which temporal fragmentation and discord are healed. The "broken lights" of immortal Love (Tennnyson's "In Memoriam") or the "broken arcs" of heaven (Browning's "Abt Vogler") are repaired by the symbol. In *She* the enchantment of Ayesha as a Circe-figure is neither permanent nor fatal, for like Ulysses, Holly and Leo possess the countercharm of a primordial vision that cannot be wholly expunged and that transforms the "madness" of imperfect love into, as Ayesha says, echoing Plato, "wings to lift us above ourselves."

※ ※

The other occult novels that do not feature Allan Quatermain's adventures, probably because Allan already has had his quota of matrimonial entanglements, are four pastoral love stories situated in north-central Africa: *The People of the Mist* (1894), *Benita* (1906), *The Ghost Kings* (1908), and *Queen Sheba's Ring* (1910). *The Yellow God: An Idol of Africa* (1908 U.S.; 1909 U.K.) has a West African setting and replaces Quatermain with a retired army major, Alan Vernon, ruined by speculators, who seeks gold in a mysterious country governed by an undying priestess and two idols. The male heroes in each of these—Leonard, Robert, Richard (like their lackluster names, each resembles the other!), Oliver (given the alliteration of Oliver Orme, a bit better) and Alan—are gentlemen, fit and alert; they do their duty to God and country, help the defenseless, and will never stoop to a dishonorable or cowardly act. But perhaps because the masculine desire of women was no stranger to Haggard's psychology, his female heroines embody a code of behavior of far greater complexity: "That woman is always potentially the noble creature, and often actually so, there can be no doubt. Thus when we imagine perfection in any shape or form we generally imagine it as female—at least men do. Also her variety is pre-eminent; this the novelist knows well. Well he knows the hopeless and baffling sameness of the average educated male of under fifty years of age, and the joy wherewith he turns to portray the women folk, no two of whom are the same."[25] Haggard's style of delineating his laudable female heroes is not unrelated to the medieval ideal of courtly love ruralized according to *pastourelle* conventions.

The People of the Mist was serialized initially in *Tit-Bits Weekly*, December 1893 to August 1894, appearing afterwards in October (London) and November (New York) issued by Longmans, Green. Leonard Outram and his brother go to Africa to find their fortune in order to buy back the family estate lost to a wealthy Jewish financier. In this calamity where historic ownership (land as an end in itself) is superseded by the wealth of commercial trade (land as a means to an end, here social status) we can glimpse a parallel with the imperial exploitation of native domains as a means to economic wealth; but the racial stereotype used by Haggard is an unfortunate reflection of British culture at the turn of his century, despite the positive influence of such major and minor cultural luminaries as Benjamin Disraeli and Israel Zangwell. One should note that this minor anti-Semitic allusion is redressed by an impartial portrait of the Abyssinian Jews in *Queen Sheba's Ring* (1910) and by the strong character of Merapi in the biblical fantasy, *Moon of Israel* (1918), even issued in a popular Yiddish edition. Digging for gold, Leonard is told by the exiled native Soa of the rubies and sapphires in her land of mist in "central South Eastern Africa."[26] If he and his native dwarf companion Otter, a Hans-like figure of fidelity to his master, will rescue Juanna from Portuguese slave traders on the Zambezi, Soa will lead them to the treasure.

Haggard's chapter on "the Yellow Devil's nest" and the saving of Juanna is brilliant in its local color and action and serves as the perfect stimulus for Leonard's romantic involvement with Juanna, called by natives the "Shepherdess." Her cognomen is probably an echo of "the virgin of the grove," Clorin, in John Fletcher's *The Faithful Shepherdess* (1610), a pastoral play of greater poetic beauty than dramatic excitement. Haggard capitalizes on the devilish practices of the slavers to segue to the weirdly demonic practices of his mist people. Although a custom of involuntary servitude had been part of African society prior to early contact with Islam and Christianity, by the nineteenth century the commercialization of chattel slavery in East Africa by Arab slavers assisted by local tribesmen was continuous and ruthless, though never as popularly noticed as the West African trade. Haggard's connection of this historical slavery to Leonard's economic impoverishment and to the fantastic religion of the people of the mist lies in the analogous loss of personal freedom that poverty, superstition, and slavery entail. But a further linkage is found when Haggard echoes the *Book of Common Prayer* to describe the slaver and his operations: "the Evil One and all his works."[27] The adventurers subsequently encounter a crocodile-devil with "yellow fangs," old, unfeeling, fat, with a vast mouth—just like the slave-trading Yellow Devil. After her rescue, that a young woman so idealized as Juanna should embark with Leonard on a raiding expedition[28] can only be excused on the grounds that the mist-people who have no use for the gems, practice "a religion of blood and human sacrifice."[29] Juanna attempts to replace this with a new creed of peace and love.[30] But because Soa, the daughter of the evil high-priest, loves Juanna to the point of insanity,[31] here recalling Hendrika's jealousy in *Allan's Wife*, she betrays Juanna and Leonard's strong but deformed retainer Otter, who are impersonating native divinities. Haggard's sociopolitical thesis is that a "secular authority"[32] embodied in an enlightened king is better than an evil priesthood cynically manipulating the tribe through devil worship.

Otter's fight with a diabolic crocodile, the tribal agent of divine punishment, is as vivid as Beowulf's struggle with Grendel's mother:

> "This is a devil that I have come to fight, a devil with magic in his eyes," he thought.... It lifted its head, fire seemed to flash from its dull eyes, its vast length began to stir. Higher and higher it reared its head, then of a sudden it leapt from the slope of rock, as alligators when disturbed leap from a river bank into the water, coming so heavily to the ground that the shock caused the cave to tremble, and stood before the dwarf with its tail arched upwards over its back.[33]

Otter springs towards his open mouth and plants two spliced daggers, points at opposite ends, in his jaws: "He felt the jaws close, but their rows of yellow fangs never touched his arm ... for the lower blade caught upon the jawbone, and at each effort it drove the sharp point on the upper knife deeper toward its brain."[34] The dwarf is tied by rawhide to his double-pointed knife and is dragged into the water of the lagoon:

> But he was as nearly amphibious as a human being can be, and could dive and swim and hold his breath, yes, and see beneath the surface as well as the animal from which he took his name.... Twice the tortured reptile sank to the bottom of the pool—and its depth was great—dragging the dwarf after it.... He felt the rough scales cut into his flesh and a sensation as though every bone in his body was breaking and his eyes were starting from his head.[35]

But the double knife saves Otter:

> Then darkness took him and he remembered no more. When the dwarf awoke it was to find himself lying on the floor of the cave, but not alone, for by his side, twisted into a last and hideous contortion, lay the Snake god—dead! The upper blade of the double knife had worked itself into its brain, and, with a dying effort, it sought the den where it had lived for centuries, dragging Otter with it, and there expired, how or when he knew not. But the dwarf had triumphed. Before him was stretched the ancient terror of the People of the Mist, the symbol and, indeed, the object of their worship, slain by his skill and valour.[36]

The treasure, however, is lost by Juanna fleeing the country; oddly, we never do learn in whose favor the pitched battle between the secular king and the cast of priests, that allows the couple to escape, is resolved.

But as in so many other tales, the real treasure won—or lost in *King Solomon's Mines*—is the woman. And to ensure that Leonard can enjoy his beloved prize free of material cares, Haggard contrives that his first love, Jane, who had deserted him to marry the tycoon who purchased his ancestral estates, dies and wills back to him his property originally lost. Her poignant letter of farewell and bequest poses the typical issue as to which woman has immortal claim upon the hero's love—the unforgettable first, she who betrayed but suffers and atones, or she who reawakens the buried passion and becomes the nurturing angel for husband and family. In *The Witch's Head*, Haggard had put forward Dolly over Eva, but in principle, the erotic and nurturiant complete each other, just as ownership of the old Outram mansion loops back in a consummating renewal.

Haggard's *People of the Mist* may have been the model for, and an enlightening contrast to, one of Bertram Mitford's best novels, the brilliantly eerie *The Sign of the Spider*, sumptuously published by Methuen in 1896. As with Haggard's adventure, Mitford's has a contemporary setting[37] and uses the same unknown territory for its demonic spider-god, who "had the head of a devil, the body and legs of a spider, and the black hairy coat of a bear; and, indeed, it was nearly as large as a fair-sized specimen of the latter."[38] If on the one hand this is a theatrical exaggeration in the vogue of Haggard, on the other it is a most worthy example in that venerable tradition of legendary fantasy monstrosities, from Grendel onwards. Economic desperation has led Mitford's Laurence Stanninghame to Johannesburg; and under the impetus of his new love—Lilith, the wife that should have been his at first—he treks into the fallen garden of the Congo. Though Conrad's Marlow has been credited with the aphorism that "this also has been one of the dark places of the earth,"[39] it was Mitford's scene of slave-hunting to which Conrad may be alluding:

> And as the whole party moves forth from the glade once more to plunge within the forest gloom, the air is alive with the circling of carrion birds; and the newly-risen sun darts his first arrowy beam upon the scene of horror, lighting up the red gore and the slain corpses, and the ghastly staring heads upon the gateway. Even as his last ray fell upon a tragedy of blood and of cruelty so now does his first, for in very truth this is one of the "dark places of the earth."[40]

Conrad transposes Mitford's allusion to Psalms 74:20 from the darkest Congo to London, broadening the theme of English slave-hunters to European imperial subjugation generally.

Mitford is far less intent than Haggard upon justifying his hero's morality. Indeed, apart from the emotional rejuvenation he gains from Lilith and his "savage" mistress, his sole principle is wealth, "the capture of the oof-bird."[41] At the adventure's close "he fell to thinking on what strange experiences had been his—of the consistent and unswerving irony of life as he had known it. Every conventionality violated, every rule of morality, each set aside, had brought him nothing but good—had brought nothing but good to him and his. Had he grovelled on in humdrum poverty-stricken respectability, what would have befallen him—and them?"[42] Even Lilith's ultimate betrayal pains Stanninghame less than Jane's hurts Leonard in *People of the Mist* because by then Laurence already has been intimate with the Ba-gcatya maiden Lindela: "young, tall, perfectly proportioned.... She wore a *mútya* or skirt of beautiful beadwork, and a soft robe of dressed fawn-skin also richly beaded but half concealed the splendid outlines of her frame."[43] Whereas Haggard's heroes never go back on gentlemanly "respectability," and whereas Conrad's Marlow is appalled by the "horror" that Kurtz acknowledges, Mitford invites us to admire Stanninghame for bravery and noble deeds; and we seem to be asked to dismiss his playing with the affections of Lilith as a married man. But as a slaver he is an even worse human predator: "It was himself or them, and he preferred that it should be them. Preyer or preyed upon—such was the iron immutable law of life, from man in his highest development to the minutest of insects: and with this law he was but complying, not in wanton cruelty, but in cold, passive ruthlessness."44 Mitford's authorial sentiments are impenetrable. Stanninghame is at least as well rewarded as Olive Schreiner's Bonaparte Blenkins; but Schreiner is explicit that Blenkins is despicable. Might Mitford's contented and revitalized protagonist be the ultimate imperial hero, he for whom slaving has paid off so safely and amply? The "take" on slavery here and in *The People of the Mist* is a fascinating contrast; one might very well prefer Mitford's narrative detachment with its ironic potentialities to Haggard's authorial guidance in moral-ethical matters.

Haggard's *Benita: An African Romance* was serialized in *Cassell's Magazine* (December 1905 through May 1906) and afterwards released in volume form by Cassell in London in September 1906, and, under Haggard's preferred title, *The Spirit of Bambatse*, on the same day by Longmans in New York. An action-fantasy that only needed Allan Quatermain to have been more widely cited, its "romancette" brevity and limited number of fully developed characters accord it secondary status even today. *Benita* opens with a vivid scene of the steamship *Zanzibar* sinking, perhaps less a prescient anticipation of the *Titanic* catastrophe than an echo of such recent past African sinkings as that of the *Teuton* of the Union Steam Ship Company bound from Cape Town to Port Elizabeth in Algoa Bay that in 1881 struck a rock in a calm sea and, with only one lifeboat lowered, sank with a loss of 236 lives.45 The plot action then moves to the Zambezi River, broadly around the years 1876–1881 in the time of Lobengula who succeeded Mzilikatzi as king of the Matabele. Partly on the basis of discussions with F. C. Selous and Theophilus Shepstone and partly from his own evidence, Haggard, as has been noted, cordially detested Lobengula because of the chief's murder of the Patterson party that included his servants, "Khiva, a Zulu boy who spoke English perfectly, and Vent-vogel or Wind Bird, a clever hottentot driver."46 In the fortress of Bambatse we have the familiar pattern of a concentric "holy of holies,"47 a womb-and-tomb site constructed by an Afro-Phoenician race whose last descendants are dying out under Matabele attack.48 In J. T. Bent's *Ruined Cities of Mashonaland* and in Wilmot's *Monomotapa*, to which Haggard contributed the preface, such ruins were described as constructed in ancient times by "Oriental" people. "Great Zimbabwe," a name that means "stone houses" in pidgin-Bantu, the largest of such ruins, was supposedly the biblical Ophir. But this and smaller ruins, not unrelated to the stone-fenced kraals of Haggard's time, were in fact part of an earlier Bantu-Arab gold-trading empire that at its height several hundred years previously had stretched between the Zambezi and Limpopo from the Indian Ocean to the Kalahari. Without doubt Wilmot's description of a great "Phoenician" structure, "half-temple, half-fortress, containing the sacred cone in its inner court, as at Paphos, Byblos, and Emesus" (Haggard's preface) was the prototype for Benita's prison. One weakness is that Haggard's citadel is more akin to that of, say, Hugh Walpole's in *The Castle of Utranto*, a tower in a country of the gothic imagination rather than any fortress we might really expect had once existed.

Also the romance recycles motifs of *King Solomon's Mines* perhaps a bit too closely: instead of the "colossal Death"[49] presiding over the past kings and the entrance to Solomon's treasure, *Benita* has a "colossal cross" with a crucified Christ, "the White One who hangs upon the cross" hovering above the ancient corpses of the Portuguese.[50] The secret entrance to the Portuguese treasure of gold, a flickering candle, a hidden passage to the outside world—all suggest what Ian Fletcher has called Haggard's repetition of "formulae of success."[51] Yet although in the total range of Haggard's romances restated actions, scenes, or themes frequently recur—such as being lost on the veld, lightning striking ferruginous rock, witch hunts, rescues of kidnaped white women, soul mates—how an artist contexualizes or deploys these favored motifs is aesthetically more important than the fact of their mere reappearance. Though chase scenes are a Haggard staple, surely Benita's initial escape from Bambatse and her flight back again pursued by Lobengula's *impi* is a brilliantly effective episode; and even though it is one of those "hair-breadth escapes" to which Olive Schreiner would have objected, it is dramatized better than anybody else could have done it.

The personality of Jacob Meyer is the most notable feature of this narrative. Like Hokosa in *The Wizard*, Jacob practices a "black art";[52] he drugs and mesmerizes Benita in his desire to discover the gold. Haggard identifies Jacob's power as an access through hypnosis to the "subconscious self which is part of the animating principle of the universe."[53] Undoubtedly Haggard chose his character's name for its Jewishness, although there was a redheaded hunchbacked Dutch artist known as Jacob Meyer (1852–1895), intriguingly painted by Gauguin as a satyr-like figure with pointed eyes, ears, and beard, holding a coiled golden snake—testimony to Gauguin's fixation with Jacob's near-demonic carnality. What makes Haggard's Jacob Meyer a villain may begin with a racial stereotype of greediness, but it is less his ethnicity than his materialistic values, his lust, and antimystical beliefs that condemn and destroy him. Although Meyer wants both the gold and Benita—in that order—he becomes less able to distinguish between love and lucre as he loses his sanity. Showering gold on his head, Jacob in his final moments becomes both Danaë and her prophetically condemned father Acrisius, King of Argos: "'A new version of the tale of Danaë,' began Robert in a sarcastic voice, then suddenly paused, for a change had come over Jacob's face, a terrible change."54 Insane with joy, then with fear, Jacob encounters the supernatural and dies, while the fair prisoner in the inaccessible tower, Benita-as-Danaë, escapes from mythic imprisonment with her father and Robert, her husband-to-be. Robert and Benita are iconically now king and queen of heaven: "Behind them was the terror of the cave, beneath them were the mists of the valley, but about them the light shone and rolled and sparkled, and above them stretched the eternal sky!"55

Serialized in *Pearson's Magazine* (October 1907 through June 1908), *The Ghost Kings* appeared in volume form with Cassell in September 1908 and later the following year in the United States. *Ghost Kings* is a story of predestined love, an attachment mystical in its essence and triumphant in its resistance to evil circumstances. The tale, reportedly plotted with Kipling's assistance, is set in the 1830s, initially in Natal and Zululand at the time of Dingaan and the Great Trek. Its action then moves "northward, ever northward"56 to the occult kingdom of the dwarf "tree people." Just as Haggard took particular pride in *Heu-Heu* anticipating "the discovery in Rhodesia of the fossilized and immeasurably ancient remains of the proto-human person who might well have been one of the Heuheua, the 'Hairy Wood-Folk,'"57 so the recent discovery of *Homo floresiensis* testifies anew to Haggard's prescient imagination in envisioning an upright-walking human dwarf species that has *not* been systematically crowded out by *Homo sapiens*, a long-cherished anthropological dogma.

Rachel Dove is the daughter of a missionary who has contracted a particularly virulent form of Anglicanism and whose single-minded rigidity and impracticality reflects all too truly the cultural failings of the European mind-set. But Rachel has inherited both her mother's levelheadedness and her "power of prescience."[58] She has the sort of distant sight such as Ayesha also possessed, a receptivity to images of past and present mirrored in still waters. Together with the visionary episodes of Thomas Owen in *The Wizard*, Haggard suggests here that Euro-Africans may regain those occult powers retained by the natives. A familiar theme in Haggard—and in nineteenth-century fiction since before Jane Austen—is that of a beautiful maiden for whose hand there are two rivals, one brimming with evil machinations and the other quietly and strongly virtuous. Rachel's two aspirants are Richard, her true love, and Ishmael, a scoundrel who plots to marry her[59] despite her hatred of him. Ishmael is very much in the mold of the repellant suitor that reaches back to such early Haggard villains as the Reverend Mr. Plowden in *The Witch's Head* or Frank Muller in *Jess*. This formula provides Haggard, and predecessors such as Dickens, a revelation of the heroine's character in the crisis of choice. Unlike Eva in *Witch's Head*, Rachel does not succumb to male pressure for marriage.

Haggard seems to be making the feminist point (and a covertly autobiographical contrast to Lilly) that women can be feminine and innocent, yet not stereotypically weak, prim, and emotional. With her gentle innocence yet strong and resourceful character, Rachel is a more mythic reembodiment of Allan Quatermain's two young wives, just as her Richard seems much like the young Allan himself. Because the masculine can only find its wholeness in the feminine, and vice versa, Rachel embodies "the Eternal Feminine that draws us ever onward"[60]—*das Ewig Weibliche* that in the figure of Gretchen had redeemed Goethe's Faust. Of course, Haggard applies Goethe's phrase neither to Rachel nor, as Freud did, to Ayesha; but in *Finished* he does describe the sorceress Nombé as "a perfect type of the eternal feminine with her graceful, rounded shape and her continual, mysterious smile which suggested so much more than any mortal woman has to give."[61] Richard and Rachel share "a 'soul affinity'" as Haggard phrased it in *Treasure of the Lake*.[62] Clearly such an affinity owes much to mystics such as Mme. Helena Blavatsky and the circle of the Society of Psychical Research established in London in the closing quarter of the nineteenth century.[63] They reintroduced into skeptical European minds—into Haggard's, if not Quatermain's more intensely doubting one—such ancient notions as reincarnation and that of Isis as a gnostic goddess, archetype of the eternal feminine. Perhaps even more pertinently, at the turning of Haggard's century, Rachel serves as an alternative to the New Woman

| SEVEN: Romances of the Lakes Region |

in man's trousers. She is the New Woman removed equally from servile submission to the patriarch yet also above a deadly militancy.

Early in the action, Rachel rescues Noie, a good witch, from Dingaan's slayers and the two young women, white and black, become companions. What remains vital in the otherwise stultifying missionary venture is transmuted in Rachel's character and appears to the natives as divine. In her, Christianity embraces paganism. She is precisely the sort of iconic, whitely clad demiurge that later J. R. R. Tolkien enshrined in his elvish figure of Galadriel, the Lady of Lórien. Because Rachel is elevated by the Zulus to the status of their white goddess, *Inkosazana-y-Zoola* who is the embodiment of the spirit of the Zulu race,[64] she is lured by Dingaan to his kraal. There Mopo, the teller of Nada the Lily's story, lurks waiting his chance to kill this tyrant as, earlier, he had assassinated Shaka. In a footnote Haggard cross-references Rachel's tale with that of Nada,[65] passing outside his story frame to a larger pattern of Zulu history and fantasy. As *Inkosazana*, Rachel replies to Dingaan's query about how the Zulus should receive the Boers: "'Those who lift the spear shall perish by the spear'"[66]—a straightforward cultural adaptation of "all they that take the sword shall perish with the sword" (Matthew 26:52) or "he that killeth with the sword must be killed by the sword" (Revelation 13:10). Though Christ's words were more a condemnation of aggressive violence than an endorsement of pacifism, the eschatological overtones of Rachel's paraphrase perhaps encouraged the Zulus, willfully, to choose not to understand her meaning. With an almost droll meticulousness they send for the priests of the ghost kings to elucidate her oracular utterance. In the romance's prefatory Extract, an anonymous letter-writer mentions the "defeats and other misfortunes"[67] of the Zulus, presumably at Blood River, that followed upon the warning of the *Inkosazana*. Rachel's admonition to the bloodthirsty king seems to be proffered by Haggard as one explanation for the decline of the Zulu nation, inasmuch as this letter from "the king's kraal, Zululand" is dated 1855, just before the battle of the Tugela in which the inferior claimant, Cetywayo, won the throne and sealed his nation's ultimate downfall.

The narrative in its final chapters shifts the scene north from Zululand to the remote interior. Among the dwarf folk, Eddo becomes Rachel's sinister suitor, candidly confessing his intention to use her selfishly as also Ishmael had intended. Rachel's captivity among the tree worshipers in this fantasy world of the ghost kings may owe much to such anthropological studies as that of Sir James Frazer. And Frederick Elworthy, for example, has noted that tree-worship originated in the interior of Africa and that the tree spirit often was embodied in living form; aborigine and tree, each is the "translation" of the other according to Elworthy.[68] The familiar Manichean pattern of struggle emerges again, here between Eddo, the evil ghost-priest, and Nya, the good Mother of the trees. By burning the mystical Tree of the Tribe[69] Noie destroys the corrupted ghost-folk along with herself, a cleansing sacrifice that saves Rachel whom she loves.[70] On its last page the narrative ends for Richard and Rachel with a hint of Milton's Adam and Eve leaving their fallen garden to enter, with sadness and hope, the quotidian world: "The World was all before them, where to choose / Their place of rest, and Providence their guide: / They hand in hand with wandering steps and slow, / Through Eden took their solitary way."[71]

Haggard's only adventure novel set in West Africa is *The Yellow God* (1908), a tightly crafted tale that unfolds in London and imaginary Asiki-land, located up-country from the port of Calabar in the Niger delta. It opens with Major Alan Vernon, a veteran Africa hand, disentangling himself from partnership with a pair of well-heeled swindlers in "the City." (Alan is *not* Allan Quatermain, but could the given names subliminally have suggested to Haggard a similarity of personality?) Barbara is the ward of one charlatan, the amorous object of the other, and is herself in love with Alan. Alan's missionary uncle had brought back from the Asikas a gold mask that looms as a living, transformative fetish.[72] Haggard did not embrace (fortunately) today's ideology that his uncle's extraordinary *object d'art* was a hegemonic, colonialist "capturing" of a tribal artifact, a deportation to an English mansion and a boardroom like some hostage or slave; but equally he is far beyond the colonial contempt for a lack of skill or slight sense of form in tribal artifacts. The origin of this mask is imputed to a long-lost ancestral race of Asikas, but by its animistic powers it obviously is not associated with the sources of Western higher culture, as had been Zimbabwe's ruins. In the manner of Picasso who first studied and emulated African masks in 1907 for *Les Demoiselles d'Avignon*, Haggard proposes the Asika mask as both art and something more: a very living reality. When one considers that Roger Fry's "Art of the Bushmen" (1910) and "Negro Sculpture" (1920), with that critic's sense of discovery and enthusiasm for African masks, were still several years in the future when *The Yellow God* was written, Haggard's fantasy-interpretation deserves to be carefully scaled against developments in the artistic and anthropological world outside of its purely generic domain.

Alan Vernon embarks from Old Calabar accompanied by his native servant and guide, Jeekie, a pragmatist in faith and life, on an upriver expedition to find the fabulous gold of Asiki-land that reportedly the natives do not value. There he is trapped by an Ayesha-like priestess, whose jealous love would sooner kill him than allow him to leave.[73] Her "evil loveliness"[74] and "immortality" through many successive incarnations[75] certainly echo *She*. The "smelling out" at the Feast of the Little Bonsa[76] is comparable to the scenes in *King Solomon's Mines*. At this Feast, the Dionysian dancing of Asika is surely one of Haggard's more erotically intense spectacles, but he carefully separates his ethnographic description of the dance itself from his commentary on Asika's voluptuous nakedness, and thus dilutes arousal.[77] Haggard's Asika seems almost an anticipation of Josephine Baker's sensual performances on the stage of the *Théâtre des Champs-Élysées* and in the *Folies Bergère* in the 1920s; at any rate, Haggard is fully aware of Asika's wild contrast, circa 1908, to "a ballet at the London music-hall."[78] A curious inverse symmetry operates in the plot, inasmuch as although both Barbara and Asika are balked by respective statutory impediments from marrying Alan immediately, the contrast between Alan's intended and the African queen, so savage and superb in her carnality, could not be greater. If Asika has the potential to destroy masculine self-control and unleash Alan's inherent capacity for an evil repressed by a structured European society, Barbara is Asika's spiritually unfallen counterpart, what may be termed the *sym + ballein* in contrast to the *dia + ballein*. The point of the parallel legal impediments to Alan's immediate nuptials is found in the antithesis of social constraints against individual desire. Just as the etymology of Barbara's name alludes antithetically to her connection with feminine chaos, so the primitive powers of darkness are not without venerable usages or cultural practices, though their precise meanings have been long since emptied of definite history and dogmatic interpretation.

Perhaps because Solomon was such a presence in Haggard's first commercial success, it is inevitable that *Queen Sheba's Ring* (1910) should echo many motifs of that narrative: the trio of adventurers (one comic, one heroic, one practical, but now with their servant Quick become a quartet); the rescue of a family member; thirst in the desert and ancient roads; tombs and a cave of ancient treasure—even a written contract at the adventure's commencement. Set somewhere around present-day Uganda, the natives and their beautiful female queen have lineally descended from Sheba's Abyssinians. Since Quick earlier had served in the Anglo-Boer war, the adventurers' mention of a camera and use of a field telephone and 3000 pounds of electrically detonated azoimide liquid to blow up a gargantuan stone Sphinx are touches in which a brash contemporary twentieth century meets Sheba's antiquity. Like the myth of the divine origin of the Egyptian pharaohs, Abyssinian rulers were supposed to have descended from Menyelek, the son of Solomon by the Queen of Sheba, and were also believed to be divine. Wallis Budge, an early friend of Haggard and translator of the *Kebra Negast*, a fourteenth-century AD Ethiopian Bible, told him stories of Egyptian archeology and spiritualism that well may have contextualized this tale.[79]

The Abati, over whom the beautiful Maqueda, called the Walda Nagasta or Child of Kings, rules are at war with the tribe of Fung. Whereas the Fung are prolific and warlike, the Abati suffer "decadence from interbreeding."[80] They live, according to the narrator, in a "fertile and mountain-ringed land" but are "a pack of effete curs."[81] As an island in a sea of hostility, their pacifism—in reality, a love of comfort and a confirmed cowardice—seems almost a veiled reference to British insularity and complacency in the years before World War I, a sentiment that may well have reached all the way back to Haggard's feelings about the retrocession of the Transvaal in 1881. When H. G. Wells played off the spineless Curate against the militaristic Artilleryman and Martians in his *War of the Worlds* (1898) or set the Eloi against the Morlocks in *The Time Machine* (1895), he was arraigning the intelligentsia for being hypocritical, abject, elitist, and lacking in courage and masculinity, comradely solidarity and self-sacrifice—and, of course, religious conviction. On the other hand, his Artilleryman and Morlocks were an uncanny anticipation of twentieth-century totalitarianism—authoritarian, immoral, racist, and regimented. The Abati are the former and the Fung are the latter; and between these poles are Queen Maqueda, a handful of mountaineers led by her captain, Japhet, and her British rescuers. Wells and Haggard may both be depicting a faltering and weakened bourgeois barely able to keep an angry proletariat at bay. As in *People of the Mist* or *Treasure of the Lake*, a corrupt priesthood and nobility control the country; the monarch, in sympathy with the feelings and opinions of ordinary decent people like Sergeant Quick, is really a hostage. Haggard's real-life model of a strong central native government based on a rule of law is lacking here, as it was in Zululand after the 1879 war and as it was fictionally both in the Kukuanaland of *King Solomon's Mines* until Ignosi came to the throne and in *She and Allan* until the defeat of Rezu. Perhaps Haggard's fictional pattern betrays his disgust with the political policies of British imperialism at its ministerial levels, if not the political exigencies and curbs on the monarchy of England itself.

She and Allan (1921) rounds out and solidifies Haggard's *mythos* of Hunter Quatermain, the Victorian skeptic who wanders after elusive Truth. Much like Olive Schreiner's central allegory of "the hunter" in *The Story of an African Farm*, so this novel concludes with Zikali's description of Allan hunting for "the Mountain of everlasting Truth, sought of all men but found by few."[82] The fear that *She and Allan*—set as a "prequel" to *She* during the reign of Cetywayo,[83] probably 1872 or just after—would exploit the success of its original, like a bad movie "remake," is groundless. If not equal to the mythopoeic *She,* this tale yet has its fine moments, its classic battles between man and nature, its occult suspense, and its authentically artistic emotional highs and lows. Certainly Quatermain's ordeal of navigating a swamp[84] compares favorably with the drama of the desert in *King Solomon's Mines*. And Quatermain's sidekick Hans, as always the quick-witted, cynical pragmatist, provides his modicum of humor. But between the Ayesha of 1887 and that of 1921, Haggard's seductive *femme fatale* has become softer, more vulnerable and complexly nuanced. Her locus is no longer a mountain morgue but the romantic ruins of Kor: "the miles of desolate streets and the thousands of broken walls, and the black blots of roofless houses and the wide, untenanted plain bounded by the battlemented line of encircling mountain crests, and above all, the great moon shining softly in the arching sky."[85] This locale reinforces Quatermain's wistful lament for the days that have gone, his constitutional *Ubi sunt* mood.

In particular, as advancing age brings to Allan a sense of the moment lost even before it can be committed to memory,[86] the insistent query arises: is love stronger than death? This is also Ayesha's question, inasmuch as she awaits the return of her Kallikrates, her Apollonian sun god consort lost in the underworld. Ayesha, we learn here for the first time, is in spiritual communion with wizards elsewhere. The plot links Ayesha to her physical opposite, Zikali, the ugly dwarf-wizard, by means of Allan's quest for a vision of his deceased wives. Zikali sends Quatermain and Umslopogaas "far across the Zambesi"[87] to Ayesha's territory to answer both Allan's yearning for explanation as well as Zikali's own question whether his vendetta against the House of Senzangakona will succeed. But Allan is reluctant to cross the Zambezi until his pursuit of a young woman kidnaped by rebellious Amahagger brings him to Ayesha's stronghold. In Haggard's romances the abduction of the white female frequently is a prelude to consecrating her as an African priestess or queen.

Ayesha here is the agent of and nearly identical with Isis, the moon-goddess of nature.[88] But her beauty and chastity have incurred the curse of Aphrodite;[89] bereft of her beloved Kallikrates and in eclipse or exile, Ayesha's powers are now challenged by Rezu, the false sun-god. After a widespread conflict, Umslopogaas, the heroic champion of the good, settles the rebellion virtually by single combat, like Sir Henry in *King Solomon's Mines*, with his magic axe, Inkosikaas.[90] His leap over the head of Rezu accompanied by a backwards stroke of his axe is surely one of the most dramatic moments in any Haggard battle scene. But since we know from *She* that Ayesha herself had killed Kallikrates, she embodies both Aphrodite and Isis and is at war with herself. In one phase she is Aphrodite, since once in ancient Greece she was a sculptor's model of Love.[91] But she notes of her statue that "mine had a mark on the left shoulder like to a mole," probably Haggard's echo of Lyly's *Euphues*: "Venus had hir Mole in hir cheeke which made her more amiable; Helen hir scarre on hir chinne."[92] Yet in her other aspect she is identified with Isis: "Do you know that the moon was a great goddess in Old Egypt and that her name was Isis and—well, once I had to do with Isis?"[93] Moreover, since she is both old and young, we have the same pattern as in Gagool and Foulata—an embodiment of the master trope of Nature's seasonal cycle of life, death, and rebirth. In Ayesha the goddesses of passion and celibacy allegorize the typical Haggard pattern of the inextricably linked good and evil powers at war:

> "All men worship their own god," she went on, "and yet none seem to know that the god dwells within them and that of him they are a part. There he dwells and there they mould him to their own fashion, as the potter moulds his clay, though whatever the shape he seems to take beneath their fingers, still he remains the god infinite and unalterable. Still he is the Seeker and the Sought, the Prayer and the Fulfilment, the Love and the Hate, the Virtue and the Vice, since all these things the alchemy of his spirit turns to an ultimate and eternal Good. For the god is in all things and all things are in the god, whom men clothe with such diverse garments and whose countenance they hid beneath so many masks."[94]

This passage also recalls the complementarity between diabolic Dukuza and symbolic Stanger in *Nada the Lily*, the typical structural pattern of Haggard's thought.

The supernatural crisis comes when Ayesha induces Quatermain's out-of-body experience[95] and he realizes that Stella, Marie, and his family seemingly have forgotten him; it is deeply disillusioning to Allan and, undoubtedly, also disturbing to the reader's sense of what Haggard may mean. Umslopogaas has an identical disappointment with the spirit of Nada. Only Mameena and Allan's heroic dog Smut (his name means a particle of soot) show an awareness of his proximity and respond with affection. Indeed, the most powerfully poignant moment, the climax to this kaleidoscope of wraiths, comes when Smut plunges into the river and swims to his master, licking his face and "yelping with mad joy."[96] Afterwards, Ayesha hints that she has controlled the manifestations to humble Allan by disabusing him of an inflated sense of his importance to the dead; however, the reader suspects Ayesha of a cynical gesture or, perhaps, a failure of theological insight. If, within Haggard's fictional world, we are to take his encounters as "actual" occult manifestations and not hallucinations produced by Ayesha's deception, then the clue to Quatermain's humiliation lies in Mameena's reference to herself as "a sinful woman with a woman's love and of the earth earthy."[97] Had Quatermain read his New Testament with the same gusto as the Old, though admittedly the former has the earthier stories, he might have understood. Mameena's imagery is Haggard's echo of I Corinthians, contrasting the "natural body" with the resurrected "spiritual body": "The first man is of the earth, earthy: the second man is the Lord from heaven. As is the earthy, such are they also that are earthy; and as is the heavenly, such are they also that are heavenly. And as we have borne the image of the earthy, we shall also bear the image of the heavenly" (15:44, 47–49). As Paulus there explains: "flesh and blood cannot inherit the kingdom of God" (15:50), so only the "natural body" and not the "spiritual body" retains a sense of fleshly love. Because "the smell of earth,"[98] its suffering and loss, is an inextricable dimension of mortal existence, the sinful woman and mongrel dog remain part of Quatermain's "natural" reality and thus express their love. But Allan's wives exist on an entirely different plane: "For in the resurrection they neither marry, nor are given in marriage, but are as the angels of God in heaven" (Matthew 22:30). And angels, as Milton observes, do not entertain the possibility of—or retain a memory of, as Allan and Mameena do—the carnal joys of kisses or greater intimacies.

In *The Holy Flower* (1915) Haggard grafts the fantasy of a holy orchid and its gorilla god onto the historical base of the East Africa slave trade in the 1870s. Haggard's slave trader Hassan-ben-Mohammed clearly is modeled upon the Zanzibari Hamed-bin-Muhammad (or Tippu Tip, 1837–1905), a notorious Swahili slave trader of mixed Arab (the so-called White or Red Arabs) and African slave parentage. Once again in Haggard's fiction the theme of deleterious miscegenation hovers in the villain's background. From the 1860s Tippu had directed long-distance slave and ivory caravans from the equatorial interior, from Lake Nyasa and from west of Lake Tanganyika, to the coastal towns where the slaves were shipped into the Arab colonies at Zanzibar or Kilwa to be sold to French or Portuguese merchants for work on sugar, coffee or rice plantations. In the wake of such protests as John Wesley's "Thoughts upon Slavery" (1774) and such economic studies as Adam Smith's *The Wealth of Nations* (1776), Parliament first restricted then ultimately outlawed English slave trading, though its actual abolition in and around Zanzibar did not occur until nearly the twentieth century. Slave ships were intercepted by the British navy, and as Haggard describes, there really was an English "man-of-war," *Crocodile*. The Royal Navy's *Crocodile* was launched in 1867—single funnel, three masts rigged for sail, white painted hull with "ram bow"—and decommissioned in 1894.

Haggard's American missionary, Brother John, whose pregnant wife is kidnaped and sold into slavery, may not be quite patterned on David Livingstone; but in the same year the *Crocodile* was under construction (1866), Livingstone trekked to Lake Nyasa with the intention of revealing the atrocities of the slave trade and, by introducing more suitable trading opportunities, to undercut the slavers. Certainly the interest of missionary societies in East Africa was roused by Livingstone's campaign. The novelistic link between this factual practice of slavery and the fantasy of the Pongo religion lies, as it did in *The People of the Mist*, in the common loss of personal freedom, physical as well as intellectual in each instance. The plot has a degree of improbability but the realistic details give the fantasy a counterbalancing authenticity. Haggard, an orchid grower himself, delightfully has interpreted an aficionado's love of *Orchidaceae*; and when Quatermain salvages a seedpod of the Holy Flower, only to lose the seeds through the fabric, the reader empathizes as acutely as he would have, had Allan lost Solomon's diamonds from the pockets of his shooting coat. In Haggard's later fantasy romances, such as this, his storytelling craftsmanship is seemingly more efficient and streamlined, pitched past pitch of presto readability.

The Ivory Child enjoyed a newspaper serialization from January 1915 onwards; it was published by Cassell in London (January 1916) and by Longmans in New York (February or April). It purports to be an explicit sequel to *The Holy Flower*, although in 1924 the adventure with Heu-Heu was interposed in Allan's order of escapades. Also, because the *The Ivory Child* apparently was nearly a decade earlier in composition than *Heu-Heu*, the former may reflect the more optimistic possibility of evil as political, external and conquerable. Although *The Holy Flower* made reference to the Zulu hunters drinking too much beer and "smoking too much of the intoxicating *dakka*, a mischievous kind of hemp,"[99] *The Ivory Child* is Haggard's first Taduki-induced story, which includes those late Quatermain tales that are not set in Africa. Taduki also seems not unrelated to the leaves of the Tree of Illusions[100] that Zikali in *Heu-Heu* requested Quatermain bring back from that accursed land. Since the mythical Taduki drug is not directly allied to the Indian hemp introduced by Dutch colonists into Africa from the East, Haggard seems to be suggesting that Zulu wizards had an indigenous, and more powerful, form of *cannabis*. Perhaps Haggard's interest in such consciousness-expanding experiences also might be related fruitfully to similar experimentation, not much later, by Aldous Huxley taking mescalin with South American Indians and to an interest in awakening the sacred in a society hostile to mystical revelation. *Ivory Child*'s African-Egyptian mythology involves Horus-the-child, the sky-god whose eyes were sun and moon. The sun-god Osiris is treacherously murdered by Set, the power of darkness and evil, and his death is avenged by his son Horus. Thus the sun is overcome by night but rises again the next morning. Isis is the sister-wife of Osiris and mother of Horus. Lady Ragnall's crescent-moon mark of Isis,[101] akin to the theurgic cicatrix of Ayesha, identifies her in the eyes of the Pongo as their next goddess; and she is kidnaped, not unlike Brother John's wife in *The Holy Flower*. As an ancient but faltering society, apparently the Pongo need a spiritual infusion of what Ruskin had called "the best northern blood,... rich in an inheritance of honour, bequeathed to us through a thousand years of noble history."[102]

Complaints about the pace of the introductory game-shooting chapters, like those concerning the scenes of orchid auctioning in the previous novel, seem misplaced. In *The Ivory Child* Haggard opens with a period vignette of a shooting party at a country manor. Is it "dated and boring"? Or is it a fantasia from history, a vintage trinket of past time, Haggard's scenes bespeaking an opulent gentility of sportsmanship and dining never to return? Whatever one's "take" on it, it also serves as a structural contrast to the primitive world opened by adventure. And another purpose of the short story-like shooting prologue may be to show how fragile the "inheritance" of a patrician way of life is when a South African confidence man, vanKoop, remakes himself in England into Sir Junius Fortescue. Lord Ragnall comments ironically to Quatermain that Sir Junius "subscribed largely to the funds of his party ... and, perhaps by coincidence, subsequently was somehow created a baronet."[103] The fraudulent manipulation of British social status is contrasted with the honesty of Hans, the publicly despised Kaffir servant. Even Lord Ragnall himself only ceases to be a conventional figure of wealth when he is galvanized by the challenge of recapturing his kidnaped wife. The centrality in this narrative of the Hottentot Hans, doubtless modeled on Haggard's own South African servant Mazooku, previously has been commented upon and noted that in this adventure he dies. In one sense Hans never dies because he is reembodied—though one always feels to a lesser extent—in divers other native servants. Hans's particular quiddity is his cynicism; he is constantly suggesting the low road—steal the wanted item, run from the approaching danger, kill the bothersome person, and so on and on. In *Treasure of the Lake* Hans hits a wonderful low in rationalizing such deeds because Quatermain and he are unlike the Africans: "'good Christians like you and me wouldn't need to bother about *them*, Baas, because, you see, they all have to do with the devil.'"[104] But this is just a pose that Hans adopts to call attention to Quatermain's "foolishness" in not being more self-regarding. For Quatermain to play the fool is to fulfill Erasmus's ideal in *Praise of Folly*: foolish in terms of the things of this world, moral in terms of the next. And, of course, when practice requires selflessness, Hans is among the greatest of moral fools. Could it be that Hans slyly articulates the morality of unreconstructed imperialism—the predatory morality of the adventurer like Olive Schreiner's Bonaparte Blenkins in *The Story of an African Farm* or Philip Hadden in Haggard's own *Black Heart and White Heart*—to point up more clearly the principles that he and Quatermain as English gentlemen will never betray?

The issue of sociopolitical freedom and the illusions of belief by which the freedom of thought is destroyed are important themes picked up again in *Heu-Heu, or The Monster.* This romance had been serialized in *Hutchinson's Magazine* (January through March of 1924) and published in book form by Hutchinson even before the serial was half finished. Although interpolated between Allan's adventures in *The Holy Flower* and *The Ivory Child*, the latter had introduced the inhaled Taduki herb and *Heu-Heu* includes a quest inspired by Zikali after a similar hypnotic drug. By this adventure Hans has already earned his cognomen, Light-in-Darkness, awarded during his exploits in the previous *Holy Flower.* Set circa 1871—we are told that diamonds had recently been discovered for "just then all Africa was beginning to talk about these stones"[105]—*Heu-Heu* is a romance concerned with superstition and the priestly power that for its own ends supports it. Like *The Holy Flower*, *Heu-Heu* is a tale of a gorilla god, though in this adventure a human priest merely wears the costume of an ape to impersonate the diabolic deity, much as Hans briefly did in *The Holy Flower.* Heu-Heu is several times alluded to as a "devil."[106] As the embodiment of the *dia + ballein*, Heu-Heu, his priests, and his tribe of "hairy folk" hold the upper hand over the dying race of the Walloo, who are under the spell of this demonic god. Annually they must sacrifice a maiden who is either accepted by the god or scorned, in which latter case they are relentlessly attacked by the hairy folk in the coming year. Narratively, the romance is not as robust as its predecessors, but in the climactic rescue of the maiden from her volcanic rock, Haggard's storytelling gift does not desert him. Harnessing one of the earth's primal forces for his purposes, Allan defeats the treacherous "heuheua" by guiding cold lake water into the island's caldera faults above its magma chambers. The eruption caused by the explosively expanding steam all but levels the island home of the spurious god. Perhaps Haggard drew upon historical descriptions of Vesuvius, Tambora or Krakatoa, though the phreatic eruption of Lassen Peak in California between 1914 and 1921 may well have been his immediate model.

When Quatermain first hears the history of Heu-Heu from Zikali, he thinks: "The story was foolishness. And yet—and yet there were so many strange peoples hidden away in the vast recesses of Africa, and some of them had these extremely queer beliefs or superstitions. Indeed, I began to wonder whether it is not possible for these superstitions, persisted in through ages, to produce something concrete, at any rate to the minds of those whom they affect."[107] This is not unlike Dorothy's belief in *The Witch's Head* that what you believe becomes your reality.[108] And indeed, Issicore dies only because of his belief in the power of the fetish.[109] The Walloo, then, are in bondage not to an outside power, but to their own inner illusions. This would seem to be an important preoccupation anticipated in Schreiner's allegory of the Hunter:

> "'Then the hunter took from his breast the shuttle of Imagination, and wound on it the thread of his Wishes; and all night he sat and wove a net. In the morning he spread the golden net open on the ground, and into it he threw a few grains of credulity, which his father had left him, and which he kept in his breast-pocket. They were like white puff-balls, and when you trod on them a brown dust flew out. Then he sat by to see what would happen. The first that came into the net was a snow-white bird, with dove's eyes, and he sang a beautiful song—'A human-God! A human-God! A human-God' it sang.'"[110]

Other birds that sing of "Immortality" and "Reward after Death" also appear, and "the hunter gathered all his birds together, and built a strong iron cage called a new creed, and put all his birds in it."[111] When at the conclusion of *Heu-Heu* Zikali speaks of "the gods men set up," he seems almost a mouthpiece for Haggard's indebtedness to Schreiner: "'when men seek a god, Macumazahn, they make one like themselves, only larger, uglier, and more evil, at least in this land, for what they do elsewhere I know not.'" And when Quatermain observes that Heu-Heu is gone and asks Zikali what will become of the Walloos, he answers bleakly: "'I cannot say, Macumazahn, but I expect they will follow Heu-Heu, who has taken hold of their souls and will drag them after him.'"[112] Allan has done battle with the giants of legend, but in the perplexed currents of modern life, no one can believe such a simple victory brings freedom from the toils of the mind itself. Modern thought knows that even in primitive experience the mind remains hostage to itself.

Structurally, the Haggardian pattern of a darkly primitive clan against a socially more agreeable tribe—the Walloos had once been "highly civilized"[113]—owes much in the first instance to Jonathan Swift's travel/adventure tale of Gulliver, to his Yahoos and Houyhnhnms who embody the two unsatisfactory extremes of passion and reason. Unlike French models of the older *voyage imaginaire* in which the traveler in the seventeenth-century *libertain* convention arrives at a simple and uncorrupted Utopian society where natural instinct and the inborn light of reason prevail, Swift tries to repel his readers with both the animality of the Yahoos and the coldness of his Houyhnhnms. Further, the nineteenth century's fascination with the vital primitive and the effete civilized represents the same polarity as that of H. G. Wells's Morlocks and Eloi in *The Time Traveller* (1895) or R. L. Stevenson's *Strange Case of Dr. Jekyll and Mr. Hyde* (1885), carried now into the first quarter of the twentieth century by Haggard. W. B. Yeats's maxim, "The worst are full of passionate intensity, / The best lack all conviction" ("Second Coming"), suggests just this failure of masculinity of which Haggard is thinking. As with Swift, having met the alien, the reader if not the narrator sees a reflection of his own human traits. Perhaps Haggard's narrative of the Walloos may be a particular and general parable of a British loss of manhood and of all humanity in bondage to the catastrophic nature of reality, aspiring to find a hero who will free them from their fallenness in order that from the depths of their self-contradiction they may reach out and find that renewal beyond their power to beget.[114]

Published posthumously in 1926, though composed as early as 1916, *Treasure of the Lake* is set prior to the death of Hans in *The Ivory Child*, though Arkle's lost letter of introduction from Lord Ragnall to Allan suggests one might place its action not long before, perhaps circa 1873. Quatermain's pride in carrying "one of the first Winchester repeaters of a sort that carried five cartridges"[115] also might suggest 1873, since that was the first year for the famous Winchester lever-action .44-40 black powder rifle which replaced the 1866 "Yellow Boy" (although the '73 full-length magazine carried fifteen cartridges and the carbine version, twelve). The location is the remote interior, loosely in the area of the great lakes, probably Uganda, given the reference to the Lado mountains.[116] Allan and Hans rescue the red-bearded John Taurus Arkle,[117] aka "Red Bull," from the primitive, violent Abanda tribe who are about to go to war with the Dabanda. This is Haggard's typical conflict of binary opposites or "doubles,"[118] quarreling twins in which the irrational energy of an Id-like antagonist confronts a more socially conditioned model of tribal life. Throughout the romances of Haggard the dynamic qualities of vision, passion, and terror ideally counterbalance the formal values of order, reason, and virtue, as displayed both in life and in imagination. In the social dynamics of tribal life, the antithetical tendencies of romantic rebellion and classic harmony are ideally each tempered by its opposite.

The concentric pattern of a mountain ring around a land in which is centered a lake with a bull's-eye island on which there is a holy of holies where divine meets human—this is a familiar organization found in several of the novels cited above. Haggard's patterned scene and its rites serve the annual cycle of nature's and man's fertility. The threatening and volatile Abanda are perishing of drought in their wilderness;

comparably, the more-ordered and repressed Dabanda teeter on the verge of a fall from their Garden of Eden and stand in need of renewal. Basically, each tribe stands in need of what the other can provide. As in *Holy Flower*, *Ivory Child*, *Heu-Heu*, *She and Allan*, and *Ghost Kings*, the fertility of the Dabanda men is "'played out.' The race has grown too ancient and too interbred. Therefore it was necessary that she who is now the Engoi upon earth [the goddess's "shadow"] should wed one of a different stock who has knowledge of the arts and laws of the great white races."[119] For this reason Red Bull has been summoned by the tribal goddess through a mutual "soul affinity"[120] based on their prior incarnations.[121] By the first decades of the new century this Ayesha-figure in Haggard remains "fair-skinned,"[122] yet resembles Nada, Mameena and other women who are racially mixed and ambiguously moral. Here the goddess of the lake is an "angel who sinned and fell from Heaven" because she "loved a white man, and that, when he was forbidden to her, she killed him to take him to Heaven with her."[123] With the return of her consort the goddess-priestess will drive out the pretender to her throne and reestablish a matriarchal authority and order between the warring tribes. The Engoi afterwards is expected to beget a yet greater earthly embodiment to lead the reunited tribes to world dominion.

In a sense, the *cor corum* or "treasure" of the lake is akin to the diamond mines of King Solomon with Foulata enshrined; but whereas in Kukuanaland the trio fails to seize the proffered renewal of nature, "Red Bull" Arkle makes the speech that Good should have made earlier in *King Solomon's Mines*:

> "Farewell, my friend whom I shall see no more. I know you believe me mad, even wicked, perhaps, and so I am, according to your judgment and that of the world we know. Yet my heart tells me that love can do no wrong and that in my madness is the truest wisdom, for yonder stands my destiny, she whom I was born to win, she who was lost and is found again. Farewell once more, and think of me at times as we shall of you, until perchance elsewhere"—and he pointed upward—"we meet again, and you, too, understand all that I cannot speak."[124]

This "wicked" "madness" of miscegenation may also be "all" that Haggard cannot say (the novel is kept until posthumous release) in the "roaring twenties" or even afterwards, inasmuch as later film scripts of *King Solomon's Mines* felt compelled to replace Good's native love interest with an Irish or similar lass. The apparent surprise of such writers as Jane Dailey in *Sex and Civil Rights* (2006) that resistance to social integration was based on a fear of miscegenation is misplaced, the two being so closely interrelated. If children are a replication of any given society's features, then the interracial child, by definition, emblematizes the erasure of that group's ongoing self-image. Yet the insipid, worn-out bloodline, sparse and faltering, needs new passion, a disturbing and antinomian energy. When the balance is only a little on one side or the other, then each group benefits and exaggerated tendencies are muted. Much of this is only cautiously suggested here in *Treasure of the Lake*, in *She and Allan*,[125] and at other sites in Haggard's novels.

Even apart from issues of racial mixing, the failure of Victorian culture to appreciate the vital role of natural instincts and passion suggests that Haggard would have read the Satan of Milton's *Paradise Lost* in much the same manner as Blake or Shelley, as a heroic rebel. Thus, for example, Mameena's rebellion becomes a daring feminist blow against the tyranny of a mundane and patriarchal law and order. Haggard's Ayesha-like women bring to the domain of a severe, wholly self-conscious intelligence the imaginative force of passion, and the humanizing side of their fallen loves makes rebellion against an overly controlled and too-rational morality a virtue. An ancient paganism can restore those powers of nature lost by an urbanized, secularized culture. Reading Haggard's tales of legendary loves and their sad losses in contemporary Western society will be for British youth a cultural rite of passage enabling them to soar to new frontiers, either imperial or spiritual:

> More and more, as what we call culture spreads, do men and women crave to be taken out of themselves. More and more do they long to be brought face to face with Beauty, and stretch out their arms towards that vision of the Perfect, which we only see in books and dreams. The fact that we, in these latter days, have as it were macadamized all the roads of life does not make the world softer to the feet of those who travel through it. There are now royal roads to everything, lined with staring placards, whereon he who runs may learn the sweet uses of advertisement; but it is dusty work to follow them, and some may think that our ancestors on the whole found their voyaging a shadier and fresher business.... [In romance] we may even—if we feel that our wings are strong enough to bear us in that thin air—cross the bounds of the known, and, hanging between earth and heaven, gaze with curious eyes into the great profound beyond.[126]

In the modern world, can the soul's journey to spiritual wealth be through diamond mining and its allied material productive forces? Rather, pale, homesick Victorians, "wandering"—in Matthew Arnold's image—"between two worlds, one dead, / The other powerless to be born,"[127] must bring their lives into contact with the dark and passionate myths of Africa's body, engendering thereby new symbols for their lost primordial identity.

❦ EIGHT

In Concluding:
"'I Have Spoken,' as the Zulus Say"

The last of Allan Quatermain's adventures, the one that concludes with his death, already had been published as early as 1887. Serialized in *Longmans' Magazine* (January through August) and outrageously pirated in the United States from pre-press copies of that initial serialization, the first authorized book edition was published in London by Longmans in June with a blue-green cover, also the same month in New York by Harper. As a sequel to *King Solomon's Mines,* it is set about 1886, some three years after the adventurers had returned to England. During the period of Quatermain's rustication at his comfortable estate in Yorkshire, he tells his "editor," H. Rider Haggard, and his old comrades in adventure, Sir Henry and Good, most of the other Quatermain tales. Of these, those set in the lakes region of central or south-central Africa seem to have a higher proportion of occult and exotic exploits—not surprisingly, since when these adventures transpired in the 1870s this area was still largely beyond the pale of empire. Although *Allan Quatermain* had followed *King Solomon's Mines* by less than two years, this original lost race adventure is located in the phantasmal, mysterious regions of *She* and the other occult novels. The possibility of a lost civilization, though unlikely in 1886–1887, still existed;[1] but that it should be a white race in a wholly self-contained country, especially in the heart of Africa, at that date required some willing suspension of disbelief.

However, current objections to *Allan Quatermain* as "a period adventure novel" unsuitable for contemporary readers, either by virtue of its style or its setting, betray a lack of historiographic curiosity and, perhaps, a culturally conditioned expectation for film-style, action-driven plot suspense. The rhetorically elegant speeches of its characters, its reported dialogue in place of "real-time" spoken words, and the lengthy descriptions of places and objects, slow the pace unacceptably for readers born in the age of the "sound bite," the jump-cut, and internet information. Such shifting of fashion carries over not just to other Haggard novels, but to some degree confronts *all* fiction no longer belonging to the sharp apex of our present moment. As to the setting, because Haggard had been pounced upon after the publication of *King Solomon's Mines* for plagiarism—more distortion than truth—he adds a postscript in *Allan Quatermain*, "Authorities," in which he cites Joseph Thomson's *Through Masai Land* (1885), a Royal Geographical Society expedition to Mount Kenya and Lake Nyanza in 1883–1884, and, as a source for his description of crabs, a review of Edward Frederick Knight's *The Cruise of the 'Falcon'* (1887), which describes a voyage in the sailing yawl *Falcon* to South American and West Indian waters in 1880. He also thanks his brother John, "consul at Madagascar, and formerly consul at Lamu, for many details furnished by him of the mode of life and war of those engaging people the Masai"[2] and, even, his sister-in-law for help in rhyming "Sorais' Song." But he insists on only a coincidental parallel with Paltock's precursory lost race novel *Peter Wilkins* (1751) and with Hardy's *Far From the Madding Crowd* (1874). As to sources of characterization, the old warrior Quatermain's resolution "to go and die as I had lived, among the wild game and the savages"[3] is just that sort of final adventure on which Tennyson's Ulysses had embarked with his aging companions. Much of Ulysses's final resolution "to seek a newer world"[4] plainly attends Allan's turning his back on a society barbarous in its vulgarity and barren in its gentility.

"I have just buried my boy, my handsome boy of whom I was so proud, and my heart is broken,"[5] begins *Allan Quatermain* just before Christmas on the 23rd of December. One of the saddest ironies—not of the fictional dating but of Haggard's actual life—is that a few years later he too would bury his son, Jock, to whom he dedicated this novel. So prescient was this passage, with its echo of David mourning Absalom, that one critic with more compassion than data took this incident in the novel as covert autobiography, a reference by Haggard to his own tragedy. The death by smallpox of Allan's son, a young and selfless physician, shows that even an affluent and advanced civilization cannot protect its members against mortality; the ravages of urban life are as dire as those of Africa's wild beasts. Thus Quatermain, Curtis, and

Good return to Africa, this time to the British-governed seaport town of Lamu, in what today is Kenya, where they are joined by Umslopogaas to go in search of a legendary white race west of Mount Kenya. The death of Allan's son or the search for a lost civilization—either could have produced a novel: in one, the noble young doctor dying of a disease infecting the urban slums; and in the other, a last and deadly safari into unknown regions. The naturalistic novel of the slums is dismissed; the novel of romantic imperial death is written instead. In this, Haggard is deliberately reactionary, and to this he owed both his initial popularity and, later, a full weight of belletristic disapproval. At the juncture in the plot where Haggard shifts from the realistic world of colonial Kenya to the visionary world of Zu-Vendis, unlike life as he really knew it, readers with a historical or political interest in imperial conquest may well find the fantasy descriptions tedious. However, the final mad dash and battle on the stairway, dramatized as well as any scenes in Haggard, even though not triggered by the historical realities in Africa, nevertheless reflect symbolic patterns and a philosophical-political ideology.

Insofar as the machine became the primary metaphor of an emergent twentieth-century aesthetic, Haggard's Zu-Vendis resisted modernity and technology, as Henry Curtis's postscript makes amply evident. And although this world at least initially is no utopia, because its temple and territory abound with real toads of evil, it is an unindustrialized alternative to the insidious smallpox of London. One need only contrast Haggard's description of the sordid town of Lamu in the opening chapter[6] with the Frowning City's[7] monumental architecture—its long boulevards and large domes, its superhuman scale and overwhelming effect—to see that in order to define an alternate social paradigm Haggard contrasts a contemporary jerry-built squalor with an ancient-futuristic architecture. Much of the literary value of the latter half of this novel derives from a social vision that combines folklore, discreet occultism, and an ecological vision linking earth to spirit, as in the public architecture of the stairway that embraces natural objects like the cliffs. Haggard has composed a novel that effectively anticipates by a big margin twentieth-century ideas of a national rebirth, a purification and reclamation of a former, past national greatness—as, for example, a reemergent Zulu national consciousness.

But the detailed description of the Zu-Vendis flower temple strikes some as narratively cumbersome. In a curiously mathematical passage, the historical elements of everyday life are stripped away here in favor of an artificial, "science fiction" architecture. The forward momentum of plot-action crashes into a marble wall of technicalities. The Temple, we are told,

> is built in the shape of a sunflower, with a dome-covered central hall, from which radiate twelve petal-shaped courts, each dedicated to one of the twelve months, and serving as the repositories of statues reared in memory of the illustrious dead. The width of the circle beneath the dome is three hundred feet, the height of the dome is four hundred feet, and the length of the rays is one hundred and fifty feet, and the height of their roofs three hundred feet, so that they run into the central dome exactly as the petals of the sunflower run into the great raised heart. The exact measurement from the midst of the central altar to the extreme point of any one of the rounded rays would be three hundred feet (the width of the circle itself) or a total of six hundred feet from the rounded extremity of one ray or petal to the extremity of the opposite one.[8]

The total length of Haggard's description of the Temple of the Sun, not to mention his schematic drawing on the page, is ten paragraphs, fourteen hundred words, strongly suggesting that Haggard himself was deeply immersed in its symbolism. The hapless reader becomes slightly frantic for air at this point. But Haggard's excursus sets up for the theorist possible conjectures as to cultural affinities investing these new versions of past styles: echoes of Syro-Phoenician sun worship, or of ancient Rome? According to Sir James Frazer in *The Worship of Nature* (1926), the Romans had a Temple of the Sun and Moon.[9] Certainly this dome imagery immediately conjures up memories of the Pantheon, though the radiating chapel-like petals suggest the choir area of a medieval cathedral.

Or maybe one could surmise that the sort of research Haggard undertook, say, for *The Virgin of the Sun* (1922) already had enlightened him that the sunflower was sacred to the old Mayans and Incans, owing to its color, shape, and heliotropic qualities. Perhaps sources such as Frederika Bremer pointed him in *Allan Quatermain* towards Incan and Mayan temple architecture: "Why do I seek for the Temple of the Sun shining aloft over earth? Is not each sunflower a temple more beautiful than that of Peru or of Solomon? And these people, who love and who worship in spirit and in truth, are not they true sunflowers—the Temple of the Sun upon earth?"[10] Apparently, too, priestesses in the Temple of the Sun wore a golden sunflower crown. If this or other possibilities are relevant, then Haggard in *Allan Quatermain* is making a point about the cultural contact of prehistoric Africa with Europe or the near East, a theory that turns back upon nineteenth-century assumptions about the origins of King Solomon's mines and Phoenician trade or evokes such odd contemporary racial conjectures as, for example, that Arab or Ethiopian warriors were the forebears of the Zulus, who were thus titular whites. Ultimately, with a jolt, one realizes that his description, composed in the luxuriant social milieu of Oscar Wilde and the 1880s, may be a set piece of *art nouveau*—a sort of ancient Pantheon and medieval Chartres transformed as if by some fantasy art-glass craftsman in Lalique's atelier. Haggard includes in his description a literal floral design typical of the period's enthusiasm for curvilinear leaves and flowers: "What makes the whole effect even more gorgeous is that a belt of a hundred and fifty feet around the marble wall of the temple is planted with an indigenous species of sunflower, which were at the time when we first saw them in a sheet of golden bloom."[11] This is an organic architecture rooted in natural forms, with external forces such as the sun acting on internal patterns to produce a continuum of design that links earth to spirit as ornament, structure and metaphor. Indeed, the repeating quasi-geometric sunflower-sunbeam radiating curves, the stylized Egyptian or pre-Columbian Americas design motifs, even the linearity of doors and other details, look forward to art deco patterns of line and curve that grew out of the earlier *nouveau* movement.

Into this ancient-futuristic world the adventurers had burst via an underground river, demonstrating rather more recklessly than in *King Solomon's Mines* their technological superiority by shooting animals. In this instance they exterminate a family of sacred hippopotami, for which understandably the Zu-Vendis priests intend to execute them. The country, however, is under the rule of Nyleptha and Sorais, two sister-queens. Nyleptha, the beautiful and gracious queen, extends protection to the adventurers and her love to Sir Henry. The fair Nyleptha's equally stunning but dark twin sister Sorais, unable to restrain the depth of her desire for Sir Henry, is whipped into a storm of discontent, and she plunges the country into civil war. Sorais is the "Lady of the Night," a title applicable equally to a prostitute or to the moon and its associated witchcraft. These sisters recapitulate the familiar Kukuanaland dialectic of the two kings or, as in Haggard's later ancient-Egyptian novel, the rivals in *The World's Desire* (1890)—the dark, snakey Meriamun and the golden, starred Helen. As Meriamun says, "Perchance she and I are *one*, Odysseus,"[12] so in some more-than-familial way the royal sisters in *Quatermain* also are akin. As so often in Haggard's novels, the narrative ends with a climactic battle, one that defeats Sorais and the forces of darkness. In her stead Nyleptha becomes the true consort of the sun, the procreator of light, reflecting in her mirroring beauty the luminous potency of her new husband, Sir Henry. Both Umslopogaas and Quatermain are mortally wounded, their deaths, as also perhaps the death of Quatermain's son had been, the price of this social-political renewal and Sir Henry's apotheosis.

※ ※

By 1900, maps that only a few decades earlier had spelled out "Unknown Interior" now confidently marked, even in the equatorial regions, rivers and swamps, railways and canals, oases and colonial capitals. The unknown had been largely tamed and the exotic adventure novel of Africa was losing its functional footing. After the century's turn the decline in Haggard's reputation is reflected by the publication of his books. Earlier volumes were often deluxe editions with decorated cloth over heavy bevel-edged boards and, as with *Allan Quatermain* for example, front and spine panels stamped in gold, with brown and pale blue ship-and-swan-patterned end papers. But later these boards became plain, without colored end papers, and the linen- or cotton-fiber printing paper of the earlier century was replaced in the twentieth with a cheaper, lighter-weight stock made from wood pulp or other vegetable fibers that turned brittle and brownish in air or light. A number of these late featherweight volumes are indeed easy to hold and highly portable, perhaps suggesting that they were understood as "light reading" in more ways than one. Because late Haggard titles were less popular and had lower print runs, his publishers in some instances overprinted the title pages of first editions, often in lighter, badly aligned type, with "Second Edition"—or "Seventh Edition" in one outrageous instance reported regarding the posthumous *Belshazzar*—to suggest better sales than occurred.

Haggard's slumping book sales were only the presenting symptom of a much larger malaise of reputation. After World War II a new political consciousness emerged, unfolding yet another threat to Haggard's reputation from a swiftly changing climate of opinion on the maintenance of empire and associated race relations. In the wake of the Anglo-Boer war, doubts relative to "the noble extension of empire" first had crept into public awareness, then accelerated. And it made little difference that Haggard's had been a progressive voice: for example, the broad comic characterization and racial stereotyping, so familiar in the popular English and American traveling vaudeville and minstrel shows of this era or earlier, are not present in Haggard's treatment of the loyal native servant. In *The Yellow God* (1908), Jeekie's common sense and self-respect trump the more genteel virtues of the house servants and the titles of their Anglo masters.[13] When Jeekie's English is not parodying the upper class, his "mission dialect" is supplemented by an awareness of the newest slang expressions. Far from the stock buffoon or swindler stereotype that persisted in performance media well into the mid-twentieth century, Jeekie may have an irreverent witty, clever bent but his survival instincts are essential for the white hero's escape. He also is the mouthpiece for Haggard's most fundamental conviction: "'Jeekie not heathen now, Major, but plenty other things true in this world, besides Christian religion.'"[14] This and other assertions reject the "superiority" of Western enlightenment based on religious or scientific-medical attainments and assert the moral-intellectual qualities and capacities of "primitive" man as commensurate with Europeans. And Jeekie is the sole architect of one of Haggard's most hilarious denouements, worthy of Evelyn Waugh's satiric caricatures. When the infatuated priestess of Asiki-land pursues Major Vernon in force to bring him back to become her love slave, Jeekie drugs and fobs off on the soldiers the wicked Sir Robert Aylward, Bart, M.P., erstwhile financier in the City of London. The white hero, of course, is too straight-arrow to allow any such efficient disposal of the villain. But Haggard's readers, who know Aylward has bought his title with the proceeds of fraud, and is about to violate the heroic Major's beloved Barbara in the African wilderness, applaud Jeekie's ironic justice. Nor does the tale end with the white hero getting all the loot; Jeekie's unsentimental version of the Major's booty suggests that maybe this native servant's rationalization is simply the more direct expression of an upper-class pursuit of wealth. Indeed, Jeekie's battlefield scavenging may pose the more difficult unspoken issue of whether Major Vernon's African fortune is so very different from the share-rigging of Aylward's "Sahara Limited," inasmuch as on some level power relations always intervene, swindling the indigenous owners. But that last enigma, of course, would be Haggard's bone for the dogs of criticism to chew on, not for the common readers.

Finally, apart from a shifting political consciousness, Haggard's reputation was tainted from the start by literary notions of a boundary between high culture and popular culture that caused the sort of fiction he wrote to be dismissed, for example, by Walter Pater as "flat and uninteresting"—even before he had begun to write it. A few years before Haggard went to Africa, Pater had this to say about modern literature and adventures of former years:

> That naïve, rough sense of freedom, which supposes man's will to be limited, if at all, only by a will stronger than his, he can never have again. The attempt to represent it in art would have so little verisimilitude that it would be flat and uninteresting. The chief factor in the thoughts of the modern mind concerning itself is the intricacy, the universality of natural law, even in the moral order. For us, necessity is not, as of old, a sort of mythological personage without us, with whom we can do warfare. It is rather a magic web woven through and through us, like that magnetic system of which modern science speaks, penetrating us with a network, subtler than our subtlest nerves, yet bearing in it the central forces of the world. Can art represent men and women in these bewildering toils so as to give the spirit at least an equivalent for the sense of freedom?... Natural laws we shall never modify, embarrass us as they may; but there is still something in the nobler or less noble attitude with which we watch their fatal combinations;... this entanglement, this network of law, becomes the tragic situation, in which certain groups of noble men and women work out for themselves a supreme *Denouement*. Who, if he saw through all, would fret against the chain of circumstance which endows one at the end with those great experiences?[15]

Pater, of course, hated mountains, enjoyed Wednesday luncheon parties on the lawn, and—as for "warfare"—when offered Rodin's bronze, "The Man with the Broken Nose," shuddered "I don't think I could *bear* to live with it!"[16] But his emphasis upon minimizing external events and optimizing the moment-by-moment perception of "fatal combinations" opened the way to Virginia Woolf's practice of the psychological novel that reached its heyday between the world wars. While Woolf was writing *The Voyage Out* (1915) or *Mrs. Dalloway* (1925), Haggard was writing *The Ivory Child* (1916) and *Heu-Heu* (1924). By the time Woolf had published "Modern Fiction" (1919), Haggard's reputation among intellectuals, as well as the fickle public, had landed firmly in the dumper.

However, the influence of Haggard upon numerous later writers of popular culture, beginning with Bertram Mitford and extending to the great battle scenes, wastelands, caverns, forests and wanderers of J. R. R. Tolkien in the *Lord of the Rings*, gave the twentieth century (and in all likelihood the twenty-first also) its definition of the exotic action-adventure. Haggard's lost-world, lost-race subgenre resonated in a host of texts, such as Arthur Conan Doyle's *Lost World* (1912). Scottish author John Buchan took his cue from Haggard and published *Prester John* (1910) based on his experiences in South Africa as private secretary to the High Commissioner, Lord Milner; Buchan's undercover mission disguised as a Boer also provided him with inspiration for his most famous character, spy-catcher Richard Hannay in *The Thirty-Nine Steps* (1915). And Allan Quatermain served as prototype for such popular icons as Edgar Rice Burroughs's Tarzan and John Carter of Mars, not to mention Tolkien's Aragorn. As an eminent adventure fantasy, did Haggard's *The Ivory Child* serve as inspiration for all those snake gods in Robert E. Howard's tales? And, as noted, the literary toughness of the harsh and primitive images in Ernest Hemingway's *The Green Hills of Africa* (1935), especially in "The Short Happy Life of Francis McComber," echoes the manly world of shooting and blood in Haggard's fiction. Not long after his inauguration, Theodore Roosevelt commented to Haggard: "It is an odd thing that you and I, brought up in different countries and following such different pursuits, should have identical ideas and aims."[17] It was no accident that the two should have felt such a keen affinity. Roosevelt was the living antidote to the dawning twentieth-century's problems: small like Allan Quatermain; energetic, virile, an attractive and boisterous personality; an explorer of wildernesses; a hunter, both of grizzlies in the U.S. west and of lions in Africa; a fighter (when needed) both of men and of the powers of darkness in high places; and, not least, a prolific writer. Haggard even dedicated the culminating volume of his Zulu trilogy, *Finished* (1917), to "Colonel Theodore Roosevelt, Sagamore Hill, U.S.A." In the final analysis Haggard's heroic or sagalike fiction undoubtedly belongs less to modernism than to modernism's precursors. But whatever the falling off of his celebrity with the capricious public and the disdainful literati, for critics to disparage his themes of the heroic and supernatural because they do not conform to realism, naturalism, or modernism's context of spiritual hollowness would be to condemn also some of the greatest imaginative works since *Beowulf.*

Outside of his chosen fictional medium, Haggard also has left his mark. He is one of the most filmed—or possibly over-filmed—authors, given that a dozen different novels have been commercially produced, some mere exploitative adaptations that should have ruined careers. There are more than a half dozen versions each of *King Solomon's Mines* and *She*, the first of which was Georges Méliès's silent black-and-white version made in France as early as 1899, entitled *La danse du feu*. Haggard has been not only a quarry for the film industry's casual borrowings—one thinks of the mummy torches in *She* and the engaging remake of *The Mummy* (1999) as a cinematic extravaganza or of the use of the Allan Quatermain's name in *The League of Extraordinary Gentlemen* (2003)—but a pervasive influence on worthier efforts, such as George Lucas's figure of Jobba the Hut modeled on the toadlike Motombo in *The Holy Flower*, or the Lucas/Spielberg *Indiana Jones* trilogy inspired by Quatermain's vocation as treasure hunter or Michael Crichton's potboiler and subsequent film, *Congo* (1995), with its rescue mission into the unknown African interior based on or adapted from *King Solomon's Mines*, complete with diamonds, ruins, volcanism, internecine fighting, and a native guide as impressive as Umbopa. Indeed, by way of earlier films based on imitators such as Conan Doyle or E. R. Burroughs, Haggard's tropes, if not a specific storyline, inspired that classic cinematic adventure, *King Kong* (1933 and the 2005 remake), with its Quatermain-type explorer, its map to an unknown territory (a bit of Stevenson, too, one admits), its gorilla god holding an island in deadly fear (as in *Holy Flower*), its kidnaped white woman, its witch doctor and sacrifice ceremony, its man-killing reptiles, caves, and jungle, and its terror of (1933) or compassion for (2005) the dark shadow self's newfound sexuality.

Although the essence of good filmmaking is not necessarily fidelity to an original text, not a single production to date has seriously attempted to convey the plot or authenticity of Haggard's narratives. Two critical assessments of *King Solomon's Mines* perhaps prove this point:

> I was once taken to see a film version of *King Solomon's Mines* [Gaumont 1937]. Of its many sins—not the least the introduction of a totally irrelevant young woman in shorts who accompanied the three adventurers wherever they went—only one concerns us here. At the end of Haggard's book, as everyone remembers, the heroes are awaiting death entombed in a rock chamber and surrounded by the mummified kings of that land. The maker of the film version, however, apparently thought this tame. He substituted a subterranean volcanic eruption, and then went one better by adding an earthquake.... There must be a pleasure in such stories distinct from mere excitement or I should not feel that I had been cheated in being given the earthquake instead of Haggard's actual scene. What I lose is the whole sense of the deathly (quite a different thing from simple danger of death)—the cold, the silence, and the surrounding faces of the ancient, the crowned and sceptred, dead. You may, if you please, say that Rider Haggard's effect is quite as "crude" or "vulgar" or "sensational" as that which the film substituted for it. I am not at present discussing that. The point is that it is extremely different. The one lays a hushing spell on the imagination; the other excites a rapid flutter of the nerves.... [T]he producer of the film substituted at the climax one kind of danger for another and thereby, for me, ruined the story.[18]

EIGHT: In Concluding

The other is Kenneth M. Cameron:

> Metro-Goldwyn-Mayer's 1950 *King Solomon's Mines* may well be the best Hollywood sound picture ever made about "Africa." This is not to say that it was about real Africa or that it dealt with real African societies or cultures. The clichés of the 1950 *King Solomon's Mines* are the familiar ones of a Victorian Africa as seen from Europe, but ... Hollywood's blackfaced whites have finally been got rid of, and lean, muscular, sometimes dangerous-looking Africans have replaced the often overweight American blacks who played Africans in other movies.... [T]he camera has matured to the point where it can see Africans, but it cannot accept them as they are.... [I]n its quest structure, the whites pursue a goal and the blacks impede them. The whites exist in individualized ones and twos; the blacks exist in masses. Whites are from outside Africa and remain separate from it; blacks are of Africa. "Jungle" is everywhere, full of snakes,... insects, and crocodiles; black Africans are close to this repellant Nature. Any treasure that Africa holds is to be grasped by whites and taken away. But now, the treasure that the two principals seek is permission to love each other, which Africa gives by killing the lost husband; it is as if imperial greed is too much to be tolerated in 1950, and so what formerly was economic ("European adventurers in search of mining concessions from the pretender to whom they give their support") has been reduced to the romantic, the general to the individual.[19]

Indeed, the fear of romance between black and white has in the commercial circles of moviedom resulted in the absurd introduction of a white girl as the romantic lead in every production of *King Solomon's Mines*. In and of itself the African liaison as handled in Haggard's novel suggests that he was a century ahead of the popular cultural curve.

Pater and his generation (not excluding Olive Schreiner) had been convinced that such action tales as Haggard's lacked "verisimilitude." But the first half of *Allan Quatermain*, for example, has a wonderful anthropological authenticity that proves Pater wrong; true, its Zu-Vendis second half, with the theatrification of the entire society, is patently fantastic—but this hardly proves Pater right. The novel is not "flat and uninteresting" because evil among the Zu-Vendi is embodied in persons with whom one can do battle. Now that we are well beyond the last century's early remodelings, those realists, naturalists, or practitioners of the *monologue intérieur* are as passé in the postmodern era as Haggard supposedly was among the moderns. To be more than a bit catty: who these days, other than a few aging professors or young *précieux*, considers James Joyce's *Finnegans Wake* anything but an experimental deadend? Yet one need not uproot Haggard's rivals to make the case for Haggard. Consider that Aristotle had deemed the homespun taste for tales of the fireside, of deeds that make men miserable or happy—that is, the happenings of the plot—essential to the nature of imitative art and the source of its intellectul pleasure. Moreover, Haggard's intellectual accomplishment was to stand against nineteenth-century notions of historical inevitability, of impersonal laws that discounted human agency and its free choices. But if heroism for Haggard is still possible, he knew also that there were no final victories, that good remained entangled with evil, a constant in human affairs. Haggard, we may claim also, fused the heterogeneous fields of comparative literature, religion, and anthropology to perfect the imperial adventure novel. This deliberate blending of motifs and themes from other disciplines and media (may we call it a protohybridization?) gave his novels more character than those of his predecessors and represented the ultimate step in the development of this genre.

Notes

Introduction

About Haggard's Works: No comprehensive scholarly edition of Haggard's works has yet been edited. Although more than twenty of his works have been reprinted in the Longmans Silver Library Edition (1890s–1910s) and about the same number (though not always the same titles) are reprinted in the MacDonald Illustrated Edition (late 1940s–1960s), neither series is complete nor authoritative by strict scholarly standards. Since the plates for U.K. and U.S. first editions, often through successive reprints, are usually paginated identically, citations within this study are to these works as originally published.

1. Sola Adeyemi, "Review of H. Rider Haggard, *Diary of an African Journey,*" H-AfrLitCine (October 2000) in H-Net Reviews in Humanities and Social Sciences (www.h-net.msu.edu), 1–2.

2. H. Rider Haggard, *Queen Sheba's Ring* (New York: Doubleday, Page, 1910), 38–39.

3. Evelyn Waugh, *Scoop: A Novel About Journalists* (London: Chapman and Hall, 1938), 101.

4. Ibid., 53–55.

5. Martin Green, *Dreams of Adventure, Deeds of Empire* (London: Routledge, 1980), 33. Brian Street, *The Savage in Literature* (London: Routledge, 1975), 11.

6. H. Rider Haggard, *The Days of My Life: An Autobiography*, (London: Longmans, Green, 1928), II: 85–86.

7. Good insisted that Quatermain read *She (She and Allan*, x-xii), which completed its serialization and was published in book form in January 1887. Thereafter, having buried his son in December (year not specified), Quatermain leaves Yorkshire and returns to Africa, dying at Zu-Vendis twelve months before the circumstances of his death are recorded in *Allan Quatermain* (June 1887; serialized in *Longman's Magazine*, from January through August 1887). Obviously one must allow some "play" in dating Allan's demise since he could not have read *She* in 1887 and then died a year *before* the publication of *Allan Quatermain*. One cannot even fantasize that *pre*-press copies of installments of *She* somehow produced an earlier pirated edition, as indeed did occur with *Allan Quatermain*; such a book could have appeared only slightly earlier than the legal edition and would have been available only in the U.S. market.

8. H. Rider Haggard, *Allan's Wife and Other Tales* (London: Spencer Blackett, 1889), 23.

9. See H. Rider Haggard, *She: A History of Adventure* (London: Longmans, Green, 1887), 227–28, 230; *Marie* (London: Cassell, 1912), 64, 251.

10. H. Rider Haggard, *King Solomon's Mines* (London: Cassell, 1885), 306.

11. Wendy Katz, *Rider Haggard and the Fiction of Empire* (Cambridge: Cambridge University Press, 1987), 135, 137.

12. H. Rider Haggard, *She and Allan* (New York: Longmans, Green, 1921), 73–75; 103. See, for example, Bertram Mitford's comments on the color bar in *Forging the Blades* (London: Eveleigh Nash, 1908), 33, 241, 270.

13. H.G. Wells, *The War of the Worlds* (New York: Random House, 1960), 1: 14.

14. Joseph Conrad, "Heart of Darkness," *Youth and Two Other Stories* (New York: McClure, Phillips, 1903), *v.i.*, chapter one; John Ruskin, "Lectures on Art" [1873], *The Complete Works*, E. T. Cook and Alexander Wedderburn, eds. (London: George Allen, 1902–1912), XX: 100–103.

15. *King Solomon's Mines*, 9.

16. Richard Rive, "Diamond Fields," *English in Africa*, 1 (March 1974), 27.

17. T. S. Eliot, "Tradition and Individual Talent," *The Sacred Wood* (London: Methuen, 1950), 226.

18. *King Solomon's Mines*, 49.

19. Andrew Lang, *Essays in Little* (New York: Scribner's, 1907), 144.

20. *Rider Haggard and the Fiction of Empire*, 31.

21. Patrick Brantlinger, *Rule of Darkness: British Literature and Imperialism, 1830–1914* (Ithaca: Cornell University Press, 1988), 230. This was certainly a major theme throughout Haggard's "About Fiction," *Contemporary Review*, 51 (February 1887), 172–80. Bertram Mitford specifically extends Brantlinger's and Katz's antithesis beyond Africa to Europe and the United States. In *Fordham's Feud* (London: Ward Lock, 1897) Mitford differentiates "the poor creatures of an effete civilisation" from Alpine denizens with "the most consummate coolness and courage with an unlimited supply of sheer physical endurance and quickness of resource" (138, 198); and in *War and Arcadia* (London: V. F. White, 1901) he contrasts the Cockney female, "puny, flat-chested, red of eye-rim, and with that unwholesome, cadaverous, dull white cuticle evolved from many generations of slum-life" (302), with Sioux braves, "tall and straight as a poplar; and as they stood, letting their clear, piercing eyes wander over the heads of the motley crowd gazing at them, no muscle of their fine aquiline countenances underwent change" (302).

22. Quoted in Brian Greene, *The Fabric of the Cosmos* (New York: Vintage Books, 2004), 9.

23. Publisher's Catalog, *She and Allan*, 3.

24. Anne McClintock, "Maidens, Maps, and Mines," *South Atlantic Quarterly,* 87.1 (1988), 23.

25. *The Days of My Life: An Autobiography,* I: 64–65.

26. Carolyn Hamilton, *Terrific Majesty: The Powers of Shaka Zulu and the Limits of Historical Invention* (Cambridge: Harvard University Press, 1998), 94, 115–29.

27. Terence Ranger, "The Rural African Voice in Zimbabwe," *Social Analysis: Journal of Culture and Social Practice*, 2 (September 1980), 100–115.

28. *Terrific Majesty: the Powers of Shaka Zulu and the Limits of Historical Invention*, 120.

29. F. B. Fynney, *Zululand and the Zulus* (Maritzburg: Horne Bros., 1880), I: 9.

30. *The Days of My Life: An Autobiography,* I: 52.

31. Laura Chrisman, *Rereading the Imperial Romance* (Oxford: Clarendon Press, 2000), 105.

32. H. Rider Haggard, *Nada the Lily* (London: Longmans, Green, 1892), ix.

33. Ibid., 33–37.

34. *The Days of My Life: An Autobiography,* I: 245.

35. *King Solomon's Mines*, 9.

36. Bertram Mitford, *Renshaw Fanning's Quest* (London: Chatto & Windus, 1894), tip-in "a" behind f.e.p.

37. Bertram Mitford, *Seaford's Snake* (London: Ward, Lock, 1912), 82, 86.

ONE: Empire and Colony

1. Nadine Gordimer, Foreword, *Olive Schreiner*, by Ruth First and Ann Scott (New Brunswick: Rutgers, 1990), 6.

2. S. C. Cronwright-Schreiner, *The Life of Olive Schreiner* (Boston: Little, Brown, 1924), 80–84.

3. Olive Schreiner [Ralph Iron, pseud.], *The Story of an African Farm* (London: Chapman & Hall, 1883), 153.

4. Olive Schreiner, *Thoughts on South Africa* (London: Unwin, 1923), 102–103.

5. H. Rider Haggard, *Jess* (New York: Harper Franklin Square, 1887), 97.

6. Homer, *The Odyssey*, Robert Fitzgerald, trans. (New York: Doubleday, 1961), Book 9: 116–35.

7. Ibid., 9: 142, 215, 350.

8. Ibid., 9: 382–94.

9. Isak Dinesen, *Out of Africa* (New York: Random House, 1938), 48–50.

10. *King Solomon's Mines*, 104–105.

11. Joseph Conrad, *The Collected Letters of Joseph Conrad*, Frederick Karl, ed. (Cambridge: Cambridge University Press, 1986), Letter of 31 December 1898, II: 139–40.

12. H. Rider Haggard, "A Zulu War-Dance," *Gentleman's Magazine*, 243 (1877), 99.

13. Betram Mitford, *A Veldt Vendetta* (London: Ward Lock, 1903), 68–69.

14. Mungo Park, *Travels in the Interior Districts of Africa, Performed under the Direction and Patronage of the Africa Association, in the Years 1795, 1796, and 1797* (London: Bulmer, 1799), 2.

15. David Livingstone, *Missionary Travels and Researches in South Africa* (New York: Harper & Brothers, 1858), x.

16. Ibid., 39–40; 207–209.

17. David and Charles Livingstone, *Narrative of an Expedition to the Zambesi and Its Tributaries* (New York: Harper, 1866), 2.

18. *The Story of an African Farm*, 3–4.

19. Bertram Mitford, *The Induna's Wife* (London: F. V. White, 1898), 150–51.

20. George Browne, *The History of the British and Foreign Bible Society, from Its Institution in 1804, to the Close of Its Jubilee in 1854* (London: Bagster, 1859), II: 255.

21. Isak Dinesen, *Shadows on the Grass* (New York: Random House, 1961), 14; J. W. Colenso, *First Steps in Zulu: Being an Elementary Grammar of the Zulu Language* (Maritzburg: P. Davis, 1882), 2.

22. *Out of Africa*, 377.

23. *Thoughts on South Africa*, 51, 108.

24. Ibid., 109. See the figure of Hendrika in Haggard's *Allan's Wife* (1889).

25. Ibid., 108–109.

26. *Missionary Travels and Researches in South Africa*, 19–20.

27. *Thoughts on South Africa*, 312.

28. *Missionary Travels and Researches in South Africa*, 20–21.

29. "Lectures on Art" [1873], *The Complete Works,* XX: 41 n.2.

30. Ibid., XX: 41–42.

31. Ibid., XX: 42.

32. Dante, *Inferno*, 3:59–60. Translation based on H. W. Longfellow, *The Divine Comedy of Dante Alighieri* (Boston: Houghton Mifflin, 1867), I: 35.

33. "Lectures on Art" [1873], *The Complete Works,* XX: 42–43.

34. Ibid., XX: 43.

35. Chinua Achebe, "The Novelist as Teacher," *New Statesman*, 29 January 1965, 162.

36. *Odyssey*, 9: 175–76.

37. Olive Schreiner, *Trooper Peter Halket of Mashonaland* (London: T. Fisher Unwin, 1897), 39–40.

38. *King Solomon's Mines*, 146.

39. *Trooper Peter Halket of Mashonaland*, 55.

40. Ibid., 64–65.

41. Ibid., 69, 232.

42. John Barrow, *An Account of Travels into the Interior of Southern Africa, in the Years 1797 and 1798* (London: Cadell & Davies, 1801), I: 272.

43. Ibid., I: 274.

44. Ibid., I: 275.

45. *Out of Africa*, 281–82.

46. Ibid., 282–83.

| Notes |

47. Jomo Kenyatta, *Facing Mount Kenya: The Tribal Life of the Gikuyu* (London: Secker and Warburg, 1938), 47–52.

48. Ibid., 51.

49. Ibid., 51–52.

50. *Odyssey*, 9: 414.

51. *Shadows on the Grass*, 14.

52. *Out of Africa*, 9.

53. H. Rider Haggard, "The Transvaal," *Macmillan's Magazine*, 36 (May 1877), 70–76.

54. "A Zulu War-Dance," 94.

55. Popularly attributed to Bishop Desmond Tutu, African spiritual leader and author (born 1931); cited by George Monbiot (www.Monbiot.com/archives/2003/08/19/stealing-nations/).

56. "A Zulu War-Dance," 96.

57. *Thoughts on South of Africa*, 82–83.

58. *Missionary Travels and Researches in South Africa*, 37.

59. "The Transvaal," 72.

60. Genesis 16:12.

61. *The Induna's Wife*, 158. Compare the Rev. H. C. Adams's negative assessment of the Boers' biblical analogy in *Perils in the Transvaal and Zululand* (London: Griffith Farran, c. 1883), 130.

62. *An Account of Travels into the Interior of Southern Africa, in the Years 1797 and 1798*, I: 312–13.

63. *The Story of an African Farm*, 11, 17–18.

64. Ibid., ix.

65. Ibid., viii.

66. *Out of Africa*, 190.

67. Ibid., 58.

68. Ibid.

69. Ella Haggard, *Life and Its Author* (London: Longmans, Green, 1890), 18–19.

70. "A Zulu War-Dance," 94, 99.

71. Ibid., 102.

72. *The Private Diaries of Sir H. Rider Haggard,* Stephen Coan, ed. (London: Cassell, 1980), 33–34, 111.

73. H. Rider Haggard, *Finished* (New York: Longmans, Green, 1917), 17.

74. *Finished*, 244.

75. H. Rider Haggard, "An Incident of African History," *Windsor Magazine* (London), December 1900, para. 22.

76. *The Days of My Life: An Autobiography*, II: 262–63; I: 194.

TWO: Heretic in Disguise

1. Virgina Woolf, *Death of the Moth and Other Essays* (New York: Harcourt, Brace, 1942), 3–6; *Collected Essays* (New York: Harcourt, Brace, 1967), II: 106, 296; *Mrs. Dalloway* (New York: Harcourt, Brace, 1925), last chapter.

2. Andrew Lang, "Literary Plagiarism," *Contemporary Review* (June 1887), 831–40.

3. C. S. Lewis, "Haggard Rides Again," *Time and Tide*, 3 September 1960, 1044–45.

4. Frank Harris, *My Life and Loves* (Paris: Author [priv. print.], 1922–1927), III: chap. 16a.

5. H. Rider Haggard, *Allan Quatermain* (London: Longmans, Green, 1887), Dedication.

6. Ian Fletcher, "Can Haggard Ride Again?" *The Listener,* 29 July 1971, 136.

7. H. Rider Haggard, *Child of Storm* (London: Cassell, 1913), vi–vii.

8. Quoted by Mbodlomani Gojwana, 4 October 2002. See website <www.inkundla.net/indonsakusa/Leadership>.

9. "About Fiction," 180.

10. *Thoughts on South Africa*, 15–16.

11. Olive Schreiner, *From Man to Man* (London: Unwin, 1926), 414–15.

12. *The Story of an African Farm*, 172–73.

13. "A Zulu War-Dance," 94.

14. H. Rider Haggard, "A Man's View of Women," review of *Woman: The Predominant Partner*, by Edward Sullivan, *African Review*, 10 (22 September 1894), 408.

15. *Child of Storm*, 83.

16. Ibid., 82–83.

17. Ibid., 75–76.

18. Ibid., 86.

19. Wilhelm Dilthey, *Pattern and Meaning in History*, H. P. Rickman, ed. (New York: Harper, 1961), 87.

20. Ibid., 79.

21. *She*, 84.

22. Ibid., 151–52; 194.

23. *She and Allan*, 288–99, 337–38.

24. H. Rider Haggard, *Benita, An African Romance* (London: Cassell, 1906), 267.

25. William James, *Varieties of Religious Experience* (New York: Longmans, Green, 1902), 389.

26. Sigmund Freud, *The Interpretation of Dreams, The Basic Writings of Sigmund Freud*, A. A. Brill, trans. (New York: Random House, 1938), 429.

27. H. Rider Haggard, *Treasure of the Lake* (New York: Doubleday, Page, 1926), 296, 310.

28. Janet Oppenheim, *The Other World: Spiritualism and Psychical Research in England, 1850–1914* (Cambridge: Cambridge University Press, 1985), 269.

29. *She and Allan*, 42.

30. H. Rider Haggard, *Allan and the Holy Flower* (New York: Longmans, Green, 1915), 73.

31. Ibid., 197.

32. H. Rider Haggard, "Lost on the Veld," *Youth's Companion* (New York), 25 (September 1902), 185. Rpt. in *Windsor Magazine* (London), December 1902.

33. *The Days of My Life: An Autobiography*, II: 160–62.

34. H. Rider Haggard, *The Ivory Child* (London: Cassell, 1916), 332–33; 303.

35. *The Poetical Works of Tennyson*, G. Robert Stange, ed. (Boston: Houghton Mifflin, 1974), 546–47.

36. *The Portable Mark Twain*, Bernard DeVoto, ed. (New York: Viking Press, 1946), 459.

37. "The Transvaal," 77.

38. Ibid., 73.

39. H. Rider Haggard, *Cetywayo and His White Neighbors; or, Remarks on Recent Events in Zululand* (London: Trubner, 1882), 220–21.

40. *Allan Quatermain*, 4–5.

41. *The Days of My Life: An Autobiography*, I: 66–67; *The Private Diaries of Sir H. Rider Haggard*, 202.

42. *King Solomon's Mines*, 9.

43. H. Rider Haggard, *The Witch's Head* (London: J. and R. Maxwell, [1884] 1887), 184, 271.

44. *Child of Storm*, vi.

45. *The Witch's Head*, 271.

46. *King Solomon's Mines*, 60.

47. F. W. Nietzsche, *The Gay Science*, Walter Kaufmann, trans. (New York: Vintage, 1974), 181–82.

48. Plutarch, "The Obsolescence of Oracles," *Moralia*, Loeb Classical Library, Frank Babbitt, trans. (London: Heinemann, 1927), 5:17.

49. *The Ivory Child*, 179–80.

50. Ibid., 35, 44.

51. Ibid., 327.

52. Ibid., 299.

53. Ibid., 303.

54. Joseph Conrad, *Heart of Darkness* (1899), *Youth: And Two Other Stories* (New York: McClure, Phillips, 1903), 170–71.

55. T. S. Eliot, "Baudelaire," *Selected Essays, 1917–1932* (New York: Harcourt, Brace, 1950), 344.

56. William Wordsworth, *Poetical Works*, Thomas Hutchinson and E. De Selincourt, eds. (London: Oxford University Press, 1967), 156.

57. *She*, 203.

58. Samuel Taylor Coleridge, *The Statesman's Manual, Collected Works*, Kathleen Coburn, ed. (Princeton: Princeton University Press, 1969), VI: 30.

59. Thomas Carlyle, *Sartor Resartus, Carlyle's Complete Works* (Boston: Estes, 1885), I: 175.

60. *Poetical Works*, 164.

61. Ibid.

62. John Milton, *Paradise Lost*, Book 2: 561.

63. Thomas DeQuincey, *Confessions of an English Opium-Eater* (Boston: Osgood, 1873), 119.

64. *Child of Storm*, vi.

65. F. C. Selous, *A Hunter's Wanderings in Africa* (London: Macmillan, 1881), 86.

66. *Heart of Darkness*, 108–109.

67. "Haggard Rides Again," 1045.

68. *The Ivory Child*, 35.

69. Edward Shanks, "Sir Rider Haggard and the Novel of Adventure," *The London Mercury*, 61 (November 1924), 74.

70. "Haggard Rides Again," 1044.

71. *She and Allan*, 131.

72. *The Oxford Book of Modern Verse, 1892–1935*, chosen by W. B. Yeats (New York: Oxford University Press, 1936), viii.

73. *Nada the Lily*, 161–62. Could Haggard be recalling his mother's verses "descriptive of the bursting of the Monsoon" that he excerpted in his memoir, *Life and Its Author*, 9–10?

74. *King Solomon's Mines*, 237.

75. H. Rider Haggard, *Allan's Wife and Other Tales* (London: Spencer Blackett, 1889), 277.

76. *The Ivory Child*, 35.

77. Graham Greene, "Rider Haggard's Secret," *Collected Essays* (New York: Viking Press, 1969), 209.

78. *The Poetical Works of Tennyson*, 101.

79. H. Rider Haggard and Andrew Lang, *The World's Desire* (London: Longmans, Green, 1890), 215.

80. H. Rider Haggard, *Maiwa's Revenge: A Novel* (London: Longmans, Green, 1888), 106.

THREE: Diamonds and Deities

1. *King Solomon's Mines*, 257.

2. *The Days of My Life: An Autobiography*, I: 136–37.

3. Anthony Trollope, *South Africa* (London: Chapman and Hall, 1878), II: 161–73.

4. Ibid., 173.

5. Quoted in *The Great Archaeologists*, Edward Brown, ed. (London: Secker and Warburg, 1976), 43.

6. A. Wilmot, *Monomotapa* (London: T. Fisher Unwin, 1896), xiii-xv.

7. *A Hunter's Wanderings in Africa*, 325.

8. *Monomotapa*, xiii–xv.

9. Ibid., xxiv.

10. *The Story of an African Farm*, 12.

11. Oliver Schreiner, *Undine* (London: Harper, 1928), 97.

12. *The Story of an African Farm*, 293.

13. Olive Schreiner, "Diamond Fields," Richard Rive, ed. *English in Africa*, 1 (March 1974), 15–16.

14. David Leslie, *Among the Zulus and Amatongas* (Edinburgh: Edmonston, 1875), 58.

15. "The Transvaal," 78.

16. *Thoughts on South Africa*, 354–55.

17. Olive Schreiner, *Dreams* (London: Unwin, 1890), 171.

18. *Nada the Lily*, 175.

19. *The Days of My Life: An Autobiography,* II: 96.

20. "About Fiction," 178; *The Days of My Life: An Autobiography*, I: 264.

21. *The Private Diaries of Sir H. Rider Haggard*, 135–37.

22. Andrew Lang, *The Poetical Works of Andrew Lang*, Mrs. Lang, ed. (London: Longmans, Green, 1923), I: 168.

23. *The Days of My Life: An Autobiography*, II: 271.

24. Roger Lancelyn Green, "The Romances of Rider Haggard," *English* 5 [1945], 145.

25. Richard Dalby, "*King Solomon's Mines*: A Centenary Remembered," *Antiquarian Book Monthly Review*, October 1985, 391–92.

26. Ibid., 391.

27. *King Solomon's Mines*, 49.

28. Stephen Coan, "A Fictional Hero in a City Grave," *The Natal Witness*, 2 November 1999, n.p.

29. *Allan Quatermain*, 18.

30. Coan, n.p.; *The Days of My Life: An Autobiography,* I: 75–76. The elongated M sound—yielding U'hlopekazi as yet another form of the above name—pales alongside the diversity and changeability possible among differing African cultural groups with Islamicized, Christianized, and hybrid spelling variants, not to mention titles, geographic origins, and even birth order included as add-ons.

31. Lloyd Siemens, *The Critical Reception of Sir Henry Rider Haggard, ELT Special Series No. 5* (1991), 422. Adrian Darter, *The Pioneers of Mashonaland* (London: Simkin, Marshall, 1914), 2, 79–80.

32. *A Hunter's Wanderings in Africa*, vii.

33. Theodore Roosevelt, foreword, *African Nature Notes and Reminiscences*, by F. C. Selous (London: Macmillan, 1908), vi.

34. *A Hunter's Wanderings in Africa*, 235.

35. Ibid., 14.

36. Ibid., 355–58.

37. Ibid., 407–12.

38. *The Days of My Life: An Autobiography*, II: 92.

39. *The Private Diaries of Sir H. Rider Haggard*, 101.

40. *The Days of My Life: An Autobiography*, I: xvii.

41. *King Solomon's Mines*, 287.

42. *A Hunter's Wanderings in Africa*, 334–35.

43. "A Zulu War-Dance," 97.

44. *King Solomon's Mines*, 43–44; no longer recommended.

45. Mary Kingsley, *Travels in West Africa* (London: Macmillan, 1897), 4.

46. *Heart of Darkness*, 126.

47. Bram Stoker, *Dracula* (1897; New York: Random House, 1996), 358.

48. H. Rider Haggard, *Marie* (London: Cassell, 1912), 66–67.

49. *King Solomon's Mines*, 115, 116.

50. Ibid., 118.

51. Ibid.

52. Ibid., 120.

53. Ibid., 144.

54. Ibid., 146.

55. Ibid.

56. Max Müller, "Comparative Mythology" [1856], in *Chips from a German Workshop* (New York: Scribner, Armstrong, 1876), II: 107, 140. Also see *Lectures on the Science of Language* [second series, 1864] (London: Longmans, Green, 1885), 565.

57. Brian Street, *The Savage in Literature* (London: Routledge, 1975), 168.

58. *King Solomon's Mines*, 259.

59. William J. Scheick, "Adolescent Pornography and Imperialism in Haggard's *King Solomon's Mines*, *English Literature in Transition*, 34:1 (1991), 19–30; Marysa Demoor, "Ritual Celebrations as Rites of Passage in Rider Haggard's Dark Romances," *Cahiers Victoriens et Edouardiens*, 39 (1994), 205–17.

60. *The Days of My Life: An Autobiography*, I: 56.

61. John B. Vickery, *The Literary Impact of The Golden Bough* (Princeton: Princeton University Press, 1973), 17.

62. Marianna Torgovnick, *Gone Primitive: Savage Intellects, Modern Lives* (Chicago: University of Chicago Press, 1990), 275.

63. *The Days of My Life: An Autobiography*, I: 254–55.

64. *King Solomon's Mines*, 8.

65. Ibid., 9.

66. Henry Callaway, *Nursery Tales, Traditions, and Histories of the Zulus* (London: John A. Blair, 1868), 193, 201.

67. H. Rider Haggard, *The Ghost Kings* (or in U.S.: *The Lady of the Heavens*) (London: Cassell, 1908), 124.

68. *King Solomon's Mines*, 27.

69. Ibid., 106.

70. Ibid., 76.

71. Ibid., 86.

72. Ibid., 125.

73. *She*, 141.

74. *King Solomon's Mines*, 258.

75. Ibid., 259.

76. James Frazer, *The Golden Bough: A Study in Magic and Religion*, Abr. ed. (New York: Macmillan, 1922), 402.

77. Walter Pater, *Greek Studies* (London: Macmillan, 1910), 105.

78. *King Solomon's Mines*, 162.

79. *Greek Studies*, 94.

80. *King Solomon's Mines*, 161.

81. Ibid., 161–62.

82. Ibid., 179, 182.

83. "A Zulu War-Dance," 101.

84. *Zululand and the Zulus*, II: 8–11.

85. *Nada the Lily*, 172; *The Ghost Kings*, 135, 137.

86. *King Solomon's Mines*, 280.

87. Ibid., 114–15.

88. Ibid., 185.

89. Ibid., 176.

90. E. B. Tylor, *Primitive Culture* (1871; New York: Harper, 1958), I: 328–35.

91. "A Zulu War-Dance," 99.

92. Ibid., 104–105.

93. *The Days of My Life: An Autobiography,* I: 76–77.

94. *The Days of My Life: An Autobiography,* II: 92; "A Zulu War-Dance," 100; *Cetywayo and His White Neighbours; or, Remarks on Recent Events in Zululand*, 3.

95. *The Private Diaries of Sir H. Rider Haggard*, 209.

96. *Primitive Culture*, I: 351–52.

97. *King Solomon's Mines*, 190, 303.

98. Ibid., 239.

99. Ibid., 239, 298.

100. *Cetywayo and His White Neighbors; or, Remarks on Recent Events in Zululand*, 9–10.

101. *King Solomon's Mines*, 306.

102. Sol Plaatje, *Mhudi* (Alice: Lovedale, 1930), 2–3.

103. *King Solomon's Mines*, 306–307.

104. *The Golden Bough: A Study in Magic and Religion*, Abr. ed., 299–300.

105. *Primitive Culture*, I: 5.

106. *King Solomon's Mines*, 281.

107. *A Hunter's Wanderings in Africa*, 194. Selous's outfit (or lack thereof) was standard for big-game hunters. One recalls how Good, dressed in trousers and gaiters, tripped in front of the charging bull elephant.

108. *King Solomon's Mines*, 308.

109. *She*, 153.

110. *Allan Quatermain*, 3. Between the first and the revised new illustrated edition of 1905 the changes in *King Solomon's Mines* are largely a genteel cleansing—"the blood spouting in fountains from the severed arteries" is nowhere to be found in chapter fourteen of 1905. The first edition represents the unretouched rendition of Haggard's love-affair with Africa—a preference supported by Haggard's axiom of romance-fantasy revision previously cited, that "wine of this character loses its bouquet when it is poured from glass to glass." Lightly revising his novel in 1887, Haggard did correct one amusing error. In the first edition in chapter eleven, "We Give a Sign," he describes a solar eclipse in England and Africa at the time of a full moon, an astronomical impossibility. Several astronomically minded readers pounced on this error, so in his revision Haggard changed it to a lunar eclipse—which then caused "violent arguments" among readers of differing editions as to whether Haggard's eclipse was solar or lunar. But astronomically impossible though it may be, the solar eclipse was part of Haggard's imagistic vision when he first told his story; and in storytelling, imagination trumps the laws of Newtonian physics.

FOUR: Zululand

1. *Marie*, xiii; *Child of Storm*, v.

2. *Marie*, xii.

3. *Zululand and the Zulus*, I: 1.

4. Donald Burness, *Shaka: King of the Zulus* (Washington: Three Continents Press, 1976), xii. Mazisi Kunene, "South African Oral Traditions," *Aspects of South African Literature*, Christopher Heywood, ed. (London: Heinemann; New York: Africana, 1976), 24–41.

5. *King Solomon's Mines*, 176, 244.

6. *Zululand and the Zulus*, I: 11–12.

7. Ibid., I: 7, 9–10.

8. *Nada the Lily*, 5.

9. Morton Cohen, *Rider Haggard: His Life and Works* (London, Hutchinson, 1960), 229.

10. Theophilus Shepstone, "Early History of the Zulu-Kafir Race," *Annals of Natal*, John Bird, ed. (Pietermaritzburg: P. Davis, 1888), I: 155.

11. Laura Chrisman, *Rereading the Imperial Romance* (Oxford: Clarendon, 2000), 103.

12. Henry Callaway, *The Religious System of the Amazulu* (1870; Cape Town: Struik, 1970), 166–68; 299–304; 40–43.

13. David Leslie, *Among the Zulus and Amatongas* (Edinburgh: Edmonston, 1875), 73; 45–57; 279–84; 85–91; *Nada the Lily*, xv, xiv.

14. *Rider Haggard: His Life and Works*, 35.

15. *Nada the Lily*, xiv, 227.

16. H. H. Parr, *A Sketch of the Kaffir and Zulu Wars* (London, 1880), 25.

17. "The Dreadful Trade," *Scots Observer*, 1 (16 February 1889), 356–57; quoted in *Rider Haggard: His Life and Works*, 187.

18. H. Rider Haggard, *Allan's Wife and Other Tales* (London: Spencer Blackett, 1889), 13–14.

19. *Nada the Lily*, 1.

20. H. Rider Haggard, *The Ghost Kings* (or in U.S.: *The Lady of the Heavens*) (London: Cassell, 1908), 133.

21. *Nada the Lily*, 295.

22. *King Solomon's Mines*, 15.

23. *Nada the Lily*, xiii, xvii.

24. *Zululand and the Zulus*, I: 9; H. Rider Haggard, *Treasure of the Lake* (New York: Doubleday, Page, 1926), 245.

25. Everett Beiler, *The Guide to Supernatural Fiction* (Kent: Kent State University Press, 1983), 90.

26. "Can Haggard Ride Again?" 138.

27. "The Romances of Rider Haggard," 146–47.

28. Nyikadzino Nkomo, "Constructing Shaka," Online posting <www.nynk.ac.tz/history.htm> as retrieved on 4 March 1997.

29. *Nada the Lily*, 210; *Marie* (London: Cassell, 1912), 271.

30. *Mhudi*, [vii].

31. Wendy Katz, *Rider Haggard and the Fiction of Empire* (Cambridge: Cambridge University Press, 1987); Nancy Armstrong, *Fiction in the Age of Photography: The Legacy of British Realism* (Cambridge: Harvard University Press, 2000); Anne McClintock, "Maidens, Maps, and Mines," *South Atlantic Quarterly*, 87.1 (1988), 147–92; Gail Low, *White Skins/Black Masks* (London: Routledge, 1996); Carolyn Hamilton, *Terrific Majesty* (Cambridge: Harvard University Press, 1998); Dan Wylie, *Savage Delight* (Pietermaritzburg: University of Natal Press, 2000); and Laura Chrisman, *Rereading the Imperial Romance*.

32. Mazisi Kunene, *Emperor Shaka the Great* (London: Heinemann, 1979), xiii.

33. *Savage Delight*, 145–52, 185–86.

34. *Nada the Lily*, 145–52.

35. E. A. Ritter, *Shaka Zulu: The Rise of the Zulu Empire* (London: Longmans, 1955), 72.

36. *Zululand and the Zulus*, I: 11.

37. *Mhudi*, 8, 22–24.

38. See Nadel and Olney; an extreme application of this principle is Passerini. Ira B. Nadel, *Biography: Fiction, Fact and Form* (London: Macmillan, 1984); James Olney, *Metaphors of Self: The Meaning of Autobiography* (Princeton: Princeton University Press,

1972); Luisa Passerini, *Autobiography of a Generation, Italy 1968* (Middletown: Wesleyan University Press, 1996).

39. *Savage Delight*, 242.

40. *Heart of Darkness*, 67.

41. *Rider Haggard: His Life and Works*, 188.

42. "Haggard Rides Again," 1045.

43. *Allan Quatermain*, 6.

44. "About Fiction," 174; *The Days of My Life: An Autobiography*, II: 244.

45. *Nada the Lily*, 157; Fynney, I: 9.

46. William Blake, *The Poetry and Prose of William Blake*, David Erdman, ed. (New York: Doubleday, 1965), 13.

47. H. Rider Haggard, *The Wizard* (New York: Longmans, Green, 1896), 50.

48. H. Rider Haggard, *Finished* (New York: Longmans, Green, 1917), 263–64.

49. *Marie*, 292.

50. H. Rider Haggard, *The World's Desire* (London: Longmans, Green, 1890), 313–14.

51. Ibid., 254.

52. *Nada the Lily*, Preface, x.

53. *White Skins/Black Masks*, 90.

54. *Among the Zulus and Amatongas*, 40, 145, 171.

55. Ibid., 275, 278.

56. *Marie*, 42.

57. Ibid., 238.

58. Bertram Mitford, *The Gun-Runner* (London: Chatto and Windus, 1882), 16.

59. *King Solomon's Mines*, 237.

60. "On Ethnographic Allegory," *Writing Culture*, James Clifford and George Marcus, eds. (Berkeley: University of California Press, 1986), 98–121; Walter J. Ong, *Orality and Literacy* (New York: Methuen, 1982).

61. *Among the Zulus and Amatongas*, 34.

62. *Nada the Lily*, 4.

63. *Mhudi*, [vii].

64. "The Novelist as Teacher," 161–62.

65. H. Rider Haggard, "Magepa the Buck," *Princess Mary's Gift Book* (London: Hodder and Stoughton, n.d. [1914]), 65.

66. The annexation of the Transvaal, however, had been strongly criticized by Colenso. Jeff Guy, *The Heretic: A Study of the Life of John William Colenso, 1814–1883* (Johannesburg: Ravan, 1983), 279.

67. Edward Corbett, *The French Presence in Black Africa* (Washington, D.C.: Black Orpheus Press, 1972), 9.

68. Gustavo Firmat, "The Facts of Life on the Hyphen," *Remembering Cuba*, Andrea O'Reilly, ed. (Austin: University of Texas Press, 2001), 175.

69. *The Days of My Life: An Autobiography*, II: 234; *Nada the Lily*, 175, 204.

70. "Haggard Rides Again," 1044; *The Days of My Life: An Autobiography,* II: 234.

71. *Finished*, 121, 232.

72. *The Ghost Kings*, 319–23.

73. *Nada the Lily*, 154.

74. Ibid., 10.

75. Ibid., xi.

76. *Savage Delight*, 33.

77. *Zululand and the Zulus*, I: 9.

78. *Nada the Lily*, 242.

79. Ibid., vi–vii.

80. "Maidens, Maps, and Mines," 183.

81. "A Zulu War-Dance," 106.

82. *Nada the Lily*, 128.

83. Callaway in *The Religious System of the Amazulu* (166) gives this name for a club, "He-who-watches-the-fords," and cites several other club names as well, including "The-groan-causer," the alternate name Haggard gives to Umslopogaas's axe.

84. *The Golden Bough: A Study in Magic and Religion*, Abr. ed., 344–76.

85. *Nada the Lily*, 126.

86. *The Golden Bough: A Study in Magic and Religion*, Abr. ed., 576.

87. See Northcote Thomas, ed. *Anthropological Essays Presented to E. B. Tylor* (Oxford: Clarendon, 1907), 210–18; Andrew Lang, *The Secret of the Totem* (London: Longmans, Green, 1905); *The Golden Bough: A Study in Magic and Religion*, Abr. ed., chapter 28.

88. *The Golden Bough: A Study in Magic and Religion* (London: Macmillan, 1890), II: 341–43; 351–52.

89. *Nada the Lily*, 108.

90. Ibid., 129, 139.

91. *The Days of My Life: An Autobiography*, II: 17.

92. *King Solomon's Mines*, 146.

93. Livy, *Historiae*, 22, 44–50.

94. *Iliad*, 9:237–39, 16:155–65; *Beowulf*, 671ff; *Henry V*, 3.1.5–9).

95. *The Poetical Works of Tennyson*, 88.

96. *The World's Desire*, 300.

97. *The Gun-Runner*, 98–101.

98. *Nada the Lily*, 16, 28.

99. *Allan Quatermain*, 62. Emphasis added.

100. *The Savage in Literature*, 57.

101. *Allan Quatermain*, 62.

102. *Nada the Lily*, 2, 3.

103. Ibid., 82.

104. *Heart of Darkness*, 62.

105. *Marie*, 114.

106. *The Poetical Works of Tennyson*, 94.

107. *King Solomon's Mines*, 281.

108. *Nada the Lily*, 5.

109. *Child of Storm*, 80.

110. *Nada the Lily*, 47; *Child of Storm*, 80, 66.

111. Lionel Johnson, *The Collected Poems of Lionel Johnson*, Ian Fletcher, ed. (New York: Garland, 1982), 53.

112. *Nada the Lily*, 155.

113. *Allan Quatermain*, 449–50.

114. Letter of 28 August 1884 to John Haggard (Lamu, Africa). H. Rider Haggard Manuscript Collection, Rare Book and Manuscript Library, Columbia University.

115. *The Days of My Life: An Autobiography*, II: 251, 255–56.

116. John Milton, *Areopagitica, Renescence Editions* <http://darkwing.uoregon.edu/~rbear/ren.htm>.

117. Ibid.

118,. *Allan Quatermain*, 2–3.

119. *Story of an African Farm*, 138–48.

120. Plato, *Phaedrus, Symposium, Laws, Plato in Twelve Volumes*, Harold Fowler, trans. (London: Heinemann, 1914), 252d–e, 254b.

121. "About Fiction," 179.

122. *Nada the Lily*, 294.

123. P. B. Shelley, *Shelley's Poetry and Prose*, Donald Reiman, ed. (New York: W. W. Norton, 1977), 405.

124. One might observe in passing, also, that in *King Solomon's Mines*, Haggard's "colossal human skeleton" seems almost a direct borrowing from Shelley's "Alastor," where Death is the "colossal Skeleton." *King Solomon's Mines* 266, 269; "Alastor," line 611.

125. *Nada the Lily*, 85, 98–99, 155, 162; *The Religious System of the Amazulu*, 40.

126. Olive Schreiner, *Dreams* (Boston: Little, Brown), 177.

127. *The World's Desire*, 263.

128. Ibid., 213, 247, 254.

129. Ibid., 215.

130. *Nada the Lily*, 180–81, 221–22, 253–54.

131. Ibid., 85.

FIVE: From the Cape to the Zambezi

1. *Marie*, 64.

2. Ibid., 251.

3. "The Transvaal," 78–79.

4. H. Rider Haggard, "The Tale of Isandhlwana and Rorke's Drift," *The True Story Book* (blue), Andrew Lang, ed. (London: Longmans, Green, 1893), 151.

5. Ibid., xiv.

6. "The Transvaal," 70–79; *The Days of My Life: An Autobiography*, II: 262–63; I:194.

7. Arthur Symons, Review of *Dreams*, *The Athenaeum* (10 January 1891), 47.

8. *The Story of an African Farm*, 116.

9. *Thoughts on South Africa*, 82–83.

10. *Missionary Travels*, 37.

11. *Thoughts on South Africa*, 150; 151–52.

12. Ibid., 272.

13. *Missionary Travels*, 100.

14. *Thoughts on South Africa*, 155.

15. *Odyssey*, 9:447, 479.

16. *Thoughts on South Africa*, 354.

17. *From Man to Man*, 198.

18. Olive Schreiner, *Trooper Peter Halket of Mashonaland* (London: Unwin, 1897), [9].

19. Olive Schreiner, "The Dawn of Civilization," *The Athenaeum* (26 March 1921), 913.

20. *Shadows on the Grass*, 381.

21. *Rhodesia* (Salisbury, Mashonaland), 12 March 1898, in Terence Ranger, *Revolt in Southern Rhodesia, 1896–1897* (London: Heinemann, 1967), 343.

22. *Out of Africa*, 263.

23. H. Rider Haggard, "Lost on the Veld," *Youth's Companion* (New York), 25 (September 1902), 185–94; rpt. *Windsor Magazine* (London), December 1902.

24. *The Days of My Life: An Autobiography*, II: 220. Emphasis added.

25. H. Rider Haggard, "An Incident of African History," *Windsor Magazine* (London), December 1900, 1–8.

26. *The Poetical Works of Tennyson*, 93.

27. H. W. Longfellow, "A Psalm of Life" (1838), in *The Complete Poetical Works of Longfellow* (Boston: Houghton Mifflin, 1893), 1: 20–22.

28. W. S. Gilbert, *Engaged* (London: Chatto and Windus, 1904), 80.

29. *The Witch's Head*, 60–61.

30. Ibid., 60.

31. *Italienische Reise*, quoted in Mario Praz, *The Romantic Agony* (New York: Meridian Books, 1960), 46.

32. *Faust*, P. B. Shelley, trans. *Complete Poetical Works* (New York: Houghton Mifflin, 1901), 761.

33. *The Witch's Head*, 62.

34. Walter Pater, *Marius the Epicurean* (London: Macmillan, 1910), I: 21.

35. Similarly Joseph Campbell has interpreted the mythic quest in *The Hero with a Thousand Faces* (1949).

36. *The Witch's Head*, 223.

37. Ibid., 239.

38. F. B. Fynney, "The Geographical and Economic Features of the Transvaal," *Proceedings of the Royal Geographical Society of London*, 22.2 (1878), 117, 119.

39. *The Witch's Head*, 224.

40. Ibid., 226, 227, 239.

41. Ibid., 238–39.

42. Ibid., 62.

43. Ibid., 329–30.

44. H. Rider Haggard, *Smith and the Pharaohs and Other Tales* (New York: Longmans, Green, 1921), 96.

45. Ibid., 130.

46. Ibid., 108.

47. Ibid.

48. Ibid., 131.

49. H. Rider Haggard, *Jess* (New York: Harper Franklin Square, 1887), 137.

50. Ibid., 189–90.

51. Ibid., 190–91, 223–24, 332–33.

52. *The Witch's Head*, 304–305.

53. H. Rider Haggard, *Swallow, A Tale of the Great Trek* (New York: Longmans, Green, 1899), 107.

54. Ibid., v–vi.

55. Katharine Woods, "The Evolution of an Artist," *Bookman* (New York), June 1899, 350–52.

56. *Swallow*, 52.

57. *Swallow*, 27–28; 227–30.

58. *The Witch's Head*, 242.

59. H. Rider Haggard, *People of the Mist* (New York: Longmans, Green, 1894), 75.

60. *Jess*, 38.

61. H. Rider Haggard, *Ayesha, The Return of She* (London: Ward Lock, 1905), 126.

62. H. Rider Haggard, *Black Heart and White Heart and Other Stories* (London: Longmans, Green, 1900), 68.

63. *Thoughts on South Africa*, 140–41.

64. *Jess*, 248.

65. *She and Allan*, 333; *Treasure Lake*, 134.

66. *Ghost Kings*, 328–29, 373–75.

67. H. Rider Haggard, *Allan's Wife and Other Tales* (London: Spencer Blackett, 1889), 211.

68. *Mhudi*, 3.

69. *Swallow*, 203.

70. *The Witch's Head*, 146.

71. "About Men and Women," *Eastern Daily Press*, 17 November 1896, Issue 7687, 8.

72. Bertram Mitford, *The King's Assegai* (London: Chatto and Windus, 1894), 7.

73. Ibid., 15, 28.

74. Ibid., 12.

75. Ibid., 33.

76. Ibid., 1, 33.

77. "Constructing Shaka," 4 March 1997.

78. *Marie*, 17, 101.

79. Ibid., 192.

80. John Van Zyl, "No God, No Morality, No History: South African Ethnographic Film," *Critical Arts*, 1980, I.1:32.

81. *Marie*, 180, 288, 300.

82. Ibid., 148, 153.

83. Ibid., 15.

84. *Allan Quatermain*, 72–83.

85. *Marie*, 65, 192.

86. *Ivory Child*, 13–33.

87. *Marie*, 90.

88. *King Solomon's Mines*, 148.

89. *Marie*, 85, 89–90, 175, 208.

90. Bertram Mitford, *John Ames, Native Commissioner* (London: F. V. White, 1900), 42.

91. Ibid., 125.

92. *Marie*, 309.

93. Bertram Mitford, *The Induna's Wife* (London: F. V. White, 1898), 171–72.

94. Ibid., 157.

95. "Lectures on Art," 42.

96. *The Induna's Wife*, 299.

97. *Marie*, 286.

98. Ibid., 292.

99. *Allan's Wife*, Catalogue of Books (September 1889), 32.

100. *Allan Quatermain*, 259–60.

101. *Allan's Wife*, 227–28.

102. Ibid., 260.

103. *King Solomon's Mines*, 319.

104. *Allan's Wife*, 311.

105. Ibid., 330.

106. *A Hunter's Wanderings in Africa*, 44, 444.

107. *Allan's Wife*, 313–15.

108. Ibid., 45.

109. Ibid., 47.

110. *Ghost Kings*, 29–30.

111. *King Solomon's Mines*, 102.

112. *Allan's Wife*, 247–48.

113. *Ivory Child*, 225–29.

114. *Allan's Wife*, 60.

115. Ibid., 211.

116. Ibid., 146.

117. Ibid., 223.

118. *Marie*, 6.

119. Ibid., 345.

120. *Allan's Wife*, 305.

121. *Maiwa*, 106.

122. Ibid., 54, 69.

123. Ibid., 129, 132, 201.

124. *Ivory Child*, 208; *Maiwa*, 215.

125. Alexander Pope, "The Rape of the Lock," Canto 1: 135–36.

126. *Maiwa*, 163.

127. Ibid., 177.

128. Ibid., 186–88.

129. Ibid., 216.

130. Ibid., 111.

131. Ibid., 112–13.

132. Ibid., 162, 195.

133. Ibid., 210.

134. Ibid., 193.

135. Ibid., 194.

136. Ibid., 214–15.

137. Ibid., 215.

SIX: From Zululand to the Far Interior

1. *The Days of My Life: An Autobiography*, II: 111.

2. *Child of Storm*, ix.

3. *Zululand and the Zulus*, I: 23–24.

| Notes |

4. *Child of Storm*, ix.

5. Ibid., 205.

6. Ibid., 99.

7. "A Zulu War-Dance," 100.

8. *Child of Storm*, 82.

9. Ibid., 85–86.

10. *Marie*, 115.

11. Ibid., 294.

12. Joseph Conrad, *Heart of Darkness: An Authoritative Text*, Robert Kimbrough, ed. (New York: W. W. Norton, 1987), 36.

13. *Zululand and the Zulus*, I: 24–26.

14. Rudyard Kipling (letter of 9 November 1912) in *Rudyard Kipling to Rider Haggard: The Record of a Friendship*, Morton Cohen, ed. (London: Hutchinson, 1965), 75.

15. *Child of Storm*, ix.

16. *The Iliad of Homer*, Alexander Pope, trans. (London: Rivington, 1760), 3.

17. Robert Graves, *The Greek Myths* (Baltimore: Penguin Books, 1955), I: 161. Compare M. I. Finley, *The World of Odysseus* (London: Chatto and Windus, 1962), 150.

18. *Child of Storm*, 158.

19. "Lectures on Art," XX: 42.

20. "Baudelaire," 380.

21. *Heart of Darkness*, 171.

22. Ibid.

23. *Child of Storm*, 67.

24. *Marie*, xii.

25. *Allan Quatermain*, 3.

26. I have spent hours trying to pin down the source of this witticism; possibly it originated in the Rider Haggard Society meetings, Cmder. Mark Cheyne, Ditchingham Lodge, Suffolk, President.

27. Oscar Wilde, *The Importance of Being Earnest*, *Complete Works of Oscar Wilde*, Vyvyan Holland, intro. (London: Collins, 1948), 338.

28. E. B. Browning, *Sonnets from the Portuguese*, William Peterson, ed. (New York: Crown Publishers, 1977), 43.

29. H. Rider Haggard, *Finished* (New York: Longmans, Green, 1917), 313.

30. Ibid., 320.

31. Ibid., 30.

32. Rev. of *Finished* by H. R. Haggard, *Punch Magazine* (London), 12 September 1917, 197.

33. *Zululand and the Zulus*, I: 27–28.

34. *Finished*, 179.

35. *Zululand and the Zulus*, I: 28.

36. *Finished*, 178–79, 197.

37. Ibid., 140, 278–86, 305.

38. *John Ames, Native Commissioner*, 87.

39. *Finished*, 36.

40. *A Hunter's Wanderings in Africa*, 276.

41. *Finished*, 241.

42. Ibid., 210–11.

43. *The Story of an African Farm*, viii.

44. Nancy Armstrong, *Fiction in the Age of Photography: The Legacy of British Realism* (Cambridge: Harvard University Press, 2000).

45. *The Story of an African Farm*, 149.

46. Francis Bacon, "Of Truth," *The Essays, Renascence Editions* <http://darkwing.uoregon.edu/~rbear/bacon.htm>.

47. *The Story of an African Farm*, 149.

48. *Smith and the Pharaohs and Other Tales*, 69–87.

49. Ibid., 81.

50. *Finished*, 244–49.

51. H. Rider Haggard, "The Tale of Isandhlwana and Rorke's Drift," *The True Story Book*, Andrew Lang, ed. (London: Longmans, Green, 1893), 137–38.

52. *Smith and the Pharaohs and Other Tales*, 70.

53. *Black Heart and White Heart and Other Stories*, 65.

54. Ibid., 34.

55. Ibid., 24.

56. Ibid., 48.

57. Ibid., 65.

58. Bertram Mitford, *The White Shield* (New York and London: Stokes, 1895), 159.

59. Ibid., 188–91, 295.

60. *Black Heart and White Heart and Other Stories, The Wizard* [1896], 238, 240–42, 250, *et passim*.

61. Ibid., 292.

62. Ibid., 294–96, 309.

63. *Allan's Wife*, 18ff.

64. *The Wizard*, 307ff.

65. Ibid., 300–301, 316.

66. Ibid., 302–303.

67. Ibid., 242–43.

68. Ibid., 275.

69. Ibid., 351.

70. Ibid., 327.

71. Ibid., 360.

72. Ibid., 260.

73. Ibid., 265–66. The shocking photograph taken in Matabeleland of the lynching that serves as a frontispiece in *Peter Halket* represents an imperial parallel to the customary hanging trees used by chiefs to execute their victims, one such tree actually sketched by Marie Lippert in *The Matabeleland Travel Letters of Marie Lippert, 1891*, Eric Rosenthal, ed. (Cape Town: Friends of the South African Library, 1960), 24.

74. John Donne, "Hymn to God, My God, in my Sickness," *Selected Poetry of John Donne (1572–1631)* <http://eir.library.utoronto.ca/rpo/display/poet98.html>.

75. *The Wizard*, 368.

76. William James, *Varieties of Religious Experience* (New York: Longmans, Green, 1902), Lectures VI and VII, "The Sick Soul."

77. *The Wizard*, 406–407.

78. *Trooper Peter Halket of Mashonaland*, 195.

79. Ibid., 220, 249. Schreiner wrote to Betty Molteno sometime in September 1896 that she hoped to finish *Peter Halket* by the next Saturday. She usually had trouble finishing projects, but apparently by 14 December 1896, the manuscript was about to go to an editor. Yet the extraordinary parallels could suggest she did not cap off her romance until she had read Haggard. Letter of September in the Olive Schreiner Collection, University of Cape Town, J. W. Jagger Library; letter of December in the Kimberley Public Library, archives.

80. Ibid., 259.

81. *The Wizard*, 236.

82. Ibid., 235.

83. Ibid., 238.

84. Ibid., 250, 297.

85. Ibid., 380–82.

86. *Smith and the Pharaohs and Other Tales*, "Little Flower," 199–200.

87. Ibid., 205.

88. Ibid., 166.

89. Ibid., 204–205.

90. Ibid., 219.

91. Ibid., 224.

92. S. C. Cronwright-Schreiner, *The Life of Olive Schreiner* (Boston: Little, Brown, 1924), 220.

93. *Trooper Peter*, 88–93.

94. *John Ames, Native Commissioner*, 190.

95. Ibid., 57–58.

96. Ibid., 308.

SEVEN: Romances of the Lakes Region

1. *The Story of an African Farm*, viii.

2. *She and Allan*, 346.

3. Ibid., 54.

4. Walter Pater, *The Renaissance: Studies in Art and Poetry* (London: Macmillan, 1910), 24–25.

5. Algernon Swinburne, *Essays and Studies* (London: Chatto and Windus, 1911), 319–20.

6. Neville Rogers, "Shelley and the Visual Arts," *Keats–Shelley Memorial Bulletin*, 12 (1960), 10; P. B. Shelley, "On the Medusa of Leonardo da Vinci," *Posthumous Poems of Percy Bysshe Shelley*, Mary Shelley, ed. (London: J. and H. Hunt, 1824), 139–40.

7. H. Rider Haggard, *Wisdom's Daughter* (New York: Doubleday, Page, 1923), 297–98, 345.

8. "About Fiction," 175.

9. Plato, *Phaedrus, Symposium, Laws. Plato in Twelve Volumes*, Harold Fowler, trans. (London: Heinemann, 1914), 252d–e, 254b.

10. Ibid., 255c–e.

11. *She*, 283.

12. *Phaedrus*, 237–56.

13. Giordano Bruno, *Of the Heroic Frenzies* (1585), Paul Memmo, trans. (Chapel Hill: University of North Carolina Press, 1964).

14. *Phaedrus*, 244c, 245b, 251d.

15. *Of the Heroic Frenzies*, "Argument of the Nolan," 75–76, "Fifth Dialogue" Pt. 2.

16. Ibid., "Fifth Dialogue," 2: 263–264.

17. Ibid., "Argument of the Nolan," 77.

18. Ibid., 7:73.

19. Ibid., "Second Dialogue," 2: 225–226.

20. *Ayesha, The Return of She*, 264.

21. H. Rider Haggard, "Who is 'She'?" *Pall Mall Gazette* (22 January 1887), 13–14.

22. *Phaedrus*, 256d; *Symposium*, 201d *et seq*.

23. *Phaedrus*, 255c–256d.

24. *Of the Heroic Frenzies*, "Argument of the Nolan," 76.

25. H. Rider Haggard, "A Man's View of Women," review of *Woman: The Predominant Partner*, by Edward Sullivan, *African Review*, 10 (22 September 1894), 407.

26. *People of the Mist*, 50.

27. Ibid., 84.

28. Ibid., 218, 228.

29. Ibid., 187.

30. Ibid., 192.

31. Ibid., 147, 230, 287.

32. Ibid., 310.

33. Ibid., 269–70.

34. Ibid., 271.

35. Ibid., 271–72.

36. Ibid., 272–73.

37. *The Sign of the Spider*, 285.

38. Ibid., 271–72.

39. *Heart of Darkness*, 54.

40. *The Sign of the Spider*, 134.

41. Ibid., 98.

42. Ibid., 310–11.

43. Ibid., 224.

44. Ibid., 172.

45. H. Rider Haggard, *My Fellow Laborer / The Wreck of the 'Copeland'* (London: George Munro, 1888), an omnibus edition of two tales in one volume, the second of which is described at length in *Days of My Life: An Autobiography*, I: 288–94.

46. H. Rider Haggard, "The Patterson Embassy to Lobengula," *The Downfall of Lobengula*, W. A. Wills and L. T. Collingridge, eds. (London: African Review, 1894), 228.

47. *Benita, An African Romance*, 14.

48. Ibid., 92, 107–8, 113.

49. *King Solomon's Mines*, 211.

50. *Benita, An African Romance*, 149, 152.

51. "Can Haggard Ride Again?" 136.

52. *Benita, An African Romance*, 260.

53. Ibid., 267.

54. Ibid., 338.

55. Ibid., 341.

56. *The Ghost Kings*, 275.

57. Author's Note in 1923 Cassell reprint.

58. *The Ghost Kings*, 28.

59. Ibid., 150, 190.

60. Johann Wolfgang von Goethe, *Faust*, final couplet.

61. *Finished*, 258.

62. *Treasure of the Lake*, 161.

63. Mitford actually cites this group by name in *Ravenshaw of Rietholme* (1910), 99.

64. *The Ghost Kings*, 86, 88.

65. Ibid., 90.

66. Ibid., 137.

67. Ibid., vii.

68. Frederick Elworthy, *The Evil Eye* (London: J. Murray, 1895), 108 n. 175.

69. *The Ghost Kings*, 371.

70. Ibid., 328–29; 373–75.

71. John Milton, *Paradise Lost*, Book 12: 646–49.

72. H. Rider Haggard, *The Yellow God* (New York: Cupples and Leon, 1908), 116–17, 204.

73. Ibid., 223–24. One recalls how Dido wanted to kill the defecting Aeneas but—not entirely unlike Ayesha—slays herself instead.

74. Ibid., 170–171, 200.

75. Ibid., 181.

76. Ibid., 213–16.

77. Ibid., 207–209.

78. Ibid., 225.

79. *The Days of My Life: An Autobiography*, II: 30–38.

| Notes |

80. *Queen Sheba's Ring*, 16.

81. Ibid., 17, 107.

82. *She and Allan*, 391–92.

83. Ibid., 30.

84. Ibid., 140–42.

85. Ibid., 250–51.

86. Ibid., vii.

87. Ibid., 54.

88. Ibid., 193, 353–54, 366.

89. Ibid., 201–205.

90. Ibid., 219–20, 227.

91. Ibid., 202.

92. John Lyly, *Euphues: The Anatomy of Wit* (1578), *The Complete Works of John Lyly*, R. W. Bond, ed. (Oxford: Clarendon Press, 1902), I: 184, ll.21–23.

93. *She and Allan*, 193.

94. Ibid., 337.

95. Ibid., 326–34.

96. Ibid., 333–34.

97. Ibid., 332.

98. Ibid.

99. H. Rider Haggard, *Allan and the Holy Flower* (New York: Longmans, Green, 1915), 352.

100. *Heu–Heu, or the Monster*, 180–81.

101. *The Ivory Child*, 64.

102. "Lectures on Art," 41.

103. *The Ivory Child*, 19.

104. *Treasure of the Lake*, 225.

105. *Heu–Heu, or the Monster*, 51.

106. Ibid., 59, 153, 231.

107. Ibid., 63.

108. *The Witch's Head*, 98, 304.

109. *Heu–Heu, or the Monster*, 234–36.

110. *The Story of an African Farm*, 139–40.

111. Ibid., 140.

112. *Heu–Heu, or the Monster*, 263–64.

113. Ibid., 113–14.

114. In Haggard, Schreiner, and Mitford the linkage between religious, political, and artistic theories was an epistemology so markedly pluralistic that man's relation to an all-encompassing eternal Logos remained inexplicable; instead, in a crisis of faith they stressed the tragic alternatives of life and the tension of truths posed against each other in their quest for the idealist's universal Author of all things.

115. *Treasure of the Lake*, 48.

116. Ibid., 8.

117. Ibid., 149.

118. Ibid., 171, 196.

119. Ibid., 298–99.

120. Ibid., 165.

121. Ibid., 177–78.

122. Ibid., 17.

123. Ibid., 20, 165–66.

124. Ibid., 291.

125. *She and Allan*, 76, 103.

126. "About Fiction," 173–74, 180.

127. Matthew Arnold, "Stanzas from the Grande Chartreuse," *The Poetical Works of Matthew Arnold*, C. B. Tinker and H. F. Lowry, eds. (London: Oxford University Press, 1961), 302.

EIGHT: In Concluding

1. *Treasure of the Lake*, 7.

2. *Allan Quatermain*, 279.

3. Ibid., 3.

4. *The Poetical Works of Tennyson*, 89.

5. *Allan Quatermain*, 1.

6. Ibid., 12.

7. Ibid., 129.

8. Ibid., 161–62.

9. Sir James Frazer, "Worship of the Sun Among Ancient Romans," *The Worship of Nature* (London: Macmillan, 1926).

10. Frederika Bremer, *The Homes of the New World* (New York: Harper, 1853), I: letter 24.

11. *Allan Quatermain*, 162–63.

12. *The World's Desire*, 254.

13. *The Yellow God*, 290–91.

14. Ibid., 100.

15. *The Renaissance: Studies in Art and Poetry*, 231–32.

16. Oliver Elton, *Frederick York Powell, A Life* (Oxford: Clarendon, 1906), I: 158–59.

17. *The Days of My Life: An Autobiography*, II: 179.

18. C. S. Lewis, "On Stories," in *Essays Presented to Charles Williams*, C. S. Lewis, ed. (London: Oxford University Press, 1947), 101.

19. Kenneth M. Cameron, *Africa on Film: Beyond Black and White* (New York: Continuum, 1994), 28–29.

❧ Appendix
Bertram Mitford: Profile of a Contrarian

Bertram Mitford is always mentioned in passing as an Anglo-African writer, yet except for Michael Lieven's essay never discussed in his own right.[1] But between 1882 and 1914 he wrote many short stories and nearly fifty novels, various ones going through multiple editions. Most are set in South Africa; and of these novels a good half dozen would clearly be considered minor classics should they be rediscovered, especially *The Gun-Runner* (1882), *The Sign of the Spider* (1896) and a quartet of Zulu tales.[2] These latter four historical tales, narrated by the Zulu Untúswa, are studies in kingship, in the conduct of men in power or struggling for power; and the climactic fall of the Zulu kingdom involves not merely the natives themselves but, as in Haggard's *Nada the Lily* (1892) and its sequels, the whole world of which they were a part. Lieven argues that Mitford's fictions are "of interest as a cross-road of various discourses in late nineteenth-century popular imperialism," citing Martin Green who in *Dreams of Adventure, Deeds of Empire* (1979) saw adventure tales as "the energizing myth of English Imperialism."[3] Perhaps Mitford's work, like Haggard's, is ultimately most interesting in the perspective of hindsight: after the disintegration of the Zulu *ancien régime*, the liberal imperialist looked forward to justice, literacy, medicine, modern communications, and relative prosperity, all under a new Anglophone dispensation. That delusion of a Europeanized Africa now stands in stark contrast to the postcolonial reality of today's stumbling giant. The meaning of Mitford's or Haggard's novels—their implicit notion that service to the empire is a noble duty, for example—has been ironized for us by our lens of self-conscious knowingness and the temporal distancing of history. One now asks how, consciously or subconsciously, these writers disavowed the popular imperial agenda of economic and military coercion or anticipated its future collapse? But beyond the fascination of political exegesis there is also in Mitford's fiction an aesthetic-moral significance. In synopsis, the action in a Mitford story perhaps seems like that in more ordinary thrillers; however, apart from his skill at dramatizing generic events in fresh and effective ways, the value of his fiction lies in its instantiation of an authorial perspective born of truly exceptional life experiences, an innovative "Catholic existentialism" that acquiesces to the tragic circumstances of life with shame and outrage but that, through the instrumentality of forgiving others, confers *upon oneself* the perfect pardon that is perfect peace.

Surprisingly, we have been told almost nothing about Mitford's private life; he seems to have passed through his times like a fish through water, with barely a trace. Such sketchy information as has been reported—scarcely comprising a few short paragraphs, since each perfunctory entry merely repeats the others—lacks even reliable fundamental statistics.[4] Where was he born? Where and for what periods did he hold Civil Service appointments in Africa? Did he marry? When? And what children did he have? Information for nearly all the incidents in Mitford's life still needs to be meticulously uncovered. In one of the scanty biographical observations, we are told that he was "a prominent member of the Anglo-African Writers' Club."[5] Haggard refers in his autobiography, *The Days of My Life* (1926), to this group of which he was elected chairman as "a pleasant and useful dining society that is now defunct."[6] Mitford, one might infer, thus socialized with Haggard who was active in the monthly dinners of the club from 1894 to (perhaps) the earliest years of the following century. Only by going back to the newspapers do we learn of several meetings in 1900, chaired by Haggard and attended by Mitford, in which the tensions of the Boer War and its future settlement—e.g., should English be the official language in the colonies?—were discussed by the members.[7] Both Mitford and Haggard began their careers as novelists by writing expository prose on Zulu-white relations; neither had attended a university and both enlisted in the Colonial Civil Service. Both belonged to the British gentry and both their mothers were by birth from the ruling class of British-Indians.[8] Moreover, prior to the Civil Service, Mitford had been a stock farmer; Haggard, subsequent to his Civil Service, had been an ostrich rancher. Yet Mitford, despite his evident qualities, never achieved Haggard's enormous popularity and is now neglected. In *The White Hand and the Black* (1907), Mitford invents a war dance at a kraal with more than a bit of applicability to real-life histories: "The boy's face flushed with delight. He had read plentifully about this sort of thing—in fact such reading had largely to do with bringing him out to the country at all. Now he was going to see it—to see the real thing."[9] The resident magistrate suggests to the young man "you might add to your pay by knocking up a description of it for one of the home magazines—or even two"[10]—precisely as Haggard had done in his first essays. But with typical Mitford irony, this dance turns real and the young trooper is "barbarously butchered. Then into his poor bleeding, mutilated body these fiends drove their assegais again and again, anointing themselves with the blood, in some instances even licking it."[11] Wishful thinking about the burgeoning career of Mitford's chief competitor in later years, one is tempted to speculate—except that Mitford himself had included just such a description in the conclusion of *Through the Zulu Country* (1883) which he clearly reused here in this novel as Haggard had reused "The Zulu War-Dance" (1877) in *King Solomon's Mines*. Thus the murdered young trooper is as much the shadowed double of a callow Mitford as of his erstwhile literary nemesis.

Although it seems likely that the absence of biographical facts will in some measure persist, the key to Mitford's vivid descriptions of colonial encounters with native otherness seems firmly rooted in his ancestry and youth. What follows will be the first functional but concise biographical account of Mitford, indispensable because of the light it sheds on the origins of his colonial mindset and on the imperial adventure genre in the hands of Haggard and others.

Mitford was born 13 June 1855 in Bath, England, the sixth of nine children of Edward Ledwich Osbaldeston-Mitford (1811–1912) and his first wife, Janet Bailey (c. 1821–1896).[12] Bertram's father Edward (with or without the hyphen in his surname, but with "Lord"—after 1895—preceding and "F.R.G.S." following) had been born in the picturesque village of Mitford, a parish in the county division of Morpeth, Northumberland, where the family had lived for over 900 years on an estate given by William the Conqueror to Sir Richard Bertram for his military support in the campaigns of 1066. Bertrams intermarried with Mitfords, living first in Mitford Castle (its ruins at present are a "scheduled monument" legally sheltered, situated on a knoll overlooking the Wansbeck River, opposite the Norman Church of St. Mary Magdalene) and later behind the ruined castle in the Old Manor House, itself now also a vestige. Edward is recorded as "of Mitford Hall," the stately mansion in Northumberland, and "of Hunmanby Hall," Yorkshire. (Much earlier, in the time of Robert Mitford [1612–1674], this line had branched from that which produced the "Mitford sisters," those scandalous ornaments to the era of Evelyn Waugh's "Bright Young Things.") In his sole novel, *The Arab's Pledge—a Tale of Marocco in 1830* (1867), Edward describes in his preface this tale as "written more than five-and-twenty years ago, after a residence of six years in Marocco."[13] Something of Bertram's future concerns may be glimpsed here: this romance does not attempt to compete with the novel of domestic Victorian realism; rather, it aims to enlarge the reader's grasp of a distant colonial world of exotic "Maroqueen customs" by telling a tale based on bona fide "tragical facts, which occurred at the time" of Edward's "residence of six years" on the scene.[14] Racial strife, racial amity: these will be Bertram's themes as well. This tale's final spectacle of an insane penitential self-immolation on a pyre has just that grotesquerie of Bertram's climactic scenes as well. Edward must have returned from Morocco to Northumberland only to leave shortly for Ceylon by what surely was the most unique route anyone hitherto had taken, which he described and illustrated with original sketches in *A Land-March from England to Ceylon Forty Years Ago* (1884). Its full title clarifies this adventurous undertaking: "through Dalmatia, Montenegro, Turkey, Asia Minor, Syria, Palestine, Assyria, Persia, Afghanistan, Scinde, and India, of which 7000 miles [were] on horseback."[15] Although Mitford does not mention Austen Henry Layard, his traveling companion, Layard in his *A Popular Account of Discoveries at Nineveh* (1854) also tells how he, aged twenty-two, and Mitford, then twenty-eight and more fluent in Arabic, covered this distance from England to Hamadan during the autumn of 1839 and winter of 1840, visiting the ruins of the ancient seats of civilization, "equally careless of comfort and unmindful of danger."[16] Both young men intended to seek a career in Ceylon, but in Persia at Hamadan, Layard chose archaeology over the Civil Service; Mitford continued on to Ceylon alone.

Once there, Edward Mitford seems to have developed a naturalist's fascination with the birds of the island. J. E. Tennent in *Ceylon* (1860) mentions his indebtedness to "Mr. Mitford, of the Ceylon Civil Service ... for many valuable notes relative to the birds of the island" and quotes Mitford's description of the Devil-Bird, not an owl but a hawk: "I never heard it until I came to Kornegalle, where it haunts the rocky hill at the back of Government-House." Its cry is "the most appalling that can be imagined, and scarcely to be heard without shuddering; I can only compare it to a boy in torture, whose screams are being stopped by being strangled."17 Even Darwin in the seventh chapter of his *Variation of Animals and Plants under Domestication* (1868) cites Mitford's study of a feral Ceylonese rooster that "visits solitary farms and ravishes" the domestic hens; Darwin retreats from this faintly ludicrous image to observe that the hybrids produced are "quite sterile" so "this species, then, may in all probability be rejected as one of the primitive stocks of the domestic fowl."18 When Edward wasn't stalking rapist roosters, he wrote plays in verse, publishing *Poems: Dramatic and Lyrical* (1869). On 1 November 1911 *The London Times* reported that King George V sent a message of congratulations to Edward on his one-hundredth birthday and on 16 May 1912 it reported a kingly message of sympathy on his death two days previously. At the time of Edward's death his widow and *relict* (Edward's second wife) was Ella Elizabeth Osbaldeston-Mitford of Sunniside, Morden, Surrey. The gross value of his personal estate at decease was £8,495.19

Our current subject, Bertram, was Edward and Janet Bailey's fourth son and is supposed, incorrectly, to have been born in Ceylon. All the other children except Bertram and his sister Sybil, apparently, were born in Ceylon, India (today Sri Lanka). Edward Mitford presumably was on the staff of the Ceylon Civil Service when in 1844 he married Janet, daughter of the Reverend Benjamin Bailey (1791-1853). Bertram's maternal grandfather, remembered as the Archdeacon of Ceylon, initially had been sent in 1816–1817 by the Church Missionary Society, sponsored by the Anglicans, to the "Syrian" Christians amid the lush hills and lakes of Kottayam, India, on the Arabian Sea. In this land of placid palm-fringed bayous and lofty mountains in the west, Bailey organized a grammar school and established at the mission the region's first printing press, publishing books including a Malayalim Bible, a dictionary, and sermons. An imposing statue of this Old Image stands at present on the grounds of Kottayam College, his original boys' and girls' academy. Bailey's translations of English texts—certainly the Gospels, but one also may conjecture such likely works as *Pilgrim's Progress*—may have served an evangelical purpose; but they worked equally well in spreading a Western sociocultural orientation toward rights and liberty which, it may be suggested, contained the seeds of the British empire's eventual dissolution. Whether Edward Mitford wanted his sons to benefit from the Britishness of an English education, avoiding their acquiring the Anglo-Indian "chi-chi" accent that carried the social stigma of mixed blood and thwarted professional opportunities, or whether it was a matter of access to schools, several sons were educated in England. One elder brother, Edward (1853–1948), and one younger brother, William (b. 1858), later became clergymen in the Church of England. Edward attended Winchester and St. John's

College, Cambridge, taking his B.A. in 1875, then served as vicar of Hunmanby, 1888–1919, and rector of Acrise, Kent, 1919–1923. William attended Durham University and afterwards was installed as rector at St. Peter's, Ickburgh, Norfolk. Bertram later stayed at the Ickburgh Rectory on at least one occasion in March 1905. St. Peter's comported well with the family background—in the Early English style with intricately carved gargoyles flanking the nave.

At the age of five young Bertram had been a "scholar" along with older siblings Frances, Edith, and Edward, living in a Kent household headed by Robert and Alicia Beevor in Ramsgate on St. Lawrence Street. (In 1862 his sister, Sybil Emma Mitford, was registered as born in this district of Thanet, suggesting that Bertram's mother was nearby at least some of this time.) At or after the age of eight he then attended the Royal Naval School in New Cross, Kent, which at modest cost principally educated upwards of 210 sons of impecunious naval and marine officers. Its curriculum qualified students "for the university, naval or military service."[20] Fittingly, it had a large swimming pool, which perhaps added to the number of Mitford's future recreations: "shooting, fishing, bicycling, walking, in early life mountain climbing, swimming when available, reading other people's novels."[21] Later, as a fifteen-year-old, Bertram is numbered among those enrolled at St. John's College, Sussex, a school for 300 boys about a mile north of the small market town of Hurstpierpoint. In Bertram's time the school's Head Master was Edward Clarke Love, D.D. He seems to have finished his secondary schooling at Hurstpierpoint College, also in west Sussex. Either before sailing to the Cape Colony or during visits back to England, Bertram apparently lodged at Tivoli, a borough of Cheltenham, Gloucestershire, with his younger brother William, who was an undergraduate at Durham University. Evidently, the Mitfords had a large branch of the family well-established in South Africa when Bertram first arrived in 1874 with the intention of stock farming. One may speculate that the reason Mitford did not attend any university but went to South Africa with the less ambitious intention of raising animals on a farm was his conversion to Catholicism. Perhaps the most evident instance of Mitford's Catholic leanings may be a covertly autobiographical exchange in *The Weird of Deadly Hollow* (1891): "'You are a Catholic, are you not?' asks the young woman, adding 'It is a grand old creed.' The protagonist replies: 'I was not brought up in it, I assure you. Very much to the contrary. When I was eighteen I began to discover that it was about the most infamously slandered creed extant, and that, I suppose, to my contrarious spirit constituted an attraction, and I began to study the whole question. When I was twenty-one I told my father I intended to enter the Catholic Church. He flew into a great rage, and vowed that the day I did so he would turn me out of doors. I was as good as my word, for I entered it without further delay, and he was as good as his, for he did turn me out of doors also without further delay.'"[22] A large number of the novels contain discreet references to Catholicism, such as the heroic Jesuit in *The King's Assegai*. But in keeping with a paucity of biographical data, Mitford is not mentioned either in W. J. Gordon-Gorman's *Converts to*

Rome (1910), nor in Madeleine Beard's *Faith and Fortune* (1997), nor does his name appear in the index of Joseph Pearce's *Literary Converts* (2000); only the *Catholic Who's Who and Yearbook* has a cursory entry.

※ ※

Mitford's South African connection comes about in this fashion: the sister of Bertram's grandfather, Robert (1780–1818), Anna Maria Mitford, born in 1782, married Miles Bowker, a Wiltshire farmer. After the British occupied the Cape, Miles led a party of settlers who sailed from Portsmouth, England, in January of 1820 for Cape Town, South Africa. These impoverished "1820 Settlers" were sent to expropriate territories from the Xhosa in the Eastern Cape and the Zulus in Natal. With his wife and nine children—his tenth child, Anna Maria Bowker was born on board the *Weymouth* while lying at anchor in Table Bay—Miles settled in the Eastern Cape, where his eleventh child James Henry was born. Miles became one of the founders there of the wool industry. Bertram perhaps apprenticed himself to learn the family trade, much as Kenrick Holt in *A Veldt Vendetta* (1903) began a new career in the Cape Colony at East London. A rare first-person narrator among Mitford's fictional protagonists, Holt alludes in the novel's last paragraph to Bertram Mitford (unnamed but recognizable) as his friend. This "settler country" of British Kaffraria was/is a turbulent, diverse region—from its sultry coast to the often snow-clad Drakensburgs it is both arid and desolate, as well as lushly green and forested, one of the most fertile regions in South Africa—in which the English built forts to maintain peace. The strongest of these bastions of imperial pacification was Fort Beaufort, which once weathered an offensive by a full Xhosa *impi*. In 1878 Bertram apparently forsook family sheep in order to enter the Colonial Civil Service of the Cape of Good Hope, assigned as a clerk to Fort Beaufort (probably the Fort Lamport in several of his novels) and to border outposts. Both the localities and the principal Zulu chiefs and *indunas* in his fiction are portrayed from first-hand experience. Possibly Mitford's first job was not stock farming but ranging and guarding the Eastern Cape frontier. Brian Stringer (email of 15 January 2006) reports that the Hurstpierpoint College register indicates Mitford had migrated to South Africa and "Joined Cape Mounted Police." This unit may have been the famed Frontier Armed Mounted Police.

Since Mitford was not a senior official appointed from London, only the voluminous and unindexed colonial records in the South African National Archives and its depositories may provide a basic outline of his postings: such sources as the Cape Civil Service Lists, the Cape General Directory, the Imperial Calendar, Civil Service Year Books, Government Gazettes and original Colonial Office correspondence. No application or correspondence between Mitford and the Colonial Office pertaining to positions or transfers has yet been found; however, he was registered in 1878 as a voter in the Karoo village of Tarkastad in the electoral division of Queenstown that included Fort Beaufort.[23] At this time, not far from Tarkastad, the Cape Colony and the Xhosas were engaged in the Ninth Border War. The reporter for the *Eastern Daily Press* (Norwich) did his homework by reading Mitford's first nonfiction publication, *Through the Zulu Country* (1883): "He was personally acquainted with King Cetewayo, John Dunn, and many of the Zulu chiefs. After the war of 1879 he travelled over the battlefields of Zululand collecting material for his literary work. The insight thus gained into Zulu life and character proved invaluable in the graphic descriptions so familiar to the many readers of his books."[24] Mitford's visit to Zululand occurred in 1881–1882, after which he says he embarked on "the homeward-bound mail steamer, having trodden South African soil for the last time."[25] Possibly Mitford may not have been an official beyond 1880, inasmuch as he is described on the title page as "Late of the Cape Civil Service." Mitford's recurrent suggestions in his later novels that natives have the fullest protection of British law, the magistrates bending over backwards to give them the benefit, are undoubtedly echoes of his own observations. His further implication that under legal protection natives become more aggressive, that access to justice empowers their resistance, may be an early and inchoate hypothesis for the end of colonialism. Several brief biographical accounts[26] say that for two years between 1886–1888, Mitford became proprietor of the *East London Advertiser*, with the implication that this was in South Africa, not the *Advertiser* in the east of London, England. The South African paper was founded in 1879 by Thomas Goodwin; Goodwin resumed control in April 1888 only to oversee the paper's liquidation in May. But having already published his travelogue of the Zululand battlefields, some poetry, and his first and best-known novel, *The Gun-Runner* (1882), at this time Mitford seems to have settled finally on a fiction-writing career.

One of Mitford's finest novels, *The King's Assegai* (1894), is dedicated to "Colonel James Henry Bowker, sometime commandant of the Cape Frontier Armed and Mounted Police, and Governor's Agent for Basutoland, whose wide knowledge of the South African native character and whose sympathy with all that is best in it are surpassed by none." As the eleventh and final child of Miles and Anna Bowker, born in 1822 on their farm "Olive Burn" in the Eastern Cape Province, Colonel Bowker was Mitford's second cousin. Bowker never married but we can assume that he must have taken a fatherly interest in the twenty-year-old Bertram. As a "convinced expansionist," not only did Bowker fight in the Seventh and Eighth Kaffir Wars; but afterwards was appointed inspector, then commandant, and finally commanding officer of the FAMP. He also was designated High Commissioner's agent in Basutoland and directed the expedition to annex the diamond fields of Griqualand West. In 1872 he led a punitive expedition against the amaHlubi and their chief, Langalibalele—Bishop Colenso decried this as a dishonestly expedient campaign but the colonists rallied to it—and in 1877 he led the suppression of Moorosi's Rebellion. Oddly, Bowker is coauthor with Roland Trimen of *South-African Butterflies: A Monograph of the Extra-Tropical Species* (1887–1889). Trimen writes there: "Colonel Bowker's debut as a votary of entomology took place in Kaffraria twenty-seven years ago.... The fine collection of native butterflies in the South-African museum owes the greater part of its treasures to his exertions,—no less than forty new species, and one most remarkable new genus (Deloneura).... The gift of specimens has been immeasurably enhanced in value by his copious notes on the haunts and habits of the insects, their distribution in South Africa, and their earlier stages."[27] If Mitford did not inherit his observant naturalist's eye from his father Edward, then surely it was a Bowker gene. The Commandant of the FAMP in Mitford's *Harley Greenoak's Charge* (1906) is clearly Colonel James's portrait. There a recent recruit is described by the subinspector as a "very black-hued Kafir" who is "rather a pet of the Commandant's; helps him to find new sorts of butterflies and creeping things that the old man is dead nuts on collecting."[28] This naturalist-warrior cousin prompted Mitford's wonderfully bizarre scene of the Commandant awaiting a massive dawn attack of assegai-wielding natives while calmly examining a lizard in a pickle bottle by the light of "a pale, wrack-swept moon, ... his thoughts running about equally on the work in front, and the latest 'specimen' he had captured."[29] At the novel's end Mitford echoes his cousin's move from what Trimen called the "productive region" of Kaffraria "to his fruitful labours in Basutoland, Griqualand West, Natal, and Zululand"[30]: "'There's some talk of giving him Basutoland.' 'Oh, well, that's not so bad. The fine old chap'll have lots of time to hunt butterflies and lizards up there.'"[31]

At what point Mitford first sailed back to England, we do not know—he returned to Africa in 1881 for his tour of the battlefields and later revisited Cape Town at least once in the spring-summer of 1898–1899—but he surely had come home by 1886 to marry at Brighton, Sussex, Zima Helen Ebden (aka "Louisa" in the 1891 census, a distorted homophone one supposes), daughter of the Honourable Alfred Ebden, a prominent surname in the southern suburbs of Cape Town. Her unusual forename—a matronymic, her mother was Decima Zima Grimley—may be a diminutive of Simon. Surely its Hebraic meaning of "evil deed" or "whoring" is unimaginable. Zima had been born at Port Elizabeth in the Cape Colony, 23 September 1854; she died in 1915 the year after her husband. Zima's first marriage had been in 1874 at barely twenty years of age to Alexander Gentle, some fourteen years her senior, a Scottish-born retail businessman and son of a clergyman in northern Scotland. That first marriage had been solemnized at Christ Church in the Parish of Paddington, Middlesex. Zima's divorce was at the suit of her husband. As a consequence of these proceedings, her mother paid a visit to England in 1882–1883 (her expenses were £640). Zima's divorce decree was dated 3 April 1884. The registration for her subsequent marriage to Mitford on 9 March 1886 describes her as "the divorced wife of Alexander Gentle" and gives the residence for both of them at the time of marriage as 60 Regency Square, Brighton, possibly a resort rooming house. Their ages then were both thirty-one years and Mitford is listed as a "bachelor" and a "gentleman" by profession. They were married in the Register Office in Brighton with no family witnesses. At that time, Zima had a son and two daughters, Zima Helen Gentle and Winifred Ebden, from her first marriage.32

Bertram and Zima's daughter Yseulte Helen was born 3 June 1887 at 40 Linden Gardens, Bayswater, London. When Bertram registered her birth several months later, his address was 3 Edward Road, St. Leonards, Hastings. Mitford's 1902 *Word of the Sorceress* was tenderly dedicated to the fourteen-year-old Yseulte: "*Nkosazana o'zandhla zimhlope...*" ("Little Chieftainess, whose hands are white..."). By 1891 the Mitfords were living at 84 Westbourne Park Road, Paddington, a district in London of substantial three-story homes, where their son Roland Bertram was born on 17 June of that year.33 In those days Bertram described his occupation rather melodramatically, or with a sense of self-irony, as a "Littérateur" of independent means. From June of 1895 forward, his other London addresses included: 21 John Street, Bedford Row; 61 Seymour Street, Hyde Park (1896); 15 Blandford Street, Portman Square (1899); 28 and, then, 11 Addison Mansions, West Kensington (from 1901 to 1907)—here also at Addison Mansions in later years Agatha Christie kept a business flat; and finally, for several years until his death, Mitford's address was 5 Furzeham Road, West Drayton.34 It is quite possible that during the 1895–1901 period of frequent address changes the Mitfords traveled abroad intermittently; no record exists of them anywhere in the 1901 British census when they may have been in Colorado. Mitford's London agent was the firm of A. P. Watt & Son, which presided over publishing's first and largest literary agency and led the trade in fiction. Describing the "pre-eminently useful institution" of the "Literary Agent," Mitford wrote Watt in a testimonial letter: "Speaking from experience I can only say—as a friend of mine said when he had learnt to ride a bicycle—I don't know how I got along all that time without one. More particularly does this hold good of a writer like myself, the very exigencies of whose especial line of fiction necessitate prolonged sojourns in far countries."35

The 1899 contract that Watt negotiated on behalf of Mitford for an edition of 2,000 copies of *The Weird of Deadly Hollow* paid him "one shilling per each and every thirteen copies sold for each shilling of the published price." His 1896 contract for *The Sign of the Spider*—arithmetically more straightforward—was ten percent of the selling price up to 2,000 copies, fifteen percent for each copy over and above that number, with an £80 advance upon publication. Later in 1899 he received for *John Ames* sixteen and two-thirds percent of the price on the first 5,000 copies; eight pence for copies over and above that number, with an advance of £150 (at the last minute he retitled this novel on the contract, crossing out the possibly puzzling native title, *The Umlimo*).36 Copies generally sold for 3/6, suggesting that with the better publishers Mitford may have cleared an initial £50–150 in the first six months (perhaps 25,000 to 75,000 USD in today's market). Some of Mitford's novels also had run serially before book publication; unpropitiously, his splendid *The White Hand and the Black* was sold for a flat rate of £150 to John Long, Ltd., Mitford complaining (30 November 1906) to Watt that Long was "not a first rate firm." Such residual royalties as his contracts produced diminished steadily. During the First World War, Yseulte (fulfilling her legendary name by nursing at the Red Cross hospital "Oaklands" in Somerset) received one of Watt's infrequent royalty payments for 5/10 (relative value today, maximally 100 USD).37 Her brother Roland, who may have been in the armed services, is not mentioned in this correspondence; Yseulte clearly was the only one who negotiated with Watt for marketing new editions.

Mitford does not seem to have given many interviews or cultivated the limelight, worse luck for his sales. In 1896 the *Eastern Daily Press* reported:

> Mr. Bertram Mitford, the author of "The Sign of the Spider," is a quick writer. He says that he "can turn out a 320 page novel in two months, if in the vein." He works best in the morning, all day long in winter, but never at night. A firm believer in outdoor exercise, he is a great walker. Twenty-three years ago he went to South Africa, and during his long stay there became personally acquainted with Cetewayo and all the prominent Zulu chiefs and leading men who engineered the Kaffir war of 1877, on the Cape border. Most of them figure in his South African novels. Mr. Mitford, before he turned his attention to fiction, had a very varied experience. He was at one time engaged in stock-farming, and he has held several Government posts. He is the third son of Mr. Osbaldeston Mitford, of Mitford Castle, Northumberland.38

Mitford's annual output fluctuated between one to three novels, exclusive of short stories. This career total of more than forty novels suggests that he made words his *métier* and by them he created a steady income stream. However, currently on the market his nineteenth-century editions are more plentiful than his twentieth-century ones, suggesting smaller press runs in the later years. Incidentally, *The Sign of the Spider* has strong affinities with Haggard's occult mysteries and appears to have been one of his best works, both commercially and as an adventure narrative. When Mitford was vacationing in October 1902 at the Hotel de Londres in Cava dei Tirreni on the Amalfi Coast, he wrote Watt that the first edition illustrations for this novel were "too vulgarly grotesque for words" and urged that with the exception of "the third in the book—showing the battle" they be excluded from the new edition being planned.39

Needless to say, Mitford, like his father, was also a Fellow of the Royal Geographical Society, the origins of which lay in the exploration of Africa. Founded in 1830, it later sent Richard Burton and J. H. Speke to discover the source of the Nile. Mitford, proposed by his friend Arthur Montefiore, was elected on April 28th, 1890 while residing at the Junior Athenaeum Club, Piccadilly; in the RGS/IBG Archives is a portrait of "B. Mitford" by Maull and Fox, Piccadilly, photographers to the Royal family—a small-framed, alert and wiry man with a bushy mustache and clean-cut features.40 Montefiore was a committed trout fisherman and a writer of exploration literature, including biographies of David Livingstone and Sir Henry Stanley; he witnessed Mitford's contract with

Sutton, Drowley for *The Weird of Deadly Hollow*. In an obituary, the *Eastern Daily Press* reported that "Mr. Mitford was a keen sportsman, and in search of adventure and information had traveled in America and India, and was very well acquainted with the Alpine districts of Switzerland, having as far back as the eighties made a successful ascent of the Matterhorn."[41]

In addition to membership in the RGS and his affiliation with the Anglo-African Writers' Club, Mitford also was a member of the Junior Athenaeum, the New Vagabond Club, the elite Wigwam Club, and the posh Savage Club, chaired by G. A. Henty.[42] This last had been founded in 1857 and remains at present one of the most unusual clubs for men of the arts, bohemian journalists, and adventurers; they refer to each other as "Brother Savage." At a typical dinner of 7 June 1893 the Club entertained H. M. Stanley, recently returned from the "Dark Continent"; an earlier dinner in 1885, just after Mitford arrived back in London, welcomed a returning group of journalists who had suffered massive casualties from the Mahdi's Dervish hordes as General Gordon fought his way up the Nile Valley. Mitford's Junior Athenaeum Club occupied the London mansion of the late Duke of Newcastle, Piccadilly West. Its roster included members of Parliament, faculty of the universities, and fellows of learned and scientific societies. One meeting (that may or may not be fantasy) followed a lecture at the Royal Institution—the discussion topic, "The End of Books": "*L'un de nous, Edward Lembroke, nous entraina a souper au Junior Athenaeum Club et, des qui le champagne eut degourdi les cerveaux songeurs, ce fut a qui parlerait de la conference de sir William Thompson et des destinees futures de l'humanite.*" Gramophone recordings will replace books: "*Jamais l'Hamlet de notre grand Will n'aura mieux dit:* Words! Words! Words! *Des mots!... des mots qui passent et qu'on ne lira plus.*"[43] Mitford seems to have stayed at the Club on a number of occasions, perhaps when his family was out of town. We are told that Mitford's New Vagabonds "in their club capacity do nothing else but dine. Periodically in the season they assemble together, the gentler sex at times included amongst them, and invite into their midst some other lady or gentleman, or both, who have won laurels in the fields of art and literature, and then there are compliments and happy speeches till the home-going time arrives."[44] One such visitor was A. Conan Doyle; on that same evening or another Fred G. Abberline, the police office in charge of the Jack the Ripper murders, attended. Finally, conceivably around the turn of the century when he published *War and Arcadia* (1901), his novel about the prelude to the last major battle of the Indian Wars, Mitford fished for rainbow trout in Colorado at the exclusive Wigwam Club on the South Platte River—probably with the split cane bamboo fly rods as in the opening scenes of *Ravenshaw of Rietholme* (1910).

Mitford's adventures are informative about the peculiarities of their regions and create characters and scenery that possess verisimilitude. In negotiating the contract for his eerie doppelgänger tale, *The White Hand and the Black*

(1907), Mitford wrote to Watt that the publisher must agree "not to alter or suppress any word, either of the copy, title page, or of the spelling of words or names of a technical or native character, but to issue the book exactly as he receives it."[45] In comparison to the mythic world of Haggard, Mitford presents a more contemporary, commonplace Africa, though certainly not as severely colorless as Olive Schreiner's. Perhaps because Mitford more often writes of the Eastern Cape Colony, not the far interior (his Zulu quartet and *The Sign of the Spider* are notable exceptions), he stresses the ordinary social realities of colonial existence—neighbors, mounted police, and towns with bicycles, tame natives, trams, judges and banks. His narratives are launched with leisurely attention to tone and feel, and not without such domestic reverberations as the role of the New Woman as in *Averno* (1913) or urban tedium as in *Sign of the Spider*; then their plots tighten toward lightning-paced dramatic action. R.W. Jones suggests that "as one of the first to transform personal colonial experience into fiction," Mitford's "long descriptive passages are an intimate and accurate record of the hazards and hardships and casual incidents of frontier life, and of the daily habits and customs of colonists and tribesmen. As such they are invaluable source material for the social historian. The passage of time may revive interest in them as contemporary historical novels."[46] Zulus and other native tribes are not sensationalized, except occasionally as with the blood-drinkers in *Gerard Ridgeley* (1894) or the cannibal orgies in *Sign of the Spider* or *The King's Assegai*. Sometimes the plots intersect by means of such reappearing figures as Cetywayo and Lorraine from *The Gun-Runner*. Lorraine may be the furtive figure who is cited again in *The Expiation of Wynne Palliser* (1896) and *The Curse of Clement Waynflete* (1894); he may be the mysterious godlike puppeteer in *John Ames* (1899), and he could be also the agent provocateur in *Forging the Blades* (1908). If so, he would be a darker alter ego for Mitford as Quatermain was for Haggard.

Though the reader takes Mitford's scenes and characters to be a model of empirical reality, on a deeper level their exoticism and conceptual novelty are symbolic sociocultural constructions of his personal vision. As much as a Mitford adventure seems at times to rely upon a low-mimetic formal realism, it in fact pushes toward extended levels of meaning, particularly in situations in which the individual escapes existential alienation and loneliness by attuning himself to his reflection in another's authentic selfhood: "The glad mirth danced in his eyes, reflected from hers."[47] A biographical profile needs only a brief, and perhaps elementary, example of Mitford's extended levels of meaning. As Renshaw Fanning, in an eponymously titled novel, lounges in his cane chair, he contemplates Marian Selwood:

> The boom of bees floated upon the jessamine-laden air, varied by the shriller buzz of a long, rakish-looking hornet winging in and out of his absurd little clay nest, wedged, like that of a swallow, beneath the eaves of the veranda. Great butterflies flitted among the sunflowers, but warily and in terror of the lurking amantis— that arrant hypocrite, so devotional in his attitude, so treacherously voracious in

his method of seizing and assimilating his prey—and a pair of tiny sugar-birds, in their delicate crimson and green vests, flashed fearlessly to and fro within a couple of yards of Renshaw's head, dipping their long needle-like bills into the waxen blossoms of the fragrant jessamine.48

This passage, opening and closing with the jasmine's fragrance, evokes all the five senses—taste and touch not least in the operations of the preying/praying mantis. Nature's fecundity is suggested by bees, butterflies and birds; and feminine grace, elegance and sensuality are foregrounded in the symbolism of the jasmine. But the Freudian imagery of "dipping ... needle-like bills into ... blossoms," in conjunction with the "terror" of the butterflies, intensifies the masculinity of Renshaw's gaze on the veranda, though his desire is still subconscious. Yet at first glance this scene is merely a transcript from domestic reality—just what one would expect to see in that semitropical latitude; and in point of fact this sugar-bird has migrated to the farm veranda from the final pages of Mitford's nonfictional *Through the Zulu Country*, feeding there without Freudian overtones and footnoted as "a species of humming bird."49 Among Mitford's favorite plot episodes are native attacks on such homesteads as this. Needless to say, the readers' *prima facie* sympathies, as controlled by the author, are all on the side of defending these colonial verandas.

Mitford's colonial philosophy is based on hard, practical considerations rather than on sentimental ethnocentrism or idealistic clichés. He believes every country gets the government it deserves, that "fortune does not favor the brave" and that "inventions have been known to make fortunes, but practically never for the inventor." He doesn't believe in "poetic justice"; or that "honesty is the best policy"; or that Zulus need missionaries.50 Mitford's typical protagonist is upper class, in his later thirties, and often some combination of a psychologically injured "renegade" (sometimes in disguise) with "a clouded and shipwrecked life" desiring revenge on society, like Lorraine in *Gun-Runner*; or he is a wanderer running from an unhappy marriage whose "life is behind him," cynical about love, which for him is "a thing of the past," as in *Palliser* or *Aletta*.51 At times a lack of money is coupled with the hardening process of despair and loss of conscience, as in Lawrence Stanninghame's pursuit of the "oof bird" of wealth in *Sign of the Spider*. Not uncommonly, this protagonist manipulates native attacks upon his countrymen for his own purposes of revenge, as in *Gun-Runner*, *Ames*, or *Palliser*. At other times he is the "victim of circumstances" who dies at end because of the "pitilessness of life."52 Within those extreme situations of suffering, struggle, guilt and death, Mitford's protagonist must make choices, take a stand, and define a place in the world. If the deeper, more sensitive heroes and heroines are destroyed, they first undergo a creative suffering and self-discovery and find in love a value that surpasses justice, happiness, or life. But often this is accompanied by ironic coincidence; in *Palliser* the tormented hero is *not* married, though his mistaken belief that he indeed was married provided the whole impetus for his tragedy.

The Mitford heroine is often a British relative sojourning with her distant colonial family, only erroneously regarded merely as a sop to his younger drawing-room readers in a pinafore. Sometimes of "Junoesque" proportions, she has a "strong passion-fraught temperament," "a free and unaffected self-possession," an "open, sunny nature," with grace, beauty, pride and puts love before socially constructed values.53 She won't scruple at courtroom perjury if the cause be love. Her romance is often set against the background of Zulu warfare, plot and subplot complicating and enriching Mitford's action. The union of the lovers, so desired by the reader, is always forestalled by new complications of social circumstance. Sometimes the woman (*vide* Lalusini in *The Induna's Wife*) is wiser or stronger-minded than her mate, and at other times she physically saves her man. Beryl in *Veldt Vendetta* (1903), Aurelle in *Seaford's Snake* (1912) and Verna in *Forging the Blades*, all shoot natives in confrontations: "Never still, Sapazani dodged the volley and laughed exultantly. But even as he did so he leaped in the air and fell flat. Those in her neighbourhood looked up at Verna Halse, who, pale as death, with a red spot on each cheek and dull eyes, after one quick glance began refilling her magazine."54 Sometimes, as in *Harley Greenoak's Charge*, *John Ames*, or *Forging the Blades*, Mitford actually seems to believe in a sentimental romanticism, though perhaps by the rule of contraries—perfect lovers who fall in love in minutes, sudden wealth, happy endings. He may be simply amusing and enriching himself by pandering to the expectations of the marketplace;55 more likely, it reflects his contrarianism. As with Olive Schreiner, more often it's the problematic whites who find a material-emotional place in Africa. In *Sign of the Spider* and *Renshaw Fanning* "the way of the transgressor" is rewarded, monetarily at least. The dual heroines in one late novel are something of an exception, though the older male—a sort of Colonel Brandon transplant from Jane Austen—is a familiar Mitford protagonist. The eponymously titled *Averno* (1913) twice cites Virgil's *Aeneid* 6:126: "The descent into Avernus is easy; the gate of Pluto stands open night and day; but to retrace one's steps, and return to the upper air, that is the toil, that is the difficulty."56 In this novel, enmeshed in the seasonal myth of the twins Kore and Persephone, Averno is a friend in England of Eva (the Greek and Latin form of Eve, "life") and in Africa of Violet (the violet-garlanded Kore-Persephone of Bacchylides's fourth lyric), who as a huntress is associated with death. Averno goes to Africa, kills the Pluto-Kaffir about to rape Violet, and returns to Eva whom he now discovers to be his predestined love.

The moral problem in a Mitford novel, for one who imperfectly knows himself and futilely tries to diagnose the poison in his soul, is how to set aside the pride or anger that blocks the deeper, truer power of love's redemption: "to melt the soured hardness of an atrophied life."57 And yet, can there be redemption without transgression? We are told in *The Gun-Runner* of Brooke Mounetney's desire for Lynette that he "loved and hated her with equal force, with the wild beast ferocity of his strong and passionately undisciplined nature."58 Precisely that same "wild beast ferocity" characterizes Brooke's successful rival Lorraine, except that his hatred is directed towards Brooke and the social hypocrisy of England. This common ontological linkage of love and hate explains the climactic gesture in *War and Arcadia* (1901). Kennion, Newlands, and Jake Rockstro all woo Adelie Wade, a lovely Wellesley graduate (thus with the sort of character constitutive of intelligence, since this was the era of the gifted professor Mary Whiton Calkins); the Britisher Kennion wins her love; Major Newlands (an almost Henry Jamesian characternym) takes defeat like a gentleman; but the lowbrow Jake tortures and intends to kill his successful rival. Rescued, Kennion allows Jake to escape, explaining to Newlands: "'He had every reason to bear me the bitterest of grudges, and if I had been in his place I might have acted in the same way, and worse. Don't you understand?' And the other understood." Earlier Adelie had reflected on Newlands that she "respected and looked up to him, taking undisguised pleasure in his society.... Yet, surely there was something more—something that was wanting."59 And, of course, what's needed is that "wild beast ferocity," found not only in Mitford's consummate lovers and haters, but in the embattled Lakotas and Zulu *isilwane* as well.

Mitford's fascination with the emotional intensity of retribution and with the incongruous "way of the world—our blessings, when they come to us, invariably do so a day too late"60 (spoken in summation by the hero of *Fordham's Feud*, whose villainy only a Corsican view of vendetta can explain)—suggests an underlying anguish in his novels with the nature of earthly justice and the silence of God, with what Miguel de Unamuno—Mitford's more-philosophical, younger contemporary—called the tragic sense of life, man's quixotic desire for the perfection that makes his life a senseless irony. Certainly in *The White Hand and the Black* a curiously relativistic morality emerges. The Zulu antagonist's power to blackmail is credible because a murder did occur, but this dark secret is ultimately nullified at the feast on Christmas. When white and black together drink a Euro-African champagne-*tywala* mix, friendship replaces hostility and absolution trumps accusation. But as lived values, neither friendship nor hostility, innocence nor guilt, is entirely good or evil. To escape from judgmental preconceptions and to embrace life requires that one absolve the other of the guilt one attributes to him, affirming that oneself and the other are ontologically linked beyond the parochial values of good and evil. Whites and blacks bury their differences and escape the self-deceptive moral, political and religious preconceptions of dogmatic and absolutist views by accepting the abyss that swallows life and by affirming existence in spite of its guilt, despair, and temporal loss. On the governmental level this also implies a relationship different from the *Weltpolitik* of "might makes right." It replaces imperial force as the definition of who the colonist is and wants to be with a softer power rooted in an awareness of what the indigenous inhabitants think and expect of him.

Because neither Mitford nor Haggard explicitly condemned the British presence in Africa, they were (and still are) considered "patriotic" writers who praised the manly virtues of the Empire against natives and Boers. Apparent statements by characters within the texts on native racial inferiority reflected historical teaching in Victorian schools and the sermons of vicars on missionary work and the white man's burden. However, this fiction, read from the authors' perspectives on their cultural environments, challenges at least some of the assumptions of jingoistic imperialism. Mitford will often put criticisms of British policy into the mouths of Boers or Zulus. Thus in *The White Shield* or *Aletta* when the Zulu Untúswa or the Afrikaner character Botma declares that the British are rapacious, Mitford either reveals an unconscious distress and uncertainty counterbalanced by a presentation of imperial power or a very conscious sympathy for the underdog that would be unpatriotic if openly acknowledged—or something of both at one time or another. One strong and direct anti-British statement occurs in *Palliser*.[61] Significantly, his plots are more often presented from the perspective of colonist or indigenous African struggling for survival in the colonized land than from Henty's transoceanic perspective of *With Buller in Natal* (1900) or *With Roberts to Pretoria* (1902). While Henty writes in the preface to this latter novel that "the Boers had not the heart to venture even once to face the British in the open," Mitford unhesitatingly burlesques this "consuming love of fair play"[62]: "Sergeant Clark's idea, you see, was thoroughly characteristic of his nationality, viz., that naked savages armed only with spears ... ought by every law of fairness to stand out and do themselves the honour of being shot down by the latest improvement in breech-loading weapons of precision in the hands of Englishmen. Failing this they were 'crawling, cowardly, greasy rascals.'"[63] Actually Mitford realized that Clark's type of warrior was also the Zulus' ancient standard,[64] so he thus credits Zulus with adapting their tactics to pragmatic necessities. The imperial scorn of the Zulu language as "monkey chatter" by those who hadn't learned it strikes the same ironic note as the popular glorification of military action as "nigger-shooting," mere "fun," or what Royston, an imperial dimwit in *The Curse of Clement Waynflete* (1894), rationalizes to Cetywayo as merely his desire for "adventure."[65]

Certainly in the final years of Bertram and Zima's marriage, a coldness had set in. On 20 November and again on 29 November 1912, Zima, writing from 60 Brompton Square, London, S.W., presses Mitford to sign a power of attorney joining her in a tangled lawsuit against several heirs and executors of her father's will. Mitford's reply, 3 December 1912, from 5 Furzeham Road, West Drayton, is harsh, probably not entirely because old Ebden clearly favored the daughters of Zima's first marriage: "I have looked through the Will and find there is no reason whatever why I should touch the affair with the tip of the tongs—my children's interests in it are so remote, and absolutely in the clouds that I don't care to join in any litigation concerning it whatever. As far as I am concerned I am afraid you must fight it out among yourselves and I decline to put my name to any document connected with it. Bertram Mitford." No salutation, no closing, and "my," not "our," children. Indeed, in a postscript Mitford even manages to cast an aspersion on his deceased father-in-law: "The whole thing is so obscurely—not to say slovenly drawn—as to be the reverse of creditable to the attorneys who drew it and the Testator who signed it." Then he adds that he is enclosing a "Cheque for this week."66

As reported in the *Eastern Daily Press*, Mitford died on 4 October 1914 at Cowfold, Sussex. His death certificate, according to the email of Brian Stringer, established "cirrhosis of the liver" and "dropsy" (edema, probably here a symptom of liver failure) as the causes. The most prevalent agent of cirrrhosis might also explain his separation from Zima, though viral hepatitis also shares a final common pathway with alcoholic liver disease. His funeral was nearby at West Grinstead on October 8 in the churchyard of the Shrine Church of Our Lady of Consolation. He lies beside his wife Zima, who died the following year, both in unmarked grave plots, numbers seven and eight according to church records; and also by his son Roland, buried there in 1932, aged forty.67 As a place of pilgrimage, the shrine may have appealed to him as a haven of meditation and spiritual strength. The earlier house of the parish priest had been used to hide clerics traveling between London and France during the Tudor persecution of Roman Catholics who refused to attend Anglican services. *The London Times* reported on 29 March 1915 that Mitford "aged 59, of Cowfold, Sussex, at one time of Mitford Castle, Northumberland, and of Hunmanby Hall, Yorks, afterwards in the Cape Colony Civil Service, author of numerous novels and descriptive stories," died intestate and left "unsettled property" of £2,196, almost a million dollars by today's values.68 By March 1915 "Zima Helen Mitford his lawful widow and *relict*" had also "died without having taken upon herself the administration of his estate," which thus devolved upon and became vested in the twenty-seven-year-old "Yseulte Helen Mitford of 7 Bedford Gardens, Campden Hill, Middlesex, spinster, natural and lawful daughter and one of the next of kin."69 When Zima died on 11 March 1915 at 31 Bedford Gardens, Kensington, London, she was sixty years, five months of age, survived by her four children and attended by Yseulte at her death.70 Later registers of British marriages (up to 1948) do not reference Yseulte; however, after the deaths of her half sisters (Winifred died in 1931 and Zima in September 1941), while residing in the medieval-renaissance village of Caldarola in the Marche region of Italy, she began to receive (or did not receive, owing to the Second World War) interest on capital left by her grandfather. According to a note in what the Mitfords call "The Brown Book" of family records, she died in July 1969.71

| Appendix A |

Notes

1. Michael Lieven, "Contested Empire: Bertram Mitford and the Imperial Adventure Story," *Paradigm*, 25 (May 1998), 1–13.

2. These four are: *The King's Assegai* (London: Chatto and Windus, 1894), *The White Shield* (London: F. A. Stokes, 1895), *The Induna's Wife* (London: F. V. White, 1898), and *The Word of the Sorceress* (London: Hutchinson, 1902).

3. "Contested Empire," 1; *Dreams of Adventure, Deeds of Empire* (New York: Basic Books, 1979), 3.

4. *Dictionary of South African Biography*, W. J. KeKock, ed. (Pretoria: National Council, 1987); *People of the Period*, Alfred Pratt, ed. (London: Neville Beeman, 1897); *Biographical and Bibliographical Record of South African Literature in English*, E. A. Seary, ed. (Grahamstown: self-published, 1938); *The Stanford Companion to Victorian Fiction*, John Sutherland, ed. (Stanford: Stanford University Press, 1989); *Cassell's Encyclopaedia of World Literature*, J. Buchanan-Brown, revised (New York: William Morrow, 1973); *Who Was Who 1897–2004*, British Library electronic database "xreferplus" (restricted to St Pancras Reading Room); *A Dictionary of Literature in the English Language*, Robin Myers, ed. (Oxford: Pergamon Press, 1970); *The Men Behind Boys' Fiction*, W. Lofts and D. J. Adley, eds. (London: Howard Baker Pubs., 1970); *Anglo-African Who's Who*, L. Weinthal, ed. (London: Routledge & Sons, 1910); *Allibone's Critical Dictionary of English Literature: A Supplement*, J. F. Kirk, ed. (Philadelphia: Lippencott, 1891); *The Catholic Who's Who and Yearbook* (London: Burns, 1910).

5. *People of the Period*, II: "Mitford."

6. H. Rider Haggard, *The Days of My Life: An Autobiography* (London: Longmans, Green, 1926), II: 110.

7. *People of the Period*, II: "Mitford"; *Days of My Life: An Autobiography*, II: 110; *The London Times*, 19 June 1900, Issue 36172, p. 11, col. E; also 18 December 1900, Issue 36328, p. 10, col. C.

8. Like Janet Bailey, Ella Doveton, Haggard's mother, was the daughter of "a prominent member of the Bombay branch of the East Indian Civil Service, and thus it came to pass that his elder daughter, Ella, spent much of her girlhood in India, a country in which she took the keenest interest during all her life, and for which she cherished a warm affection." H. Rider Haggard, "*In Memoriam*," *Life and its Author* by Ella Haggard (London: Longmans, Green, 1890), 3.

9. Bertram Mitford, *The White Hand and the Black* (London: John Long, 1907), 205.

10. Ibid., 208.

11. Ibid., 279.

12. Historical and biographical data on the Mitford family have been derived from British newspapers, from official records in England's General Register Office, part of the Office for National Statistics, from the British Probate Registry of Her Majesty's Courts Service, and from <www.FamilySearch.org> and <www.Ancestry.co.uk>; further records were located in the National Archives and Records Service of South Africa, Cape Town Archives Repository. I am indebted to Fiona Mitford, emails to the author (1 December 2005 and after), for the GRO Birth Index reference to "Mitford, Male, Bath, 5c, 741, 2Q, 1855," for the address of the family home in 1856 at 3 Marlborough Street, Bath, and other details as acknowledged below.

13. Edward Mitford, *The Arab's Pledge—a Tale of Marocco in 1830* (London: Hatchard, 1867), [iii]. So rare only one library copy exists, it is a small 8vo in bottle green sand-grained cloth boards, blocked in blind and gilt and lettered in gilt on front board, back board blocked in blind, spine plain.

14. Ibid., 32.

15. Edward Mitford, *A Land-March from England to Ceylon Forty Years Ago, Through Dalmatia, Montenegro, Turkey, Asia Minor, Syria, Palestine, Assyria, Persia, Afghanistan, Scinde, and India, of which 7000 miles on Horseback*, 2 vols. (London: W. H. Allen, 1884).

16. Austen Henry Layard, *A Popular Account of Discoveries at Nineveh* (New York: J. C. Derby, 1854), 1; see also Layard's *Adventures in Persia, Susiana, and Babylonia* (New York: Longmans, Green, 1887).

17. James Emerson Tennent, *Ceylon: An Account of the Island* (London: Longmans, Green, 1860), I: 2.

18. Charles Robert Darwin, *Variation of Animals and Plants under Domestication* (London: John Murray, 1868), I: 246.

19. *London Times*, 18 May 1912; Issue 39902; p. 11, col. B; Grant of Administration for the estate of Edward Ledwich Osbaldeston-Mitford, Probate Registry (Family Division of the High Court of Justice, England), 12 November 1912. Today's relative value of the estate would be something like USD 3-4 million. Lawrence Officer, "What Is Its Relative Value in UK Pounds?" Economic History Services <www.eh.net/hmit/ukcompare/>. Fiona Mitford, email, reports that in 1891 Janet "was living with her son William and family" and that after she died on 13 July 1896, Edward, only three months later and at age eighty-five, married the thirty-eight year old Ella who was "for her era, very outgoing, well travelled, and fluent in five languages."

20. *Cruchley's London: A Handbook for Strangers* (London: G. F. Cruchley, 1865), "Royal Naval School."

21. "Mitford, Bertram," *Who Was Who 1897–2004*, British Library electronic database "xreferplus."

22. Bertram Mitford, *The Weird of Deadly Hollow* [1891] (London: F. V. White, 1899), 144–45.

23. Colonial Office files for the period in question contain a monumental amount of unindexed material complicating the search for records: Jaco van der Merwe, principal reading room archivist, National Archives, Cape Town.

24. "Death of Mr. Bertram Mitford," *Eastern Daily Press*, 15 October 1914, Issue 14373, p. 4.

25. Bertram Mitford, *Through the Zulu Country: Its Battlefields and Its People* (London: Kegan Paul, 1883), 305.

26. See endnote 4.

27. Roland Trimen, *South-African Butterflies: A Monograph of the Extra-Tropical Species* (London: Traubner, 1887-89), I: vii–xiv.

28. Bertram Mitford, *Harley Greenoak's Charge* (London: Chatto and Windus, 1906), 177.

29. Ibid., 202; 204.

30. *South-African Butterflies*, I: vii–ix.

31. *Harley Greenoak's Charge*, 352.

32. Entries of marriage for Alexander Gentle (22 October 1874, No. 145) and Bertram Mitford (9 March 1886, No. 149), General Register Office, England. The divorce was owing to Zima's affair around 1882 in Singapore—where her husband managed the businessman's trade association—with an Irish surgeon and widower serving in the Royal Army Medical Corps: Blennerhassett Montgomerie T. Blennerhassett (1849–1926). Montgomerie had a daughter, Venice Maud (b. 1876), in the same age cohort as Zima's girls. Faced with mounting proof that when Alex was absent Monty habitually had relations with Zima at Bellevue, her home in Singapore, and that also in July of 1882 they "committed adultery" at the Bathing Pavilion at MacRitchie Reservoir four miles north of the city, Zima amended her legal response after six months of flat denial to a declaration that the Petitioner had condoned the adultery, if any, of the Respondent. But in light of the affidavits, her extenuation was discredited and custody of her son and daughters was awarded to Alex. Of the three children that Zima and Alex Gentle lost in infancy or childhood, only Eric Grant (1880–1889), who died in Amersham, Buckinghamshire, is so far identified. Ref.: WO 13 / 1606, Gentle Divorce File, National Archives in Kew; UK *Medical Register* (1859–date); Bill Jehan, email 19 February 2006 In 1885 Zima's father believed her to be married already to Mitford; her address then: Bertram Mitford, Esq., 54 St. James Street, London, S.W. National Archives of South Africa, 203 CSC 2/2/2/798 ref. 16 (76, 77).

33. Entries of births for Yseulte Helen (3 June 1887, No. 204) and Roland Bertram (17 June 1891, No. 146), General Register Office, England; "Births," *London Times*, 19 June 1891; Issue 33355; p. 1, col. A.

34. A. P. Watt & Company Records (Accession No. 11036), Manuscripts Department, Wilson Library, University of North Carolina, Chapel Hill. Although this material is entirely of a business sort, it does also supply Mitford's addresses for this paragraph.

35. Letter of 31 August 1898 (to Watt from Bertram Mitford at Kenilworth, one of Cape Town's prime residential areas in the southern suburbs), Ms. 2293B; A. P. Watt Collection, Rare Book and Manuscript Library, Columbia University. Watt was also H. Rider Haggard's literary agent; Haggard wrote Watt that "since the year 1885 some thousands of letters must have passed between us to say

nothing of countless interviews." *Letters Addressed to A. P. Watt*, A. P. Watt, ed. (London: Watt, 1929), 81.

36. Contracts of 16 January 1891; 15 June 1896; 25 August 1899; A. P. Watt & Company Records.

37. Ibid. Letters of 30 November 1906, 21 December [1917 or 1918?].

38. "About Men and Women," *Eastern Daily Press*, 17 November 1896, Issue 7687, p. 8.

39. Letter of 15 October 1902, A. P. Watt & Company Records.

40. Unfortunately, there is at least one other "B. Mitford" on the F.R.G.S. membership lists, though the common Piccadilly address for both Mitford and the photographers, *floruit* 1879–1908, suggests the portrait may be Bertram.

41. "Death of Mr. Bertram Mitford," p. 4.

42. "Mitford, Bertram," *Who Was Who 1897–2004*, British Library electronic database "xreferplus"; Joyce E. Muddock, *The Savage Club Papers* (London: Hutchinson, 1897); Matthew Norgate and Alan Wykes, *Not So Savage* (London: Jupiter Books, 1976); "London's Lesser Club-land" in *Living London*, George R. Sims, ed. vol. 3 (London: Cassell, 1906).

43. Octave Uzanne, Albert Robida, *"La fin des livres," Contes pour les Bibliophiles* (Paris: Quantin, 1895), 55.

44. "London's Lesser Club-land," III: 100.

45. A. P. Watt & Company Records, 30 November 1906.

46. "Mitford," *Dictionary of South African Biography* (1977), 3: 619. In my edition of Haggard's *King Solomon's Mines* there was a penciled slip, dated 10 March 1890, clearly left for a future reader: "Whoever reads this *great tale* should take care not to *skip* the first part—ie.: introduction and first 3 or 4 chapters—: makes story more understandable—" A voice, as so many of ours shortly will be, long gone—but that sees the necessity of grounding the exotic in the familiar, of establishing interpretive parameters, and of recognizing the complementarity of reality and fantasy.

47. Bertram Mitford, *The Gun-Runner* (London: Chatto and Windus, 1882), 23. As in Haggard, Mitford suggests the Platonic theory that the lover's search for his own best self takes place through his idealization of the beloved.

48. Bertram Mitford, *Renshaw Fanning's Quest* (London: Chatto and Windus, 1894), 98.

49. *Through the Zulu Country*, 320.

50. *Seaford's Snake* (London: Ward, Lock, 1912), 221, 103, 117; *Averno* (London: Ward, Lock, 1913), 10; *Harley Greenoak's Charge*, 100; *The Expiation of Wynne Palliser* (London: Ward, Lock, 1890), 340.

51. *The Gun-Runner*, 69; *The Expiation of Wynne Palliser*, 6; *Aletta* (London: F. V. White, 1900), 137, 125; *The Weird of Deadly Hollow*, 130–31.

52. *The Sign of the Spider*, 98; *A Veldt Official* (London: Ward, Lock, 1895), 89; *The Expiation of Wynne Palliser*, 341.

53. *The Weird of Deadly Hollow*, 20; *The Expiation of Wynne Palliser*, 11; *The Curse of Clement Waynflete* (London: Ward, Lock, 1894), 59, 244.

54. Bertram Mitford, *Forging the Blades* (London: Eveleigh Nash, 1908), 320.

55. Letter from A. P. Watt to the Northern Newspaper Syndicate (13 December 1901) intending to run a serialized version of *Raynier, Political Agent*: "I am now in receipt of yours of the 9th and now beg to return copy of the agreement between yourselves and Mr. Mitford. As you will see, I have altered the length of the story in accordance with your request. I don't think we can well deal with the nature of the novel in the agreement. Mr. Mitford quite understands that what you want is a bright love and adventure story, and that although you do not object to an African element introduced, he is to avoid all mention whatever of the present war. Unless you particularly wish an African element introduced, I think Mr. Mitford has made up his mind to write a story the scene of which shall not be laid in Africa."

56. *Averno*, 49, 135.

57. *The Heath Hover Mystery*, 246

58. *The Gun-Runner*, 88.

59. *War and Arcadia* (London: F. V. White, 1901), 293, 166.

60. *Fordham's Feud* (London: Ward, Lock, 1897), 342.

61. *The Expiation of Wynne Palliser*, 209.

62. G. A. Henty, *With Roberts to Pretoria* (London: Blackie, 1902), vi.

63. *The Curse of Clement Waynflete*, 7.

64. *Through the Zulu Country*, 145.

65. *Seaford's Snake*, 228, *The Curse of Clement Waynflete*, 284; see also *Harley Greenoak's Charge*, 76–77, 128, 136, 179, in which Dick is a caricature of the young adventure hero.

66. National Archives of South Africa, 203 CSC 2/2/2/798 ref. 16 (80, 81).

67. "Death of Mr. Bertram Mitford," p. 4; Grant of Administration for the estate of Bertram Mitford, Probate Registry (Family Division of the High Court of Justice), 24 March 1915. Father David Goddard, email to Madeleine Beard for the author, 11 June 2005: "I am able to confirm that Bertram Mitford was indeed buried here at West Grinstead. There is an entry in our Graveyard Records showing that he was buried in plot no. 7; that he was aged 50 [sic] when he died in 1914. There is also a Zima Mitford (plot no. 8) ... and a Rowland Mitford buried here in 1932, aged 40.... There are no records of memorial stones and ... I have never come across a stone bearing the name Mitford." There is no civil death record for Roland (or Rowland) Mitford for 1932, which suggests that either he died abroad, with his body brought home for burial, or that his family failed to register the death. Fiona Mitford, email, reports that Roland married Marion Huntoun, born 1891, of Springfield, Massachusetts.

68. This was the gross value; net value was £2,058; *London Times*, 29 March 1915, p. 11, col. C.

69. Grant of administration for the estate of Bertram Mitford, Probate Registry (Family Division of the High Court of Justice, England), 24 March 1915.

70. National Archives of South Africa, "Death Notice," 204 MOOC 6/9/805 ref. 3047 (1).

71. National Archives of South Africa, 205 MOOC 6/9/8995 ref. 79109 (63); Yseulte's death date provided by Fiona Mitford, email.

Index

Note: for the African novels, page numbers for the principal passages of interpretation are set in bold.

A "About Fiction" (Haggard), 41, 45, 62, 100, 143, 165, 195
Abraham (biblical figure), 134
Absalom (biblical figure), 226
Achebe, Chinua, 6, 14, 26, 29, 117, 153
Achilles (fictional character), 69, 169
Adam (biblical figure), 128, 180, 183, 210
Adeyemi, Sola, 1–2
"Adonais" (Shelley), 129
Adonis (mythic figure), 90, 96, 129
African Nature Notes and Reminiscences (Selous), 81
Aletta (Mitford), 280, 283
Allan and the Holy Flower (Haggard), 7, 8, 20, 51, 181, 192, 216–17, 219, 222, 234
Allan and the Ice Gods (Haggard), 192
Allan Quatermain (Haggard), 7, 54–55, 81, 100, 103, 111, 124, 128, 151, 155, 180, 183, **225–30**, 235
Allan's Wife and Other Tales (Haggard), 55, 106, 131, **154–59**, 178, 181, 202
Among the Zulus and Amatongas (Leslie), 105
Ancient Allan, The (Haggard), 192
Anglo-Boer War, 132, 154, 179, 212, 230
Annals of Natal (Bird), 105–06
Aphrodite or Venus (mythic goddess), 127, 168, 193–94, 214
Apocrypha, 184
Apollo (god), 198
Arab's Pledge, The (E. Mitford), 270
Ariosto, Lodovico, 106, 128
Aristotle, 1, 41, 235
Arkle, John Taurus (fictional character), 221–22
Armstrong, Nancy, 108, 176
Arnold, Matthew, 110, 195, 3, 223
"Art of the Bushmen" (Fry), 210
Ashtoreth, see Astarte
Ash Wednesday (Eliot), 62
Asika (fictional queen), 211
Astarte (goddess), 74–75, 86, 90–91
Athena (goddess), 139, 160
Augustine, Saint, 42
Austen, Jane, 48, 208, 281
Averno (Mitford), 279, 281
Ayesha (fictional character), 24, 44, 50, 59, 89, 100, 114, 128, 130, 163, 166, 172, 192–200, 208, 213–15, 217, 222–23
Ayesha, The Return of She (Haggard), 193

B Baal (god), 90–91
Babbitt, Irving, 62
Bacchylides, 281
Bacon, Francis, 176
Baggins, Bilbo (fictional character), 71
Bailey, Reverend Edward, 271
Baines, Thomas, 74
Baker, Josephine, 211
Barber, Agnes, 80
Baring-Gould, Sabine, 120
Barrow, John, 27–28, 33
Baudelaire, Charles, 8, 170
Beard, Madeleine, 273
Bede, The Venerable, 185
Belshazzar (Haggard), 230

Benita, An African Romance (Haggard), 44, 50, 192, 200, **205–207**
Bent, James, 74–75, 205
Beowulf, 2, 123, 202, 233
Berserk (mythic figure), 123
Bible, 53, 75, 82, 88, 96, 186–87, 212, 215
Billali (fictional character), 50
Black Heart and White Heart and Other Stories (Haggard), 39, 70, **178–85**, 218
Blake, William, 113, 134, 223
Blavatsky, Helena, 208
Blood River (battle), 132, 158, 209
"Blue Curtains, The" (Haggard), **142–43**
Boccaccio, Giovanni, 97
Boer War, see Anglo-Boer War
Bookman, 146
Book of Common Prayer, 202
Bottles (fictional character), 142
Bowker, James Henry, 274–75
Bramwell, J. Milne, 51
Brantlinger, Patrick, 7
Bremer, Frederika, 228
Bronker's Spruit (battle), 144
Browne, Reverend George, 21
Browning, Elizabeth, 57–58, 172
Browning, Robert, 137, 197, 200
Bruno, Giordano, 197–98, 200
Buchan, John, 232–33
Budge, Wallis, 212
Buffalo River, 177
Bulfinch, Thomas, 89
Bull, John (caricature), 136
Bulwer, Sir Henry, 35, 175
Bunn, David, 88
Bunyan, John, 117, 141
Burne-Jones, Edward, 195
Burroughs, Edgar Rice, 233–34
Burton, Richard, 2, 191, 277
Buthelezi, Gatsha, 44, 81

C Caliban (dramatic character), 110
Callaway, Henry, 105, 118
Cameron, Kenneth, 235
Cannae (battle), 123
Canova, Antonio, 88, 140
Cardus, Reginald (fictional character), 140–41
Carlyle, Thomas, 60, 134, 138, 200
Cassell's Magazine, 150
Castle of Utranto, The (Walpole), 206
Cetywayo or Cetshwayo, Cetchwayo, Cetewayo, Ketshewayo (paramount Zulu chief), 32, 95, 102, 115, 120, 149, 163–64, 167–68, 173–74, 177–79, 209, 213, 274, 277, 283
Cetywayo and His White Neighbours (Haggard), 39, 54, 132
Ceylon (Tennent), 270
Chaka (Mofolo), 108, 116
"Charge of the Light Brigade" (Tennyson), 177
Chelmsford, Lord F. A. T., 52
Cheyfitz, Eric, 114
Child of Storm (Haggard), 7, 43–44, 48, 56, 102, 150, **163–73**
Chrisman, Laura, 10, 105, 108
Christ, 24, 52, 75, 170, 180, 182–84, 187–88, 206, 209
Christie, Agatha, 276
Circe (goddess), 24, 114, 130, 193–95, 197–98, 200
Clark, Sergeant, 283

289

Clarke, Marshal, 146
Cleopatra, Queen, 48
Cohen, Morton, 105
Colenso, Bishop J. W., 10, 21, 42–43, 86, 118, 171, 274
Coleridge, Samuel Taylor, 8, 59–61, 119, 170, 200
Commerell, Nidia (fictional character), 152
Conrad, Joseph, 6, 34, 43, 62, 109, 118, 133, 148, 204
Copperfield, David and Dora (fictional characters), 48
Corinthians (biblical book), 130, 215
Cornhill Magazine, 142
Crichton, Michael, 234
Crocodile (ship), 216
Cruise of the 'Falcon,' The (Knight), 226
Crusoe, Robinson (fictional character), 166
Curse of Clement Waynflete (Mitford), 279, 283
Curtis, George (fictional character), 72, 99–100
Curtis, Sir Henry (fictional character), 36, 72–101 passim, 102, 123, 155, 171, 214, 225–27, 229–30
Custom and Myth (Lang), 87
Cyclops (mythic figure), 14, 16–17, 26–28, 30, 38, 94, 136
Cyprian, Bishop, 60

D Dalby, Richard, 79
Danaë (mythic figure), 207
Danse du feu, La (Méliès), 233
Dante, Alighieri, 59, 140, 170–71
Darwin, Charles Robert, 5, 271
DaVinci, Leonardo, 64, 194
Days of My Life: An Autobiography (Haggard), 10, 38, 55, 78, 95, 138, 269
Demeter (goddess), 90
Demoiselles d'Avignon, Les (Picasso), 210
DeMoor, Marysa, 86
DeQuincey, Thomas, 61
Descent of Man, The (Darwin), 5
Dhlomo, Rolfes, 116
"Diamond Fields" (Schreiner), 6, 76
Diana (goddess), 198
Diary of an African Journey (Haggard), 2
Dicey, A. V., 112
Dickens, Charles, 11, 48, 208
Dilthey, Wilhelm, 49
Dinesen, Isak, 6, 14, 15–17, 21, 28–30, 34, 49, 136–38
Dingaan or Dingane (paramount Zulu chief), 20, 43, 105, 107, 125, 132, 151–54, 180, 184, 207, 209
Dinizulu (paramount Zulu chief), 179
Dioscuri (mythic brothers), 121
Disraeli, Benjamin, 201
Divine Comedy (Dante), 24, 59
"Divine Image, The" (Blake), 113
Donne, John, 183
Dove, Rachel (fictional character), 48, 85, 119, 148–49, 207–10
Dowson, Ernest, 124
Doyle, Arthur Conan, 232, 234, 278
Dracula (Stoker), 85
Dreams (Schreiner), 133
Dreams of Adventure, Deeds of Empire (Green), 268
Duguza or Dukuza, 44, 112, 130, 183, 215
Duhem, Pierre, 83
Dumas, Alexandre, 8
Dunn, John (Zulu chief), 167, 274

E *Eastern Daily Press* (Norfolk), 149, 274, 277–78, 284

East London Advertiser (South Africa), 274
Eden, Garden of, 18, 141, 210, 222
Elagabalus (Roman emperor), 180
Eliot, T. S., 6, 8, 58, 62, 64, 86–87, 170
"Elissa" (Haggard), 147
Elworthy, Frederick, 210
Engaged (Gilbert and Sullivan), 139
"Eolian Harp, The" (Coleridge), 59
Ernest (fictional character), 138–42, 145
Eros (god), 195
Euphues (Lyly), 214
Eve (biblical figure), 130, 195, 210
Every, John (fictional character), 160–61
Expiation of Wynne Palliser, The (Mitford), 279–80, 283

F *Facing Mount Kenya: The Tribal Life of the Gikuyu* (Kenyatta), 29–30
Far From the Madding Crowd (Hardy), 226
Farrar, F. W., 171
Faust (dramatic figure), 140
Ficino, Marsilio, 197
Finished (Haggard), 37–39, 102, 119, **173–76**, 177, 208, 233
Finnegans Wake (Joyce), 235
Firmat, Gustavo, 118
First Principles (Spencer), 14
Fletcher, Ian, 43, 106, 206
Fleurs du mal, Les (Baudelaire), 58
Fordham's Feud (Mitford), 282
Forging the Blades (Mitford), 279, 281
Foulata (fictional character) 83, 88, 91, 98–100, 125, 130, 140, 147, 151, 161, 165–66, 174, 214, 222
Foundational Fictions (Sommer), 105
Francis of Assisi, Saint, 136
Frazer, Sir James, 63, 86–87, 89, 98–99, 110, 121–22, 209, 228
Freud, Sigmund, 50, 194, 208
From Man to Man (Schreiner), 45, 136, 143
Fry, Roger, 3, 210
Fynney, Fred, 10, 92–93, 95, 103–05, 109–10, 112, 118, 120–21, 141, 163–64, 167, 173–74

G Gagool (fictional witch doctor), 2, 68, 88, 90–100 passim, 130, 140, 151, 161, 175, 214
Galahad, Sir (fictional character), 68–69
Galazi (fictional character), 119–22, 129
Gauguin, Paul, 207
Gay Science, The (Nietzsche), 57
Genesis (biblical book), 130
Gentle, Alexander, 275
Ghost Kings, The (Haggard), 44, 48, 88, 102, 119, 149, 185, 189, 192, 200, **207–10**, 222
Gladstone, William, 79, 111
Goethe, Johann Wolfgang, 134, 139–40, 208
Golden Bough, The (Frazer), 63, 86, 110, 112, 122
Good, Captain John, 80–101 passim, 102, 125, 129, 147, 155, 165–66, 171, 174, 222, 225–27
Goodwin, Thomas, 274
Gordimer, Nadine, 14
Gore, Catherine, 62
"Grammarians's Funeral, A" (Browning), 137
Graphic, 146
Great Zimbabwe, 72–74, 147, 206, 210
Greene, Graham, 68
Green Hills of Africa, The (Hemingway), 233

Green, Martin, 268
Green, Roger Lancelyn, 79, 107
Grendel (fictional character), 123, 202, 204
Grey, Sir George, 137
Grieffenhagen, Maurice, 154
Gun-Runner, The (Mitford), 103, 115, 124, 149, 268, 274, 279–81

H Hadden, Philip (fictional character), 70, 178–79, 218
Hagar (biblical figure), 32
Haggard, Ella, 35
Haggard, "Jock," 226
Haggard, John, 226
Haggard, William, 35
Halket, Peter, (fictional character), 26–27, 188
Hamilton, Carolyn, 10, 108
Hans [the German] (fictional character), 141
Hans the Hottentot (fictional character), 20, 52, 58, 115, 125, 157–58, 213, 217, 221
Hardy, Thomas, 128, 138
Harley Greenoak's Charge (Mitford), 275, 281
Harris, Frank, 42
Hawthorne, Nathaniel, 129
Heart of Darkness (Conrad), 6, 18, 58, 70, 85, 103, 106, 109, 148, 166, 170
Hegel, Georg Wilhelm Friedrich, 50
Heine, Heinrich, 193
Helen of Troy, 48, 69, 114, 130, 168–69, 171, 229
Hemingway, Ernest, 155–56, 233
Hendrika (fictional baboon-woman), 148, 158
Henley, W. E., 79
Henty, G. A., 3, 10, 14, 278
Hero with a Thousand Faces (Campbell), 11
Heu-Heu, or The Monster (Haggard), 8, 55, 192, 207, 217, **219–21**, 222, 232
History of South Africa (Theal), 151
Hobbes, Thomas, 3, 5
Hokosa (fictional witch doctor), 180–84, 206
Holly (fictional character), 50, 89, 100, 194–97, 199–200
Holofernes (biblical figure), 63
Holy Flower, The, see *Allan and the Holy Flower*
Homer, 15–16, 26, 30, 34, 68, 169–70
Hopkins, G. M., 52, 75
Horus (god), 58, 61, 217
"Hound of Heaven, The" (Thompson), 52
Howard, Robert E., 233
"Hunter Quatermain's Story" (Haggard), 155, 157–58
Huxley, Aldous, 217

I *Idylls of the King* (Tennyson), 69
Ignosi, see Umbopa
Iliad (Homer), 168, 171
Imperial Eyes (Pratt), 18
Importance of Being Earnest, The (Wilde), 48, 188, 152, 172
"Incident of African History, An" (Haggard), 138
Induna's Wife, The (Mitford), 20, 32, 153, 164, 281
Ingoldsby Legends (Barham), 53, 177
In Memoriam (Tennyson), 112, 200
Interpretation of Dreams, The (Freud), 50
Introduction to the Science of Religion (Müller), 86
Isaiah (biblical book), 181, 186
Isis (goddess), 58, 87, 194, 214
Isandhlwana (battle), 38, 102, 141, 168, 173, 177–78

Ivory Child, The (Haggard), 7, 20, 52, **57–58**, 61, 63, 67, 126, 151, 157, 159, 181, 192, **217–18**, 219, 221–22, 232–33

J Jackson, Lilly, 35, 38, 127, 139, 208
Jacob (biblical figure), 96, 99
James, William, 50, 183
Jana (evil elephant), 157
Jeekie (fictional character), 211, 231
Jerome, Saint, 185
Jess (Haggard), 14, 41, 131, **143–45**, 147, 162
Jess (fictional character), 143–45
Jikiza the Unconquered (fictional chief), 121
John, Gospel of (biblical book), 184–85
John Ames, Native Commissioner (Mitford), **152, 174–75**, 189–90, 276, 279–81
John the Baptist (bibical figure), 180
Jones, Indiana (film character), 71
Jones, R. W., 279
Josephus, Flavius, 88
Jowett, Benjamin, 196
Joyce, James, 86, 235
Judges (biblical book), 143
Jung, Carl, 89
Jungle Book (Kipling), 122, 169

K Kallikrates (fictional character), 128, 213–14
Katz, Wendy, 5, 7, 108
Keats, John, 129, 195, 199
Kebra Negast, 212
Kelvin, Lord William Thomson, 8
Kenyatta, Jomo, 29–30, 56
Kerr, Charles, 154
Khiva (fictional and historic figure), 80, 82, 205
King Kong (Wallace/Cooper), 234
King's Assegai, The (Mitford), **149–50**, 272, 274, 279
Kingsley, Charles, 7, 89
Kingsley, Mary, 84, 166
King Solomon's Mines (Haggard), **72–101** and passim
Kipling, Rudyard, 1, 42–43, 78, 83, 122, 133, 169, 173, 207
Knudsen (colonist), 34
Koran, see *Qur'an*
Kore (mythic goddess), 140, 281
Kruger, Paul, 144, 162
Kunene, Mazisi, 104–105, 108–09
Kurtz (fictional character), 34, 118, 142, 151, 166, 170–71, 179, 204

L Lalique, René, 229
Land-March from England to Ceylon Forty Years Ago, A (Mitford), 270
Lang, Andrew, 3, 7, 39, 41, 63, 78–79, 87–89, 106–107, 110, 122, 133, 168
Langhalibalele (amaHlubi chief), 274
Layard, Austen Henry, 270
Leo (fictional character), 194–96, 199–200
Leopold III (king), 182
Leslie, David, 77, 105, 115–16, 118, 129
Lévi-Strauss, Claude, 33
Leviticus (biblical book), 181
Lewis, Clive Staples, 42, 62–64, 107, 119, 182
Liberty Leading the People (Delacroix), 160
Lieven, Michael, 268
Lilith (goddess/character), 127, 204–205
Lincoln, Abraham, 104

"Little Flower" (Haggard), **185–86**
Livingstone, David, 19–23, 42, 81–82, 110, 134, 136, 155–56, 216, 277
Livy, Titus, 123
Lobengula (Matabele paramount chief), 205–206
"Locksley Hall" (Tennyson), 125, 138
London Illustrated News, 102
London Times, 271, 284
"Long Odds" (Haggard), 155
Lord of the Rings (Tolkien), 232
Lorraine (fictional character), 281
"Lost on the Veld" (Haggard), 51, 138
Lost World, The (Doyle), 232
Low, Gail, 108, 114
Lucas, George, 234
Luck of Gerard Ridgeley, The (Mitford), 11, 279
Lyndall (fictional character), 46–49, 59, 75–76, 143, 151
Lyrical Ballads (Wordsworth), 41

M Macumazahn, see Quatermain
Madeline (fictional character), 142–43
"Magepa the Buck" (Haggard), 117, **177–78**
Maiwa's Revenge (Haggard), 7, 44, 69, 124, 131, **159–62**, 171
"Major Wilson's Last Fight" (Haggard), 138
Majuba Hill (battle), 39
Malachi (biblical book), 180
Mameena (fictional character), 2, 44, 46, 48, 52, 125–27, 147, 163–74, 181, 215–16, 222, 223
Marie (Haggard), 102, 107, 113, 115, 125, 131, **150–53**, 155, 159–60, 163, 165, 215
Marius the Epicurean (Pater), 140, 195
Marlow, Charlie (fictional character), 106, 110, 125, 166, 170–71, 204
Matthew (biblical book), 128, 141, 186–87, 189, 209, 215
Mauch, Karl, 72–74
Mazooku (native servant), 218
M'Carthy, Sir Charles, 122
McClintock, Anne, 10, 88, 108, 121
Medusa (gorgon), 139–42, 193–94
Méliès, Georges, 233
Mephistopheles (dramatic figure), 140
Meriamun (fictional character), 114, 130, 229
Metamorphoses (Ovid), 139
Meyer, Jacob (fictional character), 206–207
M'hlopekazi or Umhlopekazi (Swazi warrior), 80–81, 105
Mhudi (Plaatje), 40, 98, 109, 116, 131, 148, 154
Michelangelo Buonarroti, 197
Mill on the Floss (Eliot), 145
Milner, Lord Alfred, 233
Milton, John, 61, 127–28, 151, 195, 210, 215
Missionary Travels (Livingstone), 19, 32, 134, 156
Mitford, Bertram, 3, 9, 10, 11, 14, 133, 136, 149–50, 152–54, 189–90, 203–205, 268–88
Mitford, Edward Ledwich Osbaldeston, 270–71, 277
Mitford, Ella, 271
Mitford, Roland, 276, 284
Mitford, William, 271–72
Mitford, Yseulte Helen, 276–77, 284
Mitford, Zima Helen Ebden, 275–76, 283–84
Mnemosyne (goddess), 126
"Modern Fiction" (Woolf), 41, 232
Mofolo, Thomas, 108, 116
Monomotapa (Wilmot), 74, 206
Montaigne, Michel de, 3

Montefiore, Arthur, 277
Moon of Israel (Haggard), 201
Mopo (historical/fictional Zulu), 64–67, 105–127 passim, 149, 209
Mrs. Dalloway (Woolf), 232
Müller, F. Max, 86–87
Muller, Frank (fictional character), 143–45, 147–48, 208
Myers, Frederick, 51
Mzilikazi or Mzilikatzi, Mozelkatse, Mosilikatze, Umzilikazi (Matabele paramount chief), 74, 108–09, 111, 131, 148–49, 158, 180, 205

N Nada the Lily (fictional character), 102–30, and passim
Nada the Lily (Haggard), **102–30**, and passim
Nadel, Ira, 109
Naipaul, V. S., 14
Nanea (fictional character), 147, 178–79
Napoleon Bonaparte, 144
Narrative of an Expedition to the Zambesi (Livingstone), 19
Neil, Captain John (fictional character), 144
"Negro Sculpture" (Fry), 3, 210
Ngugi wa Thiong'o, 14
Nietzsche, Friedrich, 57–58
Nobela (fictional character), 147
Nobeta (Zulu chief), 92–93
Noie (fictional wizard), 148, 209
Noma (fictional wizard), 181–82
Nombe (fictional character), 174, 208
Novalis, 134
Nya (tree spirit), 210
Nyleptha (fictional queen), 229–30

O Odin (god), 96
Odysseus, see Ulysses
Odyssey (Homer), 16, 34, 168
O'Keefe, Georgia, 127
Olney, James, 109
"On the Medusa of Leonardo da Vinci in the Florentine Gallery" (Shelley), 140
Ophir (biblical city), 73–74, 88
Origin of Species, The (Darwin), 5
Orlando Furioso (Ariosto), 106
Osborn, Sir Melmoth, 37, 95
Osiris (god), 61, 217
Otter (fictional character), 201–202
Out of Africa (Dinesen), 30
Owen, Francis, 184
Owen, Thomas (fictional character), 179–85, 208

P Pagadi (amaChunu chief), 165
Pagan Babies (Leonard), 70
Pan (mythic figure), 57
Panda or Umpanda (Zulu paramount chief), 95, 164, 168, 173–74, 180
"Pan is Dead" (E. Browning), 57
Paradise Lost (Milton), 24, 210, 223
Park, Mungo, 19, 30
Passage to India (Forster), 35
Passerini, Luisa, 109
Pater, Walter, 64, 90, 140, 115, 128, 193, 195, 231–32, 235
Pausanias, 57
Pemberton, Sir Max, 79
People of the Mist (Haggard), 8, 192, **200–205**, 212, 216
Persephone (mythic figure), 90, 99, 281

Index

Peter Wilkins (Paltock), 226
Pereira, Hernan (fictional character), 151–52
Phaedrus (Plato), 129, 195–97, 200
Phidias, 139
Picasso, Pablo, 210
Pilgrim's Progress (Bunyan), 108, 271
Plaatje, Sol, 14, 40, 98, 108, 111, 116–17, 131, 148
Plato, 123, 195–98, 200
Plutarch, 57
Podmore, Frank, 51
Polyphemus, see Cyclops
Poems: Dramatic and Lyrical (E. Mitford), 271
Pope, Alexander, 64, 168
Popular Account of Discoveries at Nineveh, A (Layard), 270
Popular Magazine of Anthropology, 3
Praise of Folly, The (Erasmus), 218
Preller, Gustav, 154
Prester John (Buchan), 232
Pride and Prejudice (Austen), 48
Primitive Culture (Tylor), 86, 94, 96, 111
Princess, The (Tennyson), 49
Private Diaries (Haggard), 83, 96
"Psalm of Life, A" (Longfellow), 138
Psalms (biblical book), 115, 204
Punch, 173

Q Quabeet (native), 82
Quatermain, Allan (fictional character), 52–53, 67–101, and passim
Quatermain, Harry (fictional character), 100, 155, 158, 171, 227
Queen Sheba's Ring (Haggard), 2, 192, 200–201, **211–13**
Quick, Sergeant, 2, 211–12
Qur'an, 88, 99

R Ragnall, Lady (fictional character), 58, 126, 217
"Rape of the Lock, The" (Pope), 159
Ravenshaw of Rietholme (Mitford), 278
Religious System of the Amazulu, The (Callaway), 105
Renshaw Fanning's Quest (Mitford), 279–81
"Resolution and Independence" (Wordsworth), 59
Retief, Piet, 32, 150, 152–53
Revelation (biblical book), 170, 209
Rezu (fictional character), 214
Rhodesia (journal), 137
Rhodes, Cecil, 23, 25–26, 73, 132, 137, 182, 184, 189–90
Ritter, E. A., 109
Rive, Richard, 6
Romulus and Remus (mythic brothers), 121
Roosevelt, Theodore, 81, 233
Rorke's Drift (battle) 39, 52, 173, 177–78
Rose, Gregory (fictional character), 49
Rossetti, D. G., 127–28
Rousseau, Jean Jacques, 3
Ruined Cities of Mashonaland, The (Bent), 75, 205
Ruined Cities of Zulu Land, The (Walmsley), 74
Ruskin, John, 6, 23–25, 49, 73, 154, 170, 195, 217

S Sabeela (fictional character), 147
Saduko (fictional character), 48, 151, 164, 168–69
Samuel (biblical book), 181
Sartor Resartus (Carlyle), 60
Satan, 60, 127, 151, 223
Saul of Tarsus (biblical figure), 141

Scheick, William, 86, 88
Schreiner, Gottlob, 19–21, 47
Schreiner, Olive, 1, 3, 6, 9, 14, 20–22, 33, 45–47, 75–76, 118, 128, 130, 133–37, 143–45, 147–48, 151, 153, 182–84, 186–91, 205–206, 213, 220, 279, 281
Scoop (Waugh), 2
Seaford's Snake (Mitford), 11, 281
Sechele or Secheli (Bakwena chief), 22–23, 81–82, 181
Selous, F. C., 62, 74, 81–82, 84, 99, 156, 205
Sermon on the Mount, 134, 186–89
Sesame and Lilies (Ruskin), 49
Seven Types of Adventure Tale, The (Green), 11
Sex and Civil Rights (Dailey), 222
Shadow (fictional character), 147
Shaka or Chaka, Tyaka, T'shaka (Zulu paramount chief), 10, 43, 52, 94, 102–123, 125, 131, 149–51, 173, 209
Shaka: King of the Zulus (Burness), 103–104
Shakespeare, William, 110, 123, 157
"*She*" (Lang), 78
She: A History of Adventure (Haggard), 7, 10, 45, 50, 103, 114, 128, 144, 163, **191–200**, 211, 213–14, 225
She and Allan (Haggard), 5, 81, 148, 166, 192–94, **213–16**, 222–23
Sheba (biblical queen), 17, 87–100 passim, 124, 128–29, 130, 165, 211–12
Shelley, P. B., 119, 129, 194, 223
Shepstone, Sir Theophilus, 10, 32, 37, 39–40, 79, 81, 95, 97, 105, 120–21, 174, 205
"Short Happy Life of Francis McComber, The" (Hemingway), 233
Sign of the Spider, The (Mitford), **203–204**, 268, 276–77, 279–81
Sihamba (fictional witch doctoress), 148
Sitanda's Kraal, 84
Sleep and Dreams, In (Symonds), 50
Smith, Adam, 216
Smith and the Pharaohs and Other Tales (Haggard), 142, 177, 185
Smut (dog), 148, 215
Socrates, 128, 196
Soga, Tiyo, 108
Solomon (biblical king), 72–74, 89, 94, 97–100 passim, 128–29, 155, 171, 211–12, 216, 228–29
Song of Solomon (biblical book), 115
Sorais (fictional queen), 160, 229–30
South Africa (Trollope), 73
South-African Butterflies (Trimen), 274–75
Spenser, Edmund, 195
Stanley, Henry Morton, 277, 278
"Stanzas from the Grande Chartreuse" (Arnold), 110
Statesman's Manual, The (Coleridge), 60
Stella (fictional character), 155, 158–60, 215
Stephen, Saint, 141
Stevenson, R. L., 51, 78–79, 133, 195, 221
Stoker, Bram, 85
Story of an African Farm (Schreiner), 20, 33, 45–47, 75, 133–36, 143–47, 175–76, 213, 218
Strange Case of Dr. Jekyll and Mr. Hyde, The (Stevenson), 51, 195, 221
Street, Brian, 86, 124
Stringer, Brian, 273, 284
Stump (dog), 148
"Sunlight Lay Across My Bed, The" (Schreiner), 77, 130
Swallow, A Tale of the Great Trek, 102, 131, **146–49**

Swift, Jonathan, 220–21
Swinburne, A. C., 194
Symonds, J. A., 50
Symons, Arthur, 133
Symposium (Plato), 198

T Taduki (drug), 217, 219
"Tale of Isandhlwana and Rorke's Drift, The" (Haggard), 177
"Tale of Three Lions, A" (Haggard), 67, 155, 158–59
Tannhäuser (legendary figure), 193, 198
Tarzan (fictional character), 71, 233
Tempest, The (Shakespeare), 110
Tennyson, Alfred Lord, 25, 34, 49, 69, 112, 123, 125, 138, 176–77, 200
Tertullian, 51
Teuton (ship), 205
Theal, George McCall, 151
Things Fall Apart (Achebe), 117, 153, 181
Thirty-Nine Steps, The (Buchan), 233
Thompson, Francis, 52
"Thoughts on Slavery" (Wesley), 216
Thoughts on South Africa (Schreiner), 32, 134–35
Through Masai Land (Thomson), 226
Through the Zulu Country (Mitford), 269, 274, 280
"Tintern Abbey" (Wordsworth), 60
Tippu Tip, 216
Titanic (ship), 205
Tolkien, J. R. R., 107, 209, 232, 233
"To Ulysses" (Tennyson), 53
Touré, Sékou, 118
"Transvaal, The," (Haggard), 32, 36–37, 53–54, 132
Travels and Adventures in Eastern Africa (Isaac), 104
Treasure Island (Stevenson), 78–80
Treasure of the Lake (Haggard), 44, 148, 192, 208, 212, **221-23**
Trollope, Anthony, 73, 133
Trooper Peter Halket of Mashonaland (Schreiner), 7, 137, 141, 182, 188–89
True Story Book, The (Lang), 39
Tugela (river and battle), 106, 155, 163, 167, 209
Twain, Mark, 53
Twala (fictional Zulu king), 68, 85–101 passim, 180
Tylor, E. B., 86–87, 89, 94, 98, 111–12

U Ulundi (kraal and battle), 149
Ulysses (mythic hero), 15–17, 27–29, 34, 53, 69, 94, 114, 123, 130, 135–36, 169, 172, 195, 200, 226
"Ulysses" (Tennyson), 53, 123, 226
Umbelazi or Umbulazi (Zulu prince), 95, 106, 163–64, 167–69, 173
Umbopa / Ignosi (fictional character), 7, 10, 67, 80–101 passim, 106, 115, 180, 212
Umbopo, see Mopo
Umkulunkulu (Zulu goddess), 64–67, 78, 105, 111, 119, 126, 130, 175
Umslopogaas (fictional character), 2, 51, 81, 85, 105–130 passim, 149–50, 171, 213, 215, 227, 230
Unamuno, Miguel de, 282
"Uncanny, The" (Freud), 50
Undine (fictional character), 76
Untúswa (fictional character), 149–50, 153
Ushaka (Dhlomo), 116

V *Variation of Animals and Plants under Domestication* (Darwin), 271
Varieties of Religious Experience (James), 50, 183
Veldt Vendetta, A (Mitford), 18, 273, 281
Vernon, Alan (fictional character), 210–11, 231
Victoria, Queen, 45, 74, 77, 82
Virgil or Publius Vergilius Maro, 170, 281
Virgin of the Sun, The (Haggard), 228
"Visit to the Chief Secocoeni, A" (Haggard), 36
Voortrekers / Winning a Continent, Die (Preller), 154
Voyage Out, The (Woolf), 232

W Waldo Farber (fictional character), 33, 75–76, 137
Walmsley, Hugh, 74, 167
Wambe (fictional chief), 160–62
War and Arcadia (Mitford), 278, 282
War of the Worlds (Wells), 5, 212
Watt & Son, A. P., 276–77, 279
Waugh, Evelyn, 2, 63, 231, 270
Way of All Flesh, The (Butler), 138
Wealth of Nations (Smith), 216
Webster, Augusta, 195
Weird of Deadly Hollow, The (Mitford), 272, 276, 278
Wells, H. G., 5, 212, 220
Wesley, John, 216
When the World Shook (Haggard), 83
White Hand and the Black, The (Mitford), 269, 276, 278, 282
White Shield, The (Mitford), 180, 283
Wilde, Oscar, 48, 195, 229
Winchester, Oliver, 85, 221
Winters, Ivor, 52
Wisdom's Daughter (Haggard), 193
Witch's Head, The (Haggard), 39, 56, 78, 102, 131, **138–42**, 193, 203, 208, 219
With Buller in Natal (Henty), 283
With Roberts to Pretoria (Henty), 283
With Shield and Assegai (Brereton), 12
Wizard, The (Haggard), 7, 20, 52, 113, 141, 178, **179–85**
Woods, Katharine, 146
Woolf, Virgina, 41, 50, 232
Word of the Sorceress (Mitford), 276
Wordsworth, William, 52, 112, 158, 196
World's Desire, The (Haggard and Lang), 69, 106, 114, 123, 130, 229
Worship of Nature, The (Frazer), 228
Wylie, Dan, 108–09, 120

Y Yeats, W. B., 51, 64, 86–87, 134, 221
Yellow God, The, 7, 44, 192, 200, **210–11**, 231

Z Zambezi or Zambesi (river), 19, 74, 131, 142, 149, 179, 182, 186, 188, 193, 201, 205, 206, 213, 214
Zangwell, Israel, 201
Zanzibar (ship), 205
Zeus (god), 15, 17, 28, 135, 168, 196, 198
Zikali (fictional witch doctor), 2, 102, 113, 164, 171, 173–74, 213, 217, 219–20
Zola, Émile, 3
Zululand the Zulus (Fynney), 92, 103–104
Zulu War, 4, 38, 103, 110–11, 132, 138–39, 142, 155, 173, 178–79
"Zulu War-Dance, A" (Haggard), 18, 31, 36, 95, 97, 156, 269